Principles and Practice of Property Valuation in Australia

This book provides a clear outline of the key principles underlying property valuation and the current techniques and issues in the practice of valuation for the major sectors of the Australian real estate market.

Formerly titled *Valuation Principles and Practice*, this entirely new third edition comprises Australia's leading advanced valuation textbook. The first part of the book, Principles of valuation, comprises chapters written by globally recognised academics and specialists on the principles of law, economics, planning, policy and finance, all in the context of property valuation. The second part of the book, Practice of valuation, comprises chapters written by acknowledged expert valuers on the practice of valuation for key property sectors including residential, retail, commercial, industrial, leisure and rural. Further, chapters also cover valuations for purposes including lending, insurance, rating, taxation and financial reporting.

The most up-to-date valuation text for the Australian market, this book will appeal to both valuation practitioners and undergraduate/postgraduate students as well as to accountants, lawyers and professionals dealing with property valuation issues.

Dr David Parker is an internationally recognised real estate industry expert and highly regarded real estate academic (www.davidparker.com.au), and editor of *The Routledge REITs Research Handbook* (2019). He is a regular contributor to property and valuation academic journals, a Visiting Professor at the Henley Business School, University of Reading and a Visiting Fellow at the University of Ulster.

Principles and Practice of Property Valuation in Australia

Third Edition

Edited by David Parker

LONDON AND NEW YORK

Third edition published 2022
by Routledge
2 Park Square, Milton Park, Abingdon, Oxon, OX14 4RN

and by Routledge
605 Third Avenue, New York, NY 10158

Routledge is an imprint of the Taylor & Francis Group, an informa business

© 2022 selection and editorial matter, David Parker; individual chapters, the contributors

The right of David Parker to be identified as the author of the editorial material, and of the authors for their individual chapters, has been asserted in accordance with sections 77 and 78 of the Copyright, Designs and Patents Act 1988.

All rights reserved. No part of this book may be reprinted or reproduced or utilised in any form or by any electronic, mechanical, or other means, now known or hereafter invented, including photocopying and recording, or in any information storage or retrieval system, without permission in writing from the publishers.

Trademark notice: Product or corporate names may be trademarks or registered trademarks, and are used only for identification and explanation without intent to infringe.

First edition published by Australian Property Institute 1997
Second edition published by Australian Property Institute 2007

British Library Cataloguing-in-Publication Data
A catalogue record for this book is available from the British Library

Library of Congress Cataloging-in-Publication Data
Names: Parker, David, 1961- editor.
Title: Principles and practice of property valuation in Australia / edited by David Parker.
Description: Third Edition. | New York City : Routledge, 2021. | "Second edition published by Australian Property Institute 2007." | Includes bibliographical references and index.
Identifiers: LCCN 2021013398 (print) | LCCN 2021013399 (ebook) | ISBN 9780367503406 (hardback) | ISBN 9780367503413 (paperback) | ISBN 9781003049555 (ebook)
Subjects: LCSH: Valuation--Australia. | Real property--Valuation--Australia.
Classification: LCC HD1036.5 .P75 2021 (print) | LCC HD1036.5 (ebook) | DDC 333.33/20994--dc23
LC record available at https://lccn.loc.gov/2021013398
LC ebook record available at https://lccn.loc.gov/2021013399

ISBN: 978-0-367-50340-6 (hbk)
ISBN: 978-0-367-50341-3 (pbk)
ISBN: 978-1-003-04955-5 (ebk)

DOI: 10.1201/9781003049555

Typeset in Times
by KnowledgeWorks Global Ltd.

To my partner and my twin millennials. May the future with Ed recompense for that foregone.

Contents

List of figures	ix
List of tables	x
About the Author	xi
Foreword	xii
Preface	xiv

PART I
Principles of valuation   1

  1 **Legal principles**   3
      GARRICK SMALL

  2 **Economic principles**   15
      COLIN LIZIERI

  3 **Planning principles**   28
      NIGEL FLANNIGAN

  4 **Policy principles**   40
      NICKI HUTLEY

  5 **Finance principles**   49
      DAVID REES

  6 **Valuation principles**   65
      DAVID PARKER

PART II
Practice of valuation   79
Section One: Valuation practice for conventional property sectors

  7 **Residential property valuation**   81
      DAMIAN KININMONTH

Contents

8 Office property valuation — 91
PETER DEMPSEY

9 Retail property valuation — 109
BERNIE SWEENEY

10 Industrial property valuation — 124
RYAN KORDA

11 Rural property valuation — 133

Section Two: Valuation practice for specialist property sectors

12 Retirement and aged care property valuation — 146
LOIS TOWART

13 Leisure property valuation — 159
ROBERT MCINTOSH AND WESLEY MILSOM

14 Plant and equipment valuation — 170
GREG ROWE AND ROY FARTHING

15 Business and intangible asset valuation — 182
WAYNE LONERGAN

Section Three: Valuation practice for specific purposes

16 Valuation for rental purposes — 198
GREG PRESTON

17 Valuation for financial reporting purposes — 211
RICHARD STEWART

18 Valuation for secured lending purposes — 224
ROSS TURNER

19 Valuation for insurance purposes — 235
CAMERON DUNSFORD, MARK KLENKE AND ASHLEY GRANT

20 Valuation for statutory purposes — 249
DAVID PARKER

Index — *268*

Figures

1.1	Foundations of property economics	6
2.1	Quadrant model of the commercial property market	16
2.2	Adjustment in occupier markets	22
2.3	Office starts and rents in the City of London	24
3.1	Fundamental components in urban planning	31
5.1	Development finance – the capital stack: sources and uses of finance	50
5.2	Returns to debt and equity as leverage rises	52
5.3	Two investments and portfolio performance	55
5.4	The risk-return trade-off	56
5.5	The Efficient Frontier	57
5.6	Australia CBD office market performance (1990–2017)	57
5.7	Smoothed vs. unsmoothed investment returns	59
5.8	The Security Market Line	60
5.9	The ASX A-REIT sector β (May 1993 – October 2020)	62
9.1	Retail property platform	112
9.2	Trade area map	113

Tables

4.1	Methodologies for land taxes and council rates	42
5.1	The impact of a rising level of debt	51
5.2	Australia CBD office market performance (1990–2017)	58
10.1	The capitalisation approach – vacant assets	132
17.1	Australian Accounting Standards and valuation issues	213
20.1	Methodologies for land taxes and council rates	250
20.2	Matters referred to mediation 2015–2019 in Class 3	265
20.3	Matters referred to conciliation 2015–2019 in all classes	266

About the Author

David Parker is an internationally recognised real estate industry expert and highly regarded real estate academic, being a director and adviser to real estate investment groups including listed real estate investment trusts, unlisted funds and private real estate businesses (www.davidparker.com.au).

Dr Parker is a Visiting Professor at the Henley Business School, University of Reading and a Visiting Fellow at the University of Ulster. He is the former inaugural Professor of Property at the University of South Australia, a former Acting Commissioner of the Land and Environment Court of New South Wales and a Sessional Member for the South Australian Civil and Administrative Tribunal.

With over 30 years' experience in property funds management, real estate investment trusts, valuation standards and statutory valuation, Dr Parker previously held senior executive positions with Schroders Property Fund and ANZ Funds Management.

Holding a BSc, MComm, MPhil, MBA and PhD degrees, Dr Parker is a Fellow of the Royal Institution of Chartered Surveyors, the Australian Institute of Company Directors, the Australian Property Institute, the Australian Institute of Management and a Senior Fellow of the Financial Services Institute of Australasia. He is a member of the Society of Property Researchers, the American Real Estate and Urban Economics Association and the European, American and Pacific Rim Real Estate Societies.

The editor of *The Routledge REITs Research Handbook* (2018) and author of *International Valuation Standards: A Guide to the Valuation of Real Property Assets* (2016) and *Global Real Estate Investment Trusts: People, Process and Management* (2011), Dr Parker has published numerous papers in academic and industry journals. Dr Parker is a regular conference presenter around the world and Editorial Board Member for the highly ranked *Journal of Property Research*, *Journal of Property Investment and Finance*, *Pacific Rim Property Research Journal* and *Property Management*.

David Parker may be contacted by email at davidparker@davidparker.com.au.

Foreword

This edition of *Principles and Practice of Property Valuation in Australia* is an important milestone in the evolution of Australian valuation texts, which can trace their contemporary origins to Land Valuation and Compensation in Australia by R.O. Rost and H.G. Collins, published in 1971. Many of the chapters of the first edition of *Valuation Principles and Practice*, published in 1997, were updated versions of the original Rost and Collins text and were acknowledged by the authors. With this new edition Dr David Parker, an internationally recognised real estate industry expert, has produced Australia's leading advanced valuation text. Dr Parker has collaborated with 22 globally recognised academics and specialists who have contributed to a book that will guide the profession in the principles and the practice of property valuation in a most innovative way.

For example, in the first chapter, 'Legal Principles', Garrick Small has presented a sophisticated analysis of the concepts of ownership and use distinguishing between Western and indigenous cultural views and beliefs. This is a significant departure from the traditional single dimensional view of land ownership and tenure. He has successfully provided a framework where these different interpretations can be reconciled and accommodated for the purpose of valuation.

The continuous evolution of professional practice is evident in references to discounted cash flow in the first and second editions of *Valuation Principles and Practice*, once regarded as innovative and augmenting other methods of valuation, now being accepted as the primary method of valuation and analysis for larger investment properties worldwide.

This book recognises the International Valuation Standards Council's ambition for International Valuation Standards to guide the valuation profession globally. One consequence of harmonising standards is the challenge to time-honoured definitions and their interpretation. In Chapter 20, 'Valuation for Statutory Purposes', Dr Parker presents a compelling argument for why he has relegated the High Court decision in Spencer to its twenty-first century role as a significant precedent for statutory valuation. Dr Parker also eloquently advocates that the International Valuation Standards' definition of market value is more relevant in contemporary valuation practice.

The book provides valuable insight for our profession about the application of International Valuation Standards and will support the International Valuation Standards Council's goal that their standards 'underpin consistency, transparency and confidence in valuations which are key to investment decisions, financial reporting and financial market stability'.

Principles and Practice of Property Valuation in Australia will become the definitive reference for both students and for the wider profession as it has met its objective of clearly outlining the key principles underlying property valuation and the current techniques and issues in the practice of valuation for the major sectors of the Australian real estate market.

Neil Bray
Queensland Head – Government and Corporate, Herron Todd White and Australia's longest serving Valuer General, being appointed by the South Australian Government in 1999 and retiring as Queensland's Valuer General in 2020.

Preface

This book assumes that the reader already has an understanding of the fundamentals of property valuation and is seeking deeper insight into aspects of the principles and practice of property valuation. Accordingly, the principles seek to address the 'why' which underlies the 'how' of the practice, but with the 'how' assuming that the reader already understands the operation and application of the relevant valuation methods.

Further, this book is premised on the acceptance of International Valuation Standards as the principal guiding principles for valuation globally, supplemented as necessary by regional or national principles statements. Relegating *Spencer* to its twenty-first century role as a significant precedent for statutory valuation represents a major change in the Australian approach to valuation principles and practice.

This book is also premised on the now clearly evident acceptance that discounted cash flow is the primary method of valuation and analysis for larger investment properties worldwide, acknowledging that other methods of valuation may be adopted for smaller investment properties in different parts of the world.

This book comprises two parts, the first being the principles of property valuation and the second being the practice of property valuation which is divided into three sections being valuation practice for conventional property sectors, specialist property sectors and specific purposes, respectively:

Part I: Principles of valuation

- legal principles address fundamental concepts of ownership and use, reconciling indigenous concepts and Western concepts through a detailed examination of culture and belief;
- economic principles frame supply, demand and pricing in the context of property market processes as economic processes where the rational investment decisions that reflect such should be embedded in valuation practice;
- planning principles place the machinery of planning (zonings, as of right uses, prohibited uses, setbacks, height constraints and so forth) within the much wider context of planning as a facilitator for managing the realisation of a visualised future through urban development;
- policy principles identify the interconnected framework of local, State and Federal Government policies across various policy areas that individually and cumulatively impact property value and the valuation process;

- finance principles consider the role of expectations, time and risk, together with the central function of the discount rate, in the valuation process for capital market assets generally, contrasting starkly with the traditionally backward looking emphasis on prior sales and focus on the primacy of the capitalisation rate in the property valuation process; and
- valuation principles focus on the governing principles provided by the International Valuation Standards including the three key concepts of price, cost and value, the three principal valuation approaches, the five bases of value and the five premises of value.

Part II: Practice of valuation

Section One: Valuation practice for conventional property sectors

- residential property valuation practice focusing on the accepted use of technology allowing a greater focus on the distinction between marketing and market value drivers;
- office property valuation practice focusing on the structure and drivers of the institutional office property market, the principal approaches to valuation under International Valuation Standards, the central role of the occupier or tenant and future trends therein;
- retail property valuation practice focusing on the structure and drivers of the retail property market, the key variables in the retail valuation process and the principal risks for consideration;
- industrial property valuation practice focusing on the transition from manufacturing to logistics, the rise in institutional ownership, the resulting repricing of the sector and the impact on valuation methodology; and
- rural property valuation practice focusing on the structure of the rural property market, key issues affecting rural property valuation and the principal rural property market sectors for valuation.

Section Two: Valuation practice for specialist property sectors

- retirement and aged care property valuation practice focusing on the structure and operation of the market, the interaction of property and business interests and the significant role of government regulation and control;
- leisure property valuation practice focusing on the interface between property ownership and business operations, with buildings often purpose built for sole purpose which potentially creates an interdependency for the life of the asset;
- plant and equipment valuation practice focusing on identification of assets for valuation, materiality and application of the market approach and cost approach to the specialist nature of plant and equipment at both the individual asset and entire facility levels; and
- business and intangible asset valuation practice focusing on the four principal methods of business valuation, drawing parallels with the property valuation process particularly thorough the inputs to the respective methods.

Section Three: Valuation practice for specific purposes

- valuation practice for rental purposes is considered through the generic concept of rent as variously expressed (market, fair, reasonable, etc) and through specific regard to impacting lease provisions such as make good and restrictive use as well as issues such as lease incentives;
- valuation practice for financial reporting purposes is considered in the context of the inextricable link between financial reporting valuations and the interaction between accounting standards and valuation standards, requiring the valuer to have a detailed knowledge of the operation of each and their interplay;
- valuation practice for secured lending purposes is considered with particular regard to the International Valuation Standards references to scope and reporting structure together with issues associated with investment, owner-occupied and development property for secured lending purposes;
- valuation practice for insurance purposes is considered with particular regard to the central concepts of reinstatement value and Indemnity Value, focusing the valuer's attention on the important differences from the concept of market value; and
- valuation practice for statutory purposes is considered in the context of valuation for rating and taxing and valuation for compulsory acquisition, focusing the valuer's attention on the fundamental interaction between governing statute, binding Court precedent and valuation practice.

The publication of this book in the aftermath of the worldwide COVID-19 pandemic is very timely, as it reinforces the enduring relevance of the underlying principles of valuation and the need for the practice of valuation to adapt to prevailing circumstances. While COVID-19 affected property markets in different parts of the world in different ways, often with extended periods of limited or no transactional activity in certain sub-sectors, valuation practice for its many and diverse purposes adapted and continued to support the operation of global financial and capital markets despite the prevalence of the pandemic.

David Parker
Sydney, 2020

Part I
Principles of valuation

1 Legal principles

Garrick Small

Introduction

With the first part of this book addressing the principles of valuation and the second part addressing the practice of valuation, the following chapters will consider economic, planning, policy, finance and valuation principles with this chapter considering legal principles.

It is assumed that the reader already has an understanding of Western concepts such as title and Western legal applications such as *Spencer* in the context of valuation, with this chapter addressing much more fundamental concepts of ownership and use, reconciling indigenous concepts and Western concepts through a detailed examination of culture and belief.

Real property ownership is often conflated with its use, but a distinction is important for understanding how societies use and value land. Andrew Reeve (1986) recognised that it is not real property itself that is owned, but only rights to its use. Property as a 'bundle of rights' is now well accepted and the structure of those rights make up the property interests that valuers appraise. The question of property rights is complicated by the different ways that various cultures understand them, which can cause challenges for the valuer.

Australia is home to at least two distinct cultural approaches to property rights. This makes a careful understanding of the nature and significance of property rights especially relevant here. The valuer is usually called upon to value property within the English, or Anglo-Australian culture; however, the perspective of indigenous Australians has also become important, especially since 1992. This second perspective will be referred to as *customary property rights* in this chapter.

This chapter will examine the cultural foundations of property rights in general using examples from Anglo-Australia and indigenous Australia. It will outline a framework for interpreting all property rights systems and demonstrate how Anglo and indigenous property rights may be understood as parts of their respective cultures. From this framework, practical aspects relating to commerce in and valuation of property rights, both within and across the two cultures, will be considered.

Real property rights and valuation

The valuation of property may be described as the estimation of the commercial value of those property rights that are contained within a particular property interest. While this might appear to be a non-contentious definition, almost every part of it conceals controversial elements. These are most apparent when they concern intercultural property rights tensions.

Commercial value is a common enough notion within Western cultures, especially those of English, or *Anglo* origins. For many cultures *commercial values* are only one of several systems of value operating in the community and can even be looked down upon as an inferior class of value. Anglo cultures, adopting the Enlightenment thought of David Hume and Adam Smith, tend to view all values as either material or subjective.

Material values may always be equated to money, or commercial values. Subjective values relate to personal tastes and beliefs and are more difficult to express in money terms. Self-respect or family ties are values of this type. In many other cultures there are values that are objective, though neither material nor reducible to money equivalents, with Ernst Schumacher (Schumacher, 1974) arguing that these also had a place in economic thought.

Property rights and property interests differ from culture to culture. Until recently it has been too easy to assume that there is a 'best' system of property and that it is embodied in the contemporary system of private property that has dominated in the West for the last half millennia. This view has been weakened by the persistent objections of indigenous people who assert that the Western approach is inferior to their own. While this view has only gathered prominence over the last half century, they are not the only challenges to Western private property but merely the most recent and most independent.

The nineteenth century saw the beginning of a challenge to Western private property that threatened to destabilise Western economic order, before exhausting itself in the last two decades of the twentieth century. Communistic socialism was born out of the social failures of the absolute private property of the West. Its battle cry was the proclamation of Pierre-Joseph Proudhon that 'property is theft'. Despite setting out to establish its own moral, political and economic order, communistic socialism suffered from the fatal flaw of being based on the same intellectual foundations as the system is opposed. It was materialist in its metaphysics and individualist in its anthropology.

Indigenous peoples are neither materialists nor individualists. As such they are almost completely unintelligible to the modern Western mind, either on the political right or left, and even more inscrutable to the Anglo cultures who, by an accident of history, came to dominate them in many parts of the world including Australia. Despite their geographical isolation, indigenous people across the world reveal remarkable similarities in their approaches to property rights. What can be even more alarming to the Western mind is the fact that contemporary indigenous peoples also share essential resonances in their approaches to property with the West's own history that predate modern absolute private property and its accompanied economic and political strength (Simon, 1995) (Rogers, 1884).

This historical reality means that the Western approach to property rights is less secure in its claim to dominance and its merits are closely related to the persuasiveness of Herbert Spencer's theory of social evolution. It is no surprise that, as the theory of social evolution fell from popularity during the twentieth century, indigenous people gained confidence in pursuing recognition of their property rights.

Conversely, parallel forces appear to be behind the continued self-consciousness of Western economic apologists regarding private property. Richard Weaver (Weaver, 1948) asserted that property ownership was 'the last metaphysical right' in his attempt to show that private property ownership was a natural thing. Nobel Prize winner

Milton Freidman (1980) and Michael Novak (1982) are representative of the tendency for defences of capitalism to include chapters arguing the merits of absolute private property. Others such as Tom Bethell (1998) and Hernando DeSoto (2000) are more focused on arguing that private property is the foundation for economic success. Regardless of the merits of their arguments, the fact that they are arguing their cause itself implies that it is not nearly as settled as they would like it to appear.

The merits of absolute Western private property have never been unambiguously evident and a series of historians, philosophers and other intellectuals have mounted various critiques that are neither socialist nor customary. While there is a tendency for apologists for Western private property to dismiss its critics as socialists, these make up its less persuasive opponents.

Thorold Rogers (1884) was no socialist, but his analysis of English economic history demonstrated several major shortcomings of English private property and advocated instead widely distributed private property. William small had earlier arrived at a similar conclusion by a study of the architectural heritage of rural England (Cobbett, 1830). A more subtle and global view was presented by the sociologist Carle Zimmerman (1947) who observed that great civilisations rose using property systems that resembled today's indigenous customary property, but that they fell after transitioning into absolute private property of the sort now common in the West. A similar view can be seen in the work of historian Christopher Dawson (1956). Both Zimmerman and Dawson were strongly opposed to socialism, but this did not mean that they were blind to the shortcomings of Western private property.

Discussion on property rights appears to extend back into ancient history with both Plato and Aristotle considering its importance. Aristotle (Aristotle, 1981) presented a developed theory of property in the fourth century BC which has largely framed the discourse ever since. In particular, Aristotle's *dual theory of property* concluded that property should be privately owned while simultaneously still used in common. This theory provides a key tool for interpreting the appropriateness of any system of private property. Within this framework modern private property of the sort defended by Friedman, DeSoto and others is more correctly termed *absolute* private property to identify its distinction from the *conditional* private property advocated by Aristotle and manifest in property systems such as medieval feudalism. Communism took the opposite extreme by advocating *absolute common property* despite, in reality, being absolute state-owned private property.

Foundations to property rights

Indigenous people's understanding of property represents a genuinely independent approach that can be aligned with Aristotle's dictum. It is also grounded in an entirely different approach compared to both communism and capitalism. In order to understand these differences and their merits, it is necessary to understand the foundations upon which any property system is built. It has already been noted that property is influenced in some way by a society's ideas about what humanity is (its anthropology) and where it came from (its explanation for existence, or its metaphysics).

These more esoteric matters are important in discussions with indigenous people who are usually unselfconscious about linking their property rights to their spiritual beliefs. What is less obvious is that the same foundations, albeit built on different assumptions, also underlie the Western systems of private property, such as is found in

Foundations of Property Economics

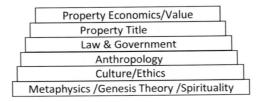

Figure 1.1 Foundations of property economics
Source: Author

Anglo-Australia. The complete set of linkages that exist between property rights and spirituality are summarised in Figure 1.1.

Anglo culture is primarily concerned with economic value and exchange. It can be said that economic action, or commerce, is the strategy adopted by a society to more efficiently fulfil the material needs of its members through material exchanges of raw materials, labour and their composites (capital, or wealth). For these exchanges to be just, the parties must hold rights to them and there must be some value equivalence in the rights exchanged.

Generally, there is little debate over a person's property rights to their own bodies and consequently personal property in the fruits of one's labour and intellectual exertions. However, property in those things that are not the result of human activity, such as land, is more difficult to justify because there is no natural connection to a human producer. This is why writers such as Bethel and De Soto acknowledge the importance of State legislation supporting private property for an effective Western economy. That is, Western private property is a product of a governmental or legal system and can change with government and legislation. It is only ever an arbitrary convention as can be seen by the way that the institution of property differs with time and place.

Cultural beliefs

The idea that property rights could be no more than a mere convention is unsettling because, somehow, property is strongly linked to people's sense of fair play and to their cultural beliefs. It betrays the underlying link that people recognise between property and fundamental moral and cultural beliefs. This should not be surprising because a country's governmental/legal system is itself an expression of its dominant cultural and moral beliefs. Democracy is fairly transparent as a political system that is no more than an expression of the cultural and moral beliefs of the majority of its members. A country's legal system is the product of its government and changes in both are reflections of changes in its moral and cultural thinking.

A culture's dominant moral system itself is not arbitrary. A moral is a principle for appropriate relations between people and to some extent it depends on what the acting moral agent understands to be the nature of the human person. Zimmerman noted that one of the changes in historical cultures as their civilisations aged was the transition from a family or tribal focus to an individual focus. If the human person is understood in terms of family connections this will result in a very different culture and moral system compared to a society where the human person is perceived as an individual. This is perhaps the greatest difference between Anglo cultures, where people tend to define themselves primarily in terms of their personal attributes and economic roles, and indigenous cultures where family, tribe and custom take precedence.

For indigenous people, the reason for their connections to tribe and family is primarily understood in terms of their beliefs about their origins. Despite there being a vast array of creation stories across the indigenous peoples of the world, there are certain commonalities. They all revolve around a creation event that generated both the land and the people. That creation event somehow set the relationships between the people, their land and each other. Most involved supernatural beings who not only made everything but also communicated the conditions on which they would give the land to the people, thus establishing the laws and customs of the tribe.

These creation accounts form the fundamental foundation for customary property rights. They proceed from what continues to be an unassailable application of logic. From two self-evident premises:

- property is naturally owned by its maker; and
- the sensible world is obviously incapable of being its own cause,

indigenous people have reasoned that agencies beyond nature have made the world and hold the original property rights to it. While the corollaries regarding the exact nature of the supernatural creators may be open to debate, positing their existence and the likely supposition that they were intelligent and intent on relating to their most intelligent creations provides a very credible foundation for indigenous customs and traditions. Amongst these are their property rights and it is for this reason that customary property rights are intimately and indissolubly connected with the entire fabric of customary law, custom and spirituality.

Terra nullius

Absolute modern Western property does not usually reach into such subtle origins. The Anglo-Australian property system owes its origin to the arbitrary action of Captain James Cook on 22 August 1770 on Possession Island, off the Queensland coast (National Archives of Australia, 2011). Just before sunset, Cook hoisted the British flag and, assuming the continent to be *terra nullius* (Latin for nobody's land), declared that the whole eastern coast of the continent was the possession of the English King George III. That declaration is the sole foundation of land title in Australia.

The fact that Cook was aware of the local residents, but disregarded them, was ignored until Eddie Mabo forced the High Court of Australia on 3 June 1992 to recognise that the people of the Murray Islands were not only residents but also owners of at least some of the land that Cook took possession of. In the simplest terms, the High Court of Australia recognised that Cook was a thief, though the legal framing of the finding was somewhat more discrete.

Creation

Indigenous peoples' accounts of the origin of the world and its people are always about connectedness. The land comes from its creator, is connected to it and is owned by it. People come from the same source, with the same connections, including connection to the land as a fundamental part of the logic of their being (Ezigbalike, 1994). Property rights are actually connections of being and life. Likewise, customary people exhibit family loyalties that are more intense and interconnected than the Western focus on biological affections can comprehend.

However, for Anglo-Australians, like other modern Westerners, the origin of the earth is linked to theories about the beginning of the universe which are examined in cosmology. The dominant cosmological explanation is the primeval and impersonal explosion of the Big Bang that sent out innumerable individual fragments to form the cosmos. Within this cosmology, complex structures, the heavier elements, planets and stars, were the result of the chance collision of individual atoms. On earth, and perhaps some other planets, the chance interactions of evolution resulted in some collections of fragments prevailing over others. Survival of the fittest, as a mechanism, may be the Western explanation for biological complexity, but it is also a metaphor for the anthropology of individualism first articulated by Thomas Hobbes (1651, reprint 1989) near the start of the modern era that reached it apogee in postmodernity's belief in the essentially oppositional nature of human interaction (Grosz, 1989).

This atomistic theory is the basis for liberal democratic theory, giving rise to the politics of pluralism. This is part of the reason why the connection back to origins is often overlooked in modern culture. However, US Supreme Court Judge Anthony Kennedy explicitly recognised the connection between Western law and people's theories of origins and humanity when he noted:

> At the heart of liberty is the right to define one's own concept of existence, of meaning, of the universe, and of the mystery of human life.

Kennedy recognised that the individualistic pluralism also applied to its own foundations (Goldstein, 1997). From an anthropology of individualism and the Big Bang's essential materialism, the utilitarian moral code of the maximisation of material benefits for the majority (Bentham and Lafleur, 1781) is the obvious choice for a moral system (Mill, 1859).

Utilitarianism and rational self-interest

Modern economic thought is based squarely on the moral logic of utilitarianism and the rational self-interested individual (Mill, 1848; Meikle, 1995). Adam Smith (1778, reprint 1910) concluded that humanity's essential self-interest is the dynamic for all economic relations and it required exclusionary, absolute private property. Thus, the absolute and exclusionary property rights of Anglo-Australia also traces its foundations back to a genesis story just as certainly as indigenous Australians do.

While the Western mind may not be aware of these connections, a different cosmology in the West would have produced a different system of property rights and this can be seen in history. The ancient Christian cosmology of the middle ages was based on the creation of the world by the Christian triune God and resulted in the theory of property rights articulated by St Thomas Aquinas (1981, II-II 66) and manifest in the feudal land property system of that era.

Likewise, Islam posits a single deity as responsible for the creation of the world and has its own distinctive property rights system where:

> Ownership and acquisition in Islam are restricted and limited by numerous obligations laid down by the Shari'ah to render them absolutely harmless. (Bashir, 2002)

This includes a preference for the social ownership of mines and reservations concerning ownership for rental (Nomani and Rahnema, 1994). Siraj Sait and Hilary Lim summarised the Islamic approach in a way which demonstrates the hierarchy outlined in Figure 1.1 when they stated:

> The land rights framework in Islamic theory is circumscribed not only by external human rights and development strategies promoting a just and equitable society, but equally by internal dynamics. These religious and moral dimensions of land may be internalised and incorporated into property transactions of many societies in multiple ways. Islam potentially impacts on all stages of the property cycle from acquisition, to management and to transmission. (Sait and Lim, 2005, p. 9)

Both these traditions are connected to the earlier Jewish religion that taught that God had said:

> "The land shall not be sold in perpetuity, for the land is mine; for you are strangers and sojourners with me". (Leviticus 25:23)

When combined with the notion that God had given the land to His people (Leviticus 25:2) this core statement of property rights and obligations fits not only into the later Christian and Islamic developments but also reveals an essential harmony with almost every customary property system known in the world. On this basis, the aspirations of Australian indigenous peoples regarding their land is not a cultural oddity, but a perspective that has wide support both geographically and historically.

Customary property rights

The key common elements in the various instances of customary property rights can be summarised as follows:

- the land is a gift from antiquity that must be passed on to its current owner's progeny;
- the land is the common possession of the customary community to whom it has been given;
- the land may be shared with others for their use, so long as ownership is understood to always remain with its traditional owners';
- exclusive possession by owners is irrelevant, so long as its ultimate owners are recognised to whom it will ultimately revert;
- property rights are one part of a more comprehensive system of custom and moral law, all of which must be maintained; and
- the land can only be used in accordance with the customs and laws of the people, even when occupied by others with permission.

These principles revolve about the two fundamental aspects of property, its ownership and its use. Ownership, as a fundamental connection, must always be maintained by the tribe or clan in customary property systems. The use of the land however may be flexibly managed for the best result. Members of most indigenous Australian tribes used their land in common with no individual or family being able to assert 'this land is mine'. However, in some cases, use rights involve apparent private allocation. In the Murray Islands for example, the success of the Mabo case was due to the traditional allocation of specific land to individual families with identifiable and durable boundaries and boundary marking. While this resembled Western exclusive property sufficiently to convince the High Court Judges that it demonstrated an 'ownership' system comparable to the West, the reality was more complex.

Murray Island customary private property normally proceeded via family lines of inheritance, but always at the ultimate discretion of the community leaders and always with ultimate reversion to the community in cases where family succession failed. It is actually private *use rights* and not *land ownership* that passes to individual Murray Island families. This is consistent with Reeve's (Reeve, 1986) observation that property rights in the West are only ever about rights to use and never actually about land ownership per se.

Intercultural land use

The Western preoccupation with exclusive rights to use property opens a very useful channel for interaction between customary and Western property systems. Indigenous customary property holders are usually comfortable with sharing the use of their land with others, provided that ultimate ownership is retained. In practice this also includes some participation in the productivity that the land is put to. In Western terms, this translates to a lease. In a lease relationship certain property rights are transferred to the lessee in return for rent. These rights include exclusive occupation and enjoyment, subject to the uses permitted by the owner as specified in the lease. Leases do not confuse the matter of ultimate ownership but respect it in the relationship between the parties, the specification of what uses are permitted and in the matter of rent.

In many countries where customary property rights are respected, workable property rights regimes have been developed based on leasehold tenure. This includes many parts of Africa and the Pacific. In Fiji a national system of leasehold is administered by the iTaukei Land Trust Board which leases land on behalf of the traditional owners. The system has been working successfully since it was established in 1940 and is structured to ensure that the land of Fiji remains in the hands of its traditional owners, even though it may be used by others on leases ranging from 30 to 99 years.

In normal circumstances, valuation of Anglo property rights is only concerned with the commercial value of the right to use property. This is especially evident in the case of the income approaches to valuation, but it is also evident in the case of compensation valuation for compulsory acquisition. The heads of compensation applicable in most jurisdictions focus primarily on compensation categories that can be interpreted in terms of lost commercial use value. This includes the market value of the land lost, any detriment to the value of the land remaining due to the severance itself (severance), or to adverse externalities suffered on the remaining land due to the use to which the lost land will be put (injurious affection).

It is only within some jurisdictions, and then only with considerable reservation, that compensation is awarded for that esoteric sense of loss (solatium) that cannot be demonstrated in commercial terms. The fact that solatium is awarded as an apparently arbitrary percentage (typically limited to 10%) suggests that our ability to actually value it is quite immature and the figure is merely a convention that achieves some level of placation between the parties. The fact that few people involved with solatium consider its magnitude as truly representing the value of the interest lost is an indication that even people of the Anglo culture can sense that some genuine human values cannot be expressed in monetary terms.

Ownership and use

Fundamentally, Anglo property value is almost entirely connected with use value. The value of the freehold interest may be notionally the present value of all the property's future rental values while the value of the leasehold interest is merely the value of some of them. Anglo ownership is no more than its material use value. In this way, ownership in Anglo culture is a very thin concept compared to its meaning to indigenous Australians.

In philosophy, the term 'property' refers to something that a thing must have in order to be itself. In chemistry, for example, a property of hydrogen is that it is lighter than air and another is that it reacts explosively with oxygen to form water. If you have a gas that lacks one of these qualities, it cannot be hydrogen. This sense of property fits well with indigenous Australian notions of land ownership. The land is something an indigenous person must have connection to in order to be an indigenous person within indigenous culture and law.

By contrast, Anglo-Australians understand that they came into the world with no necessary connection to any particular land and during their life they may buy and sell land without any fundamental attachment to it. Property's meaning is merely what comforts it can bring in a material sense.

From all of this, three principles can be concluded that relate to the valuation of property rights. The first is that the maker of a thing has natural property rights to it. Secondly, Anglo valuation is primarily connected with use values, which may be either perpetual (freehold ownership) or limited in time (leasehold). In all cases it may be expressed in monetary terms. Thirdly, indigenous Australians have a richer understanding of ownership that is intimate, perpetual and goes beyond use rights to contain real but intangible elements that cannot be equated to monetary values.

These three principles enable the valuer to address a wide spectrum of problems in property economics, especially where property straddles cultural divisions. Consider the following cases.

The leasehold land of the Wik people

This was the focus of disputes following recognition of the customary property of the Wik people in Queensland in 1996 over land that was held privately as statutory leaseholds. As a terminating interest in land with rental obligations to the State, leasehold tenure is correctly understood as a personal interest, not a real property interest. This means that at the expiry of the lease the lessee has no residual interest in the land.

A problem arose with the lessees who had taken over the leases with part of the remaining term left to run under expectations that were inconsistent with their actual legal property rights. For political reasons the rent to the State had shrunk in real terms to peppercorn levels. As a result, leases were transferred with premium payments that represented the capitalised profit rents customarily enjoyed by lessees. The lessees believed that the rents would continue at peppercorn levels and assumed that the leases would be automatically renewed on expiry. Neither of these assumptions were backed by any legal right, despite having been the common practice and expectation for some time.

The problem arose when the indigenous owners were acknowledged and it was feared that the peppercorn rents would return to market levels. The lessees never held the property rights that they had paid for, despite the established market prices for the leaseholds. This highlights the importance of valuations going beyond merely appraising market price levels to include some comment on the rational basis of the perceived value.

Jackson's Airport, Port Moresby

This airfield grew from a Royal Australian Air force runway built in 1940 and was expanded over the following three decades. Its land was *purchased* from its traditional owners. From an Anglo perspective there is no debate. The land was sold over half a century ago and the government is now the owner with no further compensation obligations.

However, the traditional owners had no concept of land sale and in recent years the descendants of those who 'sold' the land have claimed that the land is still theirs and that compensation should be given to them also. Their understanding can be interpreted in terms of a leasehold allocation with the original compensation resembling an upfront rental payment for a lease term restricted in some way to the life of the persons involved.

Present value analysis suggests that at a modest yield and discount rate of 5%, the rents over 75 years would represent about 97.4% of the upfront payment in 1940. That is, had the customary owners instead leased the land to the government in 1940 for an upfront rental payment, only 2.6% of the government's leasehold interest would have remained in 2015. On this basis the customary owners' claims start to look commercially reasonable and the current dispute turns on the meaning of a word that may well have had no meaning at all to the indigenous owners in 1940.

Summary

The distinction between concepts of ownership and use are fundamental to the International Valuation Standards and a twenty-first-century approach to property valuation. Providing the theoretical basis for such a distinction in both Western cultures and indigenous cultures, the principal contribution of this chapter is the reconciliation of such concepts between the respective cultures. The chapter offers a way of thinking about property rights that transcends the self-imposed strictures of Western society such as temporal title and offers a notion of perpetual rights to land subject to periodic derogation.

Emphasising the importance of culture and belief to concepts of ownership and use, the chapter compares and contrasts the cosmic notion of creation, the role of Christianity, Islam and other faiths, the impact of Greek philosophical foundations and customary property rights. Over two thousand years of Western philosophical debate through Adam Smith to Milton Freidman are shown to connect closely to the beliefs of indigenous cultures based on creation beliefs which establish relationships between the people, their land and each other within the notion of connectedness and a clearer spiritual bond with the land where property rights are connections of being and life.

Accordingly, the chapter provides a theoretically grounded framework within which both Western and indigenous cultural interpretations of property may be accommodated for the purposes of valuation.

With this chapter having considered foundational legal principles, the following chapters will consider economic, planning, policy, finance and valuation principles to conclude the first part of this book, addressing the principles of valuation, with the second part then addressing the practice of valuation.

References

Aquinas, T 1981, *Summa theologica*, ED Province, trans, 2nd ed, Westminster, Maryland.
Aristotle 1981, *The Politics*, TA Sinclair, trans, Penguin, London.
Bashir, AHM 2002, 'Property rights, institutions and economic development: An Islamic perspective', *Humanomics*, vol. 18, no. 3/4, p. 16.
Bentham, J and Lafleur, LJ 1781, An Introduction to the Principles of Morals and Legislation, Hafner Pub. Co, New York.
Bethell, T 1998, Noblest Triumph: Property and Prosperity through the Ages, St. Martin's Press, New York.
Cobbett, W 1830, *Rural Rides*, Nelson & Sons.
Dawson, C 1956, *The Dynamics of World History*, Mentor Omega, New York.
DeSoto, H 2000, The Mystery of Capitalism: Why Capitalism Triumphs in the West and Fails Everywhere Else, Basic Books, New York.
Ezigbalike, IC 1994, 'Cadastral "reform" – At what cultural costs to developing countries', *The Australian Surveyor*, vol. 39, no. 3, 177–186.
Friedman, M 1980, *Free to Choose*, Penguin, Harmondsworth.
Goldstein, CR 1997, 'Justice Kennedy's "notorious mystery passage"', *Liberty*, July/August.
Grosz, E 1989, *Sexual Subversions*, Allen & Unwin, Sydney.
Hobbes, T 1651, reprint 1989, *Leviathan*, Penguin, Harmondsworth.
Meikle, S 1995, *Aristotle's Economic Thought*, Oxford University Press, Oxford.
Mill, JS 1848, *Principles of Political Economy*, Routledge, London.
Mill, JS 1859, *On liberty, Fount*, London.
National Archives of Australia 2011, Secret Instructions to Lieutenant Cook 30 July 1768 (UK). *Documenting a Democracy*, www.foundingdocs.gov.au/item-did-34.html
Nomani, F and Rahnema, A. 1994, *Islamic Economic Systems*, Zed, London.
Novak, M 1982, The Spirit of Democratic Capitalism, Madison, New York.
Reeve, A 1986, *Property*, Macmillan, Houndsmills.
Rogers, JT 1884, *Six Centuries of Work and Wages*, George Allen & Unwin, London.
Sait, S and Lim, H 2005, Paper 1 – Islamic Land Theories and Applications, Islam, Land and Property Research Series, UN Habitat, Nairobi.
Schumacher, EF 1974, *Small Is Beautiful*, Abacus, London.
Simon, J (ed.) 1995. *The State of Humanity*, Blackwell, Cambridge.

Smith, A 1778, reprint 1910, *The Wealth of Nations*, JM Dent, London.
Weaver, RM 1948, *Ideas Have Consequences*, University of Chicago Press, Chicago.
Zimmerman, CC 1947, *Family and Civilization*, Harper, New York.

Biography

Garrick Small is Head of the Economics, Finance and Property Discipline Group for Central Queensland University and Associate Professor of Property. He has taught at the University of Technology, Sydney, The University of New South Wales, Western Sydney University and CQUniversity.

His career includes 18 years in the property investment and development industry with work including consulting to major developers and State departments as well as undertaking complex investment appraisals. Over three decades as an academic, he has held various leadership positions including Associate Head of School, Head of Department, Program Leader and Head of Course.

His educational background includes surveying and engineering, commerce and economics and philosophy and psychology. This has led to scholarly interests that engage the economic, cultural and philosophical aspects of the relationship between property and the community. He is recognised as an authority on property law, property rights, customary rights integration, regional development, land rights policy and valuation theory, in addition to applied questions relating to valuation, urban development policy and advanced investment appraisal.

2 Economic principles

Colin Lizieri

Introduction

With the first part of this book addressing the principles of valuation and the second part addressing the practice of valuation, the previous chapter considered legal principles, this chapter will consider economic principles and the following chapters will consider planning, policy, finance and valuation principles.

It is assumed that the reader already has an understanding of supply, demand and pricing economics in the context of valuation, with this chapter framing property market processes as economic processes where the forces of supply and demand determine rents and prices and where the rational investment decisions that reflect those forces should be embedded in valuation practice.

Economics, valuation and the market

In order to undertake a rational valuation process and to provide rigorous advice to clients, a professional valuer needs to understand the dynamics of the commercial real estate market around the subject property. Although there are important influences from government and land use regulation, those dynamic processes are essentially economic in nature: thus economics underpins a rational valuation process. This holds whether the aim is to produce a market valuation estimating likely selling price, an investment appraisal assessing a buy/sell decision or the maximum offer price or an assessment of value for bank lending purposes. Failure to account for the underlying economic processes can lead to poor advice and erroneous decision-making with over-reliance on short-term trends or noisy signals from the market.

In this chapter, the inter-connections between different parts of the market are stressed: the occupier market in which rents are formed, the investment market where prices are determined and the development market which creates new space. As economic processes, rents and prices are determined by the interaction of supply and demand. The decisions in one market produce outcomes that feed into the next market. However, because of the nature of commercial property as a real asset, these changes are not instantaneous. As a result, a full understanding of the dynamics of real estate has to acknowledge the adjustment processes operating in those markets and the frictions and lags that exist. Fundamental to conventional economics is the concept of *equilibrium*: the state where the forces of supply and demand are in balance with the price level 'clearing the market'. The interlinked real estate markets and the

DOI: 10.1201/9781003049555-2

16 Colin Lizieri

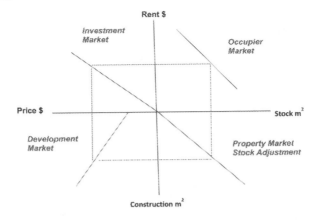

Figure 2.1 Quadrant model of the commercial property market
Source: Author, adapted from, inter alia, DiPasquale and Wheaton (1992), Ball et al. (1998), Lizieri (2009).

lags and frictions to adjustment processes means that property will rarely, if ever, be 'in equilibrium' but rather will seek to move *towards* that equilibrium state.

To provide an overall context for understanding economic processes in property markets, a number of theoretical models have been developed which set out the inter-relationship between markets. Figure 2.1 is derived from models such as those found in DiPasquale and Wheaton (1992), Fisher (1992), Ball et al. (1999) and Lizieri (2009). It shows the equilibrium linkages between four interrelated markets: the occupier, investment, development and stock adjustment markets. Before examining elements of these in more detail, this section sets out the basic linkages between the quadrants in the model.

Occupier market

The upper right quadrant details the occupier market, where rents are formed. Firms seek business premises in a location: the more desirable the location and the greater the profit that can be earned there, the more firms will seek space, pushing up rent. However, high rents deter firms (or force them to reduce their space demands). Thus the demand curve slopes downwards – the lower the rent, the more space is demanded; the more space available, the less firms need to pay. In equilibrium, the rent in the market equalises the space supplied and the economically viable demand.

Investment market

In the upper left quadrant, rents are converted to capital values in the investment market. From a valuation perspective, that conversion comes from the application of a yield or capitalisation rate to the rental income. From a market perspective, the price paid equalises the investment demand for property assets with their supply and the yield simply expresses the relationship between the rent (from the occupier market) and the price (from the investment market). Implicit in this is a required rate of return for investors, reflecting overall investment market conditions and perceptions of asset class risk.

Development market

Supply of new space in the development market (lower left quadrant) depends on the price of completed stock (determined in the investment market) compared to the cost of producing that stock (including land acquisition and clearance costs). This concept is, of course, built into development appraisals. Until price per unit area rises above the full cost of production, no development takes place – thus the chord begins away from the origin. Thereafter, as prices rise, more space is produced. It is here that the linkages and feedback mechanisms emerge, since that new supply, if not fully matched by new occupational demand, will result in lower rents and prices, affecting the profitability of development. Thus, an understanding of the dynamics of the market and lagged adjustment processes is important in the valuation and advisory process.

Property market stock adjustment

In the DiPasquale and Wheaton model, the lower right-hand quadrant represents space adjustment. New supply increases the stock of space. However, older space may become unsuitable for profitable use due to depreciation and obsolescence, while in historic urban settings, there may be few available sites, such that existing stock must be withdrawn for redevelopment. In the hypothetical equilibrium state (with no change in occupier demand), newly constructed space will equal stock that has become redundant and buildings withdrawn from the market, leaving available stock unchanged.

Thus, the overall figure shows a static equilibrium for a given level of demand in a market: the space supplied matches effective demand at a rent that attracts investors who pay prices that encourage sufficient development activity to replace redundant stock. In practice, each of the elements in this system is in motion, and it is necessary to consider the adjustment processes that result from shocks and changes in supply and/or demand in providing valuation advice. In what follows, the activity in each quadrant is examined more closely, starting with the investment market, central to the valuation process.

The investment market: rents, prices and required return

From a corporate finance perspective, the price that an investor should pay for an asset is the discounted value of the expected future cash-flows, using a discount rate that represents that investor's cost of capital. This translates straightforwardly into a discounted cash-flow investment valuation of a property. Rental values and costs associated with collecting those rents and maintaining the building are projected forward and then discounted back at a target rate of return: the resultant present value represents the maximum amount the investor should pay for a property (including all acquisition costs). For investors using an Internal Rate of Return approach, the anticipated purchase price and associated transaction costs are included in the cash-flow and the resultant IRR must be greater than the firm's target rate of return for the acquisition to proceed.

Away from the individual dwelling, prices in the marketplace should represent some consensus investment valuation. In turn, the yield on property or capitalisation rate is simply the ratio of the (current) rent to the (current) price with some adjustment needed for any reversionary elements resulting from lease contracts and rent review periods.

Yield-based valuation models may use those capitalisation rates to estimate market value but it should be recalled that the comparable evidence for those yields comes from acquisitions and rental transactions in the investment and occupier markets.

In practice, there may be many reasons for a property acquisition that does not fit such a basic model (for example: safe haven investment; acquisition for portfolio purposes; site assembly for larger projects; personal, behavioural reasons). Nonetheless, since the present value model underpins valuation, it is worth considering the economics of the elements of that calculation in more detail, starting with the target rate of return or discount rate.

Weighted average cost of capital

One approach to the target rate of return relates it to the investor's cost of capital. In the weighted average cost of capital (WACC) approach, the target rate of return is given as:

$$WACC_i = P_e R_e + P_d R_d (1 - T_c) \qquad \text{Equation 1}$$

where:
  P_e represents the proportion of equity in the firm;
  R_e represents the required return on equity;
  P_d represents the proportion of debt in the firm;
  R_d represents the marginal cost of debt; and
  T_c represents the marginal tax rate.

A firm makes a decision on the mix of capital from debt and equity. The overall cost of debt (the interest rate) is determined in capital markets as a function of capital availability and market perceptions of overall risk: the firm's marginal cost of debt also reflects the risks associated with that company and its activities relative to the overall market. The required return on equity is the return that shareholders (or equivalent stakeholders) require to persuade them to maintain investment in the company and reflects overall market perceptions of risk and the risks that arise from the activities of the firm and the leverage of the firm – with the required return increasing for higher risk activities and as the debt to equity ratio increases. In the Capital Asset Pricing Model, that risk factor is measured by the beta (β) of the firm, where a β greater than one indicates a firm whose activities and capital structure are considered systematically more risky than the overall market.

In many markets, there is a tax shield benefit from debt capital. From this it can be seen that the required return is, in considerable measure, driven by macro factors in the economy. In an environment of very low interest rates, the cost of debt falls, the relative return on equity falls and, hence, the WACC falls. Lower interest rates increase asset values, other things being equal. An investment valuation will need to consider whether that low interest rate environment will persist or is a short-run phenomenon.

Risk-free rate and risk premium

An alternative approach is to consider that the target rate of return represents a *risk-free rate* and a *risk premium* appropriate for the type of asset being valued. The risk-free rate is the return sufficient to persuade an individual to invest their wealth in a safe asset rather than to consume it now: it must compensate for the impact of expected inflation and for impatience or time preference. The risk premium is the additional return that investors demand for investing in an asset whose future cash-flow or performance is riskier than the safe asset: the greater the risk, the greater the risk premium. Thus, equities should deliver a larger risk premium than corporate bonds given stock market volatility and the greater uncertainty of dividend payments. Conventionally, investment grade real estate would be expected to have a risk premium between equities and bonds: the future capital value of a property is uncertain, but the contractual nature of rent provides greater stability in income returns.

Traditionally, the yield on government bonds has been used as a proxy for the risk-free rate (although there remains a risk of default for many governments). Bond yields in the market will reflect the inflation environment, the savings ratio in the economy and investor attitudes to overall economic risk and future prospects (greater uncertainty may lead investors to seek out the safety of government bonds forcing prices up and yields down – at the same time potentially increasing risk premiums for all assets). However, they will also reflect capital availability globally and domestically – a glut of savings will drive bond yields down as is generally thought to be the case in the asset price boom that preceded the Global Financial Crisis of 2007–2008. Government and central bank activity also influences bond yields through a number of channels including high government borrowing increasing the supply of bonds, reducing prices and raising yields, monetary policy affecting inflation expectations and specific measures such as quantitative easing which can artificially move bond yields away from their 'natural' rate. This can be seen clearly in the post-financial crisis and pandemic periods, where bond yields in many developed economies approached zero, implying negative real risk-free rates.

Capitalisation rate

The property yield or capitalisation rate (which translates rents into prices) can be interpreted directly from the idea of the target rate of return as the risk-free rate plus the risk premium. For a freehold, fee simple property, the investor is acquiring the right to receive the rental income in perpetuity: that rent may be expected to grow (at least in nominal terms) in the future. The property itself, though, will be subject to depreciation – that is it will not attract the top rents in a sub-market without capital expenditure or even redevelopment. From this, the yield can be decomposed as:

$$k = RFR + RP - g + \delta \qquad \text{Equation 2}$$

where:
  k represents the all risks yield or capitalisation rate;
  RFR represents the risk-free rate;
  RP represents the required risk premium for this type of asset;
  g represents the long-run expected rental growth; and
  δ represents the depreciation rate.

This yield decomposition is normative, in the sense that it indicates what the yield *should* be. In a property market, the observed yield comes from transactions whose prices represent the balance of supply of investment assets and (effective) demand for those assets – the balance between buyers and sellers. Where there is imbalance (for example, an excess of capital seeking investment opportunities), those market yields may diverge from fundamental yields. Rational investment decisions require careful consideration of the components of yields and their likely movement over the holding period of the investment.

Rental growth is an important component in that yield calculation. It should be stressed that this represents *long-run* stable growth and not short-run growth, whether in the recent past or forecast for the immediate future. Rental forecasts are an important component of a discounted cash-flow analysis or investment appraisal but should not have a major influence on the yield. There is a sound economic logic to this point: in the longer run, as the quadrant model indicates, higher rents (and prices) trigger new supply, absorbing any new demand. Long-run evidence points to very muted commercial rental growth after inflation (for very long-run rent and price data for Amsterdam, London and New York, see Ambrose et al. (2013), Devaney (2010), Wheaton et al. (2009).) However, supply side response to positive occupier demand shocks is not instantaneous, leading to rising rents. To explore those responses, the occupier market will be considered next.

The economics of occupational demand and rent

Demand for commercial and industrial space in a market comes from firms assessing the costs and benefits of operating in different locations and then seeking space in the most profitable of those locations. The economic drivers of profitability will vary by sector and may vary over time or with shifts in technology. The rent payable for space forms part of the cost-benefit calculation and, in principle, helps to allocate space rationally – in that more profitable businesses can outbid less profitable businesses to secure scarce space in a city or region. This competition should lead to land and property being in its 'highest and best use'.

For retail space, the best location will be that which maximises access to customers (with disposable income within the catchment area and competition from other retailers being key additional considerations). Traditionally, the point of maximum accessibility has been the central city, an idea embedded in the economic geography of central place theory. However, in developed economies dominated by car travel, the cost of providing parking space and the effects of congestion might favour out-of-town shopping malls, grocery superstores and retail parks. Retail provides an example of the influence of technology on demand, with increasing Internet sales reducing shop-based turnover and creating new demand for logistics warehousing and 'last mile' delivery points. For valuers and investment appraisers, this should sound a warning about over-reliance on historic trends in rental growth.

In similar fashion, demand for office space is driven largely by business and financial services activity. Principal factors driving locational advantage include access to a skilled labour force, access to clients and the knowledge exchanges that come from proximity to similar or complementary businesses – agglomeration economies. This has typically favoured the centres of larger cities with mass public transit access, particularly where these develop significant specialist strengths: perhaps the clearest example being international financial centres where a critical mass of activity allows deep specialist pools of labour and activity. However, there are counter-examples of more dispersed regions and smaller cities developing specialist skills, as in the high technology sector with Silicon Valley and with smaller niche cities such as Cambridge in the UK clustering activity and generating rents that are higher than their size might suggest. These accessibility advantages seem to hold even though technological developments might seem to make face-to-face contact less important in many areas of service activity and change the way that work is conducted and offices are used. In principle, new working practices and the increased use of technology and remote working might be expected to reduce the demand for floor space per worker (particularly with increases in working from home and with office intensification strategies such as hot-desking and office hotelling). However, evidence of impact remains mixed. Again, more profitable businesses can offer higher rents for space driving out the less profitable activities.

Rents and rental growth

That a specific location can attract a higher rent per square metre should not be taken to imply that rental *growth* will be higher in that market – nor even that employment growth or household income will automatically translate into rental growth. Rents are formed by supply and demand so, as demand shifts, so too can supply. Evidence suggests that *long-run* supply adjusts to demand changes. There are, though, substantial constraints that prevent short-run changes to supply: to increase the stock of space requires site assembly, planning permission, site clearance and preparation and construction. This can be a lengthy process, particularly in heavily developed city centres. While it might be argued that there are no new sites in a fully developed city and that, hence, employment growth should drive rents upwards, in practice, redevelopment allows greater density, an increase of space per plot area. By implication, economic growth will be captured in *land values*, but not in rent per unit of space: historic evidence largely confirms this. It is this lag between demand shock and supply response that can lead to rapid rental growth in response to unexpected employment or economic growth.

These short- and long-run adjustments are illustrated in Figure 2.2. Initially, demand is represented by the demand curve D-D and supply of space by S-S. The demand curve slopes downwards (with higher rents, businesses find the location less profitable and require less space, so demand falls). The supply curve slopes steeply upwards: some, but not much, space can be brought into the market in response to rising rents (for example, space in other uses or space held vacant). Balancing supply and demand results in a stock of S_1 and a rent of R_1.

If demand for space increases in the market (for example, due to rapid economic growth, an increase in profitability or deregulation), the demand curve shifts upwards to D'-D'. Since supply cannot adjust rapidly, the stock of space moves modestly to S_2 and rents jump to R_2. However, that higher rent passes into the investment market and resultant higher prices may trigger new development activity. Longer run supply adjustment is more elastic – as represented by the supply curve S'-S'. This shift results in an increase in supply to S_3 which leads to rents falling back to R_3. It is for this reason that investors, developers and valuers should take care not to over-interpret recent rental growth nor assume that immediate historic growth trends are sustainable.

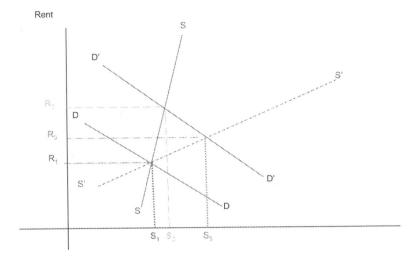

Figure 2.2 Adjustment in occupier markets
Source: author, after Ball et al. (1999) inter alia.

Vacancy rate

A key variable in understanding change in rents within a market is the vacancy rate. In a market with a low vacancy rate, lessees must compete against each other for any space available, pushing rents upwards; in a market with a high vacancy rate, lessors must compete for potential new occupiers and to retain their existing lessees, pushing rents downwards. It is generally held that, for a market to operate efficiently, there should be a reasonable amount of vacant space to allow for movement of firms, to allow refurbishment and to permit lessors to seek the optimum lessee and for lessees to seek the most appropriate space. Real estate economists have termed this the 'natural vacancy rate'. This is analogous to the natural or non-inflationary unemployment rate in labour economics which, similarly, allows for employment market flexibility, retraining and the optimal matching of workers to jobs.

Many rental adjustment models are based on the natural vacancy rate: when observed void levels in a market are above the natural rate, then rents would be expected to fall; conversely, vacancy levels below the natural rate imply a tight letting market, suggesting rising rents. As before, these are short-run adjustment processes, but provide indicators for cash-flow forecasts and investment modelling.

Finally, it should be noted that rental adjustment processes are unlikely to be symmetric due to the institutional nature of the real estate market and that there are other forces creating lags. (For a more detailed discussion, see Hendershott et al., 2010.) For example, a positive demand shock in an office market (an increase in firms seeking to locate in the market or to expand their employment) is likely to result in near immediate upward pressure on rents as firms compete for any available space. However, a negative demand shock (firms seeking to shed labour – as occurred in financial services in the aftermath of the Global Financial Crisis) may not have the same impact, due to the contractual nature of leases. A firm reducing its labour force by 10% may, nonetheless, be unable to vacate the premises it occupies until the lease term expires and may be unwilling or unable to sub-let unwanted space. This creates 'hidden vacancy' or 'grey space' in a market. Similarly, positive economic growth and rental increase may trigger a supply response – an increase in space provided in the market. What, though, is the response to negative economic and rental growth? The stock exists as a tangible asset and cannot easily be withdrawn from the market without economic loss. This illustrates a key difference in the economics of real estate compared to, for example, manufacturing, where production levels can be reduced in response to demand falls. Given the importance of the supply response, the next section will consider the economics of commercial property development.

The economics of commercial property development

From the market process described above, the decision to develop new space in a market should reflect the relationship between the costs of development (including site acquisition) and the price to be obtained for the completed development, providing an appropriate return for the developer as compensating for the risks taken. Formally, development should only take place when the ratio of the value of the completed building to the full cost of development is greater than one (technically, the ratio should exceed 1+ α where α is the option value of delaying the development decision – see Grenadier (1995) for a discussion). The calculation must account for the timing of cash-flows in the development period.

One of the major risks faced by a developer is that the development process can be lengthy. This creates a problem for developers, since they can observe rents and capital values in the *current* market but must *forecast* or anticipate what prices might be when the building is completed. Further, the decisions that developers make will affect those future prices: if many developers all decide to build at one point, then new supply may drive down rents in the occupier market and prices in the investment market, affecting profitability.

If developers react to current and recent growth in rents and capital values in a market that have resulted from a (one off) demand shock – that is, if they are *myopic* or rely on short-run trends – then it is possible that over-building will occur, triggering a familiar pattern of construction booms and slumps. Formally, if developers extrapolate current values and trends, then a cobweb cycle can arise as construction overreacts to above equilibrium price signals, over-supplying the market, driving rents below equilibrium and choking off supply in the next period (Wheaton, 1999; Lizieri, 2009). This will be exacerbated where the increase in occupier demand is, itself, cyclical: for example, if it is linked to the business cycle. Given a sufficient lag between construction starts and completion, the new space could become available just as the business cycle and demand reverses: vacancies will increase in the market and rents and values will fall, threatening the viability of the developers' business models.

Rational economic analysis should mean that developers will not take myopic decisions or be excessively influenced by current prices but will account for long-run demand and supply trends, account for adjustment processes in the market and be aware of the effect of development decisions. The persistence of property cycles in developed cities casts doubt on this and suggests that there is a strong behavioural component to development decisions. A compounding factor is capital availability. As noted in the discussion of the investment market, excess capital can drive interest rates and required returns downwards and asset prices upwards. That same excess capital may be available as development finance and funding, amplifying construction cycles.

The foregoing allows identification of conditions that will be most conducive to building and rental cycles. First, a market with a dominant economic sector will be more vulnerable to volatility in demand than one with a more diversified structure. This would be the case for cities dominated by natural resource use (for example Dallas or Houston's office sectors dominated by the oil industry) or in international financial centres. Cyclical behaviour will be exacerbated if that specialised economic activity is also volatile (thus a city dominated by global financial services will have more volatile office demand than one more reliant on stable government employment). Second, markets where the building process is lengthy will be more prone to cycles than markets where supply can adjust rapidly. Highly developed traditional city centres, particularly where there are planning and institutional constraints on development and long lags between start and completion are more vulnerable to booms and busts. Finally, markets where there are strong entry barriers for developers (perhaps due to the cost of land and construction and access to finance) will tend to be more cyclical in nature.

As an illustration of cyclical tendencies, Figure 2.3 shows new construction starts for office buildings in the City of London from 1977 to 2006 (that is, just before the onset of the Global Financial Crisis), set against real effective rental growth after accounting for inflation. The City of London fulfils all the characteristics of a market prone to cycles as outlined above. It is dominated by global financial services and associated professional services activity, characterised by significant fluctuations, site assembly and construction processes are complex given the highly developed and historic nature of the market and the planning structure and the costs of producing prime office assets in the market form a substantial entry barrier for most developers.

Two striking features of the graph are, first, the extreme cyclicality of the building cycle and, second, the apparent reaction to short-run spikes in rental growth.

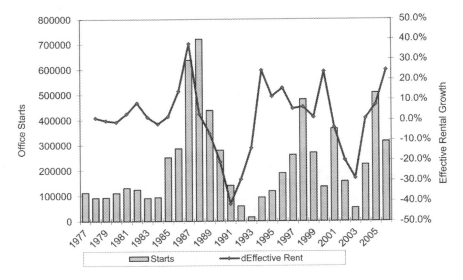

Figure 2.3 Office starts and rents in the City of London

Source: Author, utilising public data from Corporation of London, CBRE and Office for National Statistics.

The 1987–1989 building boom was driven by rising office demand as a result of financial deregulation ('Big Bang') which, following a period of subdued development, resulted in rapidly increasing rents and office capital values. However, the scale of the supply response (in part due to relaxation of planning controls) and the lag between starts and completions means that new space arrived in a more hostile economic environment, contributing to plummeting rents and values and financial distress in the property market. The subsequent spikes in development suggest that the implications of that property crash have not been learnt. Each cycle has distinct features but common characteristics: above all, over-reaction to current market information. It is worth emphasising that, in real terms correcting for inflation, office rents per square metre in the City of London in 2016 were *lower* than they were in 1986, despite 30 years of financial services industry growth in the City. Markets adjust to demand shocks.

Conclusions and further considerations

This brief survey has emphasised the importance of the inter-connectedness of markets in real estate and of the dynamics of adjustment processes. In market economies, property market processes are *economic* processes and the forces of supply and demand determine rents and prices: rational investment decisions should reflect those forces and this should be embedded in valuation practice. The nature of real estate as an asset creates complex interactions between markets since adjustment processes can be lengthy. Supply cannot react to demand shocks instantaneously – there are physical and institutional constraints that mean supply responses are sluggish while the long-lasting, physical nature of real estate means that it is difficult to reduce space if demand falls. This can lead to rental cycles, exacerbated by the actions of developers, investors and lenders reacting, perhaps over-reacting, to short-run changes in rents and prices.

The adjustment model presented here is an abstraction and simplification. A full model would need to take into account the land market and the behaviour of landowners, interactions and competition between sectors for space in a city and its hinterland, the relationship between residential and commercial real estate markets and the role of institutional and legal constraints and the planning system on market processes and adjustment. Above all, there needs to be careful consideration of the interaction between property markets and the financial system and debt markets. An understanding of the role of leverage in determining property prices, property returns and real estate market risk remains a major task for real estate economists.

Summary

The complexity of property markets that arises from the inter-connectedness of the occupier market, the investment market and the development market was considered in depth, with movement in each being both gradual and relative giving a high propensity for periods of boom through under-supply and bust through over-supply, so condemning property markets to a perpetuity of cyclicality.

By focusing on the role of the discount rate in property valuation and appraisal, the relative and over-lapping contributions of the economy, finance markets and property markets may be combined and applied in the valuation and appraisal process. The inter-connectedness of the economy, finance markets and property markets manifests in a state of constant change, compounded by the inter-connectedness with the constantly changing occupier, investment and development markets, further impacting the valuation and appraisal process.

In market economies, property market processes are *economic* processes and the forces of supply and demand determine rents and prices: rational investment decisions should reflect those forces and this should be embedded in valuation practice.

Accordingly, the chapter provides an economically-grounded framework within which to consider and interpret the impact of the roles of occupiers, investors and developers on supply and demand in the property markets and the implications that follow for value, each within the simultaneously dynamic economy and financial markets.

With this chapter having considered economic principles and the previous chapter legal principles, the following chapters will consider planning, policy, finance and valuation principles to conclude the first part of this book, addressing the principles of valuation, with the second part then addressing the practice of valuation.

References

Ambrose, B, Eichholtz, P and Lindenthal, T, 2013, 'House prices and fundamentals: 355 years of evidence', *Journal of Money, Credit and Banking*, vol. 45, pp. 477–491.
Ball, M, Lizieri, C and MacGregor, B 1999, *The Economics of Commercial Property Markets*, Routledge, London.
Devaney, S, 2010, 'Trends in office rents in the City of London: 1867–1959', *Explorations in Economic History*, vol. 47, pp. 198–212.
DiPasquale, D and Wheaton, W 1992, 'The market for real estate assets and space: A conceptual framework', *Real Estate Economics*, vol. 20, pp. 181–197.
Fisher, J 1992, 'Integrating research on markets for space and capital', *Real Estate Economics*, vol. 20, pp. 161–180.
Grenadier, S 1995, 'The persistence of real estate cycles' *Journal of Real Estate Finance and Economics*, vol. 10, pp. 95–119.
Hendershott, P, Lizieri, C and MacGregor, B, 2010, 'Asymmetric adjustment in the London office market', *Journal of Real Estate Finance and Economics*, vol. 41, pp. 80–101.
Lizieri, C, 2009, *Towers of capital*, Wiley-Blackwell, Chichester,
Wheaton, W, 1999, 'Real estate cycles: Some fundamentals', *Real Estate Economics*, vol. 27, pp. 209–230
Wheaton, W, Baranski, M and Templeton, C, 2009, '100 years of commercial real estate prices in Manhattan', *Real Estate Economics*, vol. 37, pp. 69–83.

Biography

Colin Lizieri is Grosvenor Professor of Real Estate Finance at the University of Cambridge and a Fellow of Pembroke College. Colin has a BA in geography from the University of Oxford and a PhD from the London School of Economics. He is a Fellow of the Royal Institution of Chartered Surveyors, a Fellow of the Royal Geographical Society and was elected to a Weimer Fellowship at the Homer Hoyt Institute. Colin has over 30 years' experience in real estate research and consultancy and has published widely on real estate finance, investment and office market dynamics with over 100 published works in major international journals, books and professional outlets.

Professor Lizieri's research focuses on real estate finance, risk and return in property vehicles and on the modelling of office markets. His book, *Towers of Capital* (Wiley-Blackwell), examines the linkages between international capital flows, financial crises and the office markets of major global cities. Colin's academic work has been recognised by the International Real Estate Society's Achievement Award "for outstanding achievement in real estate research, education and practice at the international level" and, in 2014, by the award of the David Ricardo medal by the American Real Estate Society, "the highest recognition by ARES of scholarly work in the real estate discipline" in recognition of "innovative and extensive publications on real estate office markets and the role of capital in urban development". Colin was the first non-US researcher to be awarded the David Ricardo medal.

3 Planning principles

Nigel Flannigan

Introduction

With the first part of this book addressing the principles of valuation and the second part addressing the practice of valuation, the previous chapters considered legal and economic principles, this chapter will consider planning principles and the following chapters will consider policy, finance and valuation principles.

It is assumed that the reader already has an understanding of the machinery of planning (zonings, as of right uses, prohibited uses, setbacks, height constraints and so forth) that so often dominate the valuation process. This allows a focus in this chapter on 'why' rather than solely on 'what' through considering planning as an allocator of public and private resources in a competitive environment to facilitate the realisation of a visualised future through urban development.

Urban development, urban planning and land

Planning is a fundamental component of most human endeavours, such as financial planning or family planning, with this chapter focusing on urban planning, being the preferred term signifying that the interest is in urban development. However, alternative terms are 'land use planning' and 'town planning'.

Distinction is made in this chapter between *urban development* and *urban planning*:

- urban development is a process by which the factors of production, such as land, labour and capital, are brought together to produce places for human habitation. The output of the process, also referred to as urban development, includes buildings such as houses and factories, infrastructure such as roads and power lines and also the modified natural environment; and
- urban planning is a process for the preparation of a plan to guide how land in a jurisdiction is to be used and developed. The output is a *statutory plan* which is a legally binding government document for the administration of urban development with its contents coming from thinking about development options for a subject area and formulation of a *strategic plan*. It should be noted that there are also urban planning consultants in the private sector who assist clients in navigating private development proposals through the statutory system.

The use and development of land is central in both urban development and urban planning and that interest in land flows through to urban development professions such as property valuation.

DOI: 10.1201/9781003049555-3

Processes of urban development

Drawing on Neutze (1981) and Wilkinson and Reid (2007), logic suggests that a community wanting to procure habitable places should first work out the locations, types and amounts of development required and then facilitate its development.

Such plan-led development has been the aspiration of urban planning since its inception. However, with few exceptions, it has never been able to inaugurate itself as undisputed leader of the urban development process. Rather the process is more of a competition of different ideas and solutions from a broad range of stakeholders about what and how much is to be developed. This corresponds with the neo-liberalism philosophy that came to ascendency in public policy during the mid-1970s with the Thatcher Government (UK) and the Reagan Administration (USA).

Major stakeholders in urban development in Australia can be categorised as:

- *Users* who are individuals, households, community groups, businesses, and government departments/agencies that have a need and will eventually occupy buildings and use infrastructure;
- *Producers* who are building companies, financiers and government agencies who contribute to the construction of urban development; and
- *Managers* who are government departments and public agencies legally empowered to regulate and manage specified components of the development process.

Such stakeholders and subcategories identified later are for the purpose of structuring ideas. Stakeholders do not have explicitly defined roles in the process and part of their competitive skill is in forging roles for themselves.

Users and Producers between them provide the basis of a market for development. The Users need habitable spaces for their lifestyle and the Producers undertake to provide them in return for payment. This market can operate with a minimum government role – for example, to ensure honesty in the mechanism of exchange. However, without government third-party regulation, stakeholders tend to operate in their own self-interest resulting in inefficient or suboptimal allocation of public and private resources.

This 'market failure', so-called, is a justification for government intervention in the provision of goods and services in society generally but it also applies to urban development. A detailed discussion of the market failure concept is beyond the scope of this chapter.

Managers

Government sector urban planners are a subset of the manager category of stakeholder, intervening in a market process on behalf of government and its constituents being commonly referred to as the 'public interest'. However, many government departments have a management role for specific components of an urban area and frequently have adopted plans separate from those of urban planning. Anything that is in the domain of habitable settlements, such as departments of transport, utilities services and sport and recreation, are a potential subset of the Manager category of stakeholder.

Urban planning is undertaken by urban planners to incorporate the disparate interests and plans of all stakeholders towards a synchronised urban settlement. This is not only a technical task but also a political one as a variety of political interests, often conflicting, have to be accommodated. Even if all government department plans are brought into a measure of agreement by negotiation, differences of opinion can remain such as, for example, priorities for action.

Ironically, urban planners are often not the opinion leaders in this competitive interaction of Manager stakeholders and have to compromise to stronger opinions, interests and political power. For example, a State transport department employs transport professionals to fulfil its responsibilities and its plans tend to wield great influence in any strategic plan. Consequently, the aspiring 'grand coordinator' role of urban planning is seldom realised fully with urban planning often more of a 'plan taker' than a 'plan maker'.

Producers

Within the Producer category there are also subcategories of stakeholders each with a different contribution to make and self-interest in doing so, being characterised as:

- *landholders* who are individuals, groups, organisations and the like that own or lease land without which land development cannot occur;
- *builders* who are individuals, groups, organisations and the like that construct infrastructure and buildings, including those who subdivide and amalgamate landholdings and who demolish urban development;
- *entrepreneurs* who are individuals, groups, companies and the like that initiate and carry the investment risk in delivering urban development to the market for sale or rent;
- *financiers* who are individuals, groups, companies, institutions and the like that lend money to stakeholders to develop or purchase infrastructure or facilities;
- *professional agents* who are architects, engineers, real estate valuers, urban planners (private sector) and the like that act as agents for other stakeholders; and
- *servicers* who are business firms, organisations, authorities and the like that provide stakeholders with services such as transport, utilities, libraries, waste disposal and so forth.

In practice, the level of influence that stakeholders have in the process depends on their personal attributes as individuals or groups rather than their role categorisation and effective powerbrokers can emerge from any category.

Urban development and redevelopment is a reaction to an existing situation that includes natural and modified landscapes, in order to provide suitable places for human habitation. In the past, the natural environment has been treated solely as a constraint on essential development and little compromise was made for its physical characteristics. In the process trees were felled, watercourses altered and swamps drained, for example, with devastating consequences such as floods, land slippage and bush fires.

Inevitably, there emerged people willing to give voice to the need for environmental sustainability and they mobilised to become major political forces in the development process. Equally inevitably, governments responded through a variety of departments and professional disciplines (including urban planning) with regulations requiring appropriate environmental sensitivity.

Short-term economic benefit of insensitive environmentalism needs to be assessed in property valuation against the expense of longer-term remediation. Apart from regulatory requirements, the ability for sensitive environmentalism to contribute marketable qualities that also increase economic returns should be factored into property valuation.

Planning principles 31

Planning process: from vision to reality

Drawing on Hack, Birch, Sedway and Silver (2009) and Godschalk, Rodríguez, Berke and Kaiser (2006), urban planning is a process of thought about how a subject area may develop into the future: planning for future urban development. In the face of uncertainty about the future, urban planners commonly think through a range of possible alternatives. That includes taking account of external shocks which are forces outside the control of policy makers but that affect urban development such as changes in economic conditions and household formations. By having worked through, in their minds, various possibilities, they reduce the likelihood of being surprised by any eventuality.

Urban planning, and urban plans, can be categorised by time perspective: long-, medium- and short-range. A long-range plan tends to be general and speculative. In practice, urban planning seldom projects a future beyond 25–30 years. A short-range future is more certain and hence a plan for it can be detailed with a short-range plan, in practice, tending to be for about five years.

Urban planning commences as a reaction to something that already exists and the aim is to create good or better places for human habitation. That commonly means changing the situation by developing new facilities or renovating existing ones.

There are two parts to Figure 3.1. The bottom part illustrates steps in generating a vision for a subject area and the top part illustrates steps in implementing that vision. A variety of plans can be used to explain a vision depending on the size and complexity

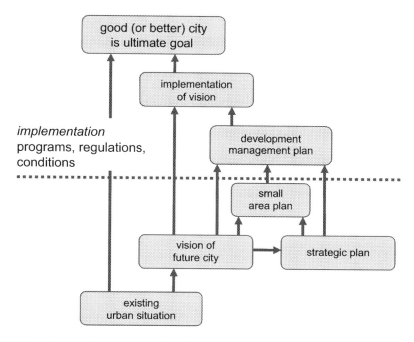

Figure 3.1 Fundamental components in urban planning

Source: Author.

Note: This diagram is not of a statutory process for any Australian State. Rather it illustrates the components that comprise urban planning as a general activity.

32 *Nigel Flannigan*

of a subject area. Figure 3.1 illustrates only two plans: a strategic plan for the whole subject area and a small area plan that contains more detail for specific parts of it.

Implementation of vision/plan

There is no point to urban planning unless there are effective means for the guidance of stakeholders and their projects in the realisation of the visualised future. This is implementation, a process in its own right, defined as the mobilisation of a society's resources to direct urban development towards a predetermined end.

The first stage in implementation is preparation of a development management plan to ensure that activities of stakeholders are mutually supportive in the development of the subject area. It sets out a sequence of actions needed to implement the vision/plan and identifies stakeholders responsible for performing each action or that are best able to do so.

The intention is to encourage stakeholders to contribute in a positive and coordinated way. This applies especially to urban managers from all levels of government that are responsible for development of specific components of urban habitation.

Stakeholder engagement in plan implementation is facilitated by the free flow of information about the prevailing development economy and this is the task of monitoring within a development management plan. It comprises the collection, analysis and dissemination of information on urban development within a government's jurisdiction, its vicinity. It is necessary to enable stakeholders to make informed development decisions as part of their contribution to efficient plan implementation.

Similarly, meaningful engagement is facilitated by ensuring that stakeholders clearly understand the content and intent of adopted plans and how to negotiate the prevailing statutory plan. It can be disseminated in hard copy or through a website and may be characterised as instruction, advice, education or whatever is most appropriate.

Recommended readings for this chapter are the publications on the website of the State Government department responsible for urban planning in the reader's Australian home State. For example, a pertinent publication of Victoria's Department of Environment, Land, Water and Planning (DELWP) is *A Guide to Victoria's Planning System*, available at: https://www.planning.vic.gov.au/guide-home/guide-to-victorias-planning-system/.

Construction and investment in implementation

The conclusion of plan implementation is commonly some new urban development, private or public. Most urban development in Australia occurs through stakeholders in the private sector with government developing some infrastructure and regulating the private urban development. In this, private sector builders, property developers, entrepreneurs and the like effectively take on roles as plan implementation agents.

Most urban development occurs with borrowed money from financiers and consequently they have a pivotal role, albeit seemingly passive. If financiers do not favour a project because of risk, economic returns or whatever, they refuse funding or place a prohibitively high cost on loans. In either case, the development is unlikely to proceed no matter how necessary other stakeholders may deem it to be. Furthermore, financiers are also influential in what gets maintained. For example, the discriminatory practice of banks 'redlining' (with a red line) geographic areas where the risk to return ratio was too high for loans to be given has the inadvertent effect of banks contributing to the creation of slums, so-called.

Governments can stimulate specific private urban development by providing economic incentives. These can be forthcoming as cash but are more likely to be as additional development permitted, lower development charges or the like, in return for specified outcomes.

Taxes, development charges and the like are not purposely devised as implementation incentives but rather are a 'user pays' mechanism to recoup government expense in the development process. However, they inevitably influence the cost of projects and their removal or reduction can be used as an incentive for particular types of project.

Initiating private and public development projects

Generally, the development process commences with an entrepreneur perceiving opportunities for developing a site in a particular location and initiating a project. Often these are economic opportunities but not necessarily so – for example, the need may be for a building to occupy so that suboptimal returns are acceptable. Either way, expectation is that a finished project will provide 'value for money'. Entrepreneurs developing for profit commonly seek a site that is undercapitalised so that they can add value by constructing new facilities or renovating dilapidated facilities.

The most direct way for government to procure needed urban development is to construct it itself – for example, through some government development authority. Once very popular, it has fallen out of favour for government departments to perform a building role. An alternative way is for government to undertake a financier role – for example, by designing its own place and then contracting it out to builders using its own funds or even borrowed funds.

In an era when the private market is seen by many policy makers as the most efficient mechanism for procuring facilities and infrastructure, even the roles of professional agent and financier may be too much for government. In that case, government can procure urban development by contracting out to private sector entrepreneurs to satisfy specified needs. That may include the entrepreneurs organising funding for government ownership and even for government to occupy as a lessee rather than an owner.

As with private financiers previously, government departments and authorities with funds and the legal power to invest it are effective implementation agents. It should be noted that urban planning is seldom in such a situation.

Planning approval subject to conformity with planning regulations

Drawing on Flannigan, Parker and Robinson (1999) and Flannigan and Domicelj (1992), urban planning has, since its inception as a knowledgeable discipline/profession, had a primary interest and role in the regulation of the use and form of urban development and administration of it. Regulation remains the most readily available and commonly used way for urban planning to implement its plan. Commonly referred to as 'development control' or 'development assessment', it dominates planning so much that it is often seen to be synonymous with it.

A development proposal needs to accord with the regulations contained in any prevailing statutory plans for it to be legal to progress with development. Specified documentation of a development proposal needs to be submitted to the responsible regulating authority or its parent government for assessment and approval.

The sought-after outcome is the issuing of a 'planning permit', a written statutory statement that a use or development may proceed, with or without cited conditions. It should be noted that a planning permit is distinct from a building permit which relates to building construction, fire safety and the like.

Clearly a regulatory authority cannot require that development of a private site occur, but only that it must conform to cited regulations if it proceeds. The ultimate decision remains with the initiating entrepreneur. Only if entrepreneurs are eager to develop and to invest in development is regulation an effective implementation tool, making it a much less positive tool than actual powers to develop or invest.

This dilemma can lead to acute negotiation between parties where a development is desired in the public interest but conditions for a development permit are claimed to make it unviable. A common tactic of proponents in this negotiation for compliance is the threat of not proceeding unless conditions are varied to ensure greater profitability.

Not only is an entrepreneur bound by the statutory plan but so are the officers assessing a proposal. Approval of any element of the proposal that violates the plan can result in a reprimand for an officer and may even trigger an expensive appeal. However, there is usually some flexibility in the regulations for each proposal to be assessed on its merits. The term 'to the satisfaction of the responsible authority', or such like, indicates provision for negotiation on specific elements of a proposal. Part of an entrepreneur's skill is in interpreting a statutory planning scheme to favour their own self-interest and then negotiate for acceptance of that interpretation.

There are indications that the assessment process operates to stifle innovation and diversity in development and therefore is a regressive influence. For example, an innovative proposal not well understood by government assessors requires more checking, research and possible appeals, with resulting delays subtly manipulating entrepreneurs towards 'tried and proven' outcomes.

Rationale for planning regulation: externalities

Value in real estate is a function of both on-site and off-site development. For example, a quality building on-site increases value but so does a public park off-site but in proximity. The social and economic impact of one development on another across site boundaries is the subject of *externalities*. An externality exists when an activity or a facility on one site causes unpriced impact, which may be unintended, on another. The effect may be negative or positive:

- a *negative externality* is where a development imposes a cost on an adjacent development thereby reducing its value; and
- a *positive externality* is where a development bestows a benefit on an adjacent development thereby increasing its value.

The self-interest of a project proponent is to exploit benefits exuding from an adjacent site and retain any benefit exuding from one's own. In this, a tangible exchange of benefits and costs can occur without any mechanism to formalise it through an exchange of money. However, government operates in the wider public interest to ensure that public and private resources are allocated efficiently or optimally. It is grossly inefficient for any investment in urban development to be wiped out, or even reduced, by subsequent development on adjacent sites.

A function of urban planning in its statutory planning mode is to minimise negative externalities and maximise positive externalities. In practice, the focus tends to be more on reducing negative externalities. It is relatively easy through regulation to require a site development not to cause harm: it is more difficult to require it to exude a benefit.

Plan implementation by regulation of land use

Drawing on Elliott (2008) and Dwight (2004), land use zoning is the most commonly used instrument for regulation of uses. The complexity of urban living is divided into a series of uses such as residential, industrial, recreation/open space and the like. These uses are allocated to different areas, called zones, with correspondingly descriptive names.

The practice is for each land use zone to be identified on a map of all developable land in a subject area. In Australia, it is common to have zones cover all land within a municipality or shire, with land not for urban development being allocated to zones such as 'open space' or 'agriculture'. Each zone is accompanied with written text including tables, schedules, diagrams and the like, necessary to clearly specify uses permitted, the type and amount of development permitted on sites within the zone to accommodate them and anything else required to inform private sector development.

Urban planning is largely a responsibility of State Government and every State has different documentation and requirements. However, zones in any planning scheme commonly cite uses as:

- prohibited: cannot be legally accommodated or permitted;
- allowed 'as of right': cannot be refused but subject to cited conditions; or
- requires a 'planning permit': may be permitted subject to approval of the regulating authority.

Even a prohibited use not allowable under the prevailing statutory planning scheme may be accommodated through an amendment to the scheme, provided the project is deemed to be in the public interest. However, the case has to be made to the governing body that retains the major sway.

Similarly, although a cited 'as of right' use cannot be prevented from being carried on, clarification should be sought from the regulating authority to confirm that a project accords with any 'as of right' conditions.

Until a permit is obtained there is no certainty that a project can proceed. Securing a planning permit brings certainty and with it a quasi-exclusive licence for additional development rights on a site, over and above the value of existing use rights, such that it is a value-adding exercise. Assessors may bargain for some of this additional value to flow back to the community in the form of various benefits such as additional open space, incorporation of art works and even particular forms of land use, such as affordable housing.

The uplift in value from securing a permit can be so substantial that entrepreneurs can earn a positive return from it without them intending to progress to development.

Called 'flipping', the permit package is on-sold to others to develop without the hassle of navigating the planning scheme.

Land use zoning is based on two fundamental rationales:

- *separation/dispersion:* to keep apart uses that are incompatible so as to avoid, reduce or minimise negative externalities of one use on another, For example, separation of noisy obnoxious industry from residential uses; and
- *agglomeration:* to cluster uses with an overt affinity, so that available positive externalities can be realised. For example, clustering shops together to form a coherent centre increases their commercial viability which can be diluted by non-compatible uses coming in between.

In zoning, distinction is made between 'highest and best use' and 'designated use'. The highest and best use is assessed on economic returns from a site without consideration of externalities; for example, a waste dump reaping a landowner the highest returns but destroying the economic potential of adjacent sites. Urban planning may take a wider public interest perspective than the self-interest of individual projects in prohibiting the highest and best use because it exudes negative externalities.

As with all plan implementation by regulation, land use zoning has been effective at stopping bad things from happening rather than being effective at making good things happen. However, since its inception, it has appealed to bureaucracies as an instrument for the regulation of use because it is both simple to establish and easy to administer. The plan has identifiable areas/zones where a wide range of uses can be carried on and regulators can easily check if a development proposal accords with the specified activities of a particular zone.

At the same time, however, there has been a bevy of criticism about zoning as an instrument for delivering quality urban development, with much of the dreariness and sterility of post-war cities being blamed on its inadequacies. Since its inception, land use zoning has progressively evolved into a more complex and sophisticated system of uses and zones to better reflect the complexity of urban habitation.

A major criticism of zoning is that the allocation of land to zones can result in a substantial uplift in land value for some landholders – for example, by allocating lower value agricultural zoned land to higher value residential zoned land. Even with an allocation to a lower value zone such as 'public open space', for example, the land has to be acquired by government at fair market value so there is no loss. However, there is an inequitable redistribution of land value and wealth with relative winners and losers. Furthermore, in the absence of government capturing the unearned increment conferred on the fortunate landowners, this gets passed on to final occupants as higher prices or rents.

This inefficient and inequitable redistribution is exacerbated by scarcity value and inflated prices created by government under-predicting demand and allocating too little land for specific uses. The corollary is that zoning too much land for a use creates an over-supply that can reduce land prices.

There are too many criticisms of the practice of land use zoning to cover adequately in this chapter. However, the shift from 'land use' to 'performance' warrants discussion. The modification is an acknowledgement that separation of uses is not an end in itself but rather a means, so that the zoning code specifies acceptable performances for location in a zone and leaves proponents to find a solution that conforms. For example, by specifying the level of acceptable noise it allows noisy factories to locate away from houses or to locate amongst them but with reduced noise or enhanced noise insulation. Many zoning codes are now versed in performance terms, albeit along with some measure of use specification.

Plan implementation by regulation of site development

Drawing on Elliott, Goebel and Meadows (2012), the specification that structures have a maximum height and a minimum setback from site boundaries are the two most popular regulations of site development. Both are based on the same logic of containment of negative externalities discussed previously.

The higher a building, the more likely it is to impact negatively on an adjacent site. The maximum height requirement is aimed at preventing an adjacent site being overpowered. Similarly, the closer a building is located to a site boundary the more likely it is to impact negatively on its neighbours. The setback specification is to create space between buildings based on the logic of physical separation of uses as with use zoning. The space left along the boundary is effectively a 'buffer strip'.

The required setbacks and their treatment tend to be most stringent along boundaries where, potentially, there is substantial conflict – for example, between industrial buildings and residential buildings, hospitals, schools or the like. Setback regulation is also applied for functional reasons, such as fire protection that is enhanced by separation of buildings making it more difficult for fires to spread and giving fire fighters access to all sides of buildings.

A setback regulation can be undermined by the buffer strip effectively being developed – for example, as an open car park or the like. Even though it is cited as not developable for the primary use of the zone, self-interest tends towards an ancillary use that adds value to the primary use. Hence, a regulating authority may specify that 'no building or works can be constructed closer to any boundary than the setback distance specified'.

Where a setback is intended to form a visual or sound barrier, a regulating authority may require that it be developed with landscaping appropriate for the intent. Commonly referred to as a 'garden buffer strip', a statutory ordinance can specify whatever landscape treatment is deemed desirable such as lawns, gardens, shrubs, trees and the like and even which party is to provide the buffer on their site. Furthermore, to protect the buffer from neglect over time, an ordinance can specify that it be 'continuously maintained to the satisfaction of the regulating authority'.

Together height and setback regulations form a notional envelope within which buildings can be built. The inter-relationship between the two is overt in a regulation such as 'setback must equal 1.5 metres plus the building height divided by 2'. A 10-metre high building, for example, would be setback 6.5 metres and a 15-metre building would be set back 9 metres.

This translates into a variable envelope where the higher a proposed building, the further into the site it has to be located and the wider the setback strip has to be, leaving more undevelopable space at ground level. In this way, the height/setback relationship determines how much real estate can be developed, albeit as a side effect, with the skill of an entrepreneur being in juggling the envelope to maximise the amount of developable real estate achieved.

The larger the site, the higher the buildings can be and the less land proportionally is taken up by the setback strip around the site periphery. Furthermore, site development regulations focus controls on impacts across site boundaries. This implicitly assumes that the relationship between on-site buildings will be protected by the self-interest of the development proponent and hence less public regulation is needed. The availability of these economies of scale is an incentive for site amalgamation.

The inability to fully develop a site to its highest and best use, boundary to boundary and as high as the heavens, has cost and value implications. Furthermore, every time special requirements are included as a 'condition of development approval', no matter how necessary or logical, there is an associated cost that must be assessed in any project valuation. In the case of any specified level of maintenance, the cost is ongoing and not just an initial capital cost.

Summary

The role of planning in shaping the human environment for the foreseeable future was considered in depth through the concept of planning as a reaction to something that already exists, potentially giving rise to positive and negative externalities requiring management for the public good.

Similarly, the role of planning as an optimal allocator of public and private resources was considered or, as may more often occur, the role of planning in managing the least suboptimal allocation of public and private resources. Balancing occupier, investor and developer interests (as considered in the previous chapter on economic principles) with the interests of the community and the aspirations of government within urban planning was discussed at length.

The relatively minor role of zonings and approvals was placed within the much wider context of planning as a facilitator for managing the realisation of a visualised future through urban development. There is no point to urban planning unless there are effective means for the guidance of stakeholders and their projects in the realisation of the visualised future.

Accordingly, the chapter provides a theoretically grounded framework within which to consider the relevance and importance of the machinery of planning (zonings, as of right uses, prohibited uses, setbacks, height constraints and so forth) that so often dominate the valuation and appraisal process, allowing a focus on 'why' rather than solely on 'what'.

With this chapter having considered planning principles and the previous chapters considering legal principles and economic principles, the following chapters will consider policy, finance and valuation principles to conclude the first part of this book, addressing the principles of valuation, with the second part then addressing the practice of valuation.

References

Dwight, M 2004, *The Complete Guide to Zoning*, McGraw Hill, New York.
Elliott, DL 2008, *A Better Way to Zone: Ten Principles to Create More Livable Cities*, Island Press, Washington DC.
Elliott, DL, Goebel, M and Meadows, C 2012, *The Rules that Shape Urban Form*, American Planning Association, Planning Advisory Service, Report No. 570.

Flannigan, N, Parker, D and Robinson, J 1999, 'Melbourne', in Berry, J and McGreal, S (eds), *Cities in the Pacific Rim: Planning Systems and Property Markets*, pp. 225–246, E & FN Spon, London.

Flannigan, N, and Domicelj, J 1992, 'Australia', in Dal Cin, A and Lyddon, D (eds), *International Manual of Planning Practice*, pp. 5–15, International Society of City and Regional Planners, The Hague.

Godschalk, DR, Rodríguez, DA, Berke, P and Kaiser, EJ 2006, *Urban Land Use Planning*, 5th ed, University of Illinois Press, Urbana.

Hack, G, Birch, EL, Sedway, PH and Silver, MJ (eds) 2009, *Local Planning: Contemporary Principles and Practice*, International City Management Association (ICMA), ICMA Press, Washington DC.

Neutze, M 1981, 'Determinants of the pattern of urban development', in Neutze, M, *Urban Development in Australia: A Descriptive Analysis*, 2nd ed, pp. 226–245, George Allen & Unwin, Sydney.

Ratcliffe, J, Stubbs, M and Keeping, M 2009, *Urban Planning and Real Estate Development*, 3rd ed, Routledge, Abingdon.

Wilkinson, S and Reed, R 2008, 'Introduction', in Wilkinson, S and Reed, R, *Property Development*, 5th ed, pp. 1–31, Routledge, Abingdon.

Biography

Nigel Flannigan was a faculty member at the University of Melbourne, Department of Town and Regional Planning (later called The School of Environmental Planning) from 1969 until 2005 when he formally retired as a Senior Lecturer and then served as a sessional staff member until 2010. Nigel's specific academic research interest was in the planning of traditional shopping districts to enable them to compete better with conventional shopping malls, where he took a micro-economic rather than design perspective. Nigel has published several papers on various topics and has given many papers at local and international conferences.

After retirement, Nigel worked part-time as a planning consultant with SGS Economic & Planning (2006–2012) where he managed and taught an Economics of Development course for the Planning Institute of Australia (PIA) as part of its Continuing Professional Development (CPD) programme. Nigel was actively engaged in professional planning throughout his career and taught numerous summer programmes for professional development at the University of Melbourne. Nigel was an active member of the Planning Institute of Australia since the 1970s until recently. He held many committee positions throughout that period and was made a Life Fellow (LFPIA) in 1992.

4 Policy principles

Nicki Hutley

Introduction

With the first part of this book addressing the principles of valuation and the second part addressing the practice of valuation, the previous chapters considered legal, economic and planning principles. This chapter will consider policy principles with the following chapters considering finance and valuation principles.

It is assumed that the reader already has an understanding of the machinery of government and the respective roles of local, State and Federal Government, allowing a focus in this chapter on both individual and interactive impacts of government policy on property value and the valuation process at the respective individual and cumulative levels of government.

Taxation

Various Commonwealth taxation arrangements have the potential to influence valuation, most notably negative gearing tax concessions, capital gains tax (CGT) and superannuation investments.

In addition to Commonwealth taxation arrangements, there are three property taxes levied by State/Territory Governments which may influence valuations, albeit to a lesser extent. These are stamp duty on property transactions, land tax and local government rates on property ownership. However, there may be differences in the way these taxes are applied to a property depending on:

- the State or Territory in which it is located;
- the nature of land use proposed by the purchaser;
- whether it is for investment purposes or if it is the principal place of residence; and
- whether or not the purchaser is a resident Australian citizen.

All these factors must be considered by the valuer as influencing the potential demand for and return on investment of the property. Each of the above taxes affecting property returns and valuation is discussed further, below.

Negative gearing

Negative gearing allows the owner of an investment property to offset any costs that exceed rental income from the property against taxable income earned from other sources. Typically, the largest cost that will result in a net income loss on a property is the interest paid on the loan to fund the purchase of the property. It is not relevant whether the property is established or newly built as long as it is available for rent.

While the property owner still bears a cash flow loss, the expectation is that the increase in the property's value over time will more than compensate for this loss. While holding the property, negative gearing provisions dampen the impact of the losses at the taxpayer's marginal tax rate.

As a simple example:

> Susan purchases a rental property. Her net rental income from lessees is $20,000 pa, while her total costs associated with owning and operating the property (interest, agent's fees, cleaning, council rates, etc) are $25,000 pa, giving a $5,000 net income loss.
>
> Susan's taxable income from her employment is $100,000. However, negative gearing allows the offset of her $5,000 net income loss, taking her effective taxable income to $95,000.

Of all taxation-related provisions, negative gearing is deemed to have the largest influence on investor returns, demand for investment properties and, therefore, valuation.

Capital gains tax

When a property is disposed of, CGT is applied to any increase in the value of the property from the time of purchase to the time of sale. Tax is paid at the seller's marginal tax rate with capital gains treated as additional income.

Where an asset has been held for more than one year, the gain is discounted by 50%. In the case of superannuation funds, the discount is 33%. Thus, the length of time an asset is held will influence the owner's perception of investment value or worth.

The costs and benefits of negative gearing and CGT concessions applied to residential property investments have been the subject of ongoing debate in the Australian Parliament and it is conceivable that changes may be introduced in the future to either remove or water-down concessions.

Superannuation

Superannuation funds – whether large organisational or self-managed (SMSFs) – can invest in property at concessional rates of taxation, increasing their potential value to the owner. Changes to rules in 2007 allowing SMSFs to borrow to invest in property has led to an increase in fund-held property. However, lending rules are restrictive – for example, loans must be limited recourse, meaning the lender has recourse only to the asset purchased with the loan.

As a non-liquid asset, an SMSF requiring a quick sale of a property asset will be likely to reduce the price of that asset. In addition, for some individuals, there are likely to be tax advantages from holding a negatively geared property outside a fund.

The complexity of superannuation rules means that valuers need to approach potential influences of superannuation on property value with extreme care.

Stamp duty

State based stamp duties are levied at the time of sale on the purchaser. This is the only State tax applying to the principal place of residence. Rates of stamp duty vary between jurisdictions and ownership types (investment versus primary residence). Stamp duty is a progressive tax, increasing with the value of the property. In the case of a primary residence, First Home Buyers (FHBS) enjoy a lower rate of duty, or a grant, in most jurisdictions.

Foreign citizens purchasing residential property in Victoria, New South Wales, Queensland, South Australia, Tasmania and Western Australia are subject to a stamp duty surcharge, with the rate varying across jurisdictions from 3% to 8%.

Land tax

Land tax is also levied by State and Territory Governments, with the exception of the Northern Territory, against the value of a land holding. In the case of strata units, the land value for each strata lot is calculated on a proportional basis.

A large number of properties are exempt from land tax, including primary places of residence. Land for primary production, rooming houses, non-profit organisations, caravan parks and retirement villages are also among exempt property types in many jurisdictions.

In cases where a land tax is applied, the definition of land assessed for taxation and the rate at which it is taxed also vary across jurisdictions. For example, in NSW the Land Value (using a three-year average) is the basis for taxation, while in Victoria it may be Site Value, Net Annual Value or Capital Improved Value. In the Northern Territory, the Unimproved Capital Value is applied as summarised in Table 4.1.

From 1 January 2016, Victoria introduced an absentee owner surcharge that applies to taxable land. An absentee owner is a person who:

- is not an Australian citizen or permanent resident;
- does not ordinarily reside in Australia; and
- was absent from Australia:
    - on 31 December of the year prior to the tax year; or
    - for more than six months in total in the calendar year prior to the tax year.

NSW, Victoria, Queensland and the ACT each charge a Foreign Land Tax surcharge of 2% (0.75% in the case of the ACT).

Table 4.1 Methodologies for land taxes and council rates

	NSW	VIC	QLD	WA	SA	TAS	NT	ACT
Land tax	LV	SV	UV	UV	SV	LV	Not levied	UV
Council rates	LV	SV, NAV, CIV	UV	Rural: UV Non-rural: GRV	LV, CV, AV	LV, CV, AAV	UCV, AV, ICV	UV

Notes: Notes: AV = Annual value, AAV = Assessed Annual Value, LV = Land Value, CV = Capital value, CIV = Capital Improved Value, GRV = Gross Rental Value, NAV = Net Annual Value, SV = Site Value, UCV = Unimproved Capital Value, UV = Unimproved Value, ICV = Improved Capital Value.

Source: Henry, K et al. (2009).

Local government charges

Local government charges, known as council rates, are typically low-value taxes applied to the value of the land to fund capital and operational requirements of local governments. As with land taxes, approaches to levying rates vary between different jurisdictions. Discounted rates or rebates are available in most regions to some property owners, for example pensioner and other concession-card holder households. A summary of current approaches is provided in Table 4.1.

Infrastructure

Policies towards infrastructure investment, in particular transport infrastructure, will have significant impacts on property valuation.

Improved access to essential economic and social or community infrastructure will, other things being equal, increase property values. Economic infrastructure includes road, rail and airports, utilities and sewerage, while social infrastructure includes libraries, swimming pools and parks.

There has been considerable research (for example, McIntosh, Trubka and Hendriks, 2016) undertaken in Australia and globally in recent years on the impact of investment in transport infrastructure (roads and rail) on property values. Indeed, governments of all levels are interested in how they can capture any land value uplift from such infrastructure investments as a means of helping to pay for them.

Other studies show the increase in value of residential properties as a result of investment in easily accessible, good quality social infrastructure such as schools and hospitals (Taylor, 2015).

However, the potential for infrastructure-related uplift (or reduction) in property values is contingent on myriad factors. As an example, depending on the location and use of a property, the development of the second airport in Sydney could increase a property's value as a result of improved access to employment and associated transport links or, alternatively, it might reduce value due to decreased amenity from noise of aircraft, increased industrial land use and increased traffic.

In addition to council rates, State and local governments impose a range of charges on developers for the construction and maintenance of economic and community infrastructure, which also has implications for valuation. It has been estimated (Master Builders Association, 2009) that these charges can amount to as much as 30% of the sale price in the North West and South West Growth Areas of Sydney, which attract local and State charges. In some instances, the infrastructure charges may add more to the cost of a property than they do to the perceived value gained.

Utilities

Access to and charges for utility services – water, energy, waste and telecommunications – will affect amenity, costs and potential usage of properties and hence valuation. These services are largely privatised in Australia, but heavily regulated in terms of rates and charges.

Properties not currently connected to utilities face significant imposts to become connected, particularly in green-field areas. Even in areas where power may be connected, if there is limited reliability in the distribution network which leads to frequent brownouts or blackouts, then this must also be considered in the valuation process.

Australia's dispersed population means that, typically, those in less densely populated regions will pay higher prices for energy and telecommunications. If geographical, topographical or other considerations prevent any access to utilities – most likely water and sewerage – then the limits imposed on the land use will reduce its potential value.

Conversely, proximity to key utility infrastructure, such as sewerage plants, television towers or concentrated, heavy overhead cabling, can reduce (visual and/or aural) amenity, with negative consequences for property values.

Water

Water in many regions of Australia is an important input to industry, particularly mining and agriculture. The arid nature of the continent, poor historical management and frequent and prolonged El Nino events that bring droughts all combine to produce water shortages in many regions.

Many agricultural properties and mining areas therefore rely on irrigation. Water may be sourced from a variety of sources and is now a tradeable commodity. In order to better manage water consumption and restore flow to certain water courses, a National Water Initiative (NWI) was implemented in 2006. Since 2013, the NWI has been managed by the Productivity Commission. Legislative and administrative aspects of water rights and water trading are the responsibility of State and Territory jurisdictions.

Access to water, including trading rights associated with land, and water management practices, such as recycling dams, will have significant implications for productive capacity and commerciality of properties and therefore land values. Drainage of land must also be taken into consideration.

Environment and climate change

Environmental considerations are now an integral part of building codes across Australia, albeit with variations between jurisdictions, potentially improving both the amenity of a property and the usage and cost of utilities.

Meeting the relevant regulations embedded in commercial and residential building codes regarding energy, water and waste efficiency involves imposts for all property types. However, recent research shows that, for commercial properties, a higher than minimum environmental rating is associated with higher rents and valuations than arise for lower rated properties that are similar in nature and location.

For properties with solar PV generators, the presence of a feed-in tariff scheme may increase the value of the property to some degree. Schemes and payment rates vary significantly between States and Territories. For example, the tariff may be gross or net, paid at a different rate and be in force for different durations.

Extreme weather events are occurring with increasing frequency and intensity, placing properties without adaptation at increasing risk of damage. Another consideration for valuers, therefore, is the proximity of a property to flood plains, bush fire prone areas and cyclone regions. Fiscal constraints on Councils mean that many flood-prone regions do not have sufficient levees in place to prevent river banks breaking during heavy rains, while previous planning policies have allowed properties to be built on flood plains. The risk of coastal inundation is also becoming an increasing risk for many areas.

Policy principles 45

Reflecting the benefits of adaptation strategies against cyclones for residential houses and apartment buildings, Suncorp Insurance now offers lower premiums for those implementing any of a number of protective measures (JCU Cyclone Testing Station and Urbis, 2015).

Contamination regulations

Residential subdivisions may be built on land that was previously used for potentially contaminating activities, such as heavy industry or service stations.

Failure to recognise that land is contaminated can have long-term consequences for both the buyer and seller including potential prosecution and obligation to pay for remediation of the land in the future.

People buying, selling or leasing land need to know if the subject land was once a contaminated site and be aware of their obligations under the relevant legislation.

Clearly, valuers should make themselves aware of the contamination status of land being valued in order to determine the impact, if any, on value.

Heritage and conservation

Governments at all levels impose controls on the determination and treatment of heritage properties. These controls range from something as small as allowable external colour schemes for residences to the need to maintain entire external or internal structures of large buildings. The latter can be extremely costly in terms of both construction costs and potential usage.

A State Heritage Authority may classify a property as being heritage under a permanent or temporary conservation order. Contravention of any legislation can result in severe penalties and even an order to reconstruct.

In addition to State bodies, the Australian Heritage Council is adviser to the Commonwealth Government on heritage matters, assessing nominations for the National Heritage List and the Commonwealth Heritage List.

The most significant impact of heritage legislation on valuation is typically in commercial office locations. A heritage building may impose severe limitations on the use of floor space when internal structures are protected. An example of this is the current site of the Powerhouse Museum in Sydney, located in the old Ultimo Power Station building.

Some governments may mitigate this impact by allowing a heritage floor space (HFS) offset:

> When a heritage item owner completes conservation works they may be awarded HFS by the City of Sydney. The awarded HFS can then be sold to a site that requires it as part of an approved development application. The money raised offsets the cost of conserving the heritage item. (City of Sydney, 2016)

The National Trust of Australia lists properties with heritage significance but has no statutory powers.

Compulsory acquisition

All levels of government in Australia have statutory powers to make compulsory acquisitions of land or an interest in land. Acquisition will be for a public purpose including road and rail corridors or, in the case of a partial interest, for an easement.

Other terms used for compulsory acquisition include resumption, expropriation, eminent domain and condemnation.

Each jurisdiction has its own legislation and approach, although there are general similarities and the valuation of a property for compulsory acquisition must make allowances for the legislation in force at the time. A person may contest an offer of compensation to acquire their property but, ultimately, they cannot prevent the acquisition where a public need is demonstrated.

Valuers should be aware of the potential for compulsory acquisition when assessing the value of a property.

Foreign investment

Changing attitudes to and policies affecting foreign investors can also have material impacts on property values, particularly in locations where these investors may cluster and create strong demand.

Foreign persons may purchase Australian property, subject to guidelines or, in the case of investments over a certain monetary threshold, an application for approval by the Foreign Investment Review Board (FIRB). When a purchase is made, relevant taxes must also be paid (as discussed in Taxation section above).

The FIRB chiefly deals with residential approval applications, for which there are clear guidelines for temporary residents, foreign residents and corporations and trusts. Further, separate guidelines are available for established dwellings and new buildings. The Commonwealth Government's priority is to encourage investment to create new dwellings so as to limit the potential impact of foreign investment on house price increases.

Following the Report on Foreign Investment in Residential Real Estate (House of Representatives Standing Committee on Economics, 2014), the FIRB has been charged with improving data collection, audit, compliance and enforcement action and addressing loopholes in the framework.

For commercial real estate, foreign persons may be required to notify and receive a no objections notification before acquiring an interest in commercial land in Australia. Different rules and thresholds for notification apply according to whether the land is vacant or not, whether the proposed acquisition falls into the category of sensitive commercial land that is not vacant and the value of the proposed acquisition.

By influencing the potential competition and demand for commercial property, FIRB regulations can influence commercial property values.

Native title

According to the Victorian Department of Justice and Regulation (2016):

> Native title is the recognition in Australian law that some Aboriginal and Torres Strait Islander people continue to hold rights and interests in land and water.

Australian law recognises that native title exists where Aboriginal people have maintained a traditional connection to their land and waters, on a continuous basis, since sovereignty and where Acts of Government have not removed it.

Native title was first recognised by the High Court of Australia in 1992 with the 'Mabo decision', which overturned the idea of 'terra nullius', being that the Australian continent did not belong to anyone at the time of European settlement.

Under the Native Title Act 1993 (Cth), Aboriginal and Torres Strait Islander people can lodge an application with the Federal Court of Australia to seek a determination of native title. Native title holders have the right to be compensated if governments acquire their land or waters for future development.

State Native Title Acts were subsequently passed to clarify aspects of Commonwealth legislation, which has also been amended.

State Governments may also have alternate systems for determining native title. For example, Victoria introduced the Traditional Owner Settlement Act 2010 (Vic), which allows for agreements to be made to recognise traditional owners' relationship to the land and to provide certain rights on Crown Land.

Native title can co-exist with some forms of land title (such as pastoral leases) but is extinguished by others (such as freehold).

The native title of a particular group will depend on the traditional laws and customs of those people. The way native title is recognised and practised will vary between groups, depending on what is claimed and what is negotiated between the people and organisations with an interest in that country.

Significant parts of rural, metropolitan and remote Australia are still subject to ongoing native title claims and more claims will likely be made in the future.

The potential for a native title claim to determine the use of land held under native title by others and/or payments to be made to native title holders can significantly impact the value of the land in question.

Social housing

State Government approaches to social (public and community) housing may also affect property prices and values. Studies have shown inconsistent findings, indicating that a number of coincident factors will influence surrounding house prices (Ahrentzen, 2008). However, it does appear that where large-scale public housing exists, prices of nearby properties are typically depressed.

Many State Governments are now pursuing a policy of decentralisation, with a greater mix of social and private housing. Understanding where redevelopment has been prioritised will be important in understanding potential value uplift to relevant properties.

Summary

Government policy is a fundamental influence on the operation of property markets, driving owner occupier, investor and occupier behaviour and decision-making. This was clearly evident in various State residential property markets over the last decade as different levels of government introduced first home owner grants, stamp duty exemptions or relief and amendment to foreign investment regulation, each of which had a direct impact on different parts of the residential property market and generated tangible and measurable outcomes in property values.

While taxation policy at all three levels of government is a high profile and so very visible influence on property markets and the behaviour of market participants, government policy regarding infrastructure, water and environmental policy all directly impact property values and require an awareness and understanding by the property valuer. While the impact of taxation policy on property values may be swift, the impact of infrastructure policy may be longer lived through an anticipation phase impacting values, followed by an implementation phase further impacting values and then a post-implementation phase again impacting property values.

As with planning policy, evolving policy principles by government shape the nature and form of the built environment thorough financial drivers and regulatory controls, each of which may have a different value impact individually and a further value impact if acting cumulatively of which the valuer should be aware.

Accordingly, the chapter provided a thematic contextual overlay within which to consider government policy principles, allowing a focus on both individual and interactive impacts of government policy on property value and the valuation process at the respective individual and cumulative levels of government.

With this chapter having considered policy principles and the previous chapters considering legal, economic and planning principles, the following chapters will consider finance and valuation principles to conclude the first part of this book, addressing the principles of valuation, with the second part then addressing the practice of valuation.

References

Ahrentzen, S 2008, *How Does Affordable Housing Affect Surrounding Property Values?* Housing Research Synthesis Project, Research Brief No. 1, August 2008.

City of Sydney 2016, www.cityofsydney.nsw.gov.au/development/application-guide/heritage-conservation/heritage-floor-space-scheme (accessed 3 November 2016).

Henry, K et al. 2009, *Australia's Future Tax System*, Report to the Treasurer, Part Two Detailed Analysis, Commonwealth Government, December 2009.

House of Representatives Standing Committee on Economics, *Report on Foreign Investment in Residential Real Estate*, Commonwealth of Australia, November 2014.

JCU Cyclone Testing Station and Urbis 2015, *Build to Last: A Protecting the North Initiative*, Suncorp Group, 2015.

McIntosh, J, Trubka, R and Hendriks, B 2016, *Transit and Urban Renewal Value Creation*, LUTI Consulting, 2016.

Master Builders Association, 2009, *Infrastructure Charges*.

Taylor, L 2015, *The Effect of School Quality on Housing Prices*, Durham, 2015 Fall.

Victorian Department of Justice and Regulation 2016, www.justice.vic.gov.au (accessed 1 November 2016).

Biography

Nicki Hutley has more than 25 years of economic, financial market and public policy experience, providing advice to public and private sector clients across a broad spectrum of public policy issues. Prior to joining Deloitte Access Economics, Nicki held senior positions with Urbis, Access Economics and KPMG.

Nicki employs economic expertise to enhance investment strategies and policy outcomes. She is skilled in complex economic, social and environmental cost-benefit analyses that meet the highest levels of government standards and rigour, including for funding applications. Throughout her career, Nicki has led large and complex economic modelling projects and policy reviews for local, State and Federal Governments. She has also prepared and reviewed numerous Regulatory Impact Statements on subjects as diverse as energy efficiency and amendments to the NSW Retirement Villages Act. She has developed particular expertise in infrastructure, social programmes, environment and climate change.

5 Finance principles

David Rees

Introduction

With the first part of this book addressing the principles of valuation and the second part addressing the practice of valuation, the previous chapters considered legal, economic, planning and policy principles. This chapter will consider finance principles with the following chapter considering valuation principles.

It is assumed that the reader already has an understanding of the mathematics of discounted cash flow valuation, allowing a focus in this chapter on basic finance functions of time, risk and return together with more advanced functions including cost of capital, correlation and diversification in their application to the property valuation process.

Real estate capital market overview

This chapter provides an overview of the financial analysts' toolkit and explains how it can be applied to real estate markets. Real estate assets deliver a range of physical and financial services. Rental income streams and capital values are real time indicators of the services that real estate provides to owners, lessees, investors and developers. In addition, the real estate sector provides a stream of payments to the public sector in the form of rates, stamp duties and taxes on income and capital gains.

The attributes of *time* and *risk* ensure that physical real estate markets are inextricably linked to financial markets. *Time* is important because investment in real estate is typically a long duration commitment. Market conditions change continuously and in real estate the costs of adjusting to change can be high. The *risks* associated with every property asset also vary over time and through its life cycle, from design and construction through to the ownership/occupancy stage, refurbishment and finally obsolescence and demolition.

Financial markets *package* and *price* these risks and associated services in ways that meet changing market circumstances, as well as the diverse requirements of real estate market participants – lessees, developers, owners and financiers.

From a real estate perspective, three major roles for financial markets may be identified:

- the market for capital – financial markets set the interest rates and discount rates that intermediate between the income stream of an asset and the capital value (CV) of that asset;
- the market for assets – financial markets fund the construction of, and investment in, individual assets; and

DOI: 10.1201/9781003049555-5

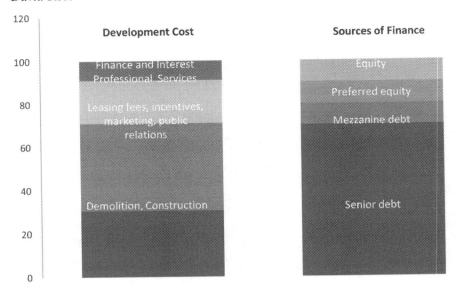

Figure 5.1 Development finance – the capital stack: sources and uses of finance

Source: Author

- the market for risk – financial markets package and price the rewards and the risks that are associated with the financial instruments (primarily equity and debt) that represent claims on individual real estate assets, as well as determining asset values in the broader context of multi-asset portfolios.

The following sections explain how financial markets fulfil each of these important roles.

The capital stack: sources and uses of finance

The capital stack is a convenient description of the range of financial instruments that can be applied to fund a development project or a passive investment. Figure 5.1 illustrates how a hypothetical office development project might be financed and how the funds might be applied.

The bottom of the capital stack represents the highest priority of claims in the event of a default and therefore the lowest risk to financiers, with risk rising as the column is ascended. Required rates of return are linked to 'seniority' – the greater the seniority, the lower the risk and therefore the lower the required return. The next section will explore how the returns for different financial instruments, in particular, debt and equity, are established.

The Capital Asset Pricing Model (CAPM)

The cost of debt and the cost of equity

In this section, the principles that determine asset pricing in financial markets are considered. The development of the Capital Asset Pricing Model (CAPM) has been one of the main agenda items in financial research over the past decades. A good starting point was the path-breaking work of Franco Modigliani and Merton Miller (1958) (MM).

With hindsight, MM's essential insight is extremely simple. Consider three identical houses, owned respectively by John Smith, Mary Jones and Fred Brown. John has paid off his mortgage, so his house is debt-free. Mary has a $100,000 mortgage on her house. Fred has a mortgage of $250,000. John offers his house for sale and secures a price of $400,000.

Question: What are the other two houses worth?
Answer: Since the houses are identical, they are also worth $400,000. This is despite the differing level of debt.

> **Principle:** The MM theorem states that in an efficient market and in the absence of extraneous factors such as taxes, bankruptcy or agency costs, assets or enterprises that deliver identical services will sell at the same price regardless of the level of financial leverage (also called 'gearing').

Importantly, consider what happens if the value of these houses rises to $500,000? John's equity stake rises by 25%; Mary's stake rises by 33.3%; Fred's stake rises by 40%. And if values fall, of course, the process applies in reverse.

> **Principle:** The volatility of financial returns to equity stakeholders rises with increasing leverage.

Consider a slightly more complex situation. Table 5.1 illustrates an enterprise that delivers a 10% return on assets invested. The value of the enterprise (V) is given by:

$$V = D + E \qquad \text{Equation 1}$$

where:
D represents debt secured against the enterprise; and
E represents the value of equity invested.

Table 5.1 The impact of a rising level of debt

Equity = E ($)	Debt = D ($)	Asset value = V = E + D ($)	Leverage = D/V (%)	Gross income ($)	Less interest ($)	Net income ($)	Return on debt (%) (r_D)	Return on equity (%) (r_E)
100	0	100	0%	10	0	10		10.0%
90	10	100	10%	10	0.4	9.6	4.0%	10.7%
80	20	100	20%	10	0.8	9.2	4.0%	11.5%
70	30	100	30%	10	1.2	8.8	4.0%	12.6%
60	40	100	40%	10	1.6	8.4	4.0%	14.0%
50	50	100	50%	10	2.0	8.0	4.0%	16.0%
40	60	100	60%	10	2.4	7.6	4.0%	19.0%
30	70	100	70%	10	2.8	7.2	4.0%	24.0%
20	80	100	80%	10	3.2	6.8	4.0%	34.0%
10	90	100	90%	10	3.6	6.4	4.0%	64.0%
0	100	100	100%	10	4.0	6.0	4.0%	

Source: Author

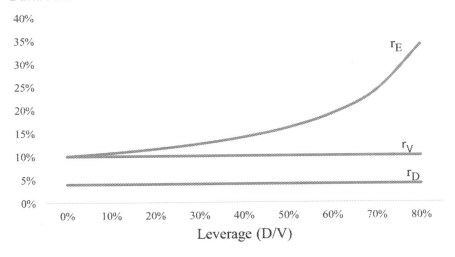

Figure 5.2 Returns to debt and equity as leverage rises
Source: Author

As with the three houses above, the value of the enterprise, V, is constant, regardless of the level of leverage.

As Table 5.1 shows, the return on the enterprise, r_V, is a constant 10% regardless of the level of debt. However, the return on equity (Net Income/E = r_E) rises and the rate of increase accelerates as leverage rises (Figure 5.2). This rising rate of return is the additional reward that the equity investor demands (or should demand) for the increase in volatility or financial risk. Financial risk rises because greater volatility in earnings follows inevitably from rising levels of debt.

> **Principle**: Replacing equity with lower cost debt enhances return on equity, but this is simply compensation for additional financial volatility (or financial risk). The value of the enterprise is *not* enhanced by increased leverage; debt may be less expensive than equity but it offers no 'free lunch'. The cost saving from 'cheap' debt finance is exactly offset by the additional return required by equity investors. This is the essential MM insight.

The weighted average cost of capital (WACC)

Equation 2 may be derived from the example above:

$$r_V = r_E\, E/V + r_D\, D/V \qquad \text{Equation 2}$$

where:
  r_V represents the overall required return;
  r_E represents the return to equity owners; and
  r_D represents the cost of debt.

So, the cost of capital, r_V, is the weighted average of the cost of debt (r_D) and the cost of equity (r_E). That's why r_V is often referred to as the **Weighted Average Cost**

Finance principles 53

of Capital (WACC). Since r_V is constant as leverage rises, as MM demonstrate, it follows that:

$$r_{EL} = r_{EU} + (D/E)(r_V - r_D) \qquad \text{Equation 3}$$

where:
r_{EL} represents required return on equity (leveraged); and
r_{EU} represents unleveraged required return on equity.

So, if leverage = 40%:

$$\begin{aligned}r_{EL} &= .10 + (0.4/0.6)(.10 - .04) \\ &= 14\%\end{aligned} \qquad \text{Equation 4}$$

Equation 2 can be expressed as:

$$V = \frac{r_E E + r_D D}{r_V} \qquad \text{Equation 5}$$

Principle: The value of the enterprise is the cash flow accruing to debt providers plus the after-tax cash flow to equity investors, discounted at the WACC.

Note that Equation 5 is simply the conventional capitalisation rate formula found in property valuation extended to include debt as well as equity in the financing mix.

There are two important qualifications to this analysis.

Firstly, it is assumed that banks will charge a fixed rate of 4.0% regardless of rising debt. Rising levels of debt increase financial risk for the lending bank too. In fact, the MM model breaks down as leverage increases – after all, at 100% leverage the bank effectively owns the entire business. As the de facto 100% equity owner of the enterprise the bank should be demanding a 10.0% return, with the rationale for the selection of a 10% return being considered in asset pricing, below.

Secondly, interest payments on debt may be tax deductible to the owners if the enterprise is profitable. The tax saving arising from interest deductibility is a genuine benefit for the owners of the business. So the statement that there is no 'free lunch' from increasing use of debt requires some adjustment – if interest payments are tax deductible, the use of debt can enhance the value of the enterprise and the WACC formula is now:

$$\begin{aligned}r_V &= r_E E/V + (1-t)r_D D/V \\ r_{EL} &= r_{EU} + (D/E)(r_{EU} - rD)(1-t)\end{aligned} \qquad \text{Equation 6}$$

where:
t represents the marginal tax rate paid by the enterprise.

Consider Equation 5 again. This can be expressed as:

$$V = \frac{r_E E + (1-t)r_D D}{r_V} \qquad \text{Equation 7}$$

Risk, return and modern portfolio theory (MPT)

To consider the characteristics of real estate as an investable asset and how it fits into a multi-asset portfolio, a further consideration of *risk* is required.

Diversifiable and non-diversifiable risk

All human activity involves risk. Some categories of risk can be limited or avoided altogether. Others cannot: a flood might close down a coal mine; a fire might destroy a shopping centre; or a hi-tech start-up company might fail to deliver a marketable product.

How are such risks priced? The answer is that in theory they can be eliminated – these are three examples of *diversifiable risks*. By holding a big portfolio comprising many coal mines or many shopping centres or stakes in many hi-tech start-ups, an investor can minimise (or diversify away) the risk of one location or one company failing. But no matter how large a portfolio of shopping centres, the investor cannot eliminate the impact of, say, an economic recession, a Global Financial Crisis or a rise in GST that adversely affects all retail spending. These are examples of *non-diversifiable risk*s:

$$\text{Total financial risk} = \text{diversifiable}(\text{or non}-\text{systemic})\text{risk}$$
$$+ \text{non} - \text{diversifiable}(\text{or systemic})\text{risk}.$$

Since diversifiable risks can be reduced (even eliminated) by actions taken by investors themselves, there is no reason why investors should be rewarded for the diversifiable risk associated with these assets. In transparent and liquid markets, coal mines, shopping centres and hi-tech start-ups are priced according to the non-diversifiable risks associated with those assets. In theory, assets do not offer higher returns to investors who choose to accept asset-specific (sometime called idiosyncratic) risks.

Portfolio diversification is not the only antidote to the problem of non-systemic risk. The insurance market provides protection against a range of non-systemic risks such as fire and earthquake. Non-diversifiable risks pose greater challenges. Insurance to cover systemic risks that have implications for real estate, such as disruptive technology and environmental liability, is an evolving market (OECD, 2003).

Risk, of course, takes many different forms – unforeseen changes to planning requirements, environmental regulations and Occupational Health and Safety (OH&S) regulations can all have a positive or negative impact on the investment performance of individual assets and on whole classes of assets. But most risks can be captured in one of these two risk categories.

The portfolio risk-return trade-off

Figure 5.3 shows two hypothetical (and extreme) scenarios. The returns to investment A vary through time, but the average return is 8% p.a. Returns to investments B and C also vary through time, with an average return of 4% p.a. Returns to all three investments A, B and C are equally volatile. The standard deviation (SD), a measure of volatility, is SD = 0.69 in all three cases.

In Case 1, two investments, A and C move together – the correlation, $R^2 = 1.0$.

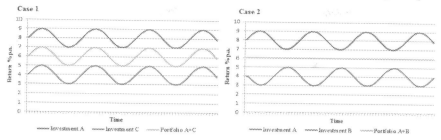

Figure 5.3 Two investments and portfolio performance
Source: Author

Now consider a portfolio comprising a 50% weighting of A and a 50% weighting of C. Intuition (and mathematics) show that this portfolio will deliver an average annual return (r_p) of 6.0% p.a.:

$$r_p = 0.50(.08) + 0.50(.04) = 6.0\%$$ Equation 8

Principle: The investment return on a portfolio of assets is the average return of the assets in the portfolio, weighted by the value of each investment held in the portfolio.

As Figure 5.3 shows, in Case 1, the 50:50 portfolio has the same volatility as A and C individually, SD = 0.69.

Now consider Case 2, where return to assets A and B are perfectly negatively correlated (R^2 = -1.0). The expected annual return is still 6.0%, as in Case 1. But variations in return for asset B now exactly offset variations in return for asset A. Volatility for a 50:50 weighted portfolio is zero (SD = 0).

Principle: The volatility of a portfolio depends not on the volatility of individual assets, but on the inter-relationship of the returns (or covariance) of all assets held in the portfolio.

The alternatives from Figure 5.3 are mapped in Figure 5.4 in risk-return space. Investments A, B and C all show the same volatility (SD = 0.69). So, too, does the portfolio (50% A + 50% C); and this portfolio shows a weighted average return of 6% p.a. But portfolio (50% A + 50% B) shows zero volatility (SD = 0).

Question: Which portfolio would an investor prefer, 50%A+ 50%B or 50%A+ 50%C?
Answer: Portfolio A+B must be preferred to A+C as both portfolios offer an average return of 6% pa, but A+B offers less (in fact, zero) volatility or risk.

Now consider an investor holding investment A. The investor gradually sells A and buys B. In Figure 4 this investor travels down the solid line from A, past P_1, eventually arriving at 50%A+ 50%B, which corresponds to a 50:50 weighting. Continuing to sell A and buy B would move the investor along the dotted line past P towards point B, C. But any point on the lower line, say P, would have the same risk but a lower return than point P_1 on the upper line. P_1 *dominates* P, with all portfolio options on the upper

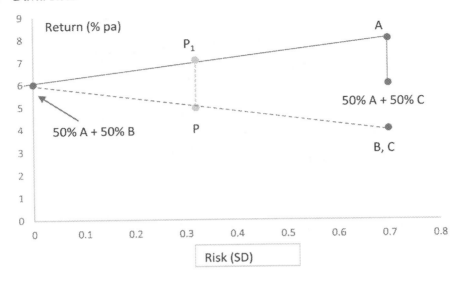

Figure 5.4 The risk-return trade-off
Source: Author

line being superior to all options on the lower line. The lower line may, therefore, be disregarded in making portfolio selections.

> **Principle**: Assets B and C have identical returns (4.0% p.a.) and identical volatility. But they behave very differently from a portfolio perspective. B has the valuable attribute that it reduces portfolio volatility, albeit at the expense of reducing portfolio return. C, on the other hand, reduces return and makes no contribution to volatility reduction.

Question: Which point on the upper line should the investor select?
Answer: We cannot definitively answer this question. Selection of the optimal point on the upper line is the task of the investor, or the investor's financial adviser. An aggressive investor would choose portfolio A, which offers the highest available return, albeit with relatively high volatility. A less aggressive investor would choose a point somewhere along the upper line, for example P_1.

The investments A, B and C are clearly extreme cases, based on correlations of +1.0 or −1.0. The real world is a good deal less precise. In the real world of many assets and a wide range of inter-correlations, the upper line typically looks more like Figure 5.5.

This is the *Efficient Frontier*. The mathematics of defining this frontier was developed by Markowitz (1959). The Efficient Frontier defines the limit of returns available to investors for each level of risk. For any level of risk (volatility), the Efficient Frontier shows the highest achievable returns from a portfolio of assets. The area below the frontier is attainable, but suboptimal. The area above the frontier is unattainable.

There is, however, a qualification here. In asset pricing the concept of a riskless or 'risk-free' asset is introduced. A portfolio comprising the risk-free asset and a combination of other assets allows investors to position themselves to the north-west of the Efficient Frontier.

Finance principles   57

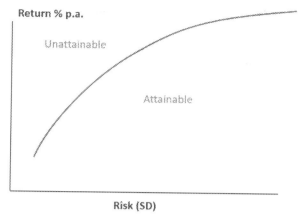

Figure 5.5 The Efficient Frontier
Source: Author

An Australian office market portfolio

How might this work in practice? Figure 5.6 shows the performance of prime office assets in some of Australia's major CBD markets (1990–2017) in risk/return space.

The portfolio, P, comprises portfolio weightings as shown in Table 5.2 (re-weighted on an annual basis). Perth is the market with the highest average total return (yield plus capital growth) of 9.1% pa over the entire period. But it also shows the highest level of volatility (standard deviation, SD). A portfolio with the constant weights as

Figure 5.6 Australia CBD office market performance (1990–2017)
Source: Author

58 David Rees

Table 5.2 Australia CBD office market performance (1990–2017)

	Total return (% pa)	Volatility (SD)	Portfolio weights (%)
Sydney	7.9	12.9	45%
Melbourne	6.5	14.3	15%
Brisbane	7.5	19.1	10%
Perth	8.5	26.4	20%
Canberra	7.3	11.7	10%
Portfolio (P)	8.1	14.2	100%

*Prime grade only

Source: Author based on JLL Research.

shown (Table 5.2) would have produced an average return of 8.1% pa over the 25-year period and volatility (SD) of 14.2%. In other words, this portfolio, over the period illustrated, would have provided an average annual return higher than all markets with the exception of Perth and volatility lower than all markets with the exception of Sydney and Canberra.

Appraisal-based indices and de-smoothing – apples and oranges

Comparisons of performance across asset classes (equities, bonds, REITs, cash, real estate) typically use market performance indices from a range of domestic and international sources – Standard & Poors, the Property Council of Australia/MSCI Australia Index or, in the United States, the NCREIF Property Index, for example. The data in Figure 5.6 are derived from the JLL Research database. The methodologies used to derive these indices may differ. Sharemarket and bond market indices typically reflect actual market transactions. In the case of direct real estate, performance indices are often based on valuations (or 'appraisals') rather than transactions. This is because transactions evidence may be sparse, out of date or unavailable. In addition, real estate assets are heterogeneous, so that even recent transactions data may not be representative of the broader market.

In real estate markets, appraisal-based indices often show a tendency to smooth out market volatility as valuers base their assessments on long-term trends rather than adopt only the most recent, and possibly unrepresentative, sales data. There is a great deal of evidence that at the individual asset level, valuers adopt an approach that partially adjusts previous valuations in light of recent evidence. The fact that valuers adjust their valuations only partially in light of new transactions evidence is not necessarily a criticism. Quan and Quigley (1991) have demonstrated that smoothed or lagged appraisals can be *optimal* in a thinly traded market. Such portfolio adjustment can be expressed as:

$$V_t = kM_t + (1-k)V_{t-1} \qquad \text{Equation 9}$$

where:
  V_t represents appraised value at time t;
  M_t represents estimated market value (established from transactions evidence) at time t;
  Vt-1 represents appraised value at time t-1; and
  k represents the adjustment factor.

Finance principles 59

When valuations are combined into market indices, the impact of the valuers' adjustment process on measured market performance is to introduce smoothing (the quarter-to-quarter or year-to-year changes are understated) and time lags (market turning points are delayed).

These two effects – a reduction in volatility and a time lag – require different adjustment processes depending on the use to which the data is applied. In the case of volatility, if the performance of direct real estate is compared against other asset classes, the systemic risk of direct real estate is likely to be understated. As a result, real estate performance looks better than it *really* is on a risk-adjusted basis. A number of alternative techniques are suggested for 'desmoothing' direct real estate index data, of which the simplest is derived from the following formula:

$$r_t = \alpha m_t + (1-\alpha) r_{t-1} \qquad \text{Equation 10}$$

where:

r_t represents the index-based return at time t;
m_t represents the 'true' (but unobservable) market return; and
α represents the de-smoothing parameter $(0 < \alpha < 1)$.

Re-arranging terms to obtain an estimate of m_t:

$$m_t = \frac{r_t - (1-\alpha) r_{t-1}}{\alpha} \qquad \text{Equation 11}$$

Evidently if $\alpha = 0$ then $m_t = r_t$. As α increases, so too does the volatility of annual returns. Figure 5.7 shows the impact of increasing α on investment returns. A range of alternative techniques are available to estimate the de-smoothing parameter, α, including regression analysis.

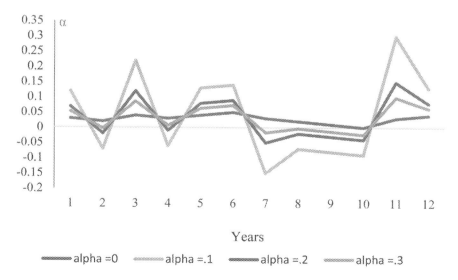

Figure 5.7 Smoothed vs. unsmoothed investment returns

Source: Author

Asset pricing, the Security Market Line (SML) and beta (β)

The Security Market Line (SML)

A broad-based portfolio (in the limit, a portfolio comprising all available investable assets) weighted by the total value of each asset, would deliver a return equal to the weighted average return of all these assets – let's call this the market return, r_m. An investor who buys this portfolio can expect to receive a return, averaged over time, of r_m. But how do the individual assets within this portfolio perform? (remember, in Table 5.1, an arbitrary assumption of a 10% return was made on that particular enterprise).

The Security Market Line (SML) establishes this relationship, being derived by Lintner (1965) and Sharpe (1966) following the work of Markowitz (1959). The SML introduces an additional asset into the discussion. We assume the availability of a *risk-free asset* (sometimes proxied as the long-term government bond rate). This risk-free asset offers a return of r_f.

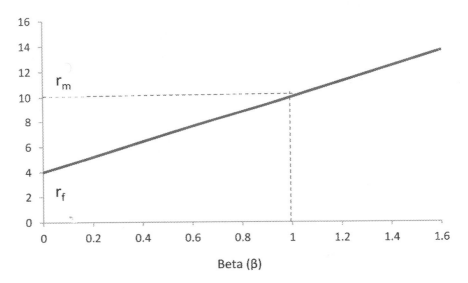

Figure 5.8 The Security Market Line

The SML establishes the formula for the Capital Asset Pricing Model (CAPM):

$$r_z = r_f + \beta(r_m - r_f) \qquad \text{Equation 12}$$

where:
   r_z represents the return required by an investor in a particular asset, *z*;
   r_f represents the return on a risk-free asset;
   r_m represents the return required by investors who select a broad asset-weighted market portfolio (in the limit, a portfolio reflecting all available investable assets); and
   β represents the volatility of the asset, z, or asset class, in comparison with the overall market. β is a measure of systemic (non-diversifiable) risk.

Finance principles 61

Principle: The insight of the Capital Asset Pricing Model (CAPM) is that the return to an individual asset is determined not by its volatility, but by the performance of that asset, or asset class, in relation to the overall market portfolio, r_m.

Beta (β) and the Equity Risk Premium (ERP)

In contrast to non-systemic risk, which is not reflected in market pricing, systemic risk is the core driver of the valuation of individual assets and asset classes. It may be contended that the correct definition of an individual asset's risk is not its statistical volatility of returns, but its contribution to portfolio risk – that is, its volatility in comparison with the volatility of the market portfolio. Statistically, for a particular asset z, β is defined as:

$$\beta z = \frac{\text{Covariance}(r_z, r_m)}{\text{Variance } r_m} \qquad \text{Equation 13}$$

Since r_f represents the return available to investors who accept no risk, it follows that $(r_m - r_f)$ is the *additional* return required by investors in the broader market. For investors in the equity market, this is called the Equity Risk Premium (ERP). It represents the additional return that investors in the sharemarket require for accepting the risk inherent in investing in shares.

The value of the ERP is elusive, being the subject of much debate and a huge literature, but 6% is often taken to be a reasonable long-term benchmark in the Australian market. (For a detailed analysis of the ERP in Australia see Bianchi, Drew and Walks (2015) *The (un)Predictable Equity Risk Premium*. The authors suggest that in current market conditions the ERP is likely to be in the range 3.0% to 4.5%.) Evidently, from Equation 12, if β = 1 then:

$$r_z = r_f + r_m - r_f = r_m \qquad \text{Equation 14}$$

The return to investors (r_z) is identical to the returns available to investors in the overall market, as shown in Figure 5.8. If r_f = 4.0% and β = 1.0 for a particular asset, z, then the required return is 4% + 6% (the ERP) = 10.0%.

Earlier, an investment return of 10% pa was assumed. It may, therefore, be concluded, using the numbers above, that for this asset β = 1.0. In other words, this asset performs strictly in line with the market portfolio.

Asset pricing and the A-REIT sector – an illustration

How does the CAPM equation apply? Consider a particular asset class – let's think about Australian REITs.

Figure 5.9 shows a stockbroker's estimate of the Australian REIT (A-REIT) sector β, derived from ASX S&P200 index data on a rolling 12-month basis between May 1993 and October 2020. Clearly the value of β fluctuates considerably over time. Although A-REITs are regarded as a defensive asset, commercial real estate has been particularly exposed to the two recent financial shocks – the Global Financial Crisis (2008) and the COVID-19 pandemic (2019).

Let's take the long-term average value of β over the period 2000 to 2020, 0.70. The average yield on ten-year Australian government bonds over this period was around 3.0%, which is conventionally adopted to represent the risk-free rate, r_f.

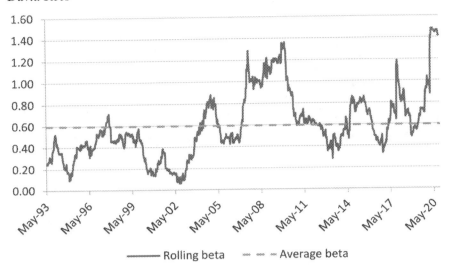

Figure 5.9 The ASX A-REIT sector β (May 1993 – October 2020)
Source: Author based on Citi Research

Then from Equation 12 the required return to the A-REIT sector is calculated as:

$$r_z = 3.0\% + 0.70(6.0\%) = 7.42\% \qquad \text{Equation 15}$$

The implied return from the A-REIT sector, r_z, is 7.42% pa. Note that this is below the required return from the overall sharemarket, which is r_f + ERP = 3.0% + 6% = 9.0%. Investors are willing to accept lower returns from A-REITs as a trade-off against the long-term relative stability of returns provided by this sector.

This, of course, is based on *historical* analysis. Markets are priced not on historical analysis but on *expected future* events. The fact that market and modelled outcomes turn out differently does not invalidate the analysis. Terrestrial navigation is accurate, even though a sailing ship may be blown off course in stormy weather.

An important qualification to this analysis is that the SML (Figure 5.8 and Equation 12) does not explicitly incorporate debt. The discussion is actually built around *asset betas* rather than *equity betas*. On the other hand, the A-REIT beta in Figure 9 reflects the behaviour of the listed A-REIT sector on the ASX, so it's an *equity beta*. As demonstrated earlier, higher levels of debt imply increased volatility and therefore a higher level of required returns. Implicitly, the returns shown in Equation 15 are for all-equity investments. The beta calculation for the A-REIT sector is based on an equity beta (β_E). A more comprehensive equation for the asset beta is:

$$\beta A = \beta E(E/V) + \beta D(D/V) \qquad \text{Equation 16}$$

where:
β_E is the equity beta; and
β_D is the debt beta, likely to be a low number (even $\beta_D = 0$ in the case of bank debt if the rate of interest is fixed for the duration of the loan).

Summary

Finance principles are tools that explain how assets are priced in the capital markets and property is no exception. As a function of time, risk, return and correlation, each asset and asset class may be priced if accurate information is available and if markets are sufficiently liquid. The proposition that 'property is different' is increasingly arguable as property markets globalise and international investors allocate capital into all asset classes around the world based on financial principles.

If valuation is to reflect the pricing of property in the capital markets, it may be contended that greater regard should be given in the valuation process to finance principles. The focus of finance principles on expectations is significant, with pricing being dependent on a view of where the economy and equity, bond and property markets may be going in the future rather than where they have been in the past. This represents a shift away from traditional property valuation approaches, where the emphasis has been on past transaction evidence with a strong aversion to 'crystal ball gazing' through consideration of the future.

The emphasis in finance principles on time, risk, return and correlation places a focus on cash flow and the discount rate as the principal ingredients for valuation, with the capitalisation rate as a by-product of financial analysis. Again, this differs significantly from traditional property valuation approaches where, historically, the capitalisation rate was considered a paramount guide to value and the discount rate a potentially unreliable secondary guide.

With REITs and funds now expanding their commercial property portfolios internationally, investment through the lens of finance principles is increasingly dominant. Therefore the same finance principles applied by financial analysts are increasingly relevant to property valuers.

With this chapter having considered finance principles and the previous chapters considering legal, economic, planning and policy principles, the following chapter will consider valuation principles to conclude the first part of this book, addressing the principles of valuation, with the second part then addressing the practice of valuation.

References

Bianchi, RJ, Drew, ME and Walk, AN 2015, 'The (un)predictable equity risk premium', *Challenger Limited*, http://www.challenger.com.au/funds/AdviserDocuments/The_Unpredictable_Equity_Risk.pdf (accessed 23 September 2016).

Lintner, J 1965, 'The valuation of risk assets and the selection of risky investments in stock portfolios and capital budgets', *The Review of Economics and Statistics*, vol. 47, no. 1, pp. 13–39.

Markowitz, HM 1959, *Portfolio Selection: Efficient Diversification of Investments*, John Wiley & Sons, New York.

Modigliani, F and Miller, M 1958, 'The cost of capital, corporation finance and the theory of investment', *American Economic Review*, vol. 48, no. 3, pp. 261–297.

OECD 2003, *Emerging Systemic Risks in the 21st Century – An Agenda for Action*, OECD, Paris.

Quan, D and Quigley, J 1991, 'Price formation and the appraisal function in real estate markets', *Journal of Real Estate Finance and Economics*, vol. 4, pp. 127–146.

Sharpe, WF 1966, 'Mutual fund performance', *Journal of Business*, vol. 39, no. 1, pp. 119–138.

Biography

Dr David Rees is a Regional Director of Research at JLL with responsibilities for advising on investment strategy and forecasting in the Asia Pacific region. David is a Fellow of the Australian Property Institute and member of the Royal Institution of Chartered Surveyors. An economist and statistician by training, prior to joining JLL, in 2008, Dr Rees was Director of Research at Mirvac Group, a leading Australian REIT.

In addition to real estate, David has experience across a range of asset and financial markets. As Head of Research at Commonwealth Bank, where he spent five years, he led a team of researchers covering economics, credit and foreign exchange markets, as well as equity research. At Bankers Trust, he held the position of Chief Equity Strategist in the investment banking division.

6 Valuation principles

David Parker

Acknowledgement

This chapter draws heavily on Parker, D (2016) *International Valuation Standards: A Guide to the Valuation of Real Property Assets* (Wiley-Blackwell, Chichester), which is duly acknowledged here rather than individually referenced through the chapter and to which readers are referred for a deeper consideration of valuation principles under International Valuation Standards.

Introduction

With the first part of this book addressing the principles of valuation and the second part addressing the practice of valuation, the previous chapters considered legal, economic, planning, policy and finance principles with this chapter considering valuation principles.

It is assumed that the reader already has an understanding of fundamental valuation principles, allowing a focus in this chapter on the governing principles of International Valuation Standards (to which the Australian Property Institute adheres) including the three key concepts of price, cost and value, the three principal valuation approaches being the cost, income and market approaches, the five bases of value being market, equitable, investment, synergistic and liquidation value and the five premises of value.

International Valuation Standards

This chapter is based on International Valuation Standards 2013 and 2019 (IVSC, 2013; IVSC, 2019) and International Financial Reporting Standards 2013 (IFRC, 2013). Given their nature, IVS's, IAS's and IFRS's are dynamic, being regularly updated and with the most recently published versions replacing previously published versions. Accordingly, readers should not rely upon this chapter as a current statement of an IVS, IAS or IFRS publication and should visit www.ivsc.org and/or www.ifrs.org to find the most recent and current version.

The advent of International Valuation Standards and their accepted dominance over regional and national standards is a result of globalisation, which has increasingly gained pace since the end of the Second World War, accelerated by the later twentieth-century developments in communications, computing and the advent of the

Internet which facilitated even greater global connectivity in banking, finance and investment contributing to the current very high level of inter-connectedness between the world's major economies, painfully evident during the contagion of the Global Financial Crisis and COVID-19 Pandemic.

In the context of property, the growth in multinational corporations, REITs and international property investors together with the international valuation service providers (such as JLL and CBRE) has driven demand for the measurement of value of operational and investment property on a common basis globally, fostered the ascendency of consistent International Valuation Standards and the demise of the dominance of idiosyncratic regional and national standards. As Gilbertson (2002) observed:

> Clients need to understand that a valuation produced in Massachusetts, Manchester, Melbourne, Moscow or Matabeleland is reliable in its standards and its methodologies. (Gilbertson, 2002)

International hierarchy

International Valuation Standards (IVS's), by definition, are of international application, being aligned with International Accounting Standards (IAS's) and International Financial Reporting Standards (IFRS's), sitting above regional and national standards.

It is through application that IVS's gain their status as, when a statement is made that a valuation has been performed in compliance with IVS, it is implicit that all relevant standards are complied with and due account is taken of any supporting guidance issued by IVSC (IVSC, 2019). Accordingly, unlike some national and regional standards issued by valuation professional organisations for their valuer members, IVS's are not mandatory on valuers unless they state that they are undertaking a valuation in accordance with the IVS's.

IVSC's role to promulgate International Valuation Standards and to act as a global focus for the valuation profession is largely operationalised through engagement with valuation professional organisations (VPO's – currently totalling round 50 and including the Australian Property Institute), regulators and other groups around the world who enforce implementation and who may also develop complementary and consistent regional and/or national standards which sit below IVS's.

Such VPO's are generally the national professional body for their country who advance the adoption and implementation of IVS's in that country, produce regional or national standards or guidance consistent with and harmonised with IVS's as may be required for that jurisdiction, act to regulate individual valuers either through self-regulation or shared regulation with government and promote the benefits of IVS's to their government and regulators (IVSC, 2014).

Structure of IVS

For the valuation of real property assets, the structure of IVS may be summarised as comprising the IVS scaffolding, the IVS General Standards and the IVS Asset Standards.

IVS scaffolding

Considered in greater detail in the following sections, the IVS scaffolding includes:

- 3 key concepts;
- 3 principal valuation approaches;
- 5 bases of value; and
- 5 premises of value.

The IVS scaffolding provides a framework or context within which the General Standards and Asset Standards sit, setting forth generally accepted valuation principles and concepts that are to be followed in the application of each but not including any procedural requirements.

IVS General Standards and Asset Standards

The IVS General Standards and Asset Standards may be briefly summarised as follows:

IVS general standards

The IVS General Standards comprise five standards, being:

- IVS101   *Scope of Work*;
- IVS102   *Investigations and Compliance*;
- IVS103   *Reporting*;
- IVS104   *Bases of Value*; and
- IVS105   *Valuation Approaches and Methods*.

IVS General Standards set forth the requirements for the conduct of all valuation assignments (except as modified by an Asset Standard), being designed to be capable of application to valuations of all types of assets for any valuation purpose to which the IVS's apply (IVS, 2019).

IVS101 *Scope of Work* specifies detailed requirements for the process of instructing the valuer. IVS102 *Investigations and Compliance* specifies detailed requirements for undertaking the valuation and IVS103 *Reporting* specifies detailed requirements for the process of reporting the valuation consistent with the original instructions.

IVS104 *Bases of Value* specifies six IVS defined bases of value and five premises of value with IVS105 *Valuation Approach and Method* specifying the market, income and cost approach and methods.

The IVS General Standards may be paraphrased as follows:

> If property investors, property lenders and property valuers around the world followed (the) pithy maxim 'say what you are going to do, do it and say what you have done', many of the problems so commonly arising in valuation could be avoided. (Bruhl, 2016)

68 David Parker

IVS asset standards

The IVS Asset Standards comprise seven standards, including:

- IVS300   *Plant and Equipment*;
- IVS400   *Real Property Interests*; and
- IVS410   *Development Property*.

IVS Asset Standards include *Bases of Value* and *Valuation Approaches and Methods*, with IVS300 *Plant and Equipment* specifying detailed requirements for the valuation of plant and equipment, IVS400 *Real Property Interests* specifying detailed requirements for the valuation of investment, owner-occupied and other property and IVS410 *Development Property* specifying detailed requirements for the valuation of contemplated or uncompleted development projects.

Three key concepts – price, cost and value

The IVS Framework (IVSC, 2013) specified three key concepts, being price, cost and value that assist with understanding the current IVS's and which are considered, sequentially, below.

Price

Distinct from value which is a matter of opinion, price is a matter of fact being the outcome of a contemplated or actual transaction:

> Price is the amount asked, offered or paid for an asset. Because of the financial capabilities, motivations or special interests of a given buyer or seller, the price paid may be different from the value which might be ascribed to the asset by others. (IVSC, 2013)

Price indicators may occur at any point during the negotiation of a transaction, effectively being a signpost, as well as an actuality at the conclusion of a transaction and may reflect the characteristics of the individual vendor and purchaser rather than the market as a whole and so not be generalisable across a market.

Accordingly, in considering price as evidence of value, users should investigate the vendor and purchaser's financial capabilities, motivations or special interests to determine the likelihood of replication by others in the market. While an observation of price in a single transaction may be of very limited use, multiple consistent observations of price in a series of transactions may be indicative of a market level.

Cost

Like price, cost is conceptually distinguishable from value in IVS's, being also a matter of fact rather than a matter of opinion. Further, like price, cost is observable but that may be the extent of the useful information contributed with potentially limited insight provided into value:

> Cost is the amount required to acquire or create an asset. When that asset has been acquired or created, its cost is a fact. Price is related to cost because the price paid for an asset becomes its cost to the buyer. (IVSC, 2013)

The parameters of the amount required to acquire an asset are not specified and may include acquisition costs such as legal fees, due diligence costs and so forth. Similarly, the parameters of the amount required to create an asset are not specified and may include such costs to create an asset as profit and risk margin, debt costs and so forth.

As with price, the financial capabilities, motivations or special interests of particular parties is not controlled and may result in a different acquisition cost or cost to create than would arise from typical market participants and so not be generalisable across a market.

Value

Within the IVS's, value can only be a judgement of one of two things, being either the most probable price in exchange or the economic benefits of ownership, broadly according with concepts of market value and concepts of investment value, respectively (IVS, 2013).

Further, this principle is extended consistently in IVS (2013) to *basis of valuation*:

> A basis of valuation can fall into one of three principal categories:
> The first is to indicate the most probable price that would be achieved in a hypothetical exchange in a free and open market. Market value as defined in these standards falls into this category.
> The second is to indicate the benefits that a person or an entity enjoys from ownership of an asset. The value is specific to that person or entity, and may have no relevance to market participants in general. Investment value and special value as defined in these standards fall into this category.
> The third is to indicate the price that would be reasonably agreed between two specific parties for the exchange of an asset. Although the parties may be unconnected and negotiating at arm's length, the asset is not necessarily exposed in the market and the price agreed may be one that reflects the specific advantages or disadvantages of ownership to the parties involved rather than the market at large. Fair value as defined in these standards falls into this category. (IVSC, 2013)

with a fourth basis of value being categories other than the three principal categories particular to a specific purpose of valuation, such as statutory, regulatory (including IFRS) or by some form of documented agreement.

Three principal valuation approaches

IVS's specify three principal valuation approaches, being the cost approach, the income approach and the market approach which are considered, sequentially, below.

Cost approach

The cost approach is the first of three principal valuation approaches recognised by IVS's and is grounded in economic theory, being based on the economic principle of 'substitution':

> The cost approach provides an indication of value using the economic principle that a buyer will pay no more for an asset than the cost to obtain an asset of equal utility, whether by purchase or by construction, unless undue time, inconvenience, risk or other factors are involved. (IVSC, 2019)

While the economic principle of substitution is relatively simple to understand as a principle, its application in practice in the context of property is much more challenging, exacerbated by the type of property for which the approach is considered most relevant within the IVS's being that where there is either no evidence of transaction prices for similar property or no identifiable actual or notional income stream that would accrue to the owner of the relevant interest, being principally 'specialised property' such as public buildings (town halls, museums and so forth) or major operating facilities (car manufacturing plants, airports and so forth).

Three cost approach methods are provided comprising the replacement cost method, the reproduction cost method and the summation method with a proposal that all of the costs that would be incurred by a typical participant should be captured (IVSC, 2019).

With valuation being a matter of opinion rather than a matter of fact, the diversity of variables within and complexity of the *cost approach* may be expected to result in a potentially wide range of opinions of value.

Income approach

The income approach is the second of the three principal valuation approaches recognised by IVS's and is grounded in economic theory, being based on the economic principle of 'anticipation of benefits':

> The income approach provides an indication of value by converting future cash flow to a single current value. (IVSC, 2019)

Consistent with the forward-looking nature of the underlying economic principle, the *income approach* conceptualises value as a single expression of future cash flows, masking within its simplicity a range of complex measurement issues and other related issues including valuation accuracy, behavioural influences and so forth.

IVS105 acknowledges that there are 'many ways' to implement the income approach but contends that they are all 'effectively based on discounting future amounts of cash flow to present value' and so focuses on the discounted cash flow method in detail, though the capitalisation method is widely used by the valuation profession in Australia.

Market approach

The market approach is the third of the three principal valuation approaches recognised by IVS's and is grounded in economic theory, being based on the economic principle of 'price equilibrium':

> The market approach provides an indication of value by comparing the asset with identical or comparable (that is similar) assets for which price information is available. (IVSC, 2019)

The market approach is dependent upon there being 'identical or comparable (that is similar) assets for which price information is available', with the absence of such sales evidence rendering the approach inapplicable.

Valuation principles 71

Consistent with recent case law in the specialist Australian Courts (see, for example, *Adams v Valuer General* [2014] NSWLEC 1005), the market approach may be contended to comprise four sequential steps in the processing of sales evidence, being:

- the accumulation step;
- the analysis step;
- the adjustment step; and
- the application step.

Five Bases of value

IVS104 specifies five bases of value, being market value, equitable value, investment value/worth, synergistic value and liquidation value which, together with market rent which IVS104 specifies to be a basis of value, are considered, sequentially, below.

Market value

Market value is defined as:

> Market value is the estimated amount for which an asset or liability should exchange on the valuation date between a willing buyer and a willing seller in an arm's length transaction, after proper marketing and where the parties had each acted knowledgably, prudently and without compulsion. (IVSC, 2019)

Accordingly, *market value* as defined by IVS's falls into the first of the three principal IVS (2103) categories of *basis of valuation*, being that which indicates the most probable price that would be achieved in a hypothetical exchange in a free and open market.

Market value may be distinguished from equitable value, investment value/worth, synergistic value and liquidation value by its adoption of a postulated market and postulated participants, being grounded in a hypothetical on market exchange.

Market rent

Market rent is defined as:

> Market rent is the estimated amount for which an interest in real property should be leased on the valuation date between a willing lessor and a willing lessee on appropriate lease terms in an arm's length transaction, after proper marketing and where the parties had each acted knowledgably, prudently and without compulsion. (IVSC, 2019)

Accordingly, *market rent* echoes *market value* with the same conditions applying and the *appropriate lease terms* being those typically agreed in the market for the type of property on the valuation date between market participants.

Market rent may be distinguished from equitable value, investment value/worth, synergistic value and liquidation value by its adoption of a postulated market and postulated participants, being grounded in a hypothetical on market agreement.

Equitable value

Equitable value is defined as:

> Equitable value is the estimated price for the transfer of an asset or liability between identified knowledgeable and willing parties that reflects the respective interests of those parties. (IVSC, 2019)

Equitable value falls into the third of the three principal IVS (2103) categories of *basis of valuation*, being that which indicates the price that would be reasonably agreed between two respective parties for the exchange of an asset.

Equitable value may be distinguished from *market value* through its basis in the actual (nominated) rather than the hypothetical (postulated). Further, *equitable value* may be distinguished from *investment value* through its dependence on participants rather than on a participant.

Investment value/worth

Investment value (often referred to in Commonwealth countries as worth) is defined as:

> Investment value is the value of an asset to a particular owner or prospective owner for individual investment or operational objectives. (IVSC, 2019)

Accordingly, *investment value* as defined by IVS falls into the second of the three principal IVS (2103) categories of *basis of valuation*, being that which indicates the benefits that a person or an entity enjoys from ownership of an asset.

Investment value may be distinguished from *market value* through its basis in the actual (nominated) rather than the hypothetical (postulated).

Synergistic value

Synergistic value is defined as:

> Synergistic value is the result of a combination of two or more assets or interests where the combined value is more than the sum of the separate values. (IVSC, 2019)

While the example often used for *synergistic value* is that value created by the combination of a freehold and long leasehold interest, it may potentially arise from any combination of two or more assets for any purpose and so requires careful distinction by the user from concepts of aggregation in the IVS's.

Significantly, for *synergistic value* to arise, there must be more than one market participant, otherwise it may be special value that arises.

Synergistic value may be distinguished from *market value* through its basis in the actual (nominated) rather than in the hypothetical (postulated). Further, *synergistic value* may be distinguished from *investment value* by its requirements for an exchange to occur in order to manifest.

Liquidation value

Liquidation value is defined as:

> Liquidation value is the amount that would be realised when an asset or group of assets are sold on a piecemeal basis. (IVSC, 2019)

Liquidation value should take into account the costs of getting the assets into saleable condition as well as those of the disposal activity, with two different premises for determination being an orderly transaction with a typical marketing period or a forced transaction with a shortened marketing period.

Liquidation value may be distinguished from *market value* through its basis in the actual (nominated) rather than the hypothetical (postulated).

Special value

While not considered in IVS (2019) to be a basis of value, IVSC (2013) included a definition of special value that helpfully assists with understanding the current IVS's:

> Special value is an amount that reflects particular attributes of an asset that are only of value to a special purchaser. (IVSC, 2013)

with special purchaser defined in IVS (2013) as:

> A special purchaser is a particular buyer for whom a particular asset has special value because of advantages arising from its ownership that would not be available to other buyers in (a/the) market. (IVS 2013)

As noted above, *special value* as defined by IVS (2013) falls into the second of the three principal IVS (2103) categories of *basis of valuation*, being that which indicates the benefits that a person or entity enjoys from ownership of an asset.

Special value may be distinguished from *market value* through its basis in the actual (nominated) rather than in the hypothetical (postulated). Further, *special value* may be distinguished from *equitable value, investment value, synergistic value* and *liquidation value* though the requirement for a *special purchaser*.

Five premises of value

IVS104 specifies five premises of value, being:

- assumed use which describes the circumstances of how an asset or liability is used;
- highest and best use which is that use, from a participant perspective, which would produce the highest value for the asset but which must be physically possible, financially feasible and legally allowable;
- current use/existing use which is the current use of an asset, liability or group of assets and/or liabilities and may differ from highest and best use;
- orderly liquidation which describes the value of a group of assets that could be realised in a liquidation sale, given a reasonable period of time to find a purchaser with the seller being compelled to sell on an as-is, where-is basis; and

- forced sale describes circumstances where a seller is under compulsion to sell and that, as a consequence, a proper marketing period is not possible and buyers may not be able to undertake adequate due diligence.

While not considered in IVS (2019) to be premises of value, IVS (2013) specified six contextual terms, being real estate, real property, investment property, trade related property, intangible asset and goodwill which helpfully inform the understanding of IVS's and are considered, sequentially, below.

Real estate

Real estate and *real property* are different in IVS's, with *real estate* being 'land' and 'things' whereas *real property* is a right, interest or benefit related to *real estate*:

> Real estate – land and all things that are a natural part of land, eg trees, minerals and things that have been attached to the land, eg buildings and site improvements and all permanent building attachments, eg mechanical and electrical plant providing services to a building, that are both below and above the ground. (IVSC, 2013)

Real property

Distinguished from *real estate* which is 'land' and 'things', *real property* is a right, interest or benefit related to *real estate*. While *real estate* is required to exist to provide the physical framework within which a right, interest or benefit may exist, it is that right, interest or benefit (*real property*) that is effectively the source of value:

> Real property – all rights, interests and benefits related to the ownership of real estate. (IVSC, 2013)

With value attaching to the property interest held rather than to the physical land and buildings, the threshold issue for the valuer to address is 'ownership' of *real estate* as the form of ownership (freehold, leasehold, licence and so forth) will determine the nature of the property interest and the extent of the 'rights, interests and benefits' arising, because, without ownership, there is no property to value.

Investment property

Echoing IAS40 *Investment Property*, the definition of *investment property* in IVS's emphasised the income and capital return characteristics while distinguishing from owner-occupied property used by a business and from property identified for sale under IFRS5 *Non-Current Assets Held for Sale*:

Investment property – property that is land or a building, or part of a building, or both, held by the owner to earn rentals or for capital appreciation, or both, rather than for:

(a) *use in the production* or *supply of goods* or *services* or for *administrative purposes*; or
(b) *sale in the ordinary course of business.* (IVSC, 2013)

with value attaching to the property interest held rather than to the physical land and buildings.

Trade related property

The definition of trade related property included two key elements, being design and a value/trading link:

> Trade related property – any type of <u>real property</u> designed for a specific type of business where the property value reflects the trading potential for that business. (IVSC, 2013)

While *trade related property* may be any type of real property, it must be designed for a 'specific' business type and the value of the property must be linked to the trading potential of that business. The traditional example usually cited is a petrol filling station, where the property was designed specifically to be a petrol filling station and the value of the property is inextricably linked to the trading potential of the petrol filling station.

Intangible asset

IVS's address the valuation of all assets including tangible and intangible assets as well as all liabilities:

> Intangible asset – a non-monetary asset that manifests itself by its economic properties. It does not have physical substance but grants rights and economic benefits to its owner. (IVSC, 2013)

In the context of property valuation, the issue of an *intangible asset* may arise in association with the valuation of a tangible asset, such as consideration of the value of the name 'Waldorf Astoria' in association with the valuation of the *real property*.

Goodwill

Traditionally considered as a component of the value of a business, *goodwill* as defined by IVS's may be applicable to the valuation of a group of properties as a portfolio:

> Goodwill – any future economic benefit arising from a business, an interest in a business or from the use of a group of assets which is not separable. (IVSC, 2013)

Accordingly, valuers should take care when instructed to value a 'group of assets' which may comprise a portfolio of properties as a portfolio and where there is market support for a premium or discount to apply at the portfolio level, as such a premium or discount may be capable of classification as *goodwill*.

Summary

The increasing pace of globalisation and the international flow of capital has seen the advent of International Accounting Standards, International Financial Reporting Standards and International Valuation Standards, often replacing previous regional and/or national valuation standards. Effectively, therefore, it is International Valuation

76 David Parker

Standards that now define valuation theory and guide valuation practice in a consistent direction around the world.

Relegating the High Court decision in *Spencer v Commonwealth* (1907) 5 CLR 418 (*Spencer*) to its twenty-first century role as a significant precedent for statutory valuation represents a major change in the Australian approach to valuation theory and practice. Valuation theory and practice are now determined by the provisions of International Valuation Standards through three key concepts, three principal valuation approaches, five bases of value and five premises of value being manifest through a series of General Standards and Asset Standards.

Therefore, valuation principles are founded in the three key concepts of price, cost and value, the three principal valuation approaches being the cost, income and market approaches, the five bases of value being market, equitable, investment, synergistic and liquidation value and the five premises of value focusing on use, supported by IVS (2103) which distinguishes between the land (*real estate*) and a right, interest or benefit related to the land (*real property*), with the latter not the former being the source of value.

Further, the valuation process is determined by IVS101, IVS102 and IVS103 with the valuation approach to plant and equipment, real property interests and development property determined by IVS300, IVS400 and IVS410, respectively.

Accordingly, this chapter provides the context for valuation principles under International Valuation Standards, highlighting that which is included and implicitly that which is not. While that which is not included in International Valuation Standards is not, necessarily, prohibited, it cannot be adopted if a valuation is to be stated as undertaken in accordance with International Valuation Standards, as may be required by an increasing number of major Australian and international valuation clients.

Previous chapters in this first part have considered legal, economic, planning, policy and finance principles. This chapter, considering valuation principles, concludes the first part, with the second part now addressing the practice of valuation.

References

Bruhl, M 2016, 'Foreword', in Parker, D (ed.), *2016 International Valuation Standards: A Guide to the Valuation of Real Property Assets*, Wiley-Blackwell, Chichester.
Gilbertson, B 2002, 'Valuation or appraisal: An art or a science?', *Australian Property Journal*, February.
International Financial Reporting Council 2013, *International Financial Reporting Standards 2013*, International Financial Reporting Council, London.
International Valuation Standards Council 2013, *International Valuation Standards 2013*, International Valuation Standards Council, London.
International Valuation Standards Council 2014, *Global Regulatory Convergence and the Valuation Profession*, International Valuation Standards Council, London.
International Valuation Standards Council 2019, *International Valuation Standards*, International Valuation Standards Council, London.
Parker, D 2016, *International Valuation Standards: A Guide to the Valuation of Real Property Assets*, Wiley-Blackwell, Chichester.

Biography

David Parker is an internationally recognised property industry expert focusing on valuation standards, compulsory acquisition and REITs, being a director and adviser to property investment groups including real estate investment trusts, unlisted funds and private property businesses (www.davidparker.com.au).

Dr Parker is currently a Visiting Professor at the Henley Business School, University of Reading and a Visiting Fellow at the University of Ulster, having been Professor of Property at the University of South Australia, an Acting Valuation Commissioner of the Land and Environment Court of New South Wales and a Sessional Member of the South Australian Civil and Administrative Tribunal adjudicating compulsory acquisition compensation and rating disputes.

Author of the authoritative *Routledge REITs Research Handbook*, *International Valuation Standards: A Guide to the Valuation of Real Property Assets* and *Global Real Estate Investment Trusts: People, Process and Management,* Dr Parker may be contacted at davidparker@davidparker.com.au

Part II
Practice of valuation

Section One
Valuation practice for conventional property sectors

7 Residential property valuation

Damian Kininmonth

Introduction

With the first part of this book addressing the principles of valuation, the second part addresses the practice of valuation being grouped into three sections comprising conventional property sectors, specialist property sectors and specific purposes. Conventional property sectors include residential, office, retail, industrial and rural property valuation practice. Specialist property sectors include retirement, leisure, plant and equipment and business and intangible asset valuation practice and specific purposes include valuation practice for rental, financial reporting, secured lending, insurance and statutory valuation purposes.

The first section of the second part of this book addresses the valuation of conventional property sectors with residential property valuation practice considered in this chapter and office, retail, industrial and rural property valuation practice considered in the following chapters.

It is assumed that the reader already has an understanding of valuation methodology for residential property, allowing a focus in this chapter on current trends in the physical, legal and financial determinants of value and the important distinction, for residential property, of what is being sold, how it is being sold and what it is being sold for.

Residential property valuation practice has been subject to significant change over the last three decades, through technology and challenges to previous paradigms. Technology is just a tool and tools will change. Just because that's how it was done in the past does not make it how it should be done either now or in the future. The real skill in valuations is understanding, what, why and how you use the tools at your disposal and how they speed you to answer to the question that your client is asking about the value of the property under review.

The purpose of the valuer is not confined to determining the value of a dwelling, they are also entrusted to assess why that particular dwelling in that unique location has that value at that point in time, under a particular set of sale conditions.

Valuations are not, therefore, a best guess but the conclusion of the valuer's analysis and understanding of all the inputs that make up the physical legal, financial and attitudinal elements that combine to determine that particular property's value in the market.

Instruction

The instruction sets out why the client has engaged the valuer and what the client needs to know from the valuation. The instruction sets out both the needs of the client in terms of knowledge and the constraints under which that knowledge may be acquired. Only after understanding the instruction can the valuer determine what tools are available to the valuer to meet the needs of that client.

The instruction sets up the framework for the valuer to determine the tools available or develop new tools to most efficiently determine that answer which meets the client's purpose for engaging the valuer. The constraints of past practices can be put aside or adapted and new practices developed to efficiently meet the client's purpose in the modern setting. Technological advancements can then be utilised to enhance the role and knowledge of the valuer and not constrain how the answer to the purpose is determined.

Market value and highest and best use principles

Valuations are founded generally on two basic concepts, being market value and highest and best use. It is important that the valuer not only know these principles but why a deviation from these principles can lead to the valuer failing to meet their obligations under their instructions.

Market value may be defined as the estimated amount for which an asset or liability should exchange on the valuation date between a willing buyer and a willing seller in an arm's length transaction, after proper marketing and where the parties have each acted knowledgeably, prudently and without compulsion.

The market value of an asset will reflect its highest and best use. Highest and best use may be defined as the use of an asset that maximises its potential and that is physically possible, legally permissible and financially feasible. The highest and best use may be for the continuation of an asset's existing use or for some alternative use. This is determined by the use that a market participant would have in mind for the asset when formulating the price that it would be willing to bid.

The key components of highest and best use, physical, legal and financial, drive how the valuer determines the appropriate method to be adopted to determine the market value of the property in question. It is the determination, description and assessment of these three components of highest and best use that provide the scope for the valuer to utilise new and emerging technologies to more efficiently complete the valuation and in so doing complete their role in answering the client's purpose for instructing the valuation.

Physical determinants of value

The principal physical determinants of value comprise location, spatial aspects and improvements.

Current trends in location analysis

The world of geocoding and spatial analysis is under constant change and is an area where the modern valuer can rapidly obtain an overview of the changing spatial dynamics that will impact on property value. Whilst Google Maps and similar have been around for many years, now the ability to apply layers of information on the desired mapping area enhances the valuer's ability to quickly review both geographical features and man-made infrastructure. The ability to then review changes in that information over time via time-lapse satellite and high resolution aerial photography is an invaluable tool. The utilisation of locational analysis and fine analysis of that information enhances the valuer's ability to determine the actual weighting that locational attributes will have on the determinants of value.

The down-side of reliance on location mapping tools is the scale utilised. The reliance by the residential valuer in utilising tools such as Google Maps and GPS navigation is that the valuer can easily navigate to the property but spatial information is limited to the screen size or scale utilised on the device carried by the valuer.

Getting to the subject property efficiently is helpful but knowing how the property sits within the broader environment is still essential. Modern mapping tools mean that the valuer does not have to drive randomly around an area but can navigate directly to points of interest they feel may impact on the property's value.

Presently, geocoding is still limited to two dimensions, which means assessing the heights of building is still problematic. However, with improvements in offset photography, this will soon be possible.

Three dimensional mapping is an emerging tool. With greater computing power, architects and planners are providing and demanding better spatial modelling of new projects that not only reveal the subject property but how it sits within the existing built environment.

Current trends in spatial analysis – land dimensions, shape and size

While the valuer is not a surveyor, it is incumbent upon the valuer to determine that the property is correctly located and that boundaries are in accordance with the surveyed Certificate of Title. The utilisation of satellite and aerial photography and spatial mapping, overlayed with geocoded title boundaries means the valuer can locate geographical features and man-made features including fencing to determine if legal and actual boundaries are in alignment.

The adoption of laser measuring devices provides an even more accurate tool for the valuer on site rather than traditional measuring tools such as tapes and wheels. Modern high-end laser devices come with magnification lens that can be utilised over long distances in any light conditions. These tools are now an essential part of the valuer's tool kit.

Current trends in improvements analysis – physical and functional

While the valuer is not a builder or architect, they should be familiar with the basic construction materials and fit-outs of the buildings that are being valued and the era in which they were developed.

This is an area that requires a basic understanding of building techniques and construction systems adopted in the area the valuer practices and also an understanding of emerging technologies and their costs and benefits. The simplest way that the valuer can keep abreast of emerging products and their cost is to attend home shows and expos. These forums have the benefit of displaying existing and new products in one place so the valuer can both view and discuss the products.

Whilst time-lapse satellite imagery is very useful to view development over the recent past, historical photos and books provide the valuer with the context as to how an area developed, over what distinct time periods and under what influences. The valuer does not have to be an historian but a keen sense of the dynamics of history can be an important influencer of current day values. Historical bias for or against an area can have significant impacts on how a location is perceived.

Recent examples of how physical products and their historical development can impact modern day values include the current cladding issues, leaky building syndrome, issues with insulation, asbestos cladding, cheap electrical wiring, pre and post bush fire constructed dwellings, fire rated buildings and their construction methods and even earthquake rated building systems. Different eras in history provide different building design elements that often influence the modern utilisation and perception of that space.

Legal determinants of value

The principal legal determinants of value comprise title, town planning and environmental aspects.

Title

The starting point for any valuation of real property is the title, the title plan and the accompanying description of restrictions that are noted on the title and plan.

In the age of PropertyPro and mass undertaking of mortgage valuations, the residential valuer can be lulled into a false complacency of not reviewing this important document thoroughly, or only undertaking partial searches. A full title search is mandatory when undertaking any valuation other than a PropertyPro valuation request. In the modern age the cost and time to undertake a full search is minimal. It should be, after receiving instructions, the first document acquired by the valuer.

Easements, covenants and agreements are all referenced in the full title search and knowing of them and how they impact on value is vital in determining the final valuation.

Town planning

The town planning constraints placed on a property must also be understood by the valuer. The differences within the various residential zones and non-residential zones and how they impact on residential development can lead to significant differences in value for physically similar properties.

Zoning maps and the accompanying overlays and schedules are readily available online. These allow the valuer to quickly determine if the subject property and comparable sales are similarly impacted by zoning constraints. When differences are noted, it is prudent that the valuer understands the difference within the zones and overlays as they may go a long way to explaining variants in value for physically similar properties.

Environmental aspects

With modern town planning and building codes, the development of residential property on environmentally contaminated land is not as prevalent as it was for previous generations of valuers. It is, however, an area of concern particularly within established areas located in close proximity to known current or previous potentially polluting industries. Just because a property is not on a designated contaminated site list does not mean it is free from potential contamination. The valuer must raise the eyes and not just look at the subject property but also the surrounding development.

With the impact of significant climate events of increasing concern to legislators and the occupiers of residential dwellings, the valuer must make themselves aware of the cost of mitigating and surviving a climate event. In Australia, the impacts of flooding, bushfire, major wind, rain and even ocean tidal events are being felt more broadly and the cost of these events is becoming more significant. The result is generally an increased cost burden for those wanting to live in these environmentally compromised locations. The cost can include increased building costs to meet new legislation, long delays in getting development approvals and increased or even no insurance coverage.

Financial determinants of value

The principal financial determinants of value comprise current use, leases, outgoings, competing uses and marketing.

Current use

One question that a valuer must ask when undertaking any valuation is whether the current use is the best use of the site. Are the improvements an under or over-capitalisation of the site? Are the improvements either physically or functionally obsolete? This may be done in two ways, first by viewing the property in the context of surrounding development and secondly by ascribing a rental to the property and therefore determining the return on the investment.

In both instances, the valuer needs a firm understanding of the expected standard of development in the local environment and the impacts on value when that standard is not met or the incremental impact of being of a greater standard. A dwelling can be habitable, but if it falls below current expectations, the improvements may be a liability. Conversely, if the improvements are significantly above local expectations, the investment in creating those improvements will not be reflected in their added value (over-capitalisation).

There is also the issue of when the current use or permitted use is not viable and how that may impact on the value of the property. Examples of this include dwellings in display villages when the builder has become insolvent, serviced apartments, hotel units or student accommodation at a time when either the operator or the economic conditions mean there is no demand for the space and no alternative legal use.

Leases

In most instances, residential leases are for short-term occupation with regular opportunities for market rent reviews. The residential valuer, however, must also be aware of other interests including life interests or even the impact on return due to long-term leases. The terms and conditions of the lease are important as they will reflect the return available to the owner.

Many areas are subject to long-term ground leases at what are currently peppercorn rents, however, the impact of what happens when such leases come to the end of their term must be considered. The assumption of always being able to sell a property with vacant possession is fraught.

Outgoings

Residential valuations of detached dwellings rarely require an in-depth knowledge of outgoings as it can be generally assumed that they will be the same across the property market under review. For statutory outgoings this is generally the case. The advent, however, of apartment living and investment over the last 25 years and, in particular, the ageing of stock means past assumptions about outgoings must be reviewed. Owner's Corporation fees will vary significantly due to the type of ancillary features offered within the building, the age of the building and the maintenance profile adopted by the management of the building.

It is, therefore, necessary for the residential valuer, particularly when reviewing high density residential accommodation, to obtain access to the latest owner's corporation minutes. These minutes should provide not just the current outgoings but also any special levies that the property will be subject to and any proposals for major future works programmes that are not covered by existing sinking funds. The minutes should state when the last building inspection was undertaken, determination of any faults, what the cost of rectification may be and, importantly, who has liability to rectify them. Particularly topical is the issue of illegal cladding products, structural faults and, for older buildings, the replacement of lifts and common air-conditioning plant which can be a significant expense.

Competing uses

With reliance placed so heavily on data bases and settled sales, the modern valuer sometimes forgets that property value is not just based on demand as reflected by the sales but also on supply. Over the last 20 years supply in many instances has struggled to keep up with the demand for new property which has resulted in an almost constant increase in values. When that dynamic changes, however, the impact on values will be significant. Property, by its very nature, is not liquid and when it comes to the development of new dwellings, be it a single houses or a high density apartment complex, there are significant time impacts as a result of planning and construction lags. This lag between when the property is sold and when it settles can see significant changes in market dynamics.

The capital city markets in particular, with their focus on overseas investment, short-term and student accommodation, have seen a significant amount of new apartment construction undertaken over the last 15 years. The lead times for these buildings can be two to three years from initial sale to final settlement. This allows for a range of competing buildings to be planned or constructed in the intervening period. It also means that a number of buildings can be settling at the one time which impacts on the rental and therefore the return that the purchaser may anticipate. The valuer must not only be aware of recent sales but of the supply pipeline and how that will impact the value of the subject property.

In 2020, the COVID-19 pandemic has caused the effective elimination of overseas migration, both short- and long-term, and the loss of overseas holiday makers. Accordingly, owners of apartments – particularly in the inner city and close to Universities – have seen rentals plummet and, in turn, values follow. If this is coupled with new products previously commenced that are now being completed also entering the market, the supply curve is one that the valuer must be cognisant of when valuing existing residential property.

A further recent example of poor supply side reporting is in regional areas that are dependent on one major industry, such as mining. Development in anticipation of a sustained mining boom may result in over-supply should such a boom falter.

Marketing

Marketing and market information has three aspects for consideration – what is being sold, how is it being sold and what is it being sold for.

Although every developer will lay claim that some aspect of their offering makes it unique, initially residential developments usually present a somewhat generic product with very little distinguishing one development from another.

As markets have matured, the occupiers of these properties do start making very distinct choices as to what they want in terms of accommodation, size and ancillary features. It is important for the valuer to distinguish what is marketing as distinct from what drives market value.

In addition to the physical aspects of the property, how the property is sold is an important consideration. Is the property a resale back into the local market? – or has it reverted to the developer pool and sold to a purchaser as part of a new campaign? Should the property be auctioned or is private sale the best method of disposal for this property type. The valuer may be asked to comment on methods of disposal and most likely purchaser profiles, not just for mortgagee or distressed sales but for all sales.

The final key is how much has a property sold for? Data bases are updated as new information is supplied, so with online data bases the valuer, in theory, has access to a wide range of sales information including marketing information and photographs supplied by marketing agents and verified sale prices as supplied by government bodies.

The danger is that the valuer will only make assumptions about the market based on data base sourced information. It is essential that all the time saved by the valuer in utilising technology platforms is used to get a deeper understanding of what has driven the sale to its conclusion and that can only be done by speaking to the participants. These include developers, selling and leasing agents, lessees, investors and owner occupiers.

Balancing data with intuition

The modern valuer has access to a plethora of information to assist in undertaking a valuation. These tools and databases speed up what have traditionally been time-consuming aspects of the valuer's role. Due to the real time updating and improved quality of information, many aspects of the residential valuer's role have become relatively easy. However, it is important to remember that if it was easy, anybody could do it and the valuer's role would be obsolete. Some data analysts will argue that on a mass scale this is already true in areas with properties having low divergence from the norm. These analysts will argue that utilising the right algorithms will produce a fairly accurate estimate of value based on a few key inputs. The valuer is, however, not just entrusted to determine the value of a dwelling but also to determine why that particular dwelling in that particular unique location has that particular value.

The valuer's role is to understand the need that the client wants fulfilled. The basis of communicating the need is the instruction. Once this has been understood, based on the principles of market value and highest and best use the valuer will review all the likely inputs, physical, legal and financial, coupled with the emotive triggers as determined by research into key buyer drivers and then determine a defendable basis for making a valuation. A valuation is not just a mathematical output, it is the result of how humans perceive a range of inputs, some empirical and some emotive, to arrive at a value that is unique to the property under review.

Technology, data bases and modern hardware such as lasers and handheld computers speed up and facilitate the valuer's role but these are just tools to aid the valuer. They are not a replacement for the ultimate skill which is recognising and assessing all the elements that are the drivers of value as perceived by the buyers and sellers of property and then presenting them to the client in a way that meets a client's need for instructing the valuer in the first instance.

Market trends

In undertaking the review of a property's features, the valuer must look not only at the legal, physical and financial constraints but also assess the features that drive potential purchasers to make the ultimate decision to choose one property over another at a particular price point. With residential property, trend waves defining particular periods can be seen and it is the valuer's role to identify those potential trends early and assess their impact.

During the late 1990s and early 2000s, new housing estates were notable for an ever increasing drive for larger sized dwellings, creating the term 'McMansion'. Houses were more often two-storey but block sizes began to shrink. Eventually the dining room was removed and the creation of the open plan kitchen/meals/family room emerged. Home theatre or entertainment rooms became popular to facilitate bigger and better TVs and sound systems.

Australians began to embrace high rise living as it reduced commute times and casual dining became the norm with small local restaurants reminiscent of Europe almost negating the need for kitchen/meals areas. Historic homes with ornate facades from the Victorian and Edwardian periods, whilst sought after, were transformed from large dark heavy spaces to light filled modern homes with extensions and renovations.

2020 and beyond will be no different and the valuer must be acutely aware of the impact that COVID-19 has had on the way people live and work and how it will continue to impact for years to come. Anticipated trends include the introduction of a separate home office space as people increasingly work more from home. Commuting will not disappear, but peak periods may be extended as people work more flexible hours. This may also facilitate the decreased reliance on the private vehicle and the rise of the auto drive electric vehicle, short-term hire vehicle or the rise of the electric bike which may see the need for garage spaces decrease or be repurposed.

One of the unexpected trends of COVID-19 was an increased movement to the regions. The changing way in which people live and work will also significantly change their property requirements. A trend that is already emerging is the desire for a main residence within close proximity to lifestyle choices such as beaches, mountains or regional towns that will be coupled with a smaller inner city house or unit which will be utilised for work and inner city entertainment. If you can work from home, you can work from anywhere so that the need to be within a reasonable commute of major centres becomes less necessary as long as there is good Internet connection.

Residential property valuation   89

In the suburban setting, the proximity to shops and local facilities has become more important as people have become reticent about gathering in larger unrestricted shopping centres. It can be anticipated that local shopping strips will reinvent themselves. This may see space that is currently underutilised reimagined with low rise residential development sitting above local shops. The trend to live, shop and play local will see the rise of the local bubble and strong local connectivity being more important when assessing the value of a property.

A trend in apartment living will be away from small one bedroom or bedsit apartments to larger two and three bedroom apartments. It will also be important for these apartments to have external connections, such that high rise apartments with no opening windows or balcony spaces may fall out of favour. Apartment complexes that have good useable passive communal spaces and gardens will find increased favour. It will also be important to plan communities with good safe passive and active community spaces including looking at developments not just as stand-alone buildings but as part of a local eco system. These building will also have to cater for the growing requirement of home delivery and online shopping. Secure cool rooms and larger temporary storage spaces along with better internal communications will be the value drivers of the future.

Residential property in its many forms and various locations is a function of legal, physical and financial constraints. However, what drives value is the perception of need. It is the valuer's role to be aware of the changing needs of the users of property so that the drivers of value may be understood. This cannot be done by solely studying a data base of sales.

Summary

In this chapter, valuation practice for residential property is considered through a contextual analysis of current trends in the physical, legal and financial determinants of value with a particular focus on marketing and the important distinction between marketing and market value drivers.

The widespread use of technology in residential property valuation is accepted with continued increasing use envisaged and embraced, facilitating time saving for reinvestment into gaining a deeper understanding of market drivers. The impact of the COVID-19 pandemic on the demand for certain types of residential property is considered together with other global issues such as defective building cladding and climate change impacts such as bushfire.

In this first section of the second part of the book, valuation practice for residential property was considered in this chapter, with valuation practice for office, retail, industrial and rural property considered in the following chapters.

The second section of the second part of this book addresses valuation practice for specialist property sectors comprising retirement, leisure, plant and equipment and business and intangible asset valuation with the third and final section of the second part addressing valuation practice for specific purposes, including rental, financial reporting, secured lending, insurance and statutory valuation purposes.

Biography

Damian Kininmonth has over 25 years' experience in the property market across Melbourne through his extensive valuation experience acting for several major commercial and retail banks and non-bank lending institutions. Damian has also been engaged to provide property consultancy services for numerous solicitors, accountants and developers as well as private clients.

During his career, Damian has undertaken the role of expert witness in various circumstances within the dispute resolution process. He has acted for local government agencies in their acquisition and disposal programmes and worked for several Commonwealth agencies in the same capacity.

Damian provides services across all property classes including retail, residential, commercial, and industrial and jointly manages the Melbourne business of Preston Rowe Patterson with an emphasis on mentoring. Utilising his diverse property experience, he provides guidance to the senior valuation staff and implements learning and training programmes for the junior members of the team.

8 Office property valuation

Peter Dempsey

Introduction

With the first part of this book addressing the principles of valuation, the second part addresses the practice of valuation being grouped into three sections comprising conventional property sectors, specialist property sectors and specific purposes. Conventional property sectors include residential, office, retail, industrial and rural property valuation practice. Specialist property sectors include retirement, leisure, plant and equipment and business and intangible asset valuation practice and specific purposes include valuation practice for rental, financial reporting, secured lending, insurance and statutory valuation purposes.

The first section of the second part of this book addresses the valuation of conventional property sectors with residential property valuation practice considered in the previous chapter, office property valuation practice considered in this chapter and retail, industrial and rural property valuation practice considered in the following chapters.

It is assumed that the reader already has an understanding of valuation methodology for office property, allowing a focus in this chapter on the structure and drivers of the office property market, the key variables in the principal approaches to the office property valuation process and future trends in the sector that will impact the assessment of value.

Background

In undertaking an office property valuation, the valuer must employ the required levels of analysis and application with particular regard to decision-making by market participants.

Analysis and application

An assessment of the market value of office property by the valuer is based on a detailed analysis of market sales evidence, including identifying the key value drivers, in order to establish those matters relevant to the market and thereby revealing how the market functions.

The individual key value drivers have a compounding impact on the outcome of the assessment when adopting the discounted cash flow methodology. Applying the results of market enquiries and analysis in relation to the key value drivers will establish, at the date of the sale, how the market rationalised market value.

The market value arises from an analysis and understanding of how the market participants value the net income being extracted from the property at the date of sale and prospectively through the application of acceptable rates of return applied to that income.

The market value of an office property reflects the present value of the net financial benefit that can be extracted from the property after allowing for all income and expenditure and capital value movement over time, based on the highest and best use of the land.

It is the valuer's role to demonstrate in the valuation how the market functions, reflected by both methodology and acceptable value drivers applied at a point in time, as distinct from how a casual observer may assume it should function. Key to this role is understanding the decision-making of office property purchasers and vendors.

Vendor and purchaser decision-making

The motivations around decision-making by vendors and purchasers in a particular market are subsumed in the outcomes of the key value drivers and ultimately the final purchase price.

The Nobel Memorial prize in Economic Sciences was awarded to Richard Thaler of the University of Chicago 'for his contributions to behavioural economics'. He introduced the study of human irrationality into the economics discipline which is based on principles of rationality. His work overlays human psychology on thinking about economic decision-making.

It is not expected that valuers fully understand the psychology, be it rational or otherwise, that overlays agreed transaction outcomes, but rather to diligently analyse these comparable transactions and to identify the assumptions relating to the key value drivers that resulted in the purchase price.

The valuer should attempt to be as fully informed as possible of the motivations of both the vendor and the purchaser in property transactions in order to understand the key assumptions which have influenced the final purchase prices at the dates of the sales.

It would be inconsistent with conventional market valuation practice if a proper analysis of the market was selectively applied or ignored in favour of the valuer's own view of the future as reflected by key value drivers not evidenced by the market. Valuers do not create values, they interpret the market and value driver trends and apply these, as appropriate, to the property being valued.

Occupier and lessee decision-making

In most office property transactions, the decision-making by the occupiers and the lessees is one of the key value drivers, particularly in the determining the value of office property being transacted for investment purposes.

As such, the valuer's due diligence will include a detailed assessment of the lease agreements that are current in the office property that is being transacted or analysed as a comparable property for the purposes of market evidence to support the valuation. The dynamics of the office leasing market are discussed further below.

Valuation standards

When valuing office buildings, it is important to follow the IVSC, RICS and API standards and guidance notes. These standards and guidance notes are an integral part of the valuation process, not something to be considered separately.

The RICS Valuation – Global Standards 2017 (incorporating IVS 2017) is a principles based document providing an important reference for the valuation of real property including office buildings. *Part 4: Valuation Technical and Performance Standards* is relevant when undertaking a valuation of an office property. The global technical and performance standards to be followed by members are set out in VPS 1 to 5 and while VPS 1, 4 and 5 focus more on technical standards, VPS 2 and 3 focus more on valuation performance and delivery standards.

Basis of value

Under VPS 4, the valuer must ensure that the basis of *value* adopted is appropriate for and consistent with the purpose of the *valuation*. If one of the bases of value defined in the global standards (including IVS defined bases) is used, then it should be applied in accordance with the relevant definition and guidance, including the adoption of any *assumptions* or *special assumptions* that are appropriate.

If a *basis of value* not defined in the global standards (including IVS defined bases) is used, it must be clearly defined and stated in the report, which must also draw attention to the fact that it is a departure if the use of the basis in the particular valuation assignment is voluntary and not mandatory. Where a *departure* is made that is not mandatory, compliance with IVS is not possible.

Market Value is defined in IVS 104 paragraph 30.1 as:

> the estimated amount for which an asset or liability should exchange on the valuation date between a willing buyer and a willing seller in an arm's length transaction, after proper marketing and where the parties had each acted knowledgeably, prudently and without compulsion.

Market Rent is defined in IVS 104 paragraph 40.1 as:

> the estimated amount for which an interest in real property should be leased on the valuation date between a willing lessor and a willing lessee on appropriate lease terms in an arm's length transaction, after proper marketing and where the parties had each acted knowledgeably, prudently and without compulsion.

Investment Value, also defined as worth, is defined in IVS 104 paragraph 60.1 as:

> the value of an asset to a particular owner or prospective owner for individual investment or operational objectives.

It should be noted that valuations undertaken for financial reporting purposes, often based on instructions from an accountant, may require a different basis of value being Fair Value which is defined by the International Accounting Standards Board (IASB) under IFRS 13 as follows:

> The price that would be received to sell an asset or paid to transfer a liability in an orderly transaction between market participants at the measurement date.

Assumptions

Under VPS 4, the valuer may be required to make an *assumption* where it is reasonable for the valuer to accept that something is true without the need for specific investigation or verification. Any such *assumption* must be reasonable and relevant having regard to the purpose for which the valuation is required.

A *special assumption* is made by the valuer where an *assumption* either assumes facts that differ from those existing at the valuation date or that would not be made by a typical market participant in a transaction on that valuation date. Where *special assumptions* are necessary, in order to provide the client with the valuation required as per their instructions, these must be expressly agreed and confirmed in writing with the client before the report is issued. *Special assumptions* may only be made if they can reasonably be regarded as realistic, relevant and valid for the particular circumstances of the valuation.

Wherever the valuer, or client, identifies that a valuation may need to reflect an actual or anticipated marketing constraint, such as a forced sale, details of that constraint must be agreed and set out in the terms of engagement.

Any *assumption or special assumption* relating to projected values must be agreed with the client prior to reporting an opinion of value. In addition, the valuation report must clearly define the *bases of value* and make reference to the higher degree of uncertainty that is likely to be implicit with a projected value where, by definition, comparable market evidence may not be available.

Independent investment evaluation

If a valuer is instructed to undertake an *Independent Investment Evaluation* of a property in the office market, rather than a *Market Valuation*, it would, in these circumstances, be open to the valuer to adopt alternative assumptions not evident in the market. These assumptions will be based on the valuer's own opinions which may only be partly informed by the current market and partly by the valuer's reasoning having regard to prospective considerations. This form of advice is not considered to be a valuation under the *RICS Valuation – Global Standards 2017*.

Office property market structure

Office property sub-markets

The office property market covers a wide spectrum of sub-markets based on the size, quality and location of the properties.

Most of the investment grade office buildings in Australia at the larger end of the spectrum are generally located in the main commercial centres (CBDs) and tend to be in the top-quality grades, being owned by Real Estate Investment Trusts (REITs), wholesale funds, investment syndicates, high net-worth individuals or international investors. Office property market valuations for the institutional investment sector are the primary consideration in this chapter.

The fundamental principle in this market is to understand how value is determined by the market participants based on an analysis and understanding of how these market participants attribute value, through analysing the net income being achieved in comparable property as at the date of sale and applying the market rates of return to that income, relevant for the property type, size, location and underlying lease conditions that underpin the net income.

The valuer's task is to then apply the analysis of these comparable property transactions and to provide the rationale that explains the results of the analysis, including adjustments necessary to that analysis, in order to account for differences when applying these factors between the comparable sales evidence and the office property being valued.

Market participant behaviours

In valuing office property, the valuer's role is not to simply apply technical skills to financial analysis but to seek, through enquiry and analysis, to properly understand, separately and in combination, the behaviours and motivations of the vendors and the purchasers in relation to the key value drivers that result in the sale prices of relevant comparable property transactions.

It is not consistent with the professional ethics and industry standards required in valuation practice if the outcomes of the analyses of the relevant property market transactions are selectively applied or ignored in favour of the valuer's own view of the future as reflected by nominated key value drivers, if these are not evidenced by the market.

However, it should be noted that the behaviour of vendors and purchasers in the office property investment market can be erratic. Howard Marks, the well-known Australian fund manager who established Oaktree Capital, expressed the concept of investment markets in the following quote:

> Developments in economies, interest rates, currencies and markets aren't the result of scientific processes. The involvement in them of people – with their emotions, foibles and biases – renders them highly unpredictable.

It is, nevertheless, the valuer's role to diligently analyse these comparable transactions and, to the extent reasonably possible, to identify the assumptions relating to the key value drivers that resulted in the purchase prices.

Office property value drivers

Interpreting the market

The valuer's role when undertaking a market value assessment is to interpret the market and to understand, based on available information, the cash flow assumptions that were adopted by the purchasers that underpinned the sale prices of comparable properties and to apply such value drivers to determine the value of the subject property. In this role, the valuer has a responsibility to reflect the office market as it exists at the date of the valuation, with all its idiosyncrasies, imperfections and uncertainties.

Underlying the purchase of income producing real estate are assumptions that are being made by the purchaser relating to forecasting future outcomes resulting from the key value drivers, adopted over the cash flow period. These value drivers will include movements in market rental values, leasing incentive levels, recoverable outgoings, inflation, vacancy and leasing-up allowances over time, current and future capitalisation rates and the need for capital expenditure to rectify the physical deterioration of the asset, minimise functional obsolescence and support the other forecasts.

Neither the purchaser in a property transaction nor the valuer preparing a market valuation knows with any reasonable certainty what, in fact, future outcomes of the key value drivers will be. To quote the Nobel laureate physicist Niels Bohr:

> Prediction is very difficult, especially if it's about the future.

with the same concept expressed differently by the economist John Kenneth Galbraith:

> We have two classes of forecasters: Those who don't know – and those who don't know they don't know.

Consequently, in the valuation process and in analysing comparable sales transactions, being able to understand the various purchasers' assumptions related to the key value drivers, including market derived forecasts, requires a combination of financial analysis skills as well as an intuition of the likely behaviours of a range of purchasers in order to identify the individual trends in the value drivers and the market generally.

This includes determining the spread between the assumed risk-free rate as represented by the ten-year government bond rate and the property return acceptable to the vendors and purchasers of the office property. This is the spread that will reflect the margin for the combined risk associated with the key value driver assumptions.

Key value drivers

Depending on the method of valuation that has been adopted, the key value drivers to be assessed for office properties are likely to be a combination of some or all of the following variables:

- rental structures (gross versus net rents) and market rental levels, compared to the rents payable under the existing lease agreements;
- assumed effective and face rental growth and the quantum of rental growth amounts based on the assumption that the property will or will not be maintained at the existing grade of accommodation by way of capital expenditure and consequently obsolescence may or may not be minimised;
- recoverable and non-recoverable outgoings based on the rental structures and projected costs of operating the property;
- capital expenditure requirement in order to keep the property within the same grade;
- discount rate to be adopted (in a discounted cash flow (DCF) valuation method) that is relevant to the specification and description of the office property being valued;
- initial equated reversionary yield or capitalisation rate to be adopted on a similar basis (in an income capitalisation valuation approach);
- vacancies, current and pending, based on existing lease agreement expiry dates and other relevant termination clauses;

- assumed lease agreement terms on renewals including down-time between tenancies, rental rates and structures;
- re-leasing and marketing costs and other expenditure required to lease the premises including leasing incentives; and
- the terminal yield of the property and assumed disposal costs at the end of the analysis period (in a DCF valuation approach).

Changing any one of these inputs may affect other inputs. By way of example, if the capital expenditure is insufficient to support the growth in rent forecasts, either the expenditure needs to be increased or the rent growth forecasts reduced.

Matters relevant to an institutional purchaser

When contemplating the purchase of an office property, the institutional purchaser of an investment grade office property will consider a range of matters in arriving at the purchase price. In addition to the normal property due diligence processes, other relevant matters that the institutional purchaser will consider, include:

- consideration of the operating environment, the economic outlook and market competition and how this will impact the transaction and why this transaction makes sense with reference to these market fundamentals;
- research on the underlying market fundamentals in a particular market including consideration of the supply and demand for office space in the target location and competing locations;
- consideration of recent comparable transactions including commentary as to the quality of the property proposed for purchase, relative to recent comparable sales;
- valuation considerations relating to the acquisition and detailed rationalisation, including capitalisation rates, terminal rate, discount rate, passing yield, ten-year IRR, hurdle rate, growth rates, letting up allowances, incentives and occupancy costs and whether the acquisition will result in accretive returns within a portfolio;
- transaction considerations including leasing assumptions such as vacancy and down-time, rent and growth rates, leasing incentives;
- forecast returns for down-side scenarios relative to the base case as well as upside scenarios; and
- scenario analysis with a sensitivity table outlining the impact of those assumptions which drive value in the transaction including the impact on returns such as the IRR if market capitalisation rates soften or if vacancies and down-time between leases increases.

Matters relevant to other purchasers

It should be noted that smaller and regionally located office properties are usually traded by less sophisticated investors including local high net-worth individuals, local syndicates and self-managed superannuation funds (SMSFs). Although the key principles supporting the purchase, due diligence and the determination of the purchase price should follow similar processes, these purchasers often proceed less formally in making purchase decisions and therefore identifying value driver trends may be more problematic.

Approaches to valuation specified in valuation standards

Under *the RICS Valuation – Global Standards 2017 (incorporating IVS 2017) Part 4: Valuation Technical and Performance Standards* VPS5, valuers are responsible for adopting and, as necessary, justifying the valuation approach(es) and the valuation methods used to fulfil specific valuation assignments. These must always have regard to:

- nature of the asset (or liability) being valued;
- purpose, intended use and context of the particular valuation assignment; and
- any statutory or other mandatory requirements applicable in the jurisdiction.

Valuers should also have regard to recognised best practice within the valuation discipline or specialist area in which they practise, although this should not constrain the proper exercise of their judgement in individual valuation assignments, in order to arrive at an opinion of value that is professionally adequate for its purpose.

Unless expressly required by statute or by other mandatory requirements, no one valuation approach or single valuation method necessarily takes precedence over another. In some jurisdictions and/or for certain purposes, more than one approach may be expected or required to be used in order to arrive at a balanced judgement. In this regard, the valuer must always be prepared to explain the approach(es) and method(s) adopted.

The overall valuation approach is usually classified into one of three main categories:

- the Market Approach, based on comparing the subject asset with identical or similar assets (or liabilities) for which price information is available, such as a comparison with market transactions in the same, or closely similar, type of asset (or liability) within an appropriate time horizon;
- the Income Approach, based on capitalisation or conversion of present and predicted income (cash flows), which may take a number of different forms, to produce a single current capital value. Among the forms taken, capitalisation of a conventional market-based income or discounting of a specific income projection can both be considered appropriate depending on the type of asset and, importantly, whether such an approach would be adopted by market participants; and/or
- the Cost Approach, based on the economic principle that a purchaser will pay no more for an asset than the cost to obtain one of equal utility whether by purchase or construction.

Further detail on the application of approaches and methods may be found in the International Valuation Standards (2019) at *IVS 105 Valuation Approaches and Methods*. It must be emphasised, however, that the valuer is ultimately responsible for selection of the approach(es) and method(s) to be used in individual valuation assignments, unless statute or other mandatory authority imposes a particular requirement.

Market (comparable unit rate) approach to office property valuation

This *Market Valuation Approach*, in the context of office property valuation, expresses the market value of a sale based on the result of dividing the purchase price by the lettable floor area of the improvements.

This is an opaque measure of value which subsumes, but does not reveal, relevant cash flow differences relating to vacancies, lease term, the need for capital expenditure, rental levels and so forth. It does not reflect the discipline and the detailed reasoning required in a DCF when rationalising all key value drivers.

However, when considering unit rates within the context of a discounted cash flow, these rates must be derived from detailed market analysis. The income analysis is a key component of this exercise. It is necessary to analyse a wide range of leasing transactions that are comparable with the subject property being valued.

This analysis requires detailed understanding of the composition of each leasing transaction including the identity of the lessee allowing, to a limited degree, an appreciation of the income covenant, the term of the lease, the face rent, the outgoings attributable to the building, the rent review provisions, the level of incentive granted and whether it was a lease to a new lessee, a lease renewal to a sitting lessee or a sub-lease under an existing head lease.

Through the analysis of the rental market, the valuer is informed of the market rental range applicable to the subject property, is able to compare levels of outgoings between buildings that are comparable and to establish the level of incentive available to lessees at the date of valuation with incentives likely to vary depending on the strength of the market.

Income approach to office property valuation

The income approach to office property valuation includes both the:

- capitalisation of income approach; and the
- DCF approach.

Capitalisation of income approach to office property valuation

The capitalisation of income approach comprises the capitalisation of the net income of an office property (after the deduction of all outgoings from the gross market rent) through the application of a relevant market yield, sourced from analysing comparable transactions, into perpetuity to derive the capital value.

Usually, in this approach, the capitalisation rate adopted is applied to the net market rental value assuming the property is fully leased and in good condition.

Deductions are then applied for vacancies and leasing-up considerations with adjustments to the passing income for committed lease rent overage (above market rents) or those which are below market rent for the unexpired term of the respective leases, as well as capital expenditure required in the foreseeable future.

Because these adjustments relate to income or capital adjustments receivable or payable in the future, these adjustments should be discounted to present value terms before the adjustment is applied to the property value determined in the capitalisation approach.

The foundation of the capitalisation approach to valuation is the assessment of the earning capacity of an investment property and adoption of an appropriate capitalisation rate, as determined through investigation and analysis of market transactions of comparable properties.

The choice of the capitalisation rate should be determined by sales analysis and discussions with investors as to their and the market's required rate of return for that particular type, location, condition and grade of office property. The accuracy in applying the capitalisation approach to valuation depends on the analysis of comparable sales and the application of appropriate value drivers.

It is vital to keep methods of analysis of comparable transactions consistent with the valuation methodology utilised.

The capitalisation rate used in valuations and applied to an income stream of an office investment property will reflect all risks related to the property within the one single all risk rate. This capitalisation rate, when divided into 100, reflects how many years of net rent are required to buy (pay for) the investment (also referred to as *the Years Purchase*).

Enquiries in the market and the determination of the capitalisation rate will reveal the risk margin for that category of office property required by market participants, relative to the assumed risk-free rate as represented by the ten-year government bond rate.

By way of example, in a buoyant market the risk margin for prime office properties may be 300 basis points spread above the bond rate while in a down cycle the risk margin may be 600 basis points.

The benefits of the income capitalisation approach to the valuation of office properties are as follows:

- subsumes all income risk considerations in a single rate;
- relatively simple to apply, particularly for single tenancy properties with long leases;
- actual known net income projections for the first year of the analysis; and
- no specific or special assumptions than other investment analysis techniques.

The risks and disadvantages of the income capitalisation approach to the valuation of office properties are as follows:

- opaque in relation to a deeper understanding of the risks associated with the various individual inputs that drive market value;
- assumes that the current net income will continue with market rental growth into perpetuity;
- ignores required capital investment decisions over time required to maintain the condition of the property;
- for properties that have income streams that fluctuate significantly, the valuation approach of capitalising the net income as at a single point in time is inappropriate. In some situations, this valuation approach may still be able to be used based on making reasonable allowances and adjustments, as would be the case with purchasers determining the price that they are prepared to offer for a property; and
- does not indicate whether or not the existing improvements on the property represent the highest and best use of the land and whether the income generating improvements support the land value based on an alternative development of the land. The income capitalisation approach to valuation is therefore inappropriate where a site is income producing but significantly underutilised or underdeveloped relative to its highest and best use potential.

Office property valuation 101

Weighted average lease expiry

One of the key measures in understanding the income risk of an asset is analysis of the weighted average lease expiry profile (WALE). This WALE is calculated based on the total income coverage expressed in years of coverage, providing a quick overview of the sum of the number of years remaining on each lease, weighted according to the total rental income derived from each lease. The longer the duration of the existing predictable income the lower the market risks associated with re-leasing, vacancy periods, market rental levels and the payment of incentives. This will influence the appropriate capitalisation rate for the asset.

Allowances and adjustments

With the capitalisation of net income valuation approach, the current market rent is capitalised into perpetuity such that allowances and adjustments usually need to be made in the process of determining property value. For example, a purchaser may make an allowance in perpetuity for vacancies related to the potential for lessee defaults, vacancies and the realisation that it is likely to be impossible to maintain 100% occupancy at market rent without allowance for income voids.

Reversionary values in leases

Properties that reflect passing rents (that is, rentals as per the existing lease agreements in the property) that are below market rents available in the market provide a positive reversionary value for the asset at the commencement of a further lease term, on the assumption that the prevailing market rents will form the basis of the further term for the existing or new lessees.

In assets where reversionary rents will be applicable, it is likely that the initial capitalisation rate adopted by the market will be lower than that which would apply if the passing rents were set at market levels. Astute purchasers are generally prepared to accept a lower yield on the basis that a higher return will ultimately be achieved through a reversion of the rents to market.

Adjusting for capital expenditure

The capitalisation approach to valuation does not partition the risks associated with the income or the possible capital expenditure payments required as a result of future physical depreciation, functional obsolescence and other causes.

A supplementary approach to adjusting for the effect of extra capital expenditures is to alter the required yield to be more reflective of the economic reality of the asset and in so doing reflect the higher risk associated with building obsolescence and associated limitations on rental growth and rental levels generally.

Discounted cash flow valuation approach to office property valuation

Being one form of the *Income Approach*, the *Discounted Cashflow Approach (DCF)* method of valuation discounts future income and reversionary value of the property to a *Net Present Value (NPV)*. The *DCF* valuation of a property asset is, therefore, the present value calculation of the future rental stream over a period, usually ten years, plus the reversionary capital value at the end of the same ten-year period, which is usually the assumed terminal value of the property based on the Year 11 forecast net income.

Therefore, the market value of an office property reflects the NPV of the net financial benefit that can be extracted from the property after allowing for all income and expenditure and capital value movement over time having regard to the highest and best use of the property. The method requires that an estimate is made of the quantum and timing of each income receivable and expenditure made. The net amounts are then discounted to an NPV at a given discount rate.

The DCF method is particularly helpful where the future income and expenditure may vary from year to year and the net income stream cannot be treated as equivalent to a level income stream. For consistency, in adopting the DCF method, reference should be made to the *International Valuation Standards Council (IVSC) Technical Information Paper 1 Discounted Cash Flow*.

Time Value of Money

Important to understanding the calculation of investment returns over longer time periods is the concept of the *Time Value of Money* (*TVM*). Simply stated, TVM is the concept that $1 today is more valuable than $1 in the future. Investors always prefer to receive money earlier, meaning that money received in the present period is more valuable than the same money received in a future period.

In general, the current principal amount is referred to as the *Present Value* with the value of that same amount in the future (after an investment for example) as the *Future Value*. Stated differently, the present value is what a given value at some point in the future is worth in today's money.

Discount Rate

The *Discount Rate* in discounted cash flows is the opportunity cost of funds or the 'required return' for the investment such as an office property. This rate should take into account the relative riskiness of the cash flows to reflect the value today of a future stream of such cash flows, as each of the future cash flows are discounted back to today at this appropriate discount rate.

The individual key value drivers have a compounding impact on the outcome of the assessment when adopting the discounted cash flow methodology. Applying the results of market enquiries in relation to the key value drivers will establish, at the date of the sale, how the market rationalised market value.

The two principal measures within a discounted cash flow are the *Net Present Value (NPV)* and *Internal Rate of Return (IRR)*.

Net Present Value (NPV)

The present value concept can be extended to any number of cash flows that may be relevant for a particular investment. Adding the individual present values of the cash flows over the period generates the *Net Present Value (NPV)* of the investment which, by definition, is the current value of that investment.

The process of *Net Present Value* involves discounting future cash flows to represent the value of these cash flows at a particular discount rate. The discount rate is the investor's required rate of return (or rate of interest) taking into account the profile of the investment related to opportunity costs, inflation and certainty of payment (risk).

Internal Rate of Return (IRR)

The other measure that is usually adopted in assessing the worth of a property, is the calculation of the *Internal Rate of Return (IRR)* which represents the annual average rate of return from the investment. The *IRR* measures the returns from both periodic income and from capital growth at the end of the cash flow period. There is no requirement that the cash flows be equally spaced or annual, these can occur at any date.

The *IRR* is defined as the rate of return that equates the present value of the expected future cash flows to the initial capital invested. The *IRR* represents the discount rate that should be applied to the *DCF* model in order to make the present value of the property inflows equal to the present value of its outflows, therefore resulting in the *NPV* equalling zero. The *IRR* is loosely analogous to an annual effective compound rate of return, although more accurately it reflects the constant year on year return.

In application to investment decisions, generally if the *IRR* is greater than the discount rate then the purchase is acceptable meeting the investment hurdle and if it is less than the discount rate then it should be rejected as it does not meet the investment hurdle. Therefore, if the hurdle rate of return required by an investor is 9%, any *IRR* in excess of 9% will indicate to the investor that the property should be acquired, while any *IRR* less than 9% would suggest that the particular investor should not buy the property. However, there are a range of investors in the market, all competing for a limited number of investment assets, hence acceptable *IRRs* for a specific property may vary between purchasers.

The key benefits of the DCF approach to valuation are as follows:

- provides a detailed consideration of the key value drivers in a transparent way allowing all assumptions to be tested and rationalised;
- uses explicit projections in the cash flows;
- accounts for the time value of money;
- makes capital investment decision-making transparent and generally more understandable and manageable; and
- fewer unstated assumptions than are incorporated within other opaque investment analysis techniques.

The key disadvantages and risks of the DCF approach to valuation are as follows:

- unsophisticated investors may misinterpret the results; and
- the process requires a considerable and lengthy expenditure of time in arriving at each of the key value drivers derived from market enquiry and research and then considering the results in combination.

Cost Approach to the valuation of office property

The *Cost Approach* is based on the economic principle that a purchaser will pay no more for an asset than the cost to obtain one of equal utility whether by purchase or construction.

It is important to recognise that cost does not necessarily equal value. In any development that provides an economic return, the value of the completed project will always be greater than the cost to produce the asset with the difference being the reward to the developer for risk represented by the profit margin.

In the case of an existing building, if it is considered that capital improvements are required, the cost of such improvements must result in a higher income which when capitalised provides an added value greater than the actual cost of completing the works.

Understanding office property occupier needs

Valuers need to understand and interpret the demand criteria of the office occupier and how office lessee's needs may change over time. Without lessees driving demand for office premises from which to conduct their business and their willingness to enter into short- and long-term lease agreements, institutional investors would not wish to invest in these forms of assets. As such, the terms and conditions and profile of the tenancy in an office property have a fundamental impact on the investment yields that investors expect from a particular property.

If investors perceive risks related to an office property, they will expect a higher risk-adjusted yield from the property and hence the value of the property will likely be lower. The risks may relate to impending lease expiry dates, multiple lessees (particularly if their financial capacity appears to be suspect), property management issues, rentals arrears, rentals rates in leases that are significantly above or below current prevailing rental rates and other similar issues.

Prospective lessees will only be prepared to sign medium- and long-term lease agreements and to pay a premium market rental based on the belief that these modern contemporary office buildings are designed to have a functionality that meets their current and potentially changing requirements over the term of their lease and are adaptable to the lessee's operational requirements.

Building obsolescence can occur when the design and specification of an existing building does not meet the evolving lessee demand criteria. As the attractiveness of the building accommodation continues to decline, so too does the market rent that lessees will be prepared to pay and hence the income earning potential and capital value of the property.

Assessing the viability of offsetting this trend and meeting lessee requirements through capital expenditure needs to be measured against the financial benefits that may be derived, such as rental increases and a lower capitalisation rate that may result.

Building occupier due diligence

Prior to committing to a new lease agreement for an office property, prospective lessees will usually undertake an extensive market search often with the assistance of a lessee representative and short list possible leasing options that may likely meet their operational requirements.

Other than key aspects related to location, office accommodation size available, the asking rental rate and the general quality standards that the office building offers, prospective lessees will more specifically undertake due diligence related to understanding the following:

- capacity of the building's services, noting that most modern existing CBD office towers have a services capacity related to air-conditioning, egress and power, based on a 1 person per 10 sqm. If new ways of working within offices means that a greater occupancy density is required, the building services will need to be upgraded and additional capital expenditure will be required;
- the performance specifications of the building need to be adequate for the manner in which the floor space is being used. This may have implications for heating and cooling systems, egress, security and BCA requirements. Building owners need to ensure that the service levels meet the requirement for the increased density need of lessees in order to preserve value;
- space planning limitations to ensure that the proposed design and resultant functionality of the building will meet requirements based on the fit out requirements. This form of planning may, for example, need to assess the ability to work around fixed points such as columns and fixed physical spaces such as reception areas, boardrooms and meeting rooms. A key assessment will be the ability to create collaboration and gathering spaces within the office tower floorplan;
- the current trend is to create attractive meeting places with appealing features such as a café-style coffee machine, drinks bar or leisure activities as interaction spaces with end of trip facilities and high-quality associated amenities;
- in addition, many organisations now opt for an internal staircase to promote the collaboration between business units and reduce lift congestion, allowing savings on energy costs;
- ability to accommodate technology requirements by ensuring that the building has the capability of incorporating evolving technologies such as wireless networks and enhanced communications connectivity; and
- sustainability, which is well established in office buildings as lessors and lessees look to improve environment quality as well as reduce waste. Prospective lessees actively assess the sustainability performance of office properties and lessors need to communicate their sustainability initiatives, including details of CO_2 levels and other air quality indicators, reusable waste campaigns and energy saving initiatives.

Future trends in occupier use of offices

It is now evident that workplace accommodation is going through significant change, with the traditional office model becoming redundant for many organisations.

Mobility and technology have evolved significantly and continue to do so with new workplace models moving from the periphery of organisational decision-making to become core decisions to support business strategy.

To preserve their value, office buildings must be able to meet these evolving functionality requirements in alignment with the demands of the operational requirements of new tenancy workplace models. To meet such lessee driven changes, office building owners need to allocate capital expenditure or risk falling to a lower grade of accommodation and rental level with potential down-side risk to the market value of the asset.

Over the last decade, businesses have been under continual pressure to drive down accommodation costs. This has partly been achieved not only by increasing the work-point density but also by reducing space utilisation per square metre allocated to each work-point. This space efficiency drives cost savings but requires businesses to find the right balance between cost reduction and staff productivity.

This trend may well be reversed with a reduction in densities following the onset of COVID-19 and social distancing guidelines incorporated into space planning. This pandemic has raised fundamental questions for the office sector, including new approaches to space utilisation, the reassessment of premises strategy and the nature and scale of office demand, combined with implications for rents and capital values. COVID-19 accelerated trends that were already established.

The office will retain a key role in corporate real estate strategy, though with greater use of rotation-based and remote working models. Home working will complement office work, not replace it. The office will continue as an anchor for collaboration and promotion of culture and mission.

Some occupiers may shift to a more diverse and employee choice-based real estate strategy. This may include remote working, flexible workspace and a hub-and-spoke model where the lessee retains its CBD headquarters, perhaps with a reduced footprint, combined with suburban satellite offices.

Flexible workspace represents an opportunity for occupiers to adopt creative models such as flex and core and reverse flex. The flexible working agenda has empowered employees to work 'anywhere, anyhow and anytime' and has allowed employees the freedom to decide when, where and how to work. This approach is more than just working remotely versus working in a primary office, allowing quality environments to be developed that foster collaboration as a primary business objective (Colliers 2020).

Activity Based Working (ABW) was considered pioneering ten years ago, yet today it is the current model of choice. *ABW* focuses on the use of floor space to align with the manner in which the business operates. *ABW* is a workplace strategy that provides people with a choice of settings for a variety of workplace activities. Rather than forcing individuals to undertake all their work at one setting, *ABW* allows people to physically locate themselves where it is most suitable for them to complete their work.

In addition, *ABW* and this agile working theme within the efficient use of space permits businesses to support increasing volatility in headcount and flexibility requirements. Currently, workspaces are being designed to create opportunities for intense, focused work through to impromptu, informal meeting spaces and formal meeting rooms depending on the work that an individual is undertaking. This approach allows not only flexibility in working style but affords the businesses some flexibility in their accommodation strategy with a workplace that allows for contraction and expansion in demand and headcount over time.

Face-to-face collaboration in the office will continue to be key to long-term business success and shaping a vibrant company culture and consequently demand for office space. Essential functions will likely remain face to face in the office to support company growth and talent development, such as induction of new employees, learning, knowledge transfer, the retention of institutional knowledge, connection to brand and the interpersonal social aspects that are the glue of any corporate culture.

In addition, new workplace and accommodation models in office buildings are now becoming a digital platform that tracks who is in the building, what they are doing and where. Using *Artificial Intelligence (AI)*, there will soon be the capability to monitor movement in order to optimise how the building is used in real time.

Digital integration in the workplace will be a core functionality that makes the workday more enjoyable and more productive. Keeping an office building relevant to these changes through capital expenditure offset by income uplift is a recurring challenge for building owners who seek to maximise asset value.

A further demand trend is the rise in the *Workplace-as-a-Service (WaaS)* model that permits businesses to only commit to fully serviced workplaces when they are needed rather than to long-term lease agreements.

This growing phenomenon will likely result in a fundamental structural change in demand dynamics for the office market. Currently, there are many co-working operators setting up business with nuanced offerings that may be subtle to the uninitiated but actually quite different when a detailed analysis of the services and offerings is provided. These are the types of trends in the occupier and tenancy markets of which the valuer needs to be aware when undertaking office property valuations.

Lease agreement trends

Based on the dictates of the office leasing market as it evolves to meet prospective tenancy requirements, the following key changes in lease terms may challenge the institutional investment market:

- rigid lease agreement terms will likely need to change to include elements of flexibility. Traditionally, occupiers sought flexibility by taking a long-term lease with options plus mechanisms to deal with expansion and contraction through the lease term.

    This level of lease flexibility came at a cost as there was a penalty in relation to break clauses that provided sufficient rental coverage to the lessor to be able to re-lease the premises. These break clauses add uncertainty in relation to the timing of cash flows and as a consequence the risk associated with the cash flow, potentially impacting the value of the property. In the future, these forms of expansion and contraction clauses may become more common; and
- with greater use of co-created space by lessees and across tenancies, with utilisation of space rather than the densification of space becoming a focus for occupiers, lessors will be required in lease negotiations to offer lessees co-working space within an office building on flexible arrangements to supplement the leased premises.

These are important trends when considering how income is extracted from the property. As it becomes viable to produce such new office buildings, significantly higher rents will be sought and obtained.

The more efficient manner in which office space is now being used in turn leads to less space being required by the lessee which may result in savings in accommodation costs. Relocating to a new building does not necessarily place an onerous burden on the total business operational cost but may have the benefit of improving productivity and consequently business profits. This demonstrates how changes in office building use may contribute to the viability of undertaking new developments.

Summary

In this chapter, valuation practice for office property is considered through a contextual analysis of the structure of the institutional office market with a focus on the importance of the occupier or lessee. Relevant aspects of International Valuation Standards are considered to provide a framework within which the valuation process may be undertaken.

In addition to the market approach and the cost approach, the combination of key variables into the principal forms of the income approach to valuation are explored, together with an analysis of occupier due diligence and future trends in occupier use, providing an holisitic view of the office valuation process.

In this first section of the second part of the book, valuation practice for residential property was considered in the previous chapter, with valuation practice for office property considered in this chapter and valuation practice for retail, industrial and rural property considered in the following chapters.

The second section of the second part of this book addresses valuation practice for specialist property sectors comprising retirement, leisure, plant and equipment and business and intangible asset valuation with the third and final section of the second part addressing valuation practice for specific purposes, including rental, financial reporting, secured lending, insurance and statutory valuation purposes.

References

Colliers 2020, *Colliers Insights – Office – Asia Pacific*, Colliers, Sydney.
International Valuation Standards Council 2019, *International Valuation Standards*, International Valuation Standards Council, London.
RICS 2017, *RICS Valuation – Global Standards 2017*, RICS, London.

Acknowledgements

The author acknowledges the assistance provided in the preparation of this chapter by the following industry leaders:

   Rodney Timm – Director at Property Beyond
   Nicholas Harris – Head of Funds Management at GPT
   Michael Cook – Group Executive, Property at Investa
   Campbell Hannan – Head of Commercial at Mirvac

Biography

Peter Dempsey provides independent expert advice in relation to real estate advisory and dispute matters relating to the assessment of the value of real estate assets. Peter acts as an expert witness in litigation matters, including those involving the Land Acquisition (Just Terms Compensation) Act 1991, that require the application of valuation principles across a range of real estate types within his expertise, knowledge and experience. Another key focus area is the commercial office sector, specialising in the Sydney CBD, where Peter provides valuation and independent advice in relation to rent reviews, rental determinations and capital values.

Peter presents lectures to students in valuation principles, the rent review and determination process and compulsory acquisition in courses conducted by UNSW, UTS and the PCA and also presents at API seminars on a range of contemporary topics.

9 Retail property valuation

Bernie Sweeney

Introduction

With the first part of this book addressing the principles of valuation, the second part addresses the practice of valuation being grouped into three sections comprising conventional property sectors, specialist property sectors and specific purposes. Conventional property sectors include residential, office, retail, industrial and rural property valuation practice. Specialist property sectors include retirement, leisure, plant and equipment and business and intangible asset valuation practice and specific purposes include valuation practice for rental, financial reporting, secured lending, insurance and statutory valuation purposes.

The first section of the second part of this book addresses the valuation of conventional property sectors with residential and office property valuation practice considered in previous chapters, retail valuation practice considered in this chapter and industrial and rural property valuation practice considered in the following chapters.

It is assumed that the reader already has an understanding of valuation methodology for retail property, allowing a focus in this chapter on the structure and drivers of the retail property market, the key variables in the retail valuation process and the principal risks for consideration.

A 'shopping centre', as discussed in this chapter, is not a 'strip' type 'centre' in which many adjoining shops, usually in individual ownership, were developed along a busy road, usually close to a railway station. The shopping centres discussed herein are a group of complementary shops on one site. The property may have two or three joint owners but is managed as a single property.

As an investment property, shopping centres differ from office buildings in one key aspect. An office building has lessees who require accommodation for essentially the same purpose – office work. They may be accountants, lawyers, insurance companies or stockbrokers. They may enjoy a grand entrance foyer, high speed lifts, water views from upper floor windows and some may refer clients to each other. The buildings investment value relies on their lease commitment and security of rental income flow, but it does not depend on their use of the floor space.

A shopping centre is a group of complementary businesses, many of competitive uses but which collaborate to provide an attractive mix of retail goods and services for the customer. A centre with excessive duplication of use and insufficient variety will find its customers drifting away to other centres in the district and will lose market share of the pool of consumer spending.

DOI: 10.1201/9781003049555-9

Shopping centre classifications

There is a wide variety of types and sizes of shopping centres which are grouped or 'classified' for comparison of various data. The following classifications from Property Council of Australia (2015) are endorsed by the Shopping Centre Council of Australia.

City centres

Retail premises within an arcade or mall development owned by one company, firm or person and promoted as an entity within a major Central Business District (CBD).
   Total Gross Leasable Area – Retail (GLAR) exceeds 1,000 sqm.
   Key features:

- dominated by specialty shops;
- likely to have frontage on a mall or major CBD street;
- generally do not include supermarkets; and
- often co-exist with large department stores.

Super regional centres

A major shopping centre typically incorporating two full line department stores, one or more full line discount department stores (DDS), two supermarkets and around 250 or more specialty shops.
   Total GLAR exceeds 85,000 sqm.
   Key features:

- one-stop shopping for all needs;
- comprehensive coverage of the full range of retail needs (including specialised retail), containing a combination of full line department stores, supermarkets, services, chain and other specialty retailers;
- typically include a number of entertainment and leisure attractions such as cinemas, game arcades and soft play centres; and
- provides a broad range of shopper facilities (car parking, food court) and amenities (rest rooms, seating).

Major regional centres

A major shopping centre typically incorporating at least one full line department store, one or more full line discount department stores, one or more supermarkets and around 150 specialty shops.
   Total GLAR generally ranges between 50,000 and 85,000 sqm.
   Key features:

- one-stop shopping for all needs;
- extensive coverage of the full range of retail needs (including specialised retail), containing a combination of full line department stores, full line discount department stores, supermarkets, services, chain and other specialty retailers;

- typically include a number of entertainment and leisure attractions such as cinemas, game arcades and soft play centres; and
- provides a broad range of shopper facilities (car parking, food court) and amenities (rest rooms, seating).

Regional centres

A shopping centre typically incorporating one full line department store, one full line discount department store, one or more supermarkets and around 100 or more specialty shops.

Total GLAR typically ranges between 30,000 and 50,000 sqm.

In some instances, all other characteristics being equal, a centre with two full discount department stores but without a department store can serve as a regional centre.

Key features:

- extensive coverage of a broad range of retail needs (including specialised retail) — however, not as exhaustive as major regional centres;
- contains a combination of full line department store, full line discount department store, supermarkets, banks, chain and other specialty retailers; and
- provides a broad range of shopper facilities and amenities.

Subregional centres

A medium-sized shopping centre typically incorporating at least one full line discount department store, a major supermarket and approximately 40 or more specialty shops.

Total GLAR will typically range between 10,000 and 30,000 sqm.

Key features:

- provides a broad range of subregional retail needs; and
- typically dominated by a full line discount department store or major supermarket.

Neighbourhood centres

A local shopping centre comprising a supermarket and approximately 35 specialty shops.

Total GLAR will typically be less than 10,000 sqm.

Key features:

- typically located in residential areas;
- services immediate residential neighbourhood;
- usually has extended trading hours; and
- caters for basic day-to-day retail needs.

Retail property platform

A commercial property has a 'two-way' relationship of owner and occupier or lessor and lessee. A shopping centre has a three-way relationship:

- property owner supplies the building;
- retail businesses provide goods and services in their tenancy; and
- customers buy goods and services from the retailers.

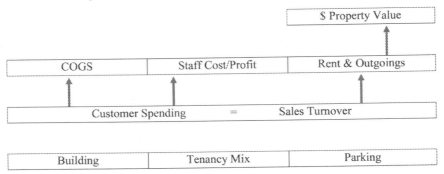

Figure 9.1 Retail property platform
Source: Author

Figure 9.1 illustrates the 'platform' of consumer spending which supports the lessee's businesses and the owner's property value, where 'COGS' is the retailers wholesale cost of goods sold.

Inspection

Apart from the usual inspection notes detailing the physical building, its condition and so forth, it is important to match each entry on the tenancy schedule to a shop in the centre. A shop may appear vacant but be closed for renovations or still fitting out before its lease commences. In a large centre, there will usually be a few tenancies in the process of relocating. This also applies to elements like automatic teller machines, kiosks, etc. Occasionally a tenancy will appear to be a kiosk but will actually be a temporary 'casual mall leasing' site.

At the inspection, remember the property is essentially a public building. A large centre will have a full-time operations team, regularly monitoring for need of repair to amenities like toilets, mall seating, rubbish bins, balustrades as well as plant, like automatic doors, lifts/escalators, air-conditioning and so forth. In a small neighbourhood centre there is not usually a full-time management presence and these elements may be not well maintained. If a centre's common area amenities, seating, toilets and indeed, the car park, appear neglected, that may have a detrimental effect on trading and consequently on rental values.

The centre manager should be interviewed about various aspects of the centre's trading, its relationship to competitive shopping centres, any prospective changes to the competition, near term capital expenditure requirements such as replacing air-conditioning or a major tenancy reconfiguration. Overdue and imminent lease expiries, lease renewal negotiations and any proposals there may be for expansion should also be identified.

It is important to inspect the nearest competitive centres to gauge their relative convenience of access, physical attractiveness, lessee mix variety, vacancies and so forth.

Trade area analysis

It is important to identify the likely 'trade catchment area' or district within which the shopping centre may expect to receive most of its customer patronage. Ideally, the client may have recently obtained a market research/analysis report from a specialist demographic consulting firm. This tends to occur with major regional centres or when a significant redevelopment or expansion is being considered.

A valuer does not have the expertise to fully relate the trade area socio-economic data to sales turnover in order to estimate a particular shopping centre's market share of total trading area spending. If the client does not have a market research report, the valuer can make some broad comparisons to get a feel for the centre's strength relative to its competitors. Population data can be found by reference to Australian Bureau of Statistics. ABS 'Quickstats' provides details such as age profile, weekly incomes, car ownership, employment and level of education on a suburb/local government area basis.

The general trade area can be estimated by measuring the distance between surrounding shopping centres of similar stature, for example the distances between neighbourhood shopping centres defines the Primary Trade Area based on the distribution of supermarkets.

The Secondary Trade Area can be defined by the distribution of discount department stores and the Tertiary Trade Area is commonly defined by the distribution of regional centres which include department stores and cinemas.

A simple, distance related observation of competitive centre locations on a map is obviously not sufficient for trade area analysis. Physical barriers, such as rivers, railway lines or valleys can make a further distant shopping centre more convenient by road. Non-residential elements, such as industrial areas, can also affect the number of people living within the normal radius of a shopping centre.

Figure 9.2 is a typical example of a trade area map produced by a specialist demographic/market research firm. It is reproduced with permission by Urbis Pty Ltd. The influence of physical barriers such as major highways and railway lines is indicated by the straight lines in the 'Secondary South' trade area.

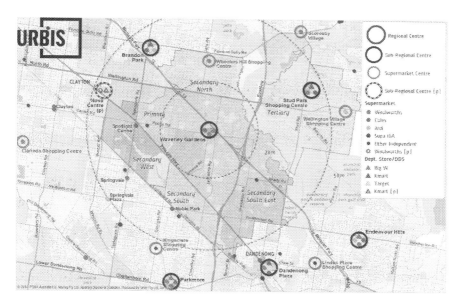

Figure 9.2 Trade area map
Source: Urbis Pty Ltd

Owner supplied information

Valuation of a shopping centre requires the valuer to obtain numerous items of information from the owner and/or the managing agent. These include a schedule summarising all tenancy lease details, budgets of 'sundry income' such as casual mall letting or other advertising and budgets of outgoings expenditure. There are also various financial reports such as the lessee's sales turnover figures, rental billings/arrears report and details of current or imminent capital repair or upgrading works that should be obtained from the owner and/or the managing agent.

Leases

Major store leases and a sample of at least half the specialty shop leases should be read and summarised in order to check the detail contained in the tenancy schedule to the 'source' documents. The leases will disclose information not always included on the tenancy schedule, such as the percentage rent factor and any special conditions.

There may well have been an incentive provided at the time of commencing the lease. Incentives have become a common feature of the retail leasing market. A retailer will usually take some months of trading to become established and is not always able to pay the full rental in the first two to three months whilst establishing its trade in the centre. There is a significant fit-out required for shelving, fixtures and fittings and so forth in a retail shop, particularly when selling cooked or fresh food. In these cases, the lessor will often provide a contribution to the lessee's fit-out. This is a reimbursement of costs for items like floor drainage for cleaning, wall linings for food preparation, additional ceilings, refrigeration plant, stainless steel cooking equipment and so forth. There may also need to be alterations to the lessor's provision of fire protection, air-conditioning and so forth. Large floor area restaurants will need extra toilets installed for the use of that particular tenancy.

These are significant capital requirements of the lessee. Owners have become willing to provide a contribution to the cost of this capital work, contingent upon proof that the lessee has paid the builder for the fit-out, signed the lease, obtained all necessary health, council and other permits and licences before the lessor makes the financial contribution. In other words, the contribution acts very much as a disciplinary requirement ensuring that the lessee complies with all these obligations. The rental level may include an amount which is effectively repayment of an interest free loan for the capital contribution. A lower rental may otherwise be paid if the lessee was provided with an empty shell and self-funded the entire fit-out works.

Retail shop leases commonly provide for fixed annual percentage increases or by Consumer Price Index or by CPI plus a figure of 1% or 2%. In most states, the lessor is no longer permitted to have rent adjusted by the greater of two alternate methods under retail leasing legislation. Market rent reviews are commonly only conducted at the commencement of a new lease by option. Many option clauses provide for a fixed increase at commencement of a new lease, thereby removing the provision for a market rent review.

There may well be 'special conditions' such as 'exclusivity' of a lessees use. These are relatively rare in modern leasing and are commonly only granted in small neighbourhood centres where the use is likely to be the only one of its kind, with only 10 to 20 shops in the property. Exclusivity is a situation where the lessor agrees not to lease another new store for the same use. It is often conditional upon the lessee recognising that the supermarket may include similar activities. Where a shopping centre has surplus land for future expansion, the owner will usually reserve the right to include one more shop of a similar competitive use in expansion onto that land.

Most leases have provision for 'percentage' or 'turnover' rental, which is payable when a lessee is trading beyond the 'threshold' or 'breakeven' level. The building owner is entitled to the extra rent payment as the quality of its building and services have contributed to the lessee's trading success. The 'threshold' is commonly a 'natural' mathematical relationship to the base rent. An 'unnatural' breakeven is any other amount, above or below the 'natural' level. For example, a butcher's shop paying $70,000 net rental with a percentage rent factor of 10% will have a natural breakeven of $700,000 sales turnover. The lease may provide that the lessee only pays percentage rent when the sales turnover exceeds $1,000,000 which means the lessee will only pay additional rent when its sales are relatively successful.

The total or 'gross occupancy cost' is the sum of base rent, any percentage rent and outgoings contribution, payable by the lessee. It is usually divided by the lessee's annual sales turnover to be a percentage that is used for rental value comparison analysis.

Leases may also have 'capped occupancy costs' where the retailer insists that it will only pay base rent to a maximum of say 12% of its annual sales turnover. In the example of a lessee paying base rental of $80,000 per annum, the 12% factor will reflect a 'breakeven' point of $666,666. If the lessee is turning over sales of $600,000, then it would only be paying rent of $72,000 per annum.

Another form of special condition is a lessee's right to 'break' or terminate the lease if its sales turnover (which must be audited) does not reach a certain minimum level within a specified period of, say, three years. In other words, a retailer (who must be of substance to successfully insist on this clause) will commit to lease a shop in the centre but reserves the right to leave in the event that it finds the sales turnover unsatisfactory.

Lessees contributions to outgoings

Outgoings 'recovery' can vary from none in the case of a pure gross lease, to 'increases' above the commencing base level, to partial 'semi-gross' leases, whereby the lessee pays council and water rates and insurance but no other operating expenses. In a 'net' lease, the lessee pays all statutory and operating expenses permissible by the relevant State retail leases legislation. In most states, this excludes land tax.

Income and outgoings

Valuation of a shopping centre requires a good working knowledge of the basics of accounting. There can be many sources of income and expenses, which may be summarised as follows:

- sources of income:
  - base rent – paid monthly by majors and specialty shops;
  - percentage rent – payable when retailer's sales turnover exceeds the 'threshold' level;

- 'sundry' – e.g. storage rooms, vending machines, children's ride machines, casual mall leasing, telecommunication aerials, mall media advertising and so forth; and
- 'recovery' of outgoings – lessee's contributing their proportionate share of outgoings, as required by their leases;
- outgoings expenditure:
  - statutory outgoings, council and water rates, fire service levy and land tax;
  - building operating expenses;
  - owner contribution to the centre's marketing fund; and
  - 'non recoverable' items, such as legal, consultant fees and infrequent capital works; and
- a long-term, typical year vacancy provision is usually deducted as a valuation allowance. This is commonly only applied to specialty shops gross income, on the basis that major leases are for longer terms and majors are much less likely to vacate or be relocated within the centre. The provision can vary from 0.5% in a prime regional centre to 2% or 3% for a small centre in a mature location or which has persistent vacancies. Deduction of this vacancy factor before capitalising the resultant net income means its deduction is made in perpetuity, as an average annual provision. The actual vacancy amount will obviously fluctuate from year to year.

The net result of deducting all expenditure and long-term annual vacancy allowance from total income is the net property income.

Valuation methods

Retail property valuations are commonly made with an income approach, being the capitalisation and discounted cash flow methods, two complementary methods employed to 'test' and support each other in approaching the valuation conclusion, as may be done for commercial and industrial buildings.

The results of the two methods can sometimes differ by a considerable amount, which acts as a 'flag' for the valuer to reconsider the essential elements of both and prepare to be able to explain the difference, as well as the rationale for choice of a rounded valuation conclusion.

Capitalisation method

The principal variables for consideration in the capitalisation method are income, adjustments and investment yield.

Income and adjustments

Capitalisation of net income is still the primary focus of attention for most investors and mortgage lenders. The annual net passing income is capitalised at a rate derived from analysis of comparable sales in the usual manner. The 'core value' will then be adjusted for above or below market rentals for leases expiring within the 'near term' of two to three years of the valuation date. There may also be vacancies which need allowance through a letting up period.

There may also be significant capital expenditure budgeted for the near term which should be taken into account. An important aspect of capital expenditure is its purpose. If the toilets, amenities, baby change rooms and common areas are to be upgraded, this will have an advantageous effect on the centres attractiveness to customers. A short-term boost in traffic and sales turnover should result from completion of those works. It is, therefore, important to consider the timing and purpose of capital expenditure works in the context of sales turnover and rental forecasting. If, on the other hand, the capital expenditure is to replace old plant, such as air-conditioning, escalators or other 'restorative' work which does not 'add value', then it is a deduction from the valuation prior to its completion but with no financial benefit thereafter.

Investment yield considerations

Investors generally consider retail property as less volatile than office property. Retail is not so affected by cyclical fluctuations in floor space supply and tenancy demand. Its rental income growth is, consequently, relatively more stable from year to year.

Lessees also have a greater degree of commitment to their leased premises than in an office building. A retail lessee has goodwill associated with its location and would not relocate as readily as an office lessee might relocate for business purposes. The major or 'anchor' retailers will typically represent about 60% of the floor area of sub-regional and regional shopping centres. They will represent 30% to 40% of the gross income of those centres. In a neighbourhood centre, the major store will be a higher percentage of floor area and of gross income, about 55% to 60% in recently developed centres.

Neighbourhood shopping centres are now developed with fewer specialty shops than in the past. Until about the year 2000, a neighbourhood shopping centre might have 18 to 20 specialty shops whereas now the number tends to be 12 to 15 and in some cases only about 6. This reflects the nature of retail, where certain activities such as newsagent's merchandise is now sold through supermarkets and people are reading newspapers online rather than purchasing a physical newspaper and therefore changing retail habits.

Larger centres have a lower proportion of weekly food/grocery spending and have a wider diversity of merchandise, a larger trade area and a greater need to keep up with market trends and customer expectations such as for attractive food courts, amenities, vertical transport and parking convenience. The decorative appeal of common areas is arguably more important in a larger shopping centre than in a neighbourhood centre, where most visits are for weekly grocery needs with the term 'non-discretionary' recently coined to characterise neighbourhood centres.

Discounted cash flow method

Discounted cash flow (DCF) is an important valuation technique which includes four key elements in the context of retail valuation:

- rental income growth expectation;
- provision for 'restorative' capital expenditure;
- redemption/terminal yield; and
- provision for vacancy risk.

It is vitally important to apply consistent and appropriate assumptions, firstly when analysing an Internal Rate of Return from a comparable property sale and then to consider application of those rates to the subject property. It is not always possible to get the full amount of information to be able to thoroughly analyse a comparable sale, for reasons of confidentiality of the contract.

The valuer who is part of the purchaser's team in appraising the acquisition will have access to this information and may provide a summary analysis of the transaction after a sale is no longer confidential. It is possible to obtain the necessary financial information from the selling agent where advising a prospective purchaser who is ultimately unsuccessful. This information is invariably subject to confidentiality agreements and cannot be reproduced. However, a summarised version of the key elements of the transaction may be released after the transaction becomes unconditional.

The discounted cash flow models all cash inflows and outflows over a ten-year period. One distinction from the capitalisation method is that acquisition and disposal costs are included. In the capitalisation approach, stamp duty on purchase is ignored for all comparable sales and the subject valuation.

Rental income growth expectation

Specialty shop rentals will usually be escalated during the lease by a fixed factor, such as 4% per annum. Market rental value may be growing at a faster or slower rate by economic demand/supply forces. If the specialty shops sales turnover is growing at a similar rate as its rental, the lessee's occupancy cost is neither becoming onerous nor advantageous in its relationship to the sales turnover. Market rental growth may, in the valuers opinion, be a different rate, having regard to prevailing inflation, expected population growth and so forth. The actual rental cash flow would increase by 4% per annum during the lease term but then be adjusted upon lease renewal to a higher or lower figure.

The major stores sales turnovers have to be individually modelled. The base rent is commonly adjusted every five years by a formula taking into account such percentage rent as may have been paid in the (two or three) years prior to the base rent adjustment. There are many different types of formula for this situation. Supermarkets usually have a natural relationship between base rent and sales turnover.

Non-food major stores such as discount department stores will usually have an 'un-natural' breakeven. It might begin as a fixed dollar figure, for example a Kmart store might have a threshold of $25,000,000. In other cases, the threshold might be set as the amount of third year sales where the lessee pays percentage rent based on the increase in the fourth year and beyond over the amount of third year sales.

It is important to remember that sales turnover is reported by lessees to the owner, including Goods and Services Tax (GST) and also excluding GST. Percentage rent is based on 'GST exclusive' sales. GST inclusive sales is the total of prices of goods and services reported by the retailer. The 'GST inclusive' data is used for comparison of trading performance by individual stores or use categories, such as clothing or footwear, with the whole centre and with peer averages.

Forecasting rental income growth should take into account expectations of local population growth being slower or faster than the State or metropolitan average forecasts. Whether a property is situated in a mature or fringe urban location will have an influence on the growth of spending per head of population.

Where a shopping centre is situated in a fringe urban location, its primary trade area population will usually be growing faster than the metropolitan average. It is also vulnerable to new competition being developed as the housing estates sprawl further afield. A supermarket may be trading at a relatively productive amount of say $50,000,000 per year and residents who live further out from the city will be travelling to that supermarket because it is the only one in the district. When another supermarket is developed further afield, its neighbouring residents will find it more convenient. The first supermarket in that district may well lose 20%, or about $10,000,000 of its turnover, to the new supermarket servicing those residents. This should be reflected in the valuer's forecasting of the subject supermarket's sales turnover and resulting percentage rent.

The risk of a new competitor being developed in a fringe urban location or an expansion of an existing supermarket is always possible. It is important to check with the local council in person or by Internet searching to establish if a planning permit or development application has recently been lodged for development of a potentially competitive store.

Provision for capital expenditure

There are two elements to capital expenditure ('capex'). Owners of larger centres will usually have a budget for capital works to be done over the next one or two financial years. Some owners have carefully designed 'life cycle' asset plans, which include estimated costs for specific projects such as refurbishing toilets, replacing mall seating, resurfacing car parks and so forth. These plans often extend for five or ten years and include broad estimates to provide for unspecified work likely to be needed in the later years.

The second element is the valuer's own provisions for capex. It is important not to 'double count' with such provisions. If the owner supplies a five- or ten-year asset plan, the valuer should be careful to only allow capex in the latter five years or allow none, accordingly. Where the owner does not provide estimated capex, or only a budget for the next financial year, the valuer may estimate:

- an annual sum bearing a sensible relationship to net rental income; or
- an annual sum estimated with reference to the total floor area, indexed by inflation over the ten-year DCF horizon; or
- a dollar rate per square metre, applied to the floor area of shop leases expiring in each year. This will provide a 'weighting' to those years, where a 'spike' of lease expiries occurs.

Redemption or terminal yield

This is the capitalisation rate used to estimate the property's likely selling price at the end of the ten-year DCF. The owner 'redeems' the investment by converting it to cash. This is commonly estimated by capitalising the anticipated net rental income receivable at the beginning of the eleventh year.

It has become a common convention to adopt a terminal capitalisation rate that is 0.25% higher than the rate applicable at the present date. Occasionally, market circumstances may warrant using the same yield for a prime centre in a well-established location. Conversely, a higher degree of 'spread' to terminal yield may be appropriate for a mature centre that is likely to incur declining trade area population and/or new competition within its trade area during the ten-year forecast. The essential rationale for this marginally higher yield at the end of the tenth year is the risk of economic conditions possibly being unfavourable at the time. Many of the leases can reasonably be expected to have been renewed during the ten-year forecast period, so the vacancy risk would not necessarily be much greater than at present date. The building will be ten years older but is expected to have had adequate restorative capital expenditure during the period.

It is also likely that there will have been some change to demographic profile of the centre's trade area during the period. The subject centre's locality may become more established as new housing is developed further from the capital city. The primary surroundings of the subject centre, in most metropolitan locations, would expect to have some redevelopment of older housing stock with new medium density apartments in future years.

Provision for vacancy risk

The DCF approach includes specific provision for future vacancies, rather than the average annual provision made in the capitalisation approach.

There are three elements to the DCF vacancy provision in the context of retail valuation:

- vacancy or 'down-time', being the absence of income while the premises are vacant;
- incentive provision of months of rent-free or a fit-out contribution granted to the incoming lessee; and
- the agency/management leasing fees payable upon commencement of a new lease.

A probability factor is provided to the down-time and incentive, recognising that many lessees will seek to renew their lease for their business continuity. A 'lessee retention' probability of 75% can be rationalised by saying three of every four shops would typically seek to renew their lease and the other one will create a vacancy by relocating or failure.

The choice of time period allowed for down-time and incentive and lessee retention probability can vary widely, by virtue of the centre's trading potential, tenancy demand and so forth. In a strong regional centre, such allowance might be:

- 2 months vacancy with 75% retention, hence deducting 0.5 months gross rental (that is, 25% loss of 2 months gross rent) for each expiring tenancy during the cash flow; and
- 6 months incentive, or 10% of a 5 year/60 month lease, with the same probability factor.

It is important to remember these are applied across all lessees and will occur twice for five-year leases during a ten-year DCF. Shops which tend to fall vacant are usually those in secondary locations on the floor plan, hence, below the average rental value per square metre.

Retail property valuation

A weaker shopping centre, such as in a mature demographic location, may warrant a greater vacancy provision, such as:

- 6 months down-time, with 50% probability, hence 3 months loss of rent applied to every lease expiry; and
- similar incentive, but with a greater probability of its application.

Specific provisions are made for major lessees which require careful consideration. It is rare for a supermarket to not exercise a lease renewal option, but it can occur for an old/small store that no longer meets modern shopping requirements. 'Non-food' major stores may be vacated, as observed with the loss of Venture Stores and McEwan's hardware in the early 1990s and recently Dick Smith Electronics. Some Myer stores have recently been closed and re-leased as smaller tenancies.

Risks to investment value

Risks to shopping centre investment value may be caused by internal or external factors. They are different to the type of risks that affect an office or industrial building and include the following.

Persistent vacancies

Some shopping centres have an excessive number of specialty shops relative to the spending capacity of the trade area population. Vacancies will occur and remain stubbornly vacant, despite the best efforts of the leasing negotiator, where a shopping centre is in a mature trade area with little population growth. Vacancies usually occur in relatively weak parts of the floor plan, such as external facing shops or shops in a long pedestrian mall.

Tenancy mix

A shopping centre could also suffer a lack of attractiveness if it does not have sufficient variety of tenancy mix to attract customers. This is the major difference in real estate value between a shopping centre and commercial property. It matters greatly to the shopping centre that it has sufficient variety of uses to make the centre competitive, relative to other centres. Only the owner knows if two floors of an office building are vacant. If a significant number of shops are vacant, it is apparent to other retailers in the centre and, importantly, to the customers. This can become quite detrimental if allowed to continue.

Trade area risk

The trade area population may be growing by construction of new housing estates. Alternatively, the age profile may be relatively mature in life cycle. Housing estates developed 20 years ago with young families moving in at the outset will now suffer a loss of population, as the young adults move away in search of tertiary education, employment and purchasing their own home elsewhere.

Issues and pitfalls in retail property valuation

The principal issues and pitfalls in retail property valuation include capital expenditure and car parking.

Capital expenditure

Major capital expenditure items such as air-conditioning and escalators will need to be replaced in major regional centres, many of which are now over 25 years old. The owners will usually endeavour to do such major capital replacements when disruption is occurring for other reasons such as an expansion or relocating multiple lessees. The work can be done under the same building contract and minimise the degree of disruption to customers during construction.

Car parking

Many large shopping centres are developed close to public transport nodes such as a railway station and/or bus interchange. Personal motor vehicle travel remains a key element of shopping, where customers are bringing home the weekly groceries or large comparison goods. In most cases, a large area of convenient car park will be a key attraction of a neighbourhood or subregional centre and the floor area will represent a relatively small (25% to 30%) proportion of the site area.

A prospective purchaser may regard a low floor/site ratio as reflecting an opportunity to expand the centre. In some cases, this has been done to the detriment of the property's trading potential as it reduces the very convenience which made the centre attractive. Expansion often adds specialty shops which dilute the consumer spending over a greater floor area and result in a fragility of tenancy demand/supply and increased number of vacancies.

Summary

Shopping centres are an interesting and challenging class of property for valuation. They can vary in size from a supermarket with a handful of shops up to a Super Regional with 500 tenancies and much greater complexity. The relationship between owner and lessees has the added focus of attention on the lessee's customers, who present the foundation of the property's market value through their spending.

In this chapter, valuation practice for retail property is considered through a contextual analysis of the structure of the shopping centre market with a focus on the importance of trade area analysis. The fundamental importance of the lease as a source of value is considered together with the key elements of income and expenditure in a retail property context.

The combination of key variables into the principal forms of the income approach to valuation are explored together with an analysis of the key risks of vacancy, tenancy mix and trade area risk prior to a consideration of the potential impacts of pitfalls such as capital expenditure and car parking, providing an holisitic view of the retail valuation process.

In this first section of the second part of the book, valuation practice for residential and office property was considered in previous chapters, with valuation practice for retail property considered in this chapter and valuation practice for industrial and rural property considered in the following chapters.

The second section of the second part of this book addresses valuation practice for specialist property sectors comprising retirement, leisure, plant and equipment and business and intangible asset valuation with the third and final section of the second part addressing valuation practice for specific purposes, including rental, financial reporting, secured lending, insurance and statutory valuation purposes.

References

Property Council of Australia 2015, *Operating Cost Benchmarks 2015: Shopping Centres*, Property Council of Australia, Sydney.

Biography

Bernie Sweeney is a National Director of Jones Lang LaSalle (JLL) Valuations and Advisory, based in its Glen Waverley office. He is responsible for valuation of retail properties, including shopping centres, supermarkets and showrooms. While based in Victoria, he has enjoyed the challenge of conducting valuations in other states, since 1997.

Bernie has more than 35 years' experience in property valuation, consultancy, investment acquisitions, valuation modelling and feasibility assignments. He began as a cadet at the City of Moorabbin in 1975, became a qualified Valuer in early 1980 and joined Jones Lang Wootton in June 1980. Bernie left to join a small valuation practice in Melbourne in August 1987 and returned to JLW in March 1988, He was made an Associate Director of JLW (VIC) Pty Limited in 1990 and Director in 1991.

Bernie has been involved in mentoring student valuers over many years and was granted the S F (Dick) Whittington Memorial Award by the API in 2004 for his role in the Graduate Seminar programme.

10 Industrial property valuation

Ryan Korda

Introduction

With the first part of this book addressing the principles of valuation, this second part addresses the practice of valuation being grouped into three sections comprising conventional property sectors, specialist property sectors and specific purposes. Conventional property sectors include residential, office, retail, industrial and rural property valuation practice. Specialist property sectors include retirement, leisure, plant and equipment and business and intangible asset valuation practice and specific purposes include valuation practice for rental, financial reporting, secured lending, insurance and statutory valuation purposes.

The first section of the second part of this book addresses the valuation of conventional property sectors with residential, office and retail property valuation practice considered in the previous chapters, industrial property valuation practice considered in this chapter and rural property valuation practice considered in the following chapter.

It is assumed that the reader already has an understanding of valuation methodology for industrial property, allowing a focus in this chapter on the evolution of the structure of the industrial property market, the fundamental determinants of value and the divergence in appropriate valuation methodology that has emerged for application across the sector.

Background

Industrial property, now also commonly now referred to as Industrial & Logistics (I&L) property, is an important and essential part of any economy. I&L property is used for a vast array of purposes, with some of the more common uses including manufacturing of goods (i.e. furniture, food, medical products), warehousing (i.e. short- or long-term palletised storage of products prior to dispatch) and transport (i.e. freight moved from one destination to the next). There are a range of other broader I&L uses, in addition to more specific uses tied to certain industries. In essence, I&L property acts as a key piece of infrastructure for physical materials and products that move through the supply chain, where goods are initially manufactured and eventually delivered to the end user or customer.

Over history there have been examples of industries which have both contracted or expanded in light of market forces, globalisation and changing consumer preferences (amongst other factors). In Australia large parts of the manufacturing sector have ceased to exist as operations have either moved offshore or, in some cases, the

DOI: 10.1201/9781003049555-10

product line has terminated completely. A well-documented and topical sector which has been relocated offshore was Australia's vehicle manufacturing sector (i.e. Holden and Ford). Conversely, as online retail sales have continued to trend upwards, this has resulted in global growth of the e-commerce sector and hence growth in the logistics assets that house these occupiers.

According to CBRE Research, e-commerce now equates to 13.3% of total retail sales. Before the Coronavirus Pandemic in March 2020 (COVID-19), online sales were less than 10% of total sales. This surge in e-commerce penetration is an example of an accelerating industry, which is a result of evolving consumer habits and the global pandemic. The COVID-19 pandemic has impacted commercial real estate in different ways. Some of these trends and impacts will be more temporary and other trends will be more permanent, such as the acceleration of e-commerce.

In recent history, say the last five or so years, I&L property has become an increasingly popular form of investment which has been a global phenomenon. It is important to note, however, I&L has not always been highly sought after and only three to five years ago the sector was viewed as an inferior form of investment compared to the office and retail sectors. However, the structural shift away from 'bricks and mortar' retail (which has been exacerbated during the pandemic) has been one of the key reasons for the popularity of the I&L sector. Whilst investor sentiment changes over time, the I&L sector in Australia is currently one of the most highly sought-after forms of commercial real estate investment (both pre-pandemic and post-pandemic announcement).

Ownership structures

I&L property has a diverse ownership structure. The two most common forms of ownership profile are the owner occupier and the investor. Owner occupiers, as the name suggest, occupy the property for their intended use. Manufacturers are generally the most likely to owner occupy a property which is partly explained by the substantial amount of plant and machinery they invest in the building and hence their preference to have full control of the asset.

Investors of I&L property are primarily looking to achieve an acceptable, risk-adjusted return on their investment. Typical investors of I&L property include private investors, syndicates and what is collectively known as 'institutional' investors. Institutional investors generally own a large number of assets usually above $10 million. The Australian real estate market has become a heavily institutionalised market in recent times (last five to ten years), whereby sophisticated investors have a clear preference to allocate more capital towards I&L property investment (compared to other investment forms). With this shift, the proportion of institutional owners has increased relative to private investors and owner occupiers. Examples of institutional investors include Australian real estate investment trusts (A-REITS), wholesale funds, fund managers, private equity, sovereign wealth funds, insurance groups and so forth.

Pricing

In Australia, pricing/values for I&L property has continued to rise since the Global Financial Crisis (GFC), for most capital cities. Broadly speaking, I&L property values (like all other investment forms) are supply and demand driven. Over the past two to three years, 'prime' I&L property values have continued to surge. A 'prime' property is loosely defined as a modern asset (less than, say, ten years old), within a well-regarded location and having the benefit of a strong lease covenant and long remaining lease term. A strong lease covenant could be defined as, say, a five-to-ten year lease to DHL (DHL being a global third-party logistics business).

The 'strength' of a lease covenant is partly determined by the credit quality of the lessee (who pays the rent) but also by the specific terms of the lease including the annual rental payments, the annual rental increases, security deposit and length of lease term remaining, amongst other factors. I&L property (more often than not) are occupied by a single lessee. As there is concentration risk through the single lessee, the quality of the lease covenant is a major aspect in determining market value for investment grade properties. Notwithstanding the comments about lease covenant, the physical attributes of the property are also important in assessing market value and cannot be overlooked.

The continual rise of most I&L property values (particularly those situated close to the capital cities on the eastern seaboard of Australia) is attributable to the significant weight of investor capital (i.e. demand for assets outweighs supply), low interest rate/risk-free rate (this usually creates lower discount rates on all forms of investment, increasing asset values), low vacancy and reasonably good occupier/leasing fundamentals (even in light of COVID-19).

As is the case with all forms of real estate investment, the underlying occupier fundamentals are a key driver of an asset's current and future financial performance. Occupier fundamentals include, but are not limited to, supply, vacancy rates, expected rental growth, performance of the sector and the ability for a lessee to pay rent.

Determinants of value

Locational attributes and physical design of an I&L property are two key determinants of value.

Location

I&L properties are located in areas which best suit the intended use and provide the most efficient output. Customer base, population/demographic, workforce, supply chain and transport nodes (roads, rail, port) will dictate what type of location is suitable for a specific user. The overall efficiency of a location impacts business cost and the operational performance, hence it is a key decision for I&L users.

Proximity to the Central Business District (CBD) may have some benefits, but most users don't necessarily require direct proximity to the CBD. Notwithstanding, generally the closer to a capital city, the higher the underlying land value due to land supply constraints and potential for higher and better uses of the land. Using Melbourne as an example, over the past 10–15 year period there has been substantial development in the western corridor (suburbs such as Derrimut, Truganina and Laverton North). These suburbs provide modern industrial estate settings and are often the preferred destination for larger scale logistics/warehouse users.

Whilst factors vary for different users, the key reasons for the west often being the preferred destination for logistics and warehouse operators can be narrowed down to the excellent road access (both freeways and major arterials), proximity to the Port of Melbourne (which makes container movements easy and direct), the availability of land (and cost of the land) and continual improvement in the surrounding work force (as urban sprawl has continued, residential subdivisions provide adequate catchment areas and employee base).

Conversely, a warehouse user may reside in the south-eastern node (say Dandenong South), as their customer base is located within the south-eastern corridor and it would not make economic sense to locate within the west. Whilst container movements from the Port of Melbourne would take longer to say Dandenong South compared to the west, the customer base and destination of the end product is also a key determinant in the most efficient location.

Building

I&L property is generally the most basic form of construction compared to other commercial real estate such as office and retail, I&L being regular in shape and having concrete floors, four walls and a roof. Whilst not contemplated in this chapter, specialised I&L properties usually have a much higher degree of building design, being purpose built for the intended user. Examples of specialised I&L buildings include cold storage, paper mills, commercial laundries and galvanising plants, amongst others.

When contemplating more generic I&L buildings, modern construction is usually always of 'portal' streel frame structure which includes dust sealed concrete floors, concrete panel and or metal deck walls and metal deck roofing with fibreglass inserts to provide natural light. More specific design features include high bay warehouse clearances (modern design is usually 10 metres minimum height), fire sprinklers, roller door access and truck loading areas (in most cases being on-grade and/or recessed loading docks).

A key part of I&L property design is having an efficient building, relative to the intended use. Using the example of a 1950s sawtooth warehouse with a 5-metre minimum clearance compared to a 2018 constructed portal frame warehouse with a 10 metre minimum clearance, and assuming they are located adjacent (i.e. both having the same locational attributes), the 1950s warehouse would provide less utility to an incoming lessee/user as the height would restrict the capacity for storage of the warehouse (i.e. pallet/cubic capacity is less than the modern building). Accordingly, an incoming lessee would pay a lower rental, say $60 psm of Gross Lettable Area (GLA). In the example of the modern warehouse, the lessee may pay $90 psm GLA.

The age of the building is always reflected in the capital value of an asset and is incorporated by way of the assessed market rental, the quoted capitalisation rate and the adopted capital value rate (dollar psm of GLA). In this example, the decreased capital value for the older 1950s building can be attributed to the much lower rent that a lessee will pay, however it could also be reflected in a higher/softer capitalisation rate giving a lower capital value and a lower direct comparison GLA rate.

Application

I&L properties usually include attached single or two level office buildings which are generally 5–10% of the GLA of the building. When valuing all forms of property, the more generic and 'user friendly' a building is, generally the tighter/lower the capitalisation rate (and the higher the capital value).

For example, in Melbourne's western node (Truganina) most users are warehousing and logistics users who require a 2–5% office area (for a 10,000 sqm building this would be an office of 200–500 sqm). For example, property A has an office ratio of 5% and a capitalisation rate is 6%. Property B has an office area of 25%, which is too large for the anticipated user profile. Valuing real estate and selecting a capitalisation rate is about assessing the risk of income, whilst also incorporating the specific physical attributes of the property being valued. Real estate investment, like any other form of investment, should be considered a 'vehicle' to generate a said return. The higher or greater form of risk attached to generating that income (i.e. the likelihood of receiving the rental income) is reflected in the capitalisation rate or discount rate for the specific asset. The market would deem property B as more risky than property A (as there is a much shallower user/lessee profile for a 25% office compared to a 5% office). Accordingly, the capitalisation rate of property B may be say 6.5% and therefore the market has factored in the higher risk profile of the asset.

For investment property, the assessed market rent and the adopted capitalisation rate (or discount rate for a DCF) are the two main levers in a valuation which are used to determine the subject property's market value. These two levers will reflect the location of the property, age/functionality of the building, underlying land value, leasing risk, strength of the lease covenant, remaining lease term, vacancy risk, liquidity and buyer depth at the time, amongst other factors.

The valuation process

The process of valuing I&L property is not dissimilar to other asset classes. A valuation instruction is initiated and the purpose and reliance of a valuation is crucial to agree up front with the client (is the valuation for financial reporting or, say, first mortgage purposes and who is relying on the report?). After the instruction is agreed, the valuation process essentially involves setting up the file, physically inspecting the property, externally inspecting the sales and rental evidence, completing the valuation 'model' (the model often being a sophisticated spreadsheet which can facilitate a discounted cash flow), followed by assessing the market value and completion of the report. Whilst this is not an exhaustive list of what is involved, these are the broad steps which result in the final report which may be anywhere between 10 and 60 pages in length.

The physical inspection is a key part of the valuation process. The first part of the inspection is correctly identifying the property (via the Certificate of Title), which is followed by a detailed inspection of all internal and external building and land areas. Whilst inspecting the property, detailed field notes will include the inspection date, age of the building, construction, finishes, design/functionality, measurements (sqm of the building and clearance height of the warehouse), amongst other notes. It is also important to interview the occupier to understand the functionality of the building, former uses/contamination risk and to gain other insights.

Valuation methodology

When the inspection and field notes have been consolidated, the methodology for valuing the property is selected. Selecting an appropriate method to value a property is dictated by the type of valuation being provided and the reliance on such valuation.

Valuation of all real estate assets is based on comparable rental and sales evidence. Comparable transactions/evidence underpin the valuation and understanding a market in detail is the key to accurate valuations. Whilst it has become more pronounced in recent years, the valuation industry is moving towards a greater degree of asset class specialisation. By specialising in a certain real estate asset classes, the valuer can become an expert in their field and value the most prestigious and complex assets. By monitoring and collecting data on a single asset class (say I&L), this gives the valuer the best opportunity to have a complete and thorough insight into that specific market.

In some valuations, comparable evidence is abundant, whilst there are other examples where evidence is scarce. For example, a 500 sqm warehouse unit within a subdivision in a metropolitan location would generally benefit from recent comparable sales within the subject development or surrounding locations, providing a sound basis for the valuation. Comparable evidence is about finding rents/sales that are as similar to the subject property as possible (similar location, size, age, income profile, etc.). On the other hand, for example, a specialised commercial laundry would have limited sales (if any) to compare to the subject property. In this instance, the search for sales evidence needs to be widened geographically where sales from other cities or states may be considered.

In the case of specialised assets, the valuer would also be required to consider other specialised asset sales. By considering other specialised asset sales, the valuer analyses the trend of the evidence and derives a risk-adjusted capitalisation rate or discount rate to assess the market value of the property (i.e. the capitalisation rate and discount rate will usually always be higher/softer for assets that are specialised, as they are deemed more risky and have a narrower lessee pool, if any).

The most commonly used valuation methods for I&L property on a market value basis are the capitalisation of net income approach (capitalisation), discounted cash flow approach (DCF) and the direct comparison approach. The summation or cost approach is less common. Two methods of valuation are usually recommended, with one approach being the primary approach and the second approach providing a check method. As a general rule, assets of less than $10 million are not valued using a DCF approach, where capitalisation and direct comparison are most widely used, whereas assets above $10 million are often valued using capitalisation and DCF methods.

Selecting appropriate methods of valuation is primarily derived by how the market participants price the asset. For example, a $50 million leased-investment property would almost always be purchased and owned by an institutional investor. Institutional investors will generally always consider the capitalisation and DCF approach (some have greater weight on DCF compared to others). Accordingly, a valuer will analyse the comparable evidence using the same methods, with a consistent form of analysis ensuring accurate valuation.

The owner occupier market is a key part of the I&L sector with many businesses electing to owner occupy as opposed to lease. Whilst the functionally of an I&L property for an owner occupier and a lessee are consistent, the owner occupier market behaves differently to the investor market when it comes to transactions or the purchasing of such assets. The investor market is focused on the income returns that the property can generate (and the quality of the lessee, lease, etc.), whilst the owner occupier market has no regard to the income profile (as the buildings are generally subject to vacant possession). Accordingly the direct comparison approach is often a primary approach to valuing a property in the typical owner occupier category. The dollar psm of Gross Lettable Area (or Land Area) is the unit of measurement most commonly used for the direct comparison approach for I&L property. The capitalisation approach is then generally considered the check approach or secondary approach. It is important to consider other vacant possession sales when valuing an asset on a vacant possession basis, similarly, the key sales for an investment property will also be key sales of leased-investment properties.

Case study 1 – valuation methodology for larger investment property

The subject property is located within Leakes Road, Truganina and comprises a 25,000 sqm office/warehouse building which was constructed in 2017. The property commenced with a 12 year pre-lease to ABC Logistics who are a large multinational lessee. The remaining lease term is 9 years and the passing annual rental paid by the lessee is $2,000,000 pa net.

In the current market, this property would be well received by institutional investors, primarily due to the core industrial location, modern nature of the building and high-quality lease covenant with long remaining term.

The property would be valued using the capitalisation and DCF approaches. A key component of the valuation is the assessment of an appropriate market rental value for the asset. Assessing a market rental ensures the true underlying attributes and quality of the building are reflected in the asset's market value. In this instance, the passing rental of $2,000,000 reflects $80 per sqm net, which is 'in line' with comparable market rental evidence. Accordingly the passing rental (rent being paid) may be adopted as 'market'. All valuations work on a 'net' rental basis, which is the rental being received by the lessor, after the deduction of all outgoings/costs associated with operating the property.

The market rent is then capitalised in perpetuity. The market rental would be capitalised at a yield (capitalisation rate) of say 5.25%, which would imply a value of $38,095,238 (which could be rounded to $38 million). The DCF approach would provide a second approach to value and discount rates in the current market generally range between 6.25% to 7%, depending on the risk profile and nature of the asset. For the subject property, the discount rate would be say 6.5% (as derived from the comparable sales). Whilst not considered a primary approach to valuing an investment grade asset, the direct comparison also provides a final check method. At the adopted value of $38,000,000, the GLA rate reflects $1,520 psm. The (hypothetical) comparable sales evidence indicates a range of say $1,400–$1,600 psm so the value is also supportable on the direct comparison basis.

Case study 2 – valuation methodology for smaller vacant possession property

The subject property is located within Greens Road, Dandenong South and comprises a 3,500 sqm office/warehouse building which was constructed in 2005. The property is not subject to any lease agreement and hence a hypothetical sale would be on a vacant possession basis.

In the current market, this property would be well received by owner occupier purchasers and some investors. The property would be valued using the direct comparison and capitalisation approaches. A DCF would not be warranted, as the purchaser profile is not sophisticated enough to be completing a DCF (nor is it warranted for an asset of this simplicity and scale).

Direct Comparison is often considered the simplest form of valuation and its most common unit of measurement is dollars per sqm of land area or dollars per sqm of

Gross Lettable Area (the building area). Again, comparable evidence is the key to valuing a property. When valuing this medium-scale generic industrial property, it would be expected that there would be a reasonably good level of comparable evidence (evidence depth can vary from time to time). The more identical a comparable sale is to the subject property, the greatest weighting the valuer will give to the said sale. In this instance, it would be reasonable to expect say 4–6 sales located within Dandenong South (or surrounding suburbs), of similar age (say built between 2000 and 2010), similar size, and having the same income profile (no income noting the subject is vacant possession).

Of key importance, particularly when the market is evolving, is to have 'current' sales. There is no set time frame on how dated or current a sale can be. Generally speaking, best practice would be to rely on key sales which have occurred in the last 1–12 months (albeit the more recent the evidence, the better). In the case of the COVID-19 recession, sales evidence from say February 2020 has much less weight than say a transaction which has occurred during the pandemic period (from March 2020 onwards).

Assume there is a key comparable sale (Sale 1) which is also located on Greens Road and is of a similar age and layout to the subject and has a warehouse clearance height of 8 metres (the subject's clearance height is 10 metres). Sale 1 reflects a GLA rate of $1,800 psm on a direct comparison basis. Sale 1 would be considered inferior to the subject, noting that all attributes of the sale and the subject are directly similar, save for the clearance height. Accordingly, Sale 1 indicates a GLA rate for the subject property would be above $1,800 psm.

Sale 2, which is also located on Greens Road and has the same income profile (vacant) and building size, albeit was constructed in 2010 (more modern than the subject). Sale 2 reflects a GLA rate of $1,900 psm. Sale 2 is deemed superior to the subject property noting it is more modern and therefore indicates/supports a GLA rate of less than $1,900 per sqm. Whilst this is very much a simplified example of the direct comparison approach, the two key sales indicate a tight value rate range of above $1,800 and below $1,900 psm. Accordingly, the valuer may then adopt $1,850 per sqm for the subject property, implying a capital value of $6,475,000.

As a check approach to value, an assessment of net market rental is required to compute the value using the capitalisation approach. The market rental assessed is, say, $385,000 pa net ($110 psm of GLA, as derived from the comparable rental evidence). The rental would be capitalised in perpetuity at a yield (capitalisation rate) of say 5.5%, which would imply a value of $7,000,000. The yield or capitalisation rate has been derived from comparable sales evidence which indicate a yield (capitalisation rates) of 5% to 6%.

As the property is subject to vacant possession and this is an income based approach, the hypothetical investor purchaser would make an allowance for vacancy to the core value. This allowance is often referred to as 'letting up' and is a capital value deduction from the $7,000,000 to reflect that the property is not generating any income. These costs are effectively market-based costs to reflect what is required to secure a lessee and produce an income. A vacancy allowance of six months rental (rental void), six months for loss of outgoings, 15% net incentive and 12% for agent's leasing fees would be appropriate allowances for this property in the current market. Table 10.1 details the capitalisation approach for such a vacant asset:

As noted above, both valuation approaches support each other and the valuer would most likely adopt the direct comparison approach as this was the primary approach to value for Case Study 2 due to the owner occupier dominated nature of the sub-market.

Table 10.1 The capitalisation approach – vacant assets

Assessed net market rent	$385,000	
Adopted capitalisation rate	5.5%	$7,00,000
Less allowances for vacancy		
6 months rental void	($192,500)	
6 months loss of outgoings	($26,250)	
15% net incentive	($288,750)	
12% agents leasing fees	($46,200)	($553,700)
Total		$6,446,300
ADOPT (rounded)		**$6,450,000**

Note: outgoings are based on $15 per sqm of GLA pa; and incentives are analysed as percentages and are displayed as a proportion of lease term. In this instance, a notional 5 year lease term (hence 15% of the five years of annual rent) is assumed. The notional lease term is the most likely lease term that would be achieved when leasing the asset (as derived from the comparable rental evidence).

Source: Author

Summary

In this chapter, valuation practice for industrial property is considered through a contextual analysis of the structure of the industrial property market with a focus on the transition from manufacturing to logistics, the rise in institutional ownership and the resulting repricing of the sector. The fundamental importance of location and the physical building are considered in the context of market examples.

The application of the DCF approach to larger investment property is compared and contrasted with the application of the capitalisation of income approach and the direct comparison approach to smaller vacant possession property, highlighting the diversity in the industrial property sector and the need for flexibility in valuation methodology adopted.

In this first section of the second part of the book, valuation practice for residential, office and retail property were considered in previous chapters, with valuation practice for industrial property considered in this chapter and valuation practice for rural property considered in the following chapter.

The second section of the second part of this book addresses valuation practice for specialist property sectors comprising retirement, leisure, plant and equipment and business and intangible asset valuation with the third and final section of the second part addressing valuation practice for specific purposes, including rental, financial reporting, secured lending, insurance and statutory valuation purposes.

Biography

Ryan Korda studied at RMIT Melbourne and has been practicing as a valuer for most of his professional career. Ryan is currently the National Director at CBRE and specialises in the valuation of Industrial & Logistics properties in Victoria. He has been with CBRE since 2012 and is a member of the Australian Property Institute.

Ryan has valued some of Australia's largest industrial estates and provides valuations for financial institutions, institutional owners, large corporate owner occupiers and developers.

11 Rural property valuation

Acknowledgement

This chapter draws heavily on chapter 13 in *Valuation Principles and Practice* (2007) (Second Edition, Australian Property Institute, Deakin) which is duly acknowledged here rather than individually referenced through this chapter and to which readers are referred for a deeper consideration.

Introduction

With the first part of this book addressing the principles of valuation, this second part addresses the practice of valuation being grouped into three sections comprising conventional property sectors, specialist property sectors and specific purposes. Conventional property sectors include residential, office, retail, industrial and rural property valuation practice. Specialist property sectors include retirement, leisure, plant and equipment and business and intangible asset valuation practice and specific purposes include valuation practice for rental, financial reporting, secured lending, insurance and statutory valuation purposes.

The first section of the second part of this book addresses the valuation of conventional property sectors with residential, office, retail and industrial property valuation practice considered in the previous chapters and rural property valuation practice considered in this chapter.

It is assumed that the reader already has an understanding of valuation methodology for rural property, allowing a focus in this chapter on the impact on value of key issues affecting the rural property market including climate, topography, soil, water and their cumulative impact on productivity through the key rural property market sectors of grazing, cropping and irrigated lands.

Structure of the rural property market

The majority of Australia's farmland is still owned and operated by families or interests associated with families though there is now an increasing level of investment by corporate and institutional investors. In the family situation, the true returns to labour and those to capital become blurred. It is known that, despite difficult times in agriculture, much of the farming land in the country remains debt-free, or with only small amounts of debt, which may be associated with operations rather than land purchases. It is also known that, in the last hundred years, those farms remaining as

DOI: 10.1201/9781003049555-11

viable units have become larger and this has been at the expense of the less profitable, smaller or poorly managed farms. Management is a critical issue in agriculture and successful farmers are those who realised that farming is a business, not a way of life, adopting sound business management practices as well as sound pasture management and animal husbandry practices to survive.

Australia by and large is a price-taker on international commodity markets and as farmer subsidies are minimal, this means that the primary sector is open to the vagaries of the world marketplace with its inherent protectionist policies, subsidies, politics and fluctuating currency exchange rates. Seasonal variations within Australia, as well as major disasters such as drought, fire or flood, make the situation worse.

Land values tend to follow the major commodity prices as the marketplace makes its assessment of potential future earnings, although there has always been a demonstrable lag.

The international situation and outlook for agricultural products has the capacity to alter very quickly. In addition to seasonal conditions, especially in the northern hemisphere, political events and actions can have a marked effect on supply, demand and price together with currency movements.

Issues influencing rural property valuation

The market for rural land is regionally influenced and may fluctuate depending on seasonal conditions, commodities outlook, general economic circumstances and rural property market participant perceptions. To value rural property, the valuer needs to fully understand the marketplace for the land, the nature of the land and farming practices.

Key factors affecting rural property valuation include:

- climate which varies by district, with rainfall, seasonal distribution, temperatures, evaporation rates, drought, wind and patterns, frost and major storms and cyclones being important considerations together with the impact of climate change;
- topography which commonly determines the use of rural land with land capable of being ploughed used to grow crops while non-arable land usually comprises land with remnant native vegetation or hilly to steep land which cannot be economically or safely cultivated;
- soil type and quality are an integral part of the agricultural production process and different soil types or land classes may result in different values. Soil characteristics across most districts fall into the following main categories such as sands, loams, non-cracking clays, cracking clays, calcareous earths, massive earths, structured earths with either smooth or rough ped fabric, duplex soils – red, brown, yellow, yellow-grey, black and grey – and organic soils;
- water plays a critical part in agriculture with areas of low rainfall often boosted by irrigation from river storages, surface water catchment or underground sources. Throughout most regions of Australia, the use of irrigation water is controlled by government through licensing. In recent times, Water Licences have been 'unbundled' from the land in most districts, meaning they form a separate legal (personal) asset. Where the water 'Entitlement' has been separated from the land, any intending financier should register an interest in the asset;

- tenure of rural property which may be freehold, Crown Land (being land that is not freehold and still held by the Crown, being regulated by the relevant State Government) or pastoral leases which cover approximately 44% of Australia's mainland allowing the use of land for grazing traditional livestock and more recently for tourism and non-traditional livestock such as kangaroos and camels; and
- productivity, being a measure that can be used to compare rural land relatively. Productivity can be measured on various bases and will vary depending on what type of enterprise is to be undertaken – such as carrying capacity for a grazing property or production or yields within a dryland cropping or irrigation property. The productivity will be closely aligned with the land types, level of improvement and infrastructure, climate and rainfall and management practices.

Valuation approach to rural property

Unlike other property types where there can be a high degree of comparability (for example houses, vacant land, industrial property), very few rural properties are identical or even closely comparable. Therefore, a degree of relative adjustment is invariably required in forming an opinion of value.

The appropriate approach to valuation will vary depending on the circumstances involved. It is usual that a suitable figure per hectare will be determined after the comparable sales have been analysed. It is often appropriate to use a combination of both the direct comparison and summation approaches where values for the land are determined using the comparison approach. The rates derived for the different land classifications within the sales are then applied to the corresponding areas of the property being valued (rate per hectare x number of hectares per classification) in a build-up or summation approach. Land is usually considered on a fenced and watered basis meaning that farm infrastructure is included in the rates per hectare derived from the sales.

The valuer would then add the value of any further assets such as farm structures and possibly water if separately tradeable (both drawn from analysed sales), to derive an overall value for the property. This build-up or summation method is a more involved approach to farm value assessment and requires a solid base of knowledge on land classifications for both the sales being analysed and the farm being valued to ensure an appropriate comparison is being made.

A useful cross-check may then be a simple direct comparison, being the total value of the farm being valued divided by the total area of the farm. This is called an improved rate per hectare and can be compared against the corresponding values for the farms analysed as appropriate evidence. All things being equal, it may be expected that the resultant rate per hectare calculated for the farm being valued would be within reasonable parity with the sales used in evidence provided they are comparable.

There are other methods of valuation including capitalisation of farm net income, unit of productive capacity (such as Dry Sheep Equivalents, Beast Area Value, Adult Equivalent, Rate per Tonne of Productive Capacity, to name a few). Each approach demands that the valuer must have equal knowledge of the attributes within the sales considered in evidence as that for the property being valued. The valuer must always follow the rule: 'As you analyse, so must you value.'

136 Rural property valuation

Basic sales information

The following check list may be useful in identifying basic sales information required for analysis:

- the name/s of the vendor and purchaser;
- check for a possible relationship between the parties;
- the Crown description and area and reconciliation of this to the property as inspected;
- the date of sale;
- consideration – gross and net and any terms including interest rates;
- inclusion of chattels – stock, plant;
- how the property was purchased/sold (e.g. auction or private sale) – if a private sale, whether there was any bargaining or whether the asking price was paid and did the purchaser have local knowledge?;
- services – power, water supply, telephone;
- the nearest town and facilities offered;
- soils – textures, types if known;
- pastures – types, areas, age, condition;
- productivity – carrying capacity, yields;
- buildings;
- drainage;
- fencing – type, number of paddocks, condition;
- stock-watering facilities – dams, tanks, mills, troughs, reticulation;
- other improvements;
- the extent of work done since sale; and
- unproductive areas – swamp, salinity, eroded gullies.

Particular focus should be given in analysis to the following:

- pastures including the need for any immediate renovation, fertiliser requirements, weeds and pests, grazing or cropping rotation and so forth;
- irrigation including specific information relating to water allocation, use of recycled water and so forth;
- drainage including extent of drainage and wet areas, swampy areas and salinity problems; and
- carrying capacity including whether the indicated carrying capacity is reasonable and sustainable, need for fodder conservation or additional fodder and so forth.

Sales analysis

Sales information can be broken down into various levels and at each step care is required to evaluate the sales for comparability. If that is considered to have been achieved, there is no need to break the information down further, though this situation may rarely arise.

One of the greatest variables on rural properties is the buildings. These may well only add 10–15% of the value of a developed farm and may often have little influence on the productive capacity of the farm itself. In rural areas the value remains in the land, because that is the productive agent, with the contribution made to the overall value of the property by the buildings varying in almost every case.

Other improvements may include physical improvements – such as fences, yards, ramps, silos – and the other common improvements such as pasture, irrigation layouts, laneways, drainage or water reticulation or provision.

There will always be a need for a 'check method' of valuation and this may often be done using the units of productivity. Information regarding carrying capacity or production of crops may be used in order to achieve a check method based on, for example, dollars per sheep area, dollars per cow area or dollars per beast area. The unit chosen will correlate with the average animal grazed in the district, or at least the most dominant form of grazing or cropping. Correlation analysis may be adopted to achieve the most appropriate unit. Conversion tables may be used to convert all other forms of grazing animal to the standard chosen.

Valuation of grazing and cropping country

Many of the moderate to higher rainfall areas of Australia, where the growing season exceeds five months, are given over to cropping and grazing. This is often done in combination if soil types, topography and economic returns to the land favour cropping. In many of these areas a form of land use rotation has traditionally been used. This technique usually incorporates leguminous plants, commonly in a pasture phase, to provide soil nitrogen for subsequent cropping phases. Nevertheless, in cropping districts there has, at various times, been premiums paid for land which can quickly be put into the cropping phase and a cash crop realised with minimum input. In times when the price expectation for a particular commodity is extraordinarily high, the date of sale and stage of the cropping cycle for land will be of particular interest.

Where grazing is undertaken as a sole activity on permanent annual or perennial-based pastures, a knowledge of pasture improvement is critical as is the ability to recognise species and weeds and to understand optimum grazing patterns. The valuer also needs to know about the land use, associated production factors, outlooks and confidence levels of the industries concerned at the time of valuation and the district itself in terms of locational factors, rainfall, soils, drainage, degradation problems and the pattern of the marketplace. This last factor comes from careful analysis of all the sales considered relevant to the property being valued.

In most districts there will be areas which are more keenly sought by knowledgeable purchasers when properties are put on the market. In other districts there may not be the same level of interest in small pockets and the whole area may be more homogeneous in its acceptance in the market, with only minor variations reflecting the perceived quality of the particular property.

In valuing mixed farmland, in particular, a valuer should make enquiries as to the past history of the land and how it has been utilised. If potatoes have been grown, for example, then dieldrin may have been used as a pesticide and the ground may not be suitable for grazing animals producing meat or milk for human consumption. In other cases, there can be soil contamination from a variety of sources such as hydrocarbons from leaking underground fuel storages or from drums and a wide variety of farm chemicals which may have been improperly stored or disposed of. The fact that a property has always been used for rural purposes is no guarantee whatsoever that the property is unlikely to be contaminated in some way. In fact, the valuer should possibly treat it as exactly the reverse.

In analysis, the critical task is to compare like with like. Various factors may be considered, usually in conjunction with each other, including size of the parcel, soil, topography, drainage, land degradation, water supply, climatic variation (rainfall, hail, frost and wind may all be marginally different within an area), pasture quality, weed infestation and levels of improvement which may all be considered by prospective purchasers.

Consistent analysis is essential to permit meaningful comparison. In those parts of Australia where relatively intensive agriculture is found, settlement patterns and homogeneous levels of development will be such that the ex-buildings level of value will frequently provide an excellent correlation, with differences in value readily reconciled with the factors listed previously. If this occurs and sales can be ranked against one another, the process of valuation is made comparatively easy.

As most land is bought and sold on the basis of dollars per hectare, this measure tends to be used in primary analysis. It is important to also look at possible other measures of productivity, as these may be considered in the marketplace. Dollars per sheep area may, at any particular time, be what a purchaser considers when actually making an offer on a dollars per hectare basis and this may well give a better understanding of comparability.

If adequate comparability cannot be realised, then it is necessary to continue the process of analysis using both per hectare approaches as well as productivity measures.

On grazing and cropping properties, it will also be necessary to assess the level of improvements, machinery sheds, storage sheds, hay sheds, milking sheds in dairying districts and fences required to operate the property at its maximum level of efficiency and to compare this with those found. While they may have a utility value, they may fail to add to the property value even though in good structural repair.

This then leads to consideration of the input of trees into farm ecosystems. In grazing country many farmers have long recognised the benefits to stock from shade trees and windbreaks. Others, in the early years, did not see any benefit from trees and deliberately went about eliminating them. Recent work has shown that, in many areas, the removal of trees has meant changing the ground water or soil hydrology to the point where saline deposits have reached the surface, destroying many hectares of previously productive land. Trees are an important part of a healthy farm and this applies to both grazing and cropping country. The existence of timber stands may take land out of immediate production, but the valuer needs to consider the input of those trees into the productivity of the rest of the farm. In some areas native trees, even if not cut down, may die because of altered land use. These would need to be replaced with trees of a different species which will adapt to the conditions. This situation is particularly noticeable in irrigation areas.

Permanent pastures may be of value and this will be a reflection of their component species, productivity, fertiliser history and also the fact that they are consolidated, fully productive pastures. In this, a quality perennial-based pasture could be expected to add more than its annual based counterpart. Where irrigation is used, pastures will reach their maximum added value not only due to their greater productivity but also because of the irrigation layout – delvers, levelling, bay formation and the like. In this, it needs to be remembered that once land is cultivated and a pasture sown, it will take several seasons for the permanent pasture to be fully consolidated and able to cope with the pressure of full stocking rates. Again, in valuation practice, like must be compared with like and in each case the district norms taken into account.

The final critical factor to consider is water supply. Without an adequate supply of water, it is not possible to carry stock on a property. Therefore, the extent and quality of water supply arrangements need to be considered. The simplest and cheapest form of water supply is a dam into which stock wade to have a drink. Because of the problems with mud, this is the least effective. It is significantly better to use a windmill, electric or solar pump to pump water into a trough beside the dam, denying stock direct access into the dam itself. At the other end of the scale is a pressurised, reticulated system serving each paddock with a trough suited to the animals. There will be many variations and each situation will have to be assessed independently and values ascribed accordingly.

Valuation of irrigation land

Whilst the area of Australia given over to irrigation is comparatively small, the productivity from irrigation districts is considerably higher and provides a significant input into the country's overall agricultural production.

The majority of irrigated land is used for pasture production, supporting dairy and beef cattle as well as sheep, primarily for meat production. Other significant areas are used for horticulture, sugar cane or fruit production. Some cropping is done under irrigated conditions, but most crops do not provide sufficient additional return to warrant the expenses involved or tying up the land in this form of agriculture. Rice production in New South Wales and the production of summer crops such as sunflowers in southern areas may be seen as exceptions to this generalisation.

Having established land use, it will be easily appreciated that the majority of irrigation is undertaken by flooding, with specialist crops utilising spray and trickle methods. For pasture production, the flood methods (principally border check) provide a cheap means of distributing water to the paddocks. In recent years the widespread use of laser levelling has meant that one of the big drawbacks with flooding, being uneven water distribution, has been largely overcome. Some farms have incorporated underground pipes with risers to bay inlets, others have looked to water monitoring devices which will electronically control the amount of water applied to any particular bay, but many farms still rely on the same primitive systems put in place many years ago. Of critical importance will be the actual farm layout, the way in which water flows across the landscape and the way in which drainage is controlled.

Economy may be the key point in the decision-making process. If money can be saved, then farmers are more likely to take greater care of the limited water resource. In many cases it is still cheaper to buy from the water authority than it is to pump from a spearpoint or deep lead bore system. This will naturally act as a disincentive if the farmer takes the short-term view on profitability. On the other hand, the existence of an assured additional water supply to a farm means that the property will be able to better withstand drought.

These differentials understood, the balance of the valuation process is exactly as previously covered in respect of grazing land. The essence is that, for sales analysis to be able to compare like with like, additional information available in irrigation country may make this comparison process easier to follow. However, in dry land valuation work, it is fair to say that the value attributes are generally simpler to understand and follow.

Valuation of specialised rural properties

In order to undertake the valuation of a specialised rural property, the peculiar production characteristics of the industry must be researched and fully understood. The process of valuation is essentially no different from that for any other rural property, except that the search for sales evidence may well take in a large area and the task of establishing comparability through the evidence offered may well be more difficult.

As with all valuation work, the task is to interpret and understand the marketplace. It may be necessary to look far beyond the actual area where the valuation is being done to identify any sales evidence. Once gained, there may be the need to look to the value of land, plus the added value of the buildings and other improvements. This may be checked by means of unit values. In the industries which use plant input and not animal input, there is less of a problem with planning control with the critical value factors being soil quality, water availability and climatic suitability.

Specialised properties may take the form of capital-intensive ventures that rely heavily on built improvements. These include piggeries, feedlots, broiler chicken production, hatcheries and egg producing farms. On other properties, the intensity may relate to the type of activity undertaken on the land and will include horticulture, orchards, citrus groves, vineyards, cane, tobacco or hop farms.

In relation to those industries which rely on buildings, care must be taken to establish what is on the property compared to what is considered the current norm for the industry. Using piggeries as an example, in the 1960s open-fronted sheds were common and a distinct improvement on farms which kept pigs in the paddocks, feeding swill and other waste. The open-fronted sheds allowed better shelter, and the separation from soil allowed improved disease control and management. Labour input was increased as feeding and waste disposal necessitated manual work. Once swill feeding was banned, nutrition was improved and a more uniform product was achieved in a shorter time. Feed tended to be of a dry nature which, once mixed, could be distributed through a mechanical feed system. Increases in labour costs and the move to larger piggeries altered design requirements and the larger production units began to incorporate full shelter housing, automation in feeding, waste disposal and water supply. The next step was to provide rudimentary climate control in the form of mechanical ventilation and even heating during winter. The old-style open-fronted sheds are, therefore, now obsolete. The value in such a piggery may be that the land upon which it stands is zoned in such a way that it can continue to be used as a piggery or be redeveloped as such.

Where planning schemes are in force, planning considerations for intensive, animal-based industries are very important. Many planning schemes specifically exclude such industries from their general farming zones. In part, this stems from the odour generated by the enterprises and the problems associated with waste disposal.

Feedlots

Feedlots are different in Australia in comparison to the colder northern hemisphere counterparts, being generally used for short-term 'finishing' of stock for the market, perhaps after range grazing or to provide 'grain fed' beef for the supermarket or specialist trade including export. Their most appropriate use may well be as adjuncts to cattle-raising properties, where they can be used as part of the finishing process for the marketplace and to ensure consistent quality where contracts may be involved.

History has shown that the economics of feed lotting is cyclical in nature, dependent on both prices paid for cattle and grain and prices received for the finished product.

A feedlot generally comprises large pens constructed on sloping land to aid drainage and waste runoff to a collection system. There are service laneways to allow access to stock and to provide feed for them. The stock have maximum feed and minimum movement, developing both intra- and inter-muscular fat, hence the term 'finishing' which refers not only to the appearance but also eating quality of the meat. A feed mixing shed is needed, storage facilities and administration areas, but generally the level of building development will be less than for a piggery or poultry farm. A feedlot of over 500 Standard Cattle Units must seek EPA approval.

Poultry enterprises

In the case of poultry enterprises, the waste is not liquid and the smell is less pervasive over a distance. There is a demand in many areas from horticulturists or processors for the waste material such that these enterprises present less potential for environmental hazard. Poultry waste has in the past been used in proprietary stock feeds, but the disease risk is obvious in such use.

In recent times, a significant moral challenge has arisen to battery/cage egg production from animal rights organisations and alternative free range systems are now the norm. This has provided opportunities for the traditional shedding systems to be retrofitted for use as a free range facility, with relatively minimal cost of conversion. Broiler production is undertaken on a deep litter system with the birds able to freely move about during their short life span of a few weeks. Sheds are climate-controlled automatically and artificially lit in most cases. Layer sheds are raised to allow manure to be collected from underneath. Modern layer sheds have fully automated egg collection systems.

Orchards and vineyards

With orchards, not only will the variety of tree be important but also the health, vigour, age and the type of pruning system will need to be considered. Pruning system refers to the trellising commonly used in new orchards – for example Tatura, Palmette, Murrumbidgee or Lincoln trellis, compared to the older vase style of pruning. Newer plantings may be on rootstock, which may offer improved disease resistance and earlier maturity. Careful enquiry will be needed to ascertain current trends and research findings and to compare these with the sales evidence available to reach a figure for added value.

Concerning contamination, some chemicals previously commonly used on orchards may now be considered harmful, often in export markets even if not in Australia. Where such chemicals have soil residues which can affect the fruit, the output from an orchard may be downgraded in its quality assessment and be unsuitable for export.

In the case of orchard, citrus grove and vineyard valuation, the concept of planted hectare should be considered. This recognises that parts of any property will be used for other activities, possibly associated with the main enterprise or even used for some other agricultural purpose. Part will also be given over to building curtilage. If these areas are separated out, what remains is the area solely used for production and this can then be used as the comparison.

The planted hectare at ex-buildings level will have two basic components, being a land value and the added value of the plantings and structures necessary to support them. There are several ways to determine planted area, such as including or excluding the headland. Although the net planted area excluding the headland and including a half width of the outside row is the most common, either can be used provided it is consistent with the sales analysed. In the valuation of such properties careful attention must be given to soil type and its suitability to the enterprise, drainage, water supply (in terms of not only quantity but also quality and reliability) and climate. On this last point, frosts and their incidence throughout the year will be important, as will the incidence of hail. Some small areas have a proven and constant history of hail storms, so being unsuitable for orchard or vineyard development. In the consideration of all these factors it would be prudent for the valuer to take expert advice from State Departments of Agriculture or their local equivalent and/or private consultants skilled in the development of such properties.

Apart from improvements such as plantings and trellising, these properties will have a need for buildings such as machinery sheds, pumphouses, packing and storage sheds. Larger properties may have cool rooms or chilled storage areas. In the case of cool stores, a controlled atmosphere storage is technologically superior and older stores may add little value, if any. As with other forms of valuation, replacement cost plus information from sales evidence will be important in ascribing added value. Further, care is needed in determining what is part of the real estate component and what constitutes plant and machinery. The time of sale may affect the price, which will be lowest after harvest and before pruning and highest just before harvest.

Vineyard valuation will present special problems in relation to the types of grapes grown and the demand for that type at the time of valuation. In the case of wine grapes, there have been substantial fluctuations over time between not only red and white varieties but also for particular varieties within these groups. As with any planting, the health, age, vigour and production levels must be taken into account, as must any disease problems. The major problem in some areas will be Phylloxera and the type of planting (being whether or not it is on resistant rootstock) will (or should) be of concern. Vineyards outside the recognised or prestige areas will usually have a lower market value, even if yields and qualities are equal. The grape supply agreement and the pricing will be a significant consideration for the market and this information is critical to determine the viability and value of the vineyard or horticultural planting.

Timber land

Timber land provides a special challenge to valuers due to the long-term nature of the activity and the risks involved in production. Here the market will be linked closely to the general economy of the State or nation as the products from forests are usually associated with the building industry. There is a significant market for pulp wood in some areas and that aspect will also need attention.

In particular, consideration should be given to:

- land tenure;
- soils and their suitability;
- climate;

- trees, including their age, species, condition, vigour and time to harvest;
- problems including disease, insects and parasites; and
- the likely land use and rehabilitation costs after felling.

Valuers often require specialised forestry assistance and this should be sought. Enquiries will also have to be made to many bodies, private and government, in order to fully satisfy all the questions relating to the industry and marketplace. Farm wood lotting may be an important source of timber in the future, as will plantations of both softwood and hardwood (native) species. Woodlots or timber plantations, therefore, will usually require separate consideration from the balance of an agricultural or grazing property.

Alternative valuation approaches to specialised properties

In each of these specialist rural property examples, the use of sales evidence has been stressed. There will be times when the valuer will be confronted with situations when sales evidence is simply not available. In these situations, the cash flow of the business may well provide some of the information needed to undertake the valuation.

Capitalisation could be considered if the information is available and could be shown to be appropriate in sales of similar enterprises. Whilst the actual cash flow may be readily available and, in some cases, show consistency over a long period, the relevant capitalisation rate is most likely to cause significant difficulty. In most operations, the income flow will vary depending not only on a fluctuating commodity market but also on how such fluctuating commodity markets affect inputs. For example, the volatility in the wheat market caused by world markets, exchange rate variation and drought have had significant impacts on poultry farms, piggeries and feedlots using wheat such that, if no substitute can readily be found, income flows will be distorted. The major difficulty remains in testing the method on sufficient sales evidence (in the market at the time of valuation) to prove its utility. In most cases, if the sales evidence is available, then the problem is likely to be solved using comparison anyway.

As distinct from capitalisation, the same information may instead be used as a guide to determining the potential viability of the property and the enterprise. The replacement costs of the improvements can then be considered with, depending on the assessment of the marketplace, appropriate rates of depreciation then applied if considered warranted before adding land value. There are considerable dangers involved in this approach due to the assumptions that are required and clearly the terms of the instruction will be critical.

In the valuation of specialised properties, the maxim of 'know the market, know the industry and the outlook' becomes paramount. Sales evidence will generally have to be searched for over a wide area and possibly interstate for some rare activities. Comparison on a direct basis is unlikely to be effective and an approach based on productivity units may be the best approach, backed by a thorough knowledge of the economic status of the particular enterprise. The approach using cost less depreciation added to land value will, in most cases, be more appropriate as a check method.

Summary

In this chapter, valuation practice for rural property is considered through a contextual analysis of the structure of the rural property market with a focus on the key issues affecting rural property including climate, topography, soil, water and their cumulative impact on productivity.

Valuation of the key rural property market sectors, being grazing, cropping and irrigation land, are considered in detail with a further review of specialised rural property valuation including feedlots, poultry enterprises, orchards and vineyards and timber lands, concluding with the consideration of alternative valuation approaches to specialised property.

In this first section of the second part of the book, valuation practice for residential, office, retail and industrial property were considered in previous chapters, with valuation practice for rural property considered in this chapter.

The second section of the second part of this book addresses valuation practice for specialist property sectors comprising retirement, leisure, plant and equipment and business and intangible asset valuation with the third and final section of the second part addressing valuation practice for specific purposes, including rental, financial reporting, secured lending, insurance and statutory valuation purposes.

Section Two

Valuation practice for specialist property sectors

12 Retirement and aged care property valuation

Lois Towart

Introduction

With the first part of this book addressing the principles of valuation, the second part addresses the practice of valuation being grouped into three sections comprising conventional property sectors, specialist property sectors and specific purposes. Conventional property sectors include residential, office, retail, industrial and rural property valuation practice, being considered in previous chapters.

Specialist property sectors include retirement property, which is addressed in this chapter, with leisure, plant and equipment and business and intangible asset valuation practice being addressed in the following chapters. The third and final section of the second part addresses valuations for specific purposes including valuation practice for rental, financial reporting, secured lending, insurance and statutory valuation purposes.

Valuation practice for retirement housing and residential aged care property is considered in detail in this chapter, including the structure of the market, the extensive information required for valuation, common methods of valuation and idiosyncratic issues impacting valuation practice.

Particular focus is placed on the interaction of the property and business aspects of the market and the significant role of government regulation and control. Retirement housing and residential aged care differ from conventional property in that the operational component is inextricably connected with the property component. Therefore, the valuer must understand the nature of these businesses.

This chapter considers the principal forms of retirement housing in Australia and residential aged care, being the provision of care in a residential setting.

Retirement housing

Retirement housing comprises congregate developments, many with communal facilities and services, requiring residents (usually) meet a minimum age requirement or be fully retired in order to enter.

Main types of properties and interests valued

Australian retirement housing includes retirement villages operated under State legislation, rental retirement complexes (rental villages) and age-segregated manufactured home estates (MHE) (also called rental parks, lifestyle villages and/or residential land

DOI: 10.1201/9781003049555-12

lease communities). Specific legislation is applicable to these types of properties and a valuer, like any operator, must be fully cognisant of current legislation.

Retirement villages

Retirement villages are regulated under State and Territory retirement village legislation. A resident on entry agrees to a residence contract with the operator, providing the right to live independently under a variety of tenures including licence, leasehold, company title (rare) and strata title. The residence contract specifies the initial capital payment (typically by way of a loan or non-refundable payment), rental (if applicable), monthly service fees, fee on exit called the deferred management fee (DMF) or exit fee and other contractual payments and obligations.

Retirement villages range from economical models with few features to luxury estates with extensive community and recreation facilities. The main types of dwellings are independent living units (ILU) and independent living apartments (ILA) providing accommodation only and serviced apartments (SA) providing additional hotel style services (commonly housekeeping, linen change and cooked meals).

The operator's interest in an established retirement village entitles them to receive a cash flow from the DMF and a share of the capital appreciation of the dwellings when residents exit and the dwellings are re-let or resold.

Rental villages

Rental villages are regulated under State and Territory tenancy legislation and residents do not reside in the dwellings under retirement village legislation. These range from smaller and older rental complexes operated by not-for-profit (NFP) organisations and governments to more recently constructed complexes with hotel style services operated by for-profit entities.

The operator's interest includes the going concern of the freehold entitling them to receive the ongoing net income from renting dwellings. A complex may be further divided into management rights and underlying land.

Manufactured home estates (MHEs)

MHEs have evolved out of caravan parks and are operated either under State tenancy or specialised MHE legislation. They feature relocatable dwellings where a resident either purchases or rents the dwelling and rents the site from the operator. An operator's interest comprises the going concern of the freehold entitling them to receive the ongoing net income from renting dwellings.

Purpose of valuation

Valuations of retirement housing are required for a number of purposes including:

- mortgage and/or finance purposes where security is required;
- listed and unlisted equity raisings where the asset is packaged for investment;
- advice for acquisition/disposal; and
- development feasibility.

The rise in institutional ownership of this asset class, particularly by listed entities, has resulted in a requirement for valuations for balance sheet reporting purposes. It is increasingly common practice that these valuations are undertaken by accountancy firms.

Deferred management fee and capital gains

The deferred management fee (DMF) results in considerable complexity in undertaking valuations of Australian retirement villages, being paid to the operator when a resident exits the village. Another complex component is the sharing of capital gains (or loss) related to the premises occupied by a resident. The DMF and capital gains may comprise a number of components:

> a percentage fee adjusted for the period of occupancy which is based on either the incoming or resale contribution or 'value' of an individual dwelling. This flat or staged percentage fee is quoted on an annual basis and is usually capped after a number of years;
> a share in the capital growth between the incoming and resale contribution from the perspective of the current resident at a specified ratio (50/50). Where the percentage fee is based on the resale contribution this contains an element of capital gain; and
> depending upon the original occupancy contract there may be further contractual payments. These are essentially cost recovery fees and include the following:
> - a refurbishment or reinstatement contribution requiring the resident to 'make good' the vacated dwelling;
> - a sales commission to meet the costs associated with marketing and selling to the next resident; and
> - a contribution to a sinking fund.

For example, a DMF and capital gain share may include the following:

- a percentage fee levied on the original purchase price of 5% per annum in years 1–4 and 2.5% per annum in years 5–8 to a maximum of 30%. If a resident were to exit after year 10, this percentage fee would still be 30%. If the unit is purchased for $120,000 and sold when the resident exited after year 10 for $160,000 the percentage fee would be $36,000 (30% of $120,000); and
- if the capital gain is shared 50/50 then the capital gain share for the operator would be $20,000 (being 50% of $160,000 – $120,000).

Therefore, simplistically, the operator would receive $56,000 when the resident exited and the dwelling was resold after 10 years plus additional contractual payments. The resident receives the balance of $104,000 ($160,000 less $56,000). If the residents were a couple, then this amount would be received when the last resident departed.

There are numerous permutations of these fees both within and between villages. It is usual for a larger village (100+ dwellings) to have up to 20 different fee structures across the individual dwellings.

In signing the residence contract on entering a village, a resident typically agrees to pay the DMF on exit. In some contracts, the DMF may be expressed as accruing and payable immediately upon entry. Any valuer or purchaser has to be aware of all individual contracts for a retirement village.

Preliminary information required

Due to the complexity of retirement village valuations, considerable preliminary information is required. Information is required from the operator and without this information it is impossible to undertake a valuation. Operators of smaller retirement villages (particularly NFP's) are notable for not keeping good records and the valuer should exercise considerable care to ensure the reliability and currency of the information provided.

In addition to the standard information provided by an owner, a resident schedule detailing the following is required for each retirement village to be valued:

- whether a unit is occupied or vacant;
- date of entry/purchase by the resident;
- ingoing contribution or rental payment;
- gender of the resident;
- current age or date of birth;
- full details of the DMF for each resident;
- share of capital gain;
- operators estimate of current prices for each dwelling; and
- contract type.

As the primary method of valuation is usually a discounted cash flow (DCF), the schedule on which calculations are based should be in an Excel format and include:

- details of any vacant dwellings, including asking prices and whether they are owned by the operator or departed resident;
- copies of standard resident agreements;
- if the village is strata titled:
  - details of the strata levies currently being paid by residents;
  - copy of the management agreement between the body corporate and the operator (if applicable);
- details of the monthly service fees payable by residents;
- details of any capital work fund or sinking fund required to be maintained under the legislation to fund capital maintenance;
- copy of the current Disclosure Statement;
- copies of the village budget for the previous three years and budget for the current year;
- details of the costs incurred by the operator's contribution to refurbishment of individual dwellings over the previous three years;
- if available, copies of the capital expenditure budget and the facilities management plan;
- site plan showing the location of dwellings and community facilities; and
- schedule of existing dwellings and typical floor plans showing:
  - the unit design;
  - level of accommodation; and
  - size (sqm).

The above information relates to an established village but, where there is land available for development, further information is required including:

- copies of development approval;
- proposed site and building plans; and
- schedule of costs (where available).

If this information is not readily forthcoming, the valuer should exercise considerable caution. This list is a minimum and, depending on location and history, further information may be required.

To determine the demand for retirement village accommodation, a demographic study of the catchment area (where most of the residents can be anticipated to originate from) must be undertaken. This determines the population over 65 (number and percentage) and projected growth in both the general population and the over-65 tranche.

As a generalisation, the incoming contribution for retirement village dwellings is less than the median house price for the surrounding area. An analysis of median house and unit prices provides an indication of whether the village is competitively priced. Transaction volumes show the depth of the residential market, which is important as many residents will have to sell their existing property in order to enter the village.

To determine market positioning, an analysis of competing supply needs to be undertaken. This requires identifying all existing and proposed retirement villages in the catchment area. Fieldwork includes not only the physical inspection of the subject property but also external inspection of competing supply.

The valuation of a rental village entails capitalisation of earnings before interest, taxation and depreciation allowances (EBITDA), requiring (preferably audited) financial accounts for the last three years including information on historic and current vacancy levels. Where the valuation is for management rights, a copy of the management agreement is required.

Rental villages, particularly those operated by for-profit entities, operate in a competitive environment requiring an analysis of competing supply. This requires identifying and externally inspecting competing supply in the surrounding area.

The valuation of a MHE entails capitalisation of EBITDA, requiring financial information similar to that for a rental village and retirement village. A further complexity of MHEs is that they may be blended comprising a tourist park and an age-segregated component. Information detailing the split of both dwellings and facilities is required. Some States allow charging a DMF to exiting residents based on the value of the dwelling, such that the information required is the same as that for retirement villages.

Major issues

Retirement villages may have co-located facilities including residential aged care (RAC) and supported accommodation. Where the operator is the same for both components, cross-subsidisation can occur. Where valuations of individual components are required, unravelling these financial arrangements can be difficult.

These assets may be valued for both for-profit and not-for-profit (NFP) operators. Convention is to undertake a valuation without individual taxation considerations except where the DMF is subject to GST. Therefore, a valuer needs to be thoroughly familiar with current taxation legislation and its interpretation.

Valuations are undertaken on a stand-alone basis for each property. Where properties have been amalgamated into a portfolio, this requires a separate adjustment.

Valuation methods

The valuation of retirement housing is based on analysis of comparable sales. To accurately analyse comparable sales, information similar to that required to undertake a valuation is needed. The sector is not noted for high transaction volumes of established properties, requiring thorough analysis of individual sales.

Valuation of established retirement villages is on a going concern basis primarily using a DCF of future cash flows. Valuation firms will usually have their own bespoke valuation model with sufficient flexibility to accommodate a variety of inputs. This DCF model has numerous inputs and a valuer needs to understand the impact of each upon the final assessment of value. It is technically possible to achieve the same final figure using significantly different inputs, requiring an understanding by the valuer of the inter-relationship of these inputs. The major inputs include the following:

- discount rate, with the net cash flows for individual years discounted at a market-driven rate;
- duration, being how long the resident stays in the village. When a resident leaves and a new resident enters (rollover), the operator receives the DMF return. While this timing is essentially unknown, industry analysis determines this duration based on historic factors and current trends. More recently, industry surveys are being developed to provide more reliable information in this area. For current residents, this is based on actuarial life tables less an x factor. For future residents, this is based on a standardised frequency which differs between ILUs and SAs. Some valuation models use a Monte Carlo simulation which incorporates the probability of different resident durations into the cash flow;
- due to the lumpy nature of the cash flows, the DCF needs to be for a longer term with the most common being:
    - 20 years plus terminal value;
    - 25 years plus terminal value;
    - 40 years plus terminal value; or
    - 50 years no terminal value,
  with this longer term incorporating estimates of the village life cycle, including redevelopment and major capital expenditure;
- escalation of prices of village dwellings and expenses. Projections of future dwelling prices are based on historical growth rates and anticipated increases. There is some correlation between the residential market and that for retirement village dwellings. Expenses are escalated at the appropriate inflation rate;
- sale of vacant dwellings:
    - for newly constructed dwellings, this is the gross realisation;
    - where the operator owns the dwelling and has paid out the previous resident, this is the net proceeds (where the contract includes a buyback provision). Under some State legislation, there are requirements to pay out exiting residents within a specified timeframe with prolonged vacancies resulting in shortfalls;
    - where the resident owns the dwelling, this is the DMF;

- refurbishment expenditure with the quantum proportional to the length of residency. Contractual arrangements determine the percentage paid by the resident and by the operator;
- sales costs and commissions;
- shortfalls between monthly fees and actual/budgeted village operating expenses. The village budget is limited by legislation to a cost recovery measure. Operator owned vacant units are required to proportionately contribute to the village budget; and
- operator's capital expenditure on village facilities.

This list is not exhaustive due to the diversity of retirement villages with a valuer's DCF model needing flexibility to accommodate potential variations.

Where the valuation includes additional land or a vacant site, the appropriate method of valuation is hypothetical development to determine residual land value. While this is mostly similar to standard residential calculations, retirement village development differs in that it is undertaken in stages (10–20 dwellings) often over years. Determining the take-up of this completed stock requires an understanding of the future demand for retirement village accommodation in this location. Where a village comprises medium to high density buildings, staging may not be possible. There is inconsistency between valuers as to whether the DMF value of the operational village on completion of development should be included in this valuation.

Valuation of the freehold of a rental village is based on capitalisation of EBITDA similar to a boarding house or motel valuation methodology. Where interests have been split into management rights and underlying land, the management rights are valued on the basis of capitalisation of net operating income (NOI) after deducting rental for the site. The value of the underlying land is based on capitalisation of the rental.

Valuation of MHEs is based on capitalisation of EBITDA but, where a DMF is charged, a DCF valuation similar to a retirement village is required.

Direct comparison may be used as a check method for rental villages and MHEs on a $/dwelling basis.

Residential aged care

Residential aged care (RAC) facilities comprise supported living for older people who need daily assistance (personal and medical) and cannot live alone. In addition to accommodation, RAC facilities provide hotel style services and personal and medical assistance.

Aged care in Australia is subject to regular reviews, policy reinterpretations and changing acronyms. As these can significantly alter the profitability of RAC facilities, a valuer must be thoroughly familiar with the most up-to-date legislation and its impact upon a RAC business.

Legislative and regulatory control

Aged care in Australia is predominantly regulated under the Aged Care Act 1997 (Cth). This legislation facilitates funding for the provision of aged care services and regulates the providers of these services. Commonwealth Government funding is determined by the Aged Care Funding Instrument (ACFI). Providers and RAC facilities must constantly adhere to standards in order to receive government funding for providing care.

Providers of aged care are overseen by the Department of Health (Department). This requires all RAC facilities which receive Commonwealth funding to be accredited in order to receive Commonwealth funding plus resident fees and accommodation payments. The business providing the aged care must be an approved provider holding government issued places (previously called licensed beds) in respect of the services that they provide.

The Commonwealth Government also funds home care to recipients not living in a RAC facility where such recipients may be living in the general community or in retirement housing. To receive this government funding, a recipient must be assessed by an Aged Care Assessment Team (ACAT) as requiring such assistance. This ACAT assessment details the level of required care and assistance and hence the level of government supported funding.

Following the Productivity Commission's *Caring for Older Australians* report in 2011, the Commonwealth Government introduced the Living Longer Living Better Reforms in 2012. These reforms comprised a series of changes to the delivery of aged care over a ten-year period.

In July 2014, new subsidy and fee arrangements for those entering RAC commenced. These removed the classifications of high and low care and replaced them with a matrix of funding depending upon ACAT classification (needs-based). Low care accommodation bonds were removed and Refundable Accommodation Deposits (RAD) and Daily Accommodation Payments (DAP) to pay for all levels of accommodation were introduced. Refundable Accommodation Contributions and Daily Accommodation Contributions were introduced for lower means residents.

In March 2017, allocated places for government-funded Home Care Packages ceased resulting in lower barriers to entry for new entrants to become registered providers of aged care services. Retirement housing operators prepared for these changes by becoming providers and purchasing care and service providers.

By 2022, the distinction between RAC and home care and allocated places for RAC will cease. Recipients of government-funded care may receive this in a RAC facility or other type of accommodation. These recipients will have a choice of care providers and it may technically be possible for a resident in a RAC facility to receive care from another provider.

Interests valued

The most common interest in a RAC facility is that of a going concern where the approved provider is also the property owner. Interests may be further divided into the lessor owning the land and buildings and a management company operating the facility (lessee).

This division into operating company and property company can increase the risk, particularly for the lessor and operator. Where the operating company is the approved provider and holds the approved places, the lessor owns a specialised property requiring a very specialised lessee. If the current operating company were to be placed into receivership, in order to continue to provide services to the residents the lessor (or the operating company's receiver) would have to source a new operating company that was both an approved provider and had the capacity to obtain the allocated places for the facility or had sufficient places. In the event that the lessor or operating company's receiver could not find an alternative operator, alternative accommodation would need to be found for the current residents and the lessor may as a result lose the benefit of receiving government funding. A situation could well arise where the lessor ends up owning a vacant specialised property with few prospects of taking full advantage of its commercial potential.

A further difficulty can arise where the lease is for 30 years or more. The aged care sector is noted for regular policy changes which have the potential to impact upon operating revenue. If market reviews are not sufficiently frequent, the lease has the potential to move into an uncommercial arrangement for either party.

Moreover, under current legislation, the operating company cannot use the RADs to pay the rent and must do so out of operating revenue. They can, however, use the DAPs to pay rent.

Purpose of valuation

Valuations of RAC facilities are required for a number of purposes including the following:

- mortgage and/or finance purposes where security is required;
- listed and unlisted equity raisings:
  - the facility as a going concern; or
  - the underlying land and buildings value where the property is subject to a head lease;
- advice for acquisition/disposal; or
- development feasibility.

Preliminary information required

In addition to the standard information provided by an owner, further information is required for each RAC facility valued including:

- site plan of the property indicating the location of the facility;
- building floor plans showing the location of rooms, back-of-house facilities and community or common areas;
- a schedule of building gross floor areas or building plans to scale;
- a schedule of the current ACFI classifications of residents in the facility;
- details of the number of concessional residents currently in the facility (and the average levels of concessional residents for the past three years);
- a schedule of the number of places available in each facility for the past three years, type of care provided and occupancy levels achieved over the past three years;
- income and expense statements for the previous three financial years and the budget for the current year. This should show government funding received, resident fees received, accommodation charges received, other revenue received and a breakdown of expenses into operational, staff and fixed expenses;
- a schedule of current and historic occupancy levels;
- a schedule of accommodation payments received for the facility, indicating the name of the resident, the total amount and the balance owing (if any);
- copy of the standard resident agreement;

Retirement and aged care property valuation 155

- copy of the latest accreditation report;
- copy of the planning consent for each facility;
- copies of the certificates of accreditation and certification for each facility (as applicable) including the facilities assessment score;
- details of any immediate capital works required if not covered under existing building warranties; and
- copies of any outstanding notices or relevant correspondence from the Department of Health.

Again, some operators are not noted for keeping comprehensive records and, if this information is not readily forthcoming, the valuer should exercise caution. This list is a minimum and, depending on location and history, further information may be required.

Similar to retirement housing, an analysis of competing supply to determine market positioning needs to be undertaken. The Department publishes lists annually of all aged care providers on its website including the number of licensed places. Further, approved providers are required to publish information, usually on their website.

Major issues

A significant proportion of RAC facilities have NFP owners and approved providers. Many NFPs operate RAC facilities at less than commercially optimal levels. It is not unusual to find a facility where accommodation payments and revenue are not being maximised from residents. Convention is to value these properties on the basis of stabilised EBITDA. This requires valuing the property on the basis of average levels of management and then deducting the present value of the shortfall for the time taken to achieve this.

Valuation methods

Valuation of RAC facilities is based on analysis of comparable sales. However, there is significant variation in size, specialisation, quality, age, location and operation of such RAC facilities. Analysis of transactions to determine key metrics requires considerable expertise and skill. Moreover, quoted sale prices may or may not include value attributable to allocated places, plant and equipment.

Valuation of a RAC facility as a going concern is based on the capitalisation of EBITDA, therefore understanding the cash flows is of major importance. The main revenue items comprise DAPs, payments for care, hotel services (linen, meals, cleaning) and accommodation:

- payments for care and hotel services are based on the required level of care as determined by the ACAT assessment. This comprises the following fees:
  - a basic daily care fee, which is paid by all residents (set at a percentage of the age pension);
  - a means tested care fee, where residents are required to contribute to the cost of their care which is means tested. There is a lifetime cap (indexed) on this care fee. For residents with insufficient income and/or assets, the government contributes to bring the total to that required under the ACAT assessment. Residents with insufficient income and/or assets who do not pay the means tested care fee are deemed concessional residents.

The provider receives the level of funding determined by the ACAT assessment, with the proportion paid by the government and by the resident being determined by the resident's financial position;
- payments for other care or hotel services, including enhanced linen change, meals and cleaning of rooms. These comprise the following fees:
  - extra service fees and service packages – some providers have been granted extra service status to allow them to provide an enhanced range of services for which an extra service fee is charged. Similarly, other providers have introduced packages comprising a range of enhanced services; and
  - residents may pay for optional services over and above the general standard offered at that facility. Examples of optional services include pay TV and wine with meals;
- payments for accommodation, with residents expected to pay for their own accommodation, except for concessional residents. The cost of this is partially set by market forces or agreed between the resident and provider on entry into a RAC facility. This can be paid in the following ways:
  - RAD (Refundable Accommodation Deposit) comprising a lump sum agreed between the resident and provider on entry into a RAC facility. It is subject to government set parameters in that a resident must be left with a minimum level of assets after paying the RAD. On exiting the facility, the RAD is refunded less deductions. The permitted deductions include:
    - any accrued daily payment fees (DAPs);
    - any other fees agreed with the resident. These may be described as retention sums or refurbishment fees; and
    - any outstanding fees under the agreement including any means tested care fee;

    A RAD is not a general contribution to capital and there are restrictions as to what it may be used for. It is not permitted to pay down debt for working capital or, where the facility is subject to a lease, it cannot be used for rental payments. A RAD is both an asset and a liability due to the repayment requirement;
  - DAP (Daily Accommodation Payment), comprising a regular payment which a resident may elect to pay out of their existing assets. It is determined by multiplying the maximum accommodation payment agreed with the resident (typically the RAD) by a maximum permissible interest rate (set by the government). The benefit of the DAP is that it may mean residents do not have to sell the family home in order to fund the entry into a RAC facility; and
  - a combination of RAD and DAP. Residents may elect to contribute through a combination of a RAD and a DAP, again agreed with the provider.

Where these payments are subject to parameters set by the Department, these parameters are changed on a six month/annual basis.

Expenses to operate an RAC facility include the following:

- care expenses including health and hygiene supplies, medications, aids and equipment, physiotherapy;
- hotel expenses including catering, food supplies, dietary consultant services, laundry (usually contracted out), cleaning supplies; and

- accommodation expenses including building repairs and maintenance, fire services, air-conditioning, security and fixed utilities such as insurance, electricity, water and council rates.

In addition, there are administration expenses including telephones, computers, legal fees, office supplies, postage and printing. Convention is that payroll expenses are a separate item amalgamating nursing and administrative staff. To fully understand profitability, these need to be apportioned to the relevant classification. RAC is a service industry, consequently salaries constitute the highest expense item in most facilities.

Consultancy companies compile profitability data for a range of RAC facilities and regularly publish benchmarking data with specialist RAC valuers subscribing to these publications. These benchmarks, plus industry experience, enable valuers to determine the appropriate level of profitability for an individual facility.

After determining the stabilised EBITDA, this is then capitalised at an appropriate rate. Further adjustments for shortfalls are then made to derive the final assessment of value.

While the total value of RAD's may be noted in the valuation report, they are not part of the net value of the facility.

Where an RAC facility is the subject of a head lease, the lessee's interest is based on the capitalisation of the NOI less rental expenses. Sufficient numbers of RAC facilities are subject to head leases, therefore there is rental evidence to determine appropriate benchmarks.

The lessor's interest is based on the capitalisation of the net rent. While it is possible to undertake this calculation without details of the operations of the RAC facility, this is not ideal.

Direct comparison is used as a check method on a $/place basis.

Future trends

Future changes to RAC in Australia are expected to facilitate greater flexibility in delivering care to older Australians. Funding of care will be through the recipient not the provider, giving recipients the flexibility to choose (and change) their provider. This is anticipated to open up the provision of aged care services to more innovative models of delivery. RAC is not expected to disappear, however it is anticipated to cater for residents with increasingly higher needs.

Retirement and aged care is a constantly evolving industry, consequently new business models and ways of providing services and accommodation are continually explored. Valuers need to be up to date with current and potential business trends.

Summary

In this chapter, valuation practice for retirement housing and residential aged care property is considered, being a specialist property sector of considerable complexity subject to significant local, State and Commonwealth Government regulation and control.

For each of the key sectors, the principal types of property therein are identified together with the interests to be valued and the typical purposes of the valuation.

Comprehensive guidance is provided concerning the type of information required to undertake a valuation and the common methods of valuation are considered in detail. Complexities such as deferred management fees and the treatment of capital gains are explained in the context of valuation practice.

Retirement housing and residential aged care valuation practice is a particularly dynamic specialism subject to almost continual change of regulation by government to which the market responds through variations to the prevailing models of operation. Being at the interface of valuation as a property and/or as a business, the valuer requires a detailed working knowledge of the sector and the trends prevailing therein.

In the first section of the second part of the book, valuation practice for residential, office, retail, industrial and rural property was considered. In this second section of the second part of this book, valuation practice for specialist property sectors is considered comprising retirement property in this chapter with leisure, plant and equipment and business and intangible asset valuation considered in the following chapters.

The third and final section of the second part of this book addresses valuation practice for specific purposes, including rental, financial reporting, secured lending, insurance and statutory valuation purposes.

Biography

Lois Towart has over 30 years' experience in the real estate and financial services industries. She has extensive experience in the valuation and analysis of different types of retirement housing, residential aged care and medical properties.

The author acknowledges the assistance of Arthur Koumoukelis at Thomson Geer.

13 Leisure property valuation

Robert McIntosh and Wesley Milsom

Introduction

With the first part of this book addressing the principles of valuation, the second part addresses the practice of valuation being grouped into three sections comprising conventional property sectors, specialist property sectors and specific purposes. Conventional property sectors include residential, office, retail, industrial and rural property valuation practice, being considered in previous chapters.

Specialist property sectors include leisure property, which is addressed in this chapter, with retirement property considered in the previous chapter and plant and equipment and business and intangible asset valuation practice being addressed in the following chapters. The third and final section of the second part addresses valuations for specific purposes including valuation practice for rental, financial reporting, secured lending, insurance and statutory valuation purposes.

Valuation practice for leisure property is considered in detail in this chapter, including the range of occupancy forms and the importance of financial data and capital expenditure to the valuation process. Emphasis is placed on the interface between property ownership and business operations in the leisure property sector, where buildings are often purpose built for sole purpose, potentially creating an interdependency for the life of the asset.

Leisure properties

Leisure properties cover a wide range of property types from hotels, motels, pubs, casinos and so forth to theme parks, backpacker hostels and entertainment venues. They are distinguished by being trade related. In other words, they comprise not just real estate but also a business together with all the relevant fixtures, fittings and equipment.

In most cases the properties will be sold with the benefit of the business. The properties may be owner occupied, leased to an operator or the business may be managed by an operator on behalf of the owner under a management agreement.

The location and nature of the properties are extremely varied from luxury hotels in CBD locations to campsites within national parks. Each has its own unique characteristics and appropriate approaches to business. Some may be focused on the quality of improvements, others on technology and service levels while some are entirely reliant on domestic demand and others on that from overseas.

It is essential that the valuer understands the nature of the business and the property as well as the opportunities and the risks. This requires more than a simple

DOI: 10.1201/9781003049555-13

understanding of real estate. It requires, amongst other things, knowledge of the business operations, the demand drivers and the buyers' rationale and motivation.

There are several characteristics that distinguish leisure properties from commercial real estate. These include:

- the short-term nature of the income (usually daily) compared with leased properties;
- the resultant relative volatility of the income;
- the even greater volatility of the net income since many of the costs are fixed and comprise a higher proportion of revenue than for commercial buildings;
- the need for active management – even if there is a manager, the asset management relates to the business not just the maintenance of the property; and
- the need for regular capital expenditure at a much higher level than for commercial property.

In most cases, leisure properties can be valued using similar principles but valuers should not attempt such work without the appropriate expertise in the relevant area.

Understanding the financials

Each business type in the leisure industry will have its own format and key measures and terms. The valuer needs to know these in order to comprehend the business and its potential. In pubs it may be revenue per department per week, in hotels the ADR (average daily rate), occupancy and RevPAR (revenue per available room), in gaming venues it may be turnover or win rate. Each industry has its own benchmarks which enable comparison between properties and businesses to provide a better understanding of the operations.

In hotels, for example, there is a globally recognised and adopted accounting approach called the Uniform System of Accounts. This covers all aspects of hotel accounting including what income and costs should be allocated to each department (room, food and beverage, telephones etc.) as well as central costs such as administration, maintenance and utilities. This enables comparison to be made between different revenue and cost items quickly and efficiently. The methods of comparison include analysis as a percentage of either total or departmental revenues or per available room or per occupied room.

In many businesses there will be parts that are relatively profitable and others less so. In hotels, the rooms usually produce a much higher profit as a percentage of revenue compared with food and beverage. Understanding the sources of the revenues and matters such as the proportion of fixed and variable costs and, particularly in Australia, personnel costs can all be more easily achieved using industry benchmarks and standardisation helps with this. Therefore, knowing that in a luxury hotel housekeepers may only clean between 10 and 12 rooms a day and that in economy hotels the figure may be closer to 20 enables a rapid analysis of historic figures and permits the valuer to identify areas for improvement or existing excellence.

This is true in all types of leisure properties. In gaming venues, understanding which elements are the highest revenue earners and which have the greatest margins is vital, as is knowing where the clients come from, why and their capacity to spend? In theme parks, it may be what are the key attractions, how to capture additional spend, what are the holiday cycles and how often do rides need to be replaced?

Hotel financials

Hotel financial reports prepared in accordance with the Uniform System of Accounts separate income and costs into specific areas.

Revenues are divided between Rooms, Food, Beverage, Other Food and Beverage, Telephones and Communications and other specific areas such as Spas, Rentals and so forth. Costs relating directly to these departments are then allocated. All the labour, costs of sales (in Rooms this could be room's supplies, in Food the cost of the food itself) and other costs are carefully allocated. Each department then has its own P&L, targets and budgets. All of this can be analysed in detail down to how many covers there are for lunch, the cost of that food and so forth.

The central costs of Administration, Sales and Marketing, Property Maintenance and Utilities are then each deducted to give a gross profit. From this is deducted the management fees and the owner's costs such as rates and taxes, property insurance and property rental to give the EBITDA. Finally, the Furniture, Fittings and Equipment (FF&E) allowance is made to give the net income. It is this net income that is normally used when valuing hotels.

The proportion of revenues and costs vary significantly depending upon many factors such as the nature of the hotel and its location. In summary, however, in Australia Rooms usually comprise the largest revenue item and the most profitable (departmental costs are 15% to 35% of room revenues). Food and Beverage profits on the other hand tend to be in the 15% to 35% level. The combined central or undistributed costs may be 15% to 25% of revenues. Management costs have been coming down and Base Fees are now commonly 1% to 1.5% of revenue and Incentive Fees 5% to 9% of Gross Operating Profit (GOP) after the Base Fee has been deducted.

The result is that the net income tends to be in the range of 25% to 55% of total revenue with the lower proportions achieved by luxury hotels and the higher figures by limited service hotels (albeit off a lower revenue figure).

Other leisure property financials

Other leisure operations typically provide their financials in accordance with a financial reporting format whereby the revenue lines are reported separately to the costs. Revenue and costs are generally benchmarked against comparable operations on a weekly or percentage basis.

A pub, for example, could have Bars, Bottles, Gaming, Food, Accommodation and so forth as revenue lines which, after an allowance for the cost of goods, gaming taxes and so forth are combined to provide the GOP for the venue. Cost items including Accounting, Payroll, Subscriptions, Replacements and Utilities are then deducted to provide an EBITDA for the property. The profitability of pubs can vary greatly depending on the mix of the business, for example being predominately a gaming venue or a food and beverage operation.

Management structures – the pros and cons

As indicated earlier, it is important to identify the way in which a property is managed and the structure, with the main alternatives comprising the following aspects.

Owner operated

In this case, the owner also runs the business. This means that there is no separation of roles. The owner may employ a manager to act on his or her behalf but the success or otherwise of the enterprise rests with the owner. This is, therefore, capital-intensive and, in the case of many leisure properties, requires considerable time and effort. The owner needs expertise in the relevant business in order to optimise results and this means both marketing and operations.

Leased

In this case, the business is run by a lessee who, in effect, owns the business. The property owner has only the real estate. This offers a degree of separation and specialisation. The lessee does not tie up capital in real estate and can therefore invest more in marketing and management. The lessor takes less risk and therefore receives a lower return but a more stable income stream. The lessee bears the risk of having to ensure that the business is profitable enough to be able to pay the rental on a regular basis, with the profitability of the lessee critical to operations and overall valuation.

Since most hotel owners wish to maximise returns, this structure is not common in Australia with operators preferring to enter into management agreements. However, there are a large number of pubs that operate subject to a lease. Historically, a number of lessees had entered into agreements that became unaffordable due to a change in business such as the introduction of smoking legislation. Agreements now typically provide the lessee greater scope to ensure the viability of the business and success of the investment.

It is crucial for a valuer undertaking a valuation of a leased asset to understand the viability of the business and not just apply a yield to the rental income. If the lessee does not provide the business trade for analysis, then the valuer should proceed with caution, benchmarking the business assuming fair average management.

Management agreement

In this structure the business is managed by a specialist operator as an agent on behalf of the owner. It is the owner's business but there is a contract with a company that will assume management responsibility in return for a fee (usually a percentage of revenue and gross profit). The owner has little say in the business, other than an annual review of the budgets. The owner has access to specialised marketing and management systems (either domestic or international) and has a relatively passive role. However, the owner is reliant upon the success of the operator and the income is variable.

Others

There are other structures such as franchise or, more recently, manchise. In these structures, the owner has more direct control of the operations but uses a hotel management company to market the property or provide room bookings.

Understanding the supply and demand issues

The performance of leisure properties is highly dependent upon the business operations. Unlike many other property types, such as offices and industrial which are dependent upon the general levels of supply and demand and the local economy, leisure properties depend upon the success of the individual businesses run within them. There are, therefore, several key issues to consider when valuing such assets.

Demand drivers

A good understanding of the sources and nature of demand is vital. Is the general demand international or domestic? Where does it come from specifically, is it corporate or leisure, what is the proportion of group business or air crew, how cyclical is the demand (by season, month, week or even day of the week)? For example, a specific focus on a high yielding sector may maximise profits in the short term but what are the risks of this continuing? Would greater diversity improve sustainability of the business? Such considerations need analysis from the viewpoint of the market as a whole and then from the viewpoint of the property specifically.

Reviewing and understanding historical trends

The first step in understanding leisure properties is to review and investigate the trends in the location. What is the existing business in the region and for the property and what are the trends, opportunities and challenges? For example, a gaming venue may benefit from surrounding businesses that have recently opened such that relying on the historical performance could be incorrect. The valuer needs to establish whether the increased revenue is sustainable and likely to continue.

Valuers need to consider the relationship between supply and demand and the impact of each. For example, for accommodation hotels there is often a balance point for occupancy in each market. Below this, ADR rates tend to fall and above this they rise. For resorts this may be only 60% to 65% but in city hotels it may be 80% to 85%. A review of the trends will indicate key factors such as whether changes to accessibility (such as more flights or a new motorway) have changed total demand levels. Interestingly, leisure properties also have the propensity to create their own supply induced demand. In other words, the creation of a new property could increase the total level of demand in that location.

Forecasting

Once a good understanding of historical trends has been completed, the valuer is in a position to estimate the future supply and demand levels. Whilst based on factual information, this requires a degree of careful subjective judgement. Normally supply is easier to estimate, at least in the short term, than demand. Demand can be highly volatile and in the short term uncertain. For example, a disruption to airlines due to matters such as volcanic activity or terrorism events can, and does, have an immediate impact on demand. Likewise, the introduction of a new bar could have significant impacts on the overall performance of an established business. Investigating the trends and likely events is fraught with difficulty but an essential part of a valuer's role, since that which buyers consider when bidding for properties is the likely future income of the property.

Capital expenditure in leisure properties

Capital expenditure (capex) in leisure properties is an issue of major significance. Most other property types require some regular upgrade but, since leisure properties are let on a daily basis rather than for several years, it is essential to keep them up to date and operating efficiently. Also, since leisure properties include the business, there are more elements involved than in most other property types.

When valuing pubs, motels and the like, it is normal to project the income based on the assumption that the property is in reasonable condition and then make an allowance for any expenditure necessary. For international hotels, casinos and major tourism properties, there is a clear need for regular upgrade (for hotels, this is often considered to be a period of five to seven years). Since this is regularly required, it is normal to reflect by allowing a percentage of total revenue on an annual basis.

This has been reinforced by the fact that most management agreements provide for the owner to make a regular provision for an FF&E replacement reserve which is usually 3% to 4% of total revenue. In reality, this probably understates the total requirement. Research in the United States indicates that, for properties over ten years of age, the actual expenditure averages 6% to 9%. It is, therefore, normal to allow for a deduction of 3% to 4% of revenue when both analysing sales and valuing hotels.

Trends in operations and developments

In recent years there have been many changes in the hospitality industries. There has been an increased emphasis on maximising returns and minimising costs in all sectors and this has led to various changes. For example, labour costs in Australia are high compared with the rest of Asia. Therefore, there is increased emphasis on multiskilling and productivity. An Australian hotel may have only 20% to 25% of the number of employees of some Asian hotels which means that the service levels may be very different. This becomes a challenge for operators who wish to provide a global standard level of service. Some of the major changes in the hospitality industries are considered further, below.

Demand

Demand levels and requirements are constantly evolving. What was acceptable ten years ago in terms of facilities and experiences is no longer valid. For motels, it may be the TV and movie services and the accessibility of Wi-Fi. For gaming venues, it may be the types of games and the ambience. In hotels, the changes are numerous and the rate of change is increasing. There has been a trend away from large and often tired rooms to smaller rooms with better facilities and increased modernity. There is now an emphasis on communal space for working, more lifestyle products and luxury has a different meaning.

Changes in demand sources are leading to significant alterations in service offerings. In particular, the rapid and substantial growth of visitors from China has meant changes in staffing skills, menu selections and the mix of accommodation. Such changes have occurred before such as in the late 1980s when Japanese visitors all required bathtubs and not showers, meaning that many hotel rooms were simply not suitable for what were then the highest-yielding guests.

Newly developing demand segments from different generations are also encouraging alterations in the product offerings and new brands are being created to match these needs and the increased affluence of younger generations.

Ensuring operational efficiency

The costs of running hotels have been increasingly under pressure. Those operators who can provide the best returns are expanding and others have had to change their business models. This has included such changes as:

- the outsourcing of housekeeping and other services – with hoteliers, in many but not all cases, increasing their emphasis on marketing and service levels with more flexibility in terms of staffing levels if the outsourcing model is used;
- laundry and associated services – a large laundry was a normal feature of many quality hotels but this is no longer the case. External providers have proved more efficient and the capital cost of the equipment is so high and the labour issues so significant that the move to close laundries has, in many cases, been an easy decision;
- the multiskilling of staff – there is less emphasis on working on the front desk or being a waiter and more on being a service provider to guests and being able to switch from one role to another; and
- central services – operators are increasingly adopting a shared service centre for marketing and accounting in particular and in many cases for HR and even management, if hotels under one management company are in close vicinity to each other. Procurement has also been improved dramatically with the move away from individual hotels buying goods and services being relentless and rapid. Whether it be insurance, beds or utilities, the freeing up of markets has pushed prices down, particularly if the benefits of scale can be used.

An absolute focus on operational efficiency has led to a number of new hotels being added to supply. These tend to be in the limited service sector and, in many cases, have standardised smaller rooms, consistent service standards, limited food and beverage and can be operated with fewer staff than traditional hotels. This has enabled developers of hotels to compete for sites which previously achieved better returns for alternative uses.

Developments

Changes in design and finishes have helped reduce construction costs. New building techniques have led to faster construction times and standardisation has enabled facilities, such as bathrooms, to be manufactured off-site and delivered as a completed product.

Disruptive technologies

Much has been made recently of the threat of peer to peer accommodation providers such as Airbnb. Such challenges are not new. When Internet marketing first started there was much concern amongst hoteliers as rooms were being sold at heavy discounts on a last minute basis. It took a little while for operators to fully embrace the changes and now Internet marketing is regarded as one of the best and cheapest distribution channels (though the commission costs for booking through an operators own website are probably the lowest of all).

This new challenge is somewhat different, comprising an alternative form of accommodation competing with hotels. There are still many differentiators such as service levels, the question of legality in some markets, location and so forth. There is no doubt, however, that they are now part of the tourism market. Research in more mature markets such as the United States indicates that the new variety of offerings are creating new demand levels and are not having a significant impact on hotel performance. However, the new offerings market is still in a nascent stage and could change.

Operators

Reference has already been made to the creation of new brands. Many of the major operators now have multiple brands and there is increasing pressure to merge and obtain greater efficiencies using larger businesses. Part of this is driven by the increased cost of technology but also by the pressure to reduce costs. Some groups now have over 20 brands in their stable and this number is growing. The recent mergers of Marriott Hotels & Resorts with Starwood Hotels and of Accor Hotels with Fairmont Raffles International Hotels are examples.

Operators have also become 'asset-lite' with most selling all their properties as investors and analysts prefer to see specialisation in either hotel operations or investment but not the two mixed together. This has led to the disposal of many hotels and resorts.

The investment market and purchasers

Probably the most important element in preparing the valuation of leisure properties is understanding the purchaser. This includes their capacity to buy, motivation and exactly what they require. A simple analysis of sales without a good understanding of the motivation of individual buyers can lead to a complete misunderstanding of the market.

Leisure properties are quite unlike other commercial property types in terms of buyer demand, as illustrated in the following examples:

- a few years ago a major Sydney hotel was rejected by Asian high net worth individuals due to certain Feng Shui elements. It sold to an American corporation. It has since resold to an Asian group that was more institutional in nature and where the main motivation was returns;
- the sale of a very similar hotel to one that had sold for a record price. The market had improved but the second hotel attracted much more limited demand as it was subject to a long-term management contract, whereas the former property's agreement had only one year to run and the buyer was an operating company which was very keen to become established in that market and could take over operations when the agreement ended;
- the recent trend in the lowering of yields to near record levels for top tier hotels in Sydney and Melbourne has been driven by Asian buyers with a lower cost of

capital than Australians. Should their ability to buy be reduced, a new type of buyer could have a very different pricing rationale; and
- one key issue in hotels is not only the return on investment but also the return on ego. The wish to own a hotel of quality and substance, particularly if attractive, can drive investors to buy more than income.

It is, therefore, apparent that an understanding of the motivation and reasoning of each investor is vital. Leisure assets are not homogeneous products. Each has its own characteristics and advantages and disadvantages and the valuer needs to understand these and how they match buyers' expectations.

Valuing a leisure property

There are several well-established steps in valuing a leisure property and in matters that should be addressed in a valuation report, including the following.

Tourism and leisure market

A review of the market in which the property sits and competes is normally undertaken and provided. This may address historic supply and demand trends at national, State and local levels. This can include the economy, exchange rates, access, sources of demand, supply trends, ADR, occupancy and RevPAR changes and trends as well as competitive and complementary properties.

Historic trading

If the business has a trading record, this is normally reviewed in detail and compared with other competitors not just in terms of revenues and costs but also positioning, operations, standards and so forth. There is always inherent risk with new hotels, as operations typically take three years to reach a mature level. Conversely, a new pub could actually perform at higher levels in its initial year of operation, as patrons wish to utilise the new facilities. The risk for a valuer, therefore, is to determine if the levels achieved are sustainable or may reduce once the 'honeymoon' period concludes.

Sales

The review of historic sales may include not only matters such as initial yields and IRRs as well as direct comparison approaches (such as value per room) but also discussion of the motivation and rationale of buyers and the trends. Understanding any capital expenditure, plans to reposition the asset or future development opportunities must also be considered.

Forecasts

It is now normal in most business-related valuations for the valuer to prepare a forecast of the likely operations. For pubs, this may only be for one year under 'normal' management. For accommodation hotels, forecasts of up to ten years are common. Such projections are often intended to reflect the expectation of likely buyers and are related to the specific manager – not just the 'normal' manager. As with understanding a comparable sale, the impacts of any capital expenditure or future development opportunities must also be considered. Any major capital expenditure reflected in the cash flow forecast should not only reflect any possible improvements in trade once the works have been completed but also impacts on the business while the works are being undertaken.

Valuation

It is normal for valuers to adopt a range of approaches and achieve a balance of these or at least to reflect the approach taken by the most likely buyers for the property. Typical approaches include the initial yield approach, stabilised yield approach, discounted cash flow and direct comparison.

COVID-19

The impact on the demand for, the operation of, the resultant cash flows from and the values of leisure properties due to the COVID-19 pandemic has been considerable and varied. Substantial changes in the guest profiles, particularly from the international and conference sectors, have occurred and are likely to be continued for some time. Contemporaneously intrastate, domestic leisure demand has increased substantially. As a result of the pandemic, hoteliers are looking to change business practices such as cleaning protocols, reducing staff numbers and removing some facilities such as self-service restaurants.

The major difference when leisure assets are compared to other property sectors is that the cash flow of the property can, quite literally, be reduced to zero overnight (as happened with government intervention closing hospitality venues) but can also bounce back to previous levels just as quickly (or even greater than before as experienced in regional locations due to pent up travel demands).

The length and depth of the impact of the pandemic is unclear at the time of writing, hence there is considerable uncertainty as to future cash flows. The result is an inevitable reduction in buyer interest in most properties. However, specific segments have continued to perform well and this, coupled with low interest rates, has prevented drops in value similar to those seen in the United States or Europe. The valuation of such properties has seldom been as challenging and complex. The need to discuss the implications and effects with operators, vendors and buyers has never been greater to ensure a proper understanding of the market.

Summary

In this chapter, valuation practice for leisure property is considered, being a specialist property sector of considerable complexity within a fast moving, dynamic and global property market. With a wide range of occupancy forms found across different types of leisure property, the significance of the business operating within the leisure property is emphasised through a detailed analysis of that financial and capital expenditure data required to undertake a valuation.

Reflecting the interface between property ownership and business operations, the importance of supply and demand together with market trends, evolving user preferences and investor preferences are explored and their impact on the leisure property market considered.

In the first section of the second part of the book, valuation practice for residential, office, retail, industrial and rural property was considered. In this second section of the second part of this book, valuation practice for specialist property sectors is considered comprising leisure property in this chapter with retirement property considered in the previous chapter and plant and equipment and business and intangible asset valuation considered in the following chapters.

The third and final section of the second part addresses valuation practice for specific purposes, including rental, financial reporting, secured lending, insurance and statutory valuation purposes.

Biography

Robert McIntosh is the Executive Director responsible for advisory and valuation work in CBRE Hotels in Asia Pacific. Based in Sydney, he has over 40 year's property experience, 30 of which are in hotels. He has spent eight of these years living in Asia and valuing leisure properties across the continent. His experience includes resorts in the Maldives and French Polynesia, City hotels in many countries, golf courses, casinos in Singapore, Macau and Australia, theme parks, pubs, hotels and motels.

Robert's experience has been wide ranging in terms of geography, property type and skills. He has been involved in advisory, valuation, operator selection, consulting and sales assignments throughout the Asia Pacific region. In addition, he has advised on the restructuring of various portfolios, due diligence assignments and the listing of real estate assets.

Robert has developed advanced financial models for commercial, retail and hotel properties. He has also been involved in numerous conferences as a speaker and moderator. He has also provided expert evidence in respect of various property-related matters. Robert has considerable experience in related associations, having been a board member of the Sydney Visitors and Convention Bureau and serving on various professional committees of organisations such as the API and RICS.

Wesley Milsom is the Director of Investments at Elanor Investors, focusing on hotel and leisure assets. Previously he was the National Director of CBRE Hotels responsible for advisory and valuation work for hotels in Australia and the Pacific. Based in Sydney, he has over 15 year's property experience, 13 of which are in hotels. His experience includes major international hotels, resorts, motels, golf courses, casinos, theme parks, pubs, clubs and motels across Australia and the Pacific including destinations such as, Fiji, Vanuatu, PNG, French Polynesia and Samoa.

Wesley's experience has been wide ranging in terms of geography, property type and skills. He has been involved in advisory, valuation, consulting and sales assignments throughout the Pacific region.

14 Plant and equipment valuation

Greg Rowe and Roy Farthing

Acknowledgement

This chapter draws heavily on chapter 19 in *Valuation Principles and Practice* (2007) (Second Edition, Australian Property Institute, Deakin) by Roy Farthing which is duly acknowledged here rather than individually referenced through this chapter and to which readers are referred for a deeper consideration.

Introduction

With the first part of this book addressing the principles of valuation, the second part addresses the practice of valuation being grouped into three sections comprising conventional property sectors, specialist property sectors and specific purposes. Conventional property sectors include residential, office, retail, industrial and rural property valuation practice, being considered in previous chapters.

Specialist property sectors include retirement property and leisure property, which were addressed in previous chapters, plant and equipment which is considered in this chapter and business and intangible asset valuation practice which is addressed in the following chapter. The third and final section of the second part addresses valuations for specific purposes including valuation practice for rental, financial reporting, secured lending, insurance and statutory valuation purposes.

Valuation practice for plant and equipment is considered in detail in this chapter, focusing on identification of assets for valuation, materiality and application of the market approach and cost approach to the specialist nature of plant and equipment at both the individual asset and entire facility levels.

Purpose and scope of valuation

Plant and equipment valuation may be required primarily for a range of purposes, including:

- financial reporting;
- tax compliance;
- stamp duty;
- regulatory pricing;
- insurance;

DOI: 10.1201/9781003049555-14

- loan security;
- acquisition; and
- disposal,

which are each considered further, below.

To determine the scope of the valuation, the valuer should identify those assets which are to be the subject of the valuation. This task will normally be completed by a combination of physical inspections of the assets and a reconciliation of the company's fixed asset records with the assets in existence.

Building fixtures should be carefully identified and separately classified, with consultation between the different specialist valuers, the client and the client's advisers sometimes required to determine the appropriate classification.

Plant, machinery and equipment assets are non-realty assets that manifest themselves by their physical presence. They are tangible assets that usually generate income (provide economic returns) for their owner. Plant, machinery and equipment assets can be categorised as tangible assets and often as personal property and may exist as individual items or as part of a system of items that perform a specific function.

Tangible assets are assets that are of a physical and material nature. Personal property assets are tangible assets that are not permanently affixed to real estate and can be moved. A general definition of personal property is anything and everything except intangibles, that is not real estate and/or not permanently attached to real estate. System assets are assemblies of items, related by their proximity, interconnection and/or integration that perform a function collectively.

A fundamental requirement of the plant and equipment valuation process is to adequately record and describe the subject assets, with the valuer noting the following data:

- description;
- manufacturer;
- model or type number;
- size and/or capacity;
- serial number; and
- description of modifications and attachments.

Certain other additional information may be required such as the asset number, asset class or category, date of manufacture, condition, amount of use and so forth. Such additional information will be determined by the nature of the valuation required and the scope of work agreed with the client.

The technical information recorded by the valuer is required to ensure that comparable sales information or current replacement cost information obtained during the research phase of the project is relevant.

Materiality

Valuations of plant and equipment can range from a valuation of a single asset to a valuation of literally thousands of individual assets spread across a number of sites (possibly worldwide). To apply the same level of rigour to the low-value assets within a client's portfolio as to the high value assets can be counter-productive and might be interpreted as over-servicing a client.

Accordingly, valuers will generally place greatest emphasis on those assets that are material in the context of the valuation they are completing. What is material in one valuation may be immaterial in another. In considering the question of materiality, valuers should ensure that the way in which they focus on the assets does not impact on the reliability of the overall valuation conclusion.

Valuations for financial reporting purposes

Valuation for financial reporting purposes generally is addressed in Chapter 17, including details of relevant International Accounting Standards, Australian Accounting Standards, International Financial Reporting Standards and International Valuation Standards.

From the viewpoint of plant and equipment, assets for valuation should be classified by directors or senior officers of the instructing entity as either operational assets or non-operational assets, as this will determine the appropriate valuation method for the particular asset.

Operational assets are those assets being used in the operation of the entity and which are held for their continued use or service potential for the foreseeable future. Non-operational assets are those assets which are not integral to the operation of the entity and may be further classified as surplus assets (held for sale) or investments.

Bases of value

The Australian Accounting Standards allow reporting entities to record values using either the cost or revaluation model. Valuers are principally concerned where the revaluation model has been adopted with the value of the assets required to be reported at Fair Value.

AASB 13 – Fair Value Measurement mirrors IFRS 13; however, it includes notes to Australian circumstances. The Standard, which commenced in 2015, defines Fair Value, sets out a single framework for measurement and requires various disclosures. AASB 13 applies when other standards require or permit Fair Value Measurement. It does not apply in some instances relating to AASB 117 Leases and AASB 136 Impairment of Assets. The Standards also require that the acquisition cost of assets acquired as part of a business combination be determined based on Fair Value.

AASB 13 defines fair value as:

> The price that would be received to sell an asset or paid to transfer a liability in an orderly transaction between market participants at the measurement date.

It goes on to further define Fair Value as the price that would be received to sell an asset or paid to transfer a liability in an orderly transaction in the principal (or most advantageous) market at the measurement date under current market conditions regardless of whether that price is directly observable or estimated using another valuation technique.

AASB 13 also includes a section on application to non-financial assets, noting the principle of highest and best physically possible, legally permissible and financially feasible use. The Standard also discusses valuation techniques noting that an entity shall use valuation techniques that are appropriate in the circumstances and for which sufficient data are available to measure Fair Value, maximising the use of the relevant observable inputs and minimising the use of unobservable inputs. The Standard also discusses Level 1, Level 2 and Level 3 inputs to the assessment of Fair Value.

For the majority of specialised plant and equipment assets, highest and best use will usually be the existing use of the assets installed and operating as part of a continuing business. However, this will not always be the case.

Underlying the definition of Fair Value is a presumption that the entity is a going concern without any intention or need to liquidate, to curtail materially the scale of its operations or to undertake a transaction on adverse terms. It has been generally interpreted that this should only apply to the extent that the entity is in fact a going concern.

Whilst the accounting standards require the use of Fair Value for financial reporting purposes, International Valuation Standards use and define Market Value. In most circumstances, the terms Fair Value and Market Value can be used interchangeably as they are premised upon very similar valuation principles.

IVS (2019), which is adopted by API, defines market value as follows:

> Market Value is the estimated amount for which an asset or liability should exchange on the valuation date between a willing buyer and a willing seller in an arm's length transaction, after proper marketing and where the parties had each acted knowledgeably, prudently and without compulsion.

The IVSC definition of 'market value' is applied in accordance with the following conceptual framework:

a 'The estimated amount' refers to a price expressed in terms of money payable for the asset in an arm's length market transaction. Market value is the most probable price reasonably obtainable in the market on the valuation date in keeping with the market value definition. It is the best price reasonably obtainable by the seller and the most advantageous price reasonably obtainable by the buyer. This estimate specifically excludes an estimated price inflated or deflated by special terms or circumstances such as atypical financing, sale and leaseback arrangement, special considerations or concessions granted by anyone associated with the sale, or any element of special value available only to a specific owner or purchaser;

b 'An asset or Liability should exchange' refers to the fact that the value of an asset or liability is an estimated amount rather than a predetermined amount or actual sale price. It is the price in a transaction that meets all the elements of the market value definition at the valuation date;

c 'On the valuation date' requires that the value is time-specific as of a given date. Because markets and market conditions may change, the estimated value may be incorrect or inappropriate at another time. The valuation amount will reflect the market state and circumstances as at the valuation date, not those at any other date;

d 'Between a willing buyer' refers to one who is motivated, but not compelled to buy. This buyer is neither over eager nor determined to buy at any price. This buyer is also one who purchases in accordance with the realities of the current market and with current market expectations, rather than in relation to an imaginary or hypothetical market that cannot be demonstrated or anticipated to exist. The assumed buyer would not pay a higher price than the market requires. The present owner is included among those who constitute 'the market';

e   'And a willing seller' is neither an over eager nor a forced seller prepared to sell at any price, nor one prepared to hold out for a price not considered reasonable in the current market. The willing seller is motivated to sell the asset at market terms for the best price attainable in the open market after proper marketing, whatever that price may be. The factual circumstances of the actual owner are not a part of this consideration because the willing seller is a hypothetical owner;

f   'In an arm's length transaction' is one between parties who do not have a particular or special relationship, e.g. parent and subsidiary companies or landlord and tenant that may make the price level uncharacteristic of the market or inflated. The market value transaction is presumed to be between unrelated parties, each acting independently;

g   'After proper marketing' means that the asset has been exposed to the market in the most appropriate manner to effect its disposal at the best price reasonably obtainable in accordance with the market value definition. The method of sale is deemed to be that most appropriate to obtain the best price in the market to which the seller has access. The length of exposure time is not a fixed period but will vary according to the type of asset and market conditions. The only criterion is that there must have been sufficient time to allow the asset to be brought to the attention of an adequate number of market participants. The exposure period occurs prior to the valuation date;

h   'Where the parties had each acted knowledgeably, prudently' presumes that both the willing buyer and the willing seller are reasonably informed about the nature and characteristics of the asset, its actual and potential uses and the state of the market as of the valuation date. Each is further presumed to use that knowledge prudently to seek the price that is most favourable for their respective positions in the transaction. Prudence is assessed by referring to the state of the market at the valuation date, not with benefit of hindsight at some later date. For example, it is not necessarily imprudent for a seller to sell assets in a market with falling prices at a price that is lower than previous market levels. In such cases, as is true for other exchanges in markets with changing prices, the prudent buyer or seller will act in accordance with the best market information available at the time;

i   'And without compulsion' establishes that each party is motivated to undertake the transaction, but neither is forced or unduly coerced to complete it.

While the IVSC and API consider that Market Value will be synonymous with Fair Value in the vast majority of situations, valuers will not be in a position to determine whether this is the case where the value of tangible assets has been determined using the depreciated replacement cost approach subject to the test of adequate profitability (or test of service potential in the case of a not-for-profit enterprise). This is because to be able to make that judgement, one must be able to compare the total value of all assets and liabilities used by a cash-generating unit with the Net Present Value of the cash flows generated by that cash-generating unit.

The Appendix of AASB 5 defines a cash-generating unit as follows:

> The smallest identifiable group of assets that generates cash inflows that are largely independent of the cash inflows from other assets or groups of assets.

Therefore, to be able to make that comparison it is necessary to have access to the valuations of all tangible and intangible assets, all current and non-current assets and liabilities and the cash flows of the cash-generating unit. In the majority of cases, only the management of the reporting entity will be in a position to make that judgement. However, valuers should be cognisant of the process that the reporting entity is required to follow and be prepared to assist management in reaching an appropriate conclusion.

The test of adequate profitability in the case of a for-profit enterprise is required because the value of specialised assets that rarely trade separate from the business in occupation is usually inextricably tied to the net cash flows that can be generated from the use of those assets.

Where a going concern does not exist, or where the assets are surplus to the business, the assets should be valued on the basis of Net Realisable Value. Net Realisable Value is a term referring to the estimated selling price of an asset in the ordinary course of business, less selling costs and costs of completion. As such, it is akin to Market Value less disposal costs, only where all requirements of the Market Value definition are met.

In certain circumstances, surplus non-operational assets will be valued on the basis of Salvage Value or Scrap Value as appropriate. The American Society of Appraisers defines Salvage Value as follows:

> An opinion of the amount, expressed in terms of money that may be expected for the whole property or a component of the whole property that is retired from service for possible use elsewhere, as of a specific date.

and defines Scrap Value as follows:

> An opinion of the amount, expressed in terms of money that could be realised for the property if it were sold for its material content, not for a productive use, as of a specific date.

The International Valuation Standards provide three acceptable valuation approaches to determine Market Value for plant and equipment:

- market approach;
- cost approach; and/or
- income approach,

which will be considered further, below.

Market approach

In applying the Market Approach (or market comparison approach), the valuer should research both the national and international markets (as applicable) to determine whether any recent sales of similar equipment have occurred. The valuer should seek to identify sales of assets of the same make, model or type, age and condition. In analysing such comparable sales information, it is critical that the valuer be aware of the different qualities and capacities of alternative makes and models of equipment.

Sources of comparable sales evidence may include:

- publicly reported sales;
- published value guides;
- the Internet;
- trade journals advertising assets for sale;
- attendance at auction sales;
- client records of second-hand purchases and disposals; and
- manufacturer's suggested trade-in prices.

For assets which are exchanged commonly in the marketplace, there is an abundance of suitable market evidence. In those instances, the Market Approach provides a reliable valuation tool for the valuer.

Adjustments may need to be made to those recorded transactions to take account of differences in the timing, location, background and subject matter of the recorded transactions as compared to the assets being appraised.

Comparable sales evidence may arise from the sale of comparable individual machines or assets (to which an amount equal to the depreciated replacement cost of the installation of the asset should be added) or from the sale of entire facilities that are comparable (to which adjustment for location, timing and other factors that may affect the level of value should be made).

Comparable sales of entire facilities may be available and useful for process plants such as abattoirs, petrochemical plants, power stations and so forth but would generally not be appropriate for facilities such as engineering works and specialised manufacturing plants where the type and configuration of equipment and product are not generally comparable from one facility to the next. Naturally, the context, location and circumstances surrounding the transaction must be fully investigated in order to establish its relevance for market comparison purposes.

Cost approach

The Cost Approach (or depreciated replacement cost (DRC) approach) is generally used to determine the value of specialised assets which rarely, if ever, trade in the open market except as part of a business in occupation. Many types of plant and equipment fall into this category which is considered extensively in API (2007).

Various State and Federal Treasuries and regulatory authorities, such as the Australian Competition and Consumer Commission (ACCC), have adopted the term 'Optimised Depreciated Replacement Cost' (ODRC). This approach is the same in practice as a properly applied DRC approach. It merely places a greater focus on the optimisation process which should be inherent in any DRC valuation.

The DRC approach involves establishing the Gross Current Replacement Cost (GCRC) of the asset after determining any optimisation factors and then depreciating this value to reflect the anticipated effective working life of the asset from new, the age of the asset and the estimated residual value at the end of the asset's working life. The resultant figure is referred to as the Net Current Replacement Cost (NCRC) and represents the market value of the asset.

When adopting the DRC approach, the valuer should also establish whether the asset in its current form represents the optimum replacement given technological and functional changes since construction.

Gross Current Replacement Costs

In assessing Gross Current Replacement Cost (GCRC), valuers should adopt the lower of replacement cost and reproduction cost. Replacement cost is the current cost of a similar new asset having the nearest equivalent utility to the asset being valued. Reproduction cost is the current cost of reproducing a new replica of the asset being valued using the same, or closely similar, materials.

The cost elements may differ depending on the type of the asset and should include the direct and indirect costs that would be required to replace/recreate the asset as of the valuation date. Some common items to consider include:

direct costs:

1 materials; and
2 labour.

indirect costs:

1 transport costs;
2 installation costs;
3 professional fees (design, permit, architectural, legal, etc.);
4 other fees (commissions, etc.);
5 overheads;
6 taxes;
7 finance costs (e.g. interest on debt financing); and
8 profit margin/entrepreneurial profit to the creator of the asset (e.g. return to investors).

The GCRC is generally established by contacting manufacturers or their agents and making due allowance for freight, duty, local delivery, crane hire, installation, engineering costs and so forth. It is also possible to estimate the GCRC by inflating or indexing the historical cost of an asset.

Manufacturers and their agents supply costs on a number of different bases. It is important that the valuer understands the terminology and what additional costs must be provided for. Typically, manufacturers will supply costs either ex-works, free on board (FOB) or free into store (FIS). Additional costs such as freight/transport costs, duty, delivery, procurement, installation, design and engineering costs and interest incurred during construction must be incorporated into the final figures.

Valuers should take particular care with Special Purpose Machinery which includes custom-built machines and machines built to perform a unique function.

These may have been manufactured by specialist engineering companies or made in-house by the client's engineering department. Special Purpose Machinery may be valued with regard to the GCRC of a proprietary machine that performs substantiality the same function as the special purpose machine, to which adjustment may be required.

Valuers may also be required to determine values for a class of assets known as 'Product Specific Items'. These include items such as press tools, welding jigs, injection moulds, blow moulds, cutting knives, patterns, dies and so forth. Because much of the information required to value such assets will be held by the client, the value of items such as these is usually determined with some client involvement and discussions with specialist tool makers.

Effective lives or useful lives

The effective working life of an asset is the estimated life of the asset, assuming continued use in its present function as part of a continuing business. It is considered to be at an end when profitability is exceeded by operating and maintenance costs.

The standard and frequency of maintenance is a significant factor in the determination of effective lives. All other things being equal, a regularly and well-maintained item of equipment will have a longer effective life than an identical item of equipment which is subjected to poor and infrequent maintenance.

Clearly no valuer can estimate the exact date when the effective working life of an asset will end, but a reasonable estimate must be made and in arriving at this estimate all forms of obsolescence should be considered together with amount of use, type of use, rebuilding or reconditioning and maintenance.

It should be noted that the preceding discussion relates to the consideration of effective lives in the context of Market Value. For accounting depreciation purposes, effective life may be determined by a company's depreciation policy and may be substantially different to that adopted by the valuer for valuation purposes.

Residual values

The residual value of an asset must be estimated to perform a depreciation calculation. This residual value reflects the fact that the asset may no longer be an economic proposition in its present role. However, it may remain in use but with profitability impaired due to increased maintenance costs and lack of efficiency compared with more modern assets.

Depreciation

Depreciation can be a useful tool to the valuer, but it is to be remembered that depreciation gives a factor based only on age, working life and residual value, expressed as a percentage of GCRC, the answer being calculated on a purely mathematical basis. The valuer must take account of all available information in his assessment of depreciation. Market transactions should be carefully researched and used as a check method against the DRC approach wherever possible.

Selection of the appropriate method of depreciation is critical with the following methods most commonly used:

- diminishing value or reducing balance;
- straight-line or prime cost;
- production units; and
- market derived.

The objective of using depreciation for valuation purposes is different to that for accounting purposes. The latter is concerned with the allocation of costs over the effective life of the asset whilst the former is concerned with the quantification of obsolescence.

In addition to physical obsolescence which measures the consumption of life or service potential, there are three kinds of obsolescence which may affect the value of plant and equipment being technological, functional and economical.

It is most important that whichever method of depredation is adopted, it reflects market behaviour in the appropriate industry and recognises the pattern of consumption of the service potential embodied in the asset.

The final selection of the rate and method of depreciation is based on the valuer's assessment of the economic working life of the asset and the level of residual value at the end of the economic working life.

IVSC Standards require that any value calculated by a DRC approach must be expressed as subject to adequate profitability or service potential in the case of public assets or assets devoid of free cash flows, related to the value of the enterprise as a whole.

Income approach

The Income Approach seeks to determine the current (present) value of anticipated future economic benefits associated with the asset. In reality, it is rarely possible to identify an income stream and allocate it to individual pieces of equipment. As a result, it is generally very difficult, if not impossible, to assess values for individual plant and equipment assets by reference to the income approach.

Valuations for other purposes

In addition to valuation for financial reporting purposes, plant and equipment valuation may be undertaken for a range of other purposes which are detailed in API (2007) and briefly summarised below:

- valuations for tax compliance purposes – while valuations for Federal tax compliance purposes are generally completed similarly to financial reporting purposes (with allowance for 'tax-only' assets), valuations for tax consolidation purposes should follow the Commissioner's guidelines;
- valuations for stamp duty purposes – while valuations for State and Territory stamp duty purposes follow relevant statute and are generally completed similarly to those for financial reporting purposes, regard should be given to 'land rich' provisions and the classification of fixtures and chattels;

- valuations for regulatory pricing purposes – valuations may be required by regulators as part of the assessment of reasonable consumer charges for power stations, electricity transmission and distribution networks, gas transmission and distribution networks, rail networks and so forth, with a DRC approach commonly adopted;
- valuations for insurance purposes – with the general concepts and principles considered in Chapter 19 in the context of real property, valuation of plant and equipment for insurance purposes is a highly specialised area of valuation which is considered at length in API (2007) to which the reader is referred for a comprehensive explanation; and
- valuations for loan security and disposal purposes – banks, lenders and corporate insolvency practitioners are major users of plant and equipment valuation services, commonly requiring valuations based on an assumed need to liquidate, materially curtail the scale of operations or undertake a transaction on adverse terms. Regard is required to the form of sale (private treaty, tender or public auction) and sale as a whole in situ or partially in situ or either ex-situ, with valuations for sale by auction undertaken on the basis of 'auction realizable value' which is consistent with Market Value but with a curtailed marketing period. In certain circumstances, the valuer may be required to assume a liquidation or forced sale scenario premised on a short time period which should be nominated in the valuation report.

Summary

In this chapter, valuation practice for plant and equipment is considered, being a specialist property sector of considerable complexity encompassing a diverse range of individual assets and operating facilities from, for example, individual engines to whole trains to an entire railway network.

Identifying the asset, assets or facility to be valued is addressed, together with issues of materiality, prior to focusing on plant and equipment valuation for financial reporting purposes. Application of the market approach and cost approach are considered in detail, with the latter addressing Gross Current Replacement Cost and the challenging issues of useful lives, residual values and deprecation, concluding with a brief consideration of plant and equipment valuation for other purposes.

The plant and equipment valuation profession, like so many others, is ever changing. New valuation techniques and improved standards of service will be sought by clients and it will be incumbent upon the valuer to maintain and improve skill levels accordingly. Similarly, there are increasing statutory requirements and standards that the professionals must keep abreast of.

In the first section of the second part of the book, valuation practice for residential, office, retail, industrial and rural property was considered. In this second section of the second part of this book, valuation practice for specialist property sectors is considered comprising plant and equipment in this chapter with retirement property and leisure property considered in the previous chapters and business and intangible asset valuation considered in the following chapter.

The third and final section of the second part addresses valuation practice for specific purposes, including rental, financial reporting, secured lending, insurance and statutory valuation purposes.

References

API 2007, *Valuation Principles and Practice*, 2nd ed, Australian Property Institute, Deakin.

Biographies

Greg Rowe is the Managing Director of Preston Rowe Paterson Sydney, having significant experience in the valuation of not only real estate but also plant, machinery and equipment, primarily focusing on financial reporting.

Greg is actively involved in major asset, plant, machinery and equipment valuation projects undertaken by the firm. He has also been involved in API originated short courses and committees relevant to the valuation of plant, machinery and equipment.

In addition to being actively involved in the firm's asset, plant, machinery and equipment valuation division, Greg is also responsible for the growth and direction of the business, in conjunction with the firm's other directors.

Roy Farthing is the principal of Roy Farthing Consulting and a former partner of EY, where he led their Capital Equipment Valuation team. Roy has over 45 years' experience providing valuations of plant and equipment in the mining, oil and gas, utilities, infrastructure, manufacturing and public service sectors in over 25 countries around the world. He is considered an expert in plant and equipment valuations for financial reporting, tax, stamp duty, insurance and dispute resolution purposes.

Roy is active in raising and developing standards in the valuation profession and has served as vice Chair of the Professional Board of the International Valuation Standards Council (IVSC) and is a current member of the IVSC's Standards Review Board, former member of the API Standards Steering Committee, and current member of the AASB Fair Value Advisory Panel. He is a Life Fellow of the Australian Property Institute and is accredited as a Certified Practising Valuer (Plant & Machinery).

15 Business and intangible asset valuation

Wayne Lonergan

Introduction

With the first part of this book addressing the principles of valuation, the second part addresses the practice of valuation being grouped into three sections comprising conventional property sectors, specialist property sectors and specific purposes. Conventional property sectors include residential, office, retail, industrial and rural property valuation practice, being considered in previous chapters.

Specialist property sectors include business and intangible assets, which are addressed in this chapter, with retirement property, leisure property and plant and equipment considered in previous chapters. The third and final section of the second part addresses valuations for specific purposes including valuation practice for rental, financial reporting, secured lending, insurance and statutory valuation purposes.

The valuation of business and intangible assets is considered in this chapter which comprehensively addresses the four principal methods of business valuation, drawing parallels with the property valuation process particularly thorough the inputs to the respective methods. Applicability of different methods to different types of businesses is considered together with a range of significant valuation issues and common errors arising in business valuation.

Property valuation and corporate finance

Property valuers are increasingly interacting with senior executives and Board members in corporations regarding property investment decisions, whether they be for the businesses' own use or as a separate investment class. Many senior executives are now well versed in, or experienced with, the principles and practice of modern corporate finance and, in particular, discounted cash flow (DCF) valuations. This is certainly the case in larger investment institutions who see commercial property as just another asset class. In today's interrelated capital markets, property valuers need to be able to understand and use DCF methods of valuation.

Understanding the approaches taken by other business executives to value a business and its assets can assist valuers in putting forward their own business cases regarding property investments, property ownership relative to leasing and other property-related matters.

This chapter outlines the basic approaches which are commonly used in the valuation of businesses and shares and explains some of the issues associated with each approach. Some of the principles underlying approaches to the valuation of company

DOI: 10.1201/9781003049555-15

shares, companies and other 'going concern' type assets, such as infrastructure projects, are also highlighted.

It is not the intention of this chapter to provide a detailed discussion of important matters such as estimating rates of returns, the relevance, or otherwise, of capital structure, alternative capital budgeting techniques and so forth. Numerous texts are available which contain greater detail on such subjects, provide a general guide, or focus on specific aspects such as capital budgeting, portfolio management and the more esoteric approaches to finance and valuation such as the theory and practice of option pricing. The purpose of this chapter is to provide a simple introduction to the basics of valuation from a corporate finance perspective.

However, it is emphasised that equity and business valuation is a highly litigious area and property valuers should not perform business or equity valuations unless they are qualified, experienced and, in the case of advising or dealing in securities (e.g. Independent Expert Reports (IERs)), licensed to do so.

Basic approaches from the corporate finance perspective

The maxim 'all value is the present value of future cash flows' is true both in business and equity valuations and in commercial property valuations. Hence the importance and prevalence of DCF valuations.

In business and equity valuations, other methods of valuation may be used, for example, the capitalisation of future maintainable profits or asset-based methods of valuation. However, these methods are actually surrogates for the DCF method of valuation.

Why the surrogates mirror basic DCF principles

In the case of capitalised profit methods of valuation, the surrogate for future cash flows is after-tax profits. In the case of the capitalised EBIT method of valuation, the surrogate future cash flows is EBIT, which is shared between shareholders and interest bearing debt holders. To calculate equity value using the capitalised EBIT method of valuation, the market value of interest bearing debt is deducted from the capitalised EBIT value.

Similarly, where it is appropriate to use an asset-based method of valuation, the source of cash flow is from the sale of assets (e.g. if liquidation is likely) or the cash flows required to acquire the assets (e.g. a company with a property or share portfolio which is going to be retained).

In business valuations, it is generally necessary to consider more than one method of valuation. It is also important to check the implied value of goodwill, or 'blue sky' element, for reasonableness.

Equity and business valuations may vary significantly depending on the ownership entity (e.g. company, partnership, unit trust etc.), the percentage interest held (e.g. controlling or minority interest, size of holding, etc.), any relevant idiosyncratic tax characteristics and the purpose of the valuation. However, the fundamental test of market value is the price that would be negotiated by a knowledgeable willing but not anxious buyer (WBNAB) and a knowledgeable willing but not anxious seller (WBNAS) acting at arm's length.

Determinants of value

DCF valuations (and thus other share valuation methods) are based on the following, common-sense propositions:

- an investor can invest in so-called 'risk-free' investments, such as Commonwealth Bonds. In fact, such bonds are really only risk-free as to credit risk. They are not risk-free as to interest rate risk (unless they are held to maturity) nor to inflation risk (although inflation has not been a material issue in Australia for more than two decades);
- to invest in higher risk assets, rational investors seek a higher rate of return consistent with that risk;
- money received today is more valuable than money received in the future;
- business valuations are forward-looking (e.g. *future* maintainable profits). However, past and current profit performance often provides useful information about likely future trends; and
- business based valuations primarily depend upon data from actual 'comparable sales' and ASX data. Daily turnover on the ASX is some $5 billion to $10 billion, a much more active and liquid market, with much higher levels of information disclosure and the subject of much more analyst and academic research, than the commercial property market.

Fortunately, in business valuations most technical terms can be translated literally to understand their meaning. However, business valuations are a much more complex area than may, at first, appear. Furthermore, it is emphasised that litigation risks for valuers are very high.

Business valuation methodologies

The four principal valuation methodologies comprise:

- DCF;
- capitalisation of future maintainable profits (FMP);
- asset-based valuations; and
- capitalisation of future maintainable dividends (FMD) – for minority interests.

Each of the above techniques requires:

- estimating the quantum and timing of future economic benefits to be derived from the asset or business; and
- assessing the risks relevant to the asset and the business.

The most theoretically appropriate approach to valuation is the DCF method. This is because a DCF calculates the market value of a business or security as the present value of the (reasonably) expected future cash flows from the business or security, adjusted for the level of risk involved. The DCF technique is widely used and widely accepted by the business community and securities industry and relevant regulators.

Selecting the appropriate methodology

The choice of an appropriate methodology depends on:

- any legal requirements as to the methodology to be used;
- the availability of information;
- a clear understanding of the nature of the business, its key strengths and weaknesses and its operating environment; and
- a clear understanding of the practical limitations of alternative methodologies which may impact on their use and weighting to assess market value.

If there are surplus assets or liabilities owned by, or owed by, the entity being valued, it may be appropriate to value them using an asset-based method of valuation. However, where the business is dependent upon less tangible factors, such as people or brand names, an earnings or cash-flow basis of valuation is usually more appropriate than an asset-based valuation.

It is important to recognise that equity and business valuations are not a precise science. A valuer should consider using all applicable methodologies and preferably provide some insight as to the decision process used in accepting or rejecting the use of the various approaches.

The following are examples of circumstances where one valuation methodology may be more applicable than others.

A service industry

Businesses such as advertising agencies or professional practices generally do not have substantial tangible assets and most of their income producing potential is generated through intangible assets such as their people and the goodwill attached to their or the firm's name. Accordingly, it will generally be appropriate to apply a capitalised earnings or a DCF methodology rather than an asset-based method of valuation.

An underperforming business

Generally a business is conducted with a view to deriving future earnings sufficient to provide the proprietor with an adequate rate of return on the investment. A business may be so embryonic or may deteriorate to such a degree that the value of the business will be maximised by ceasing operations and realising the assets of the business. In such a situation, a net assets based (notional liquidation) valuation approach would be the most appropriate methodology to adopt.

An asset-based business

Some operations are dependent upon specific capital-intensive assets which in their own right have a readily determinable market value. For example, property investment companies are frequently valued using net asset values as a going concern. There are increasing calls from experienced property practitioners and investors for the application of DCF techniques for all commercial property valuations.

Start-up businesses

New enterprises and companies changing the nature of their business are often valued on an earnings or cash flow basis due to the perception that the business's value lies in the future cash flows which may be generated from the 'idea'. With such businesses, it is unlikely that an asset-based valuation approach will be relevant. The valuation of technology assets and other identifiable intangible assets requires a deep understanding of the appropriate valuation methods to use. Frequently this will link back to an earnings or cash flow basis. The risk related to this type of business is even greater. There may be few relevant precedents in the marketplace to assist with the risk assessment.

Methodologies employed in public documents

When assessing the value of shares or businesses, Independent Expert Reports (IERs) are required by ASIC to consider a number of alternative valuation methods, stating the reasons for their selection or explaining why certain methodologies were not selected.

It is usually instructive to review other IERs to gain an appreciation of the logic underlying those valuations and the approaches used. IERs should contain sufficient detail as to the key underlying assumptions so that another independent expert can replicate the work and achieve the same result. It is important to note that only licensed securities advisers can prepare IERs.

DCF method of valuation

The principal focus of a DCF valuation is to quantify the extent, timing and risk of future cash flows.

Inputs

The DCF model takes as its inputs those factors which directly affect the expected future economic benefits shareholders will receive:

- recognising that shareholders returns comprise dividends plus capital gains from share price increases, and not accounting profits, which are a function of accounting conventions;
- recognising economic cash flows and not just accounting earnings;
- recognising that money has a time value – a dollar in the future is worth less than a dollar today;
- explicitly allowing for both the business risk (the nature of the industry in which the company operates) and financial risk (the extent to which debt funding is used to finance operations) of the enterprise to be reflected in the discount rate; and
- allowing for both incremental working capital and incremental capital investment requirements.

The essential premise of the DCF technique is that a business should at least be able to generate a return on its operations equivalent to the cost of raising debt and equity funds to operate in its line of business. This cost constitutes the firm's cost of capital which is used as the discount rate in the DCF. If the business or asset cannot generate this return, shareholders will invest elsewhere to obtain a return appropriate to the degree of risk involved.

A DCF calculates the value of equity of a business by assessing total business value (called enterprise value) and subtracting from this the market value of debt used to fund operations:

Total equity value = enterprise value less market value of net debt

Enterprise value comprises the following components:

- the present value of cash flows from operations during a forecast period of operating the business plus the value of any excess assets such as shares and other assets not essential to operations;
- an assessment of the 'terminal value' which is the present value of that component of the business value attributable to operations beyond the forecast period; and
- forecast periods of, ideally, ten years (to avoid the terminal value comprising an excessive proportion of total value).

Cash flow from operations is the difference between operating cash inflows and cash outflows adjusted for the cash taxes payable. The after-tax cash flow represents cash available to pay back debt holders and pay dividends to shareholders (or reinvest for future capital gains).

Discount rate

The discount rate to be used to discount each forecast period's cash flows to the present is generally calculated using the Capital Asset Pricing Model (CAPM).

The CAPM calculates the required return on equity based on stock market data and the sensitivity of the share price of comparable companies to market movements (the average stock market return exceeds the risk-free rate in Australia by some 6% pa).

This comparison provides a single measure of relative risk, known as the 'beta' factor, to be applied to calculate the appropriate cost of equity. A number of professional services provide beta data. The return on equity is combined with the required after-tax cost of debt, with each weighted in accordance with its relative weighting in the business' capital structure, to derive the weighted average cost of capital (WACC).

This is the rate used as the discount rate in DCF valuations applied to discount future cash flows after tax (but before interest costs) to their present value.

Terminal value

The terminal value of the business at the end of the forecast period is its market value at that time.

If the business is expected to continue as a going concern, the terminal value is the value of the expected annual cash flow, divided by the cost of capital:

$$\text{Terminal value at the end of the forecast period} = \frac{\text{Expected annual cash flow}}{\text{Cost of capital}}$$

This value is then discounted back to the valuation date.

The terminal value is often a significant contributor to the overall value of the business or equity being valued. Thus, caution needs to be exercised in determining growth rates in cash flows and/or dividends beyond the forecast period chosen and assumptions used should be clearly stated.

Limitations

The DCF approach to valuation is both technically and economically sound.

The two major areas of difficulty in its use are the assessment of future cash flows and the assessment of the appropriate discount rate. Careful judgement should be exercised in assessing which factors are most likely to affect future cash flows.

It should be noted that the market value of debt in the capital structure is not necessarily equal to its book value. The relevance of book value depends on whether or not the interest rate and terms of the debt instrument are consistent with the market at the time.

The assessment of the cost of equity for firms whose shares are not actively traded in a public marketplace can be difficult. A reasonable comparator is a company whose equity is publicly traded and whose business characteristics are reasonably similar to those of the entity being valued.

When assessing the cost of equity capital by using a proxy listed firm or industry average, material differences in the degree of financial leverage together with other market factors (e.g. the company either operates overseas, rather than in Australia, or is internationally diversified) between the proxy firm and the company which is being valued need to be considered.

The sensitivity of the DCF to changes in key assumptions regarding future cash flows and the discount rate should then be assessed to calculate the probability adjusted or 'central best estimate' of market value.

Capitalisation of future maintainable profits (FMP)

The valuation of a company based on future maintainable profit (FMP) requires the determination of two company-specific parameters, the earnings that the company can sustain in the future and the applicable price earnings ratio (PER).

Future maintainable profits (after tax) is the return to equity. If EBIT is being capitalised, this is the return to debt and equity combined.

Technically, the only truly observable integers are FMP after tax and the PER. Other levels of income, for example EBIT, are derived by calculation (based on publicly disclosed information) and therefore more prone to error. EBIT valuations are easy to understand but should still be cross-checked to the value determined by multiplying FMP after tax by the appropriate PER.

Normalising income levels

Having ascertained the earnings base most appropriate for the valuation, the earnings should be normalised by excluding abnormal, non-recurring and non-arms-length transactions but including any unrecognised costs and income which are not reflected in the results.

Items which may require adjustments include:

- compensation to owners and spouses, so that these are representative of arms-length arrangements;
- depreciation rates;
- non-recurring items, such as business interruptions, discontinued operations, abnormal market conditions;
- adjustments of rental or lease payments to an arms-length basis;
- adjustments of any related party transactions to an arms-length basis (e.g. management fees);
- non-operating income or expenses that are not related to the principal business; and
- interest on shareholder loans other than on an arms-length basis.

The aim is to determine future maintainable profit. This is done by examining the:

- trend and cyclicality of current profits;
- previous and (reasonably) forecast normalised profits;
- industry and economic trends;
- risk factors affecting the business;
- liquidity position;
- security of tenure in respect of premises, agency rights, franchises, licences;
- asset support to the capitalised value;
- debt/equity ratios;
- continuity and experience of management; and
- experiences (success/failure) of entities of a similar nature.

Factors suggesting a lower multiple or a higher rate of return may include:

- public companies used for comparison may be more diversified than the company being valued, thus spreading and lowering overall risk;
- the entity being valued may not be fully operational, such that there may be risks and uncertainties in developing products and penetrating new markets; and
- the entity being valued may have a significantly higher debt/equity ratio than the industry average, indicating a higher level of financial risk.

Factors suggesting a higher multiple may include:

- substantial growth potential; and
- experience, expertise and continuity of management.

Inflation

Inflation has not been a material valuation issue in Australia for the last two decades.

Determination of the capitalisation rate

A reference point, in selecting the capitalisation rate for an unlisted entity, is the multiple for 'comparable' companies in the same or similar industries and other specific firm characteristics (less depth of management, etc.).

PE or EBIT multiples of 'comparable' companies or 'comparable' sales need to be adjusted for size (smaller multiples apply to smaller entities), growth prospects (higher multiples for higher growth prospects) and negotiability (lower multiples apply to less negotiable assets).

Limitations

The capitalisation of FMP method of valuation is widely used in the financial community.

The adoption of Australian equivalents to International Financial Reporting Standards (AIFRS) by reporting entities provides some assurance that disclosed accounting profits are derived on a reasonable basis. Having said this, it is nevertheless important to note that accounting measures of earnings may not measure the true economic value of the business due to:

- differences and changes in accounting standards between entities and over time;
- exclusion of adequate explicit consideration of both business and financial risk; and
- inadequate consideration of the time value of money.

Further complications arise in share valuations with respect to recognition of other factors such as illiquidity, blockage, voting control considerations, different voting rights attaching to different classes of shares and specific aspects of Articles of Association (for older companies, now called constituent documents) and Shareholder Agreements.

Asset-based valuations

Asset-based valuations are generally used in the following circumstances:

- where a company is not expected to remain a going concern – e.g. where the sale value of individual assets are greater than the value on a going concern basis; or
- where assets are of prime importance to the company's operations and are marketable in their own right (e.g. property companies, investment companies).

There are principally three types of asset-based valuations:

- liquidation basis;
- orderly realisation of assets-basis; and
- net tangible assets.

Liquidation based valuation

Using this approach, assets are valued on the basis of securing a sale in the short term.

Orderly realisation of assets

An orderly realisation period is the highest price obtainable for assets within a reasonable time frame. What constitutes a reasonable period of realisation will depend on the condition of the company, the nature of its assets, the costs and the perceived benefits of prolonging the realisation. Selling expenses, employee and other contract termination costs, tax on realised gains and lease termination costs should be deducted from the gross realisable values.

Net tangible assets

Using this approach assets are valued on an in-situ going concern basis. Liquidation and sale costs are not taken into account. Since this method relies upon accounting measures of asset values, rather than on market-based indicators, it has little theoretical support. It can, however, be used as a check on other valuation methodologies, particularly if some reliable benchmark is available for the industry in which the company operates.

Optimised depreciated replacement value

This is a valuation technique commonly used for infrastructure assets such as gas transmission pipelines or electricity transmission and distribution networks. As the term implies, it is the replacement cost today, in today's dollars, of the existing asset(s), but with an optimal configuration for its current use, both technically and functionally depreciated to reflect the elapsed useful life of the asset. This method often requires significant input from engineers and other specialist technical experts.

Capitalisation of future maintainable dividends (FMD)

The dividend valuation model is also a surrogate for a DCF based valuation wherein future cash flows are in the form of dividends and/or sale of the shares to a willing but not anxious buyer who will, in turn, receive dividends. This method only applies to minority interests.

Future maintainable dividends are a function of future maintainable earnings and the expected dividend payout ratio.

The basic capitalised income model can be adapted to incorporate growth in dividends. If it is assumed that a firm will adopt a constant dividend payout ratio, then estimating the growth rate in dividends is equivalent to estimating the growth rate in profits.

When a constant growth in dividends is assumed, this can be expressed mathematically as:

$$P = \frac{d}{r - g} \qquad \text{Equation 1}$$

where:
    P = the current share price
    d = the next expected dividend
    r = the required rate of return for the shares
    g = the expected constant growth rate in dividends

This is a simplification of more complex discounting formulae which can allow for various rates of growth (for example, start-up, maturity and decline) over specific periods in the future.

Intangible assets

The valuation of tangible assets such as receivables, property, plant and equipment and so forth is relatively straightforward. However, the valuation of intangible assets is generally much more difficult.

Intangibles include trademarks, patents, brand names, business systems and proprietary technology, as well as 'goodwill'. Whilst there are a number of valuation approaches adopted in valuing intangibles, they generally fall into the following three categories:

- market approach (e.g. comparable transactions);
- cost approach (e.g. current replacement cost, dollars per line of code); or
- assessment of future economic benefits (e.g. relief from royalties).

The approach adopted depends on the purpose of the valuation and the availability of relevant information.

There are often few, if any, sales of individual intangible assets. Consequently, market value information is scarce. In addition, it is also difficult as a practical matter to distinguish the actual identifiable intangible asset, such as a brand name, from the assets supporting them, such as the management team, superior marketing or distribution channels, which contribute to the value of the intangible asset.

However, identifiable intangibles may be valued if it can be demonstrated that a separate market for the property rights in question does exist (e.g. patents, broadcast licences, etc.). Great care must be exercised to ensure that there has been adequate and justifiable separation of all of the contributing factors to intangible value, or, at the very least, the valuer is specific in indicating the 'bundle' of intangibles which have been valued.

Other significant valuation issues

Other significant valuation issues for consideration include diversification, income tax losses, imputation franking credits, control, synergy, investment alternatives and barriers to entry.

Valuing a diversified group

In a group, or a company comprising a range of businesses operating in different industries, a valuation will normally be conducted of each material individual business unit with the individual valuations then being aggregated.

It is important to ensure that each unit does, in fact, operate on a stand-alone basis. If it does not, appropriate financial statement adjustments should be made to reflect a stand-alone operation. Each business unit should bear its own costs and overheads and notional financing structure adjustments should be made if its capital structure is substantially different from a structure considered normal for a similar business.

Valuing income tax losses

Income tax losses may, in certain cases, have potential value. However, under Australia's dividend imputation system, the value of income tax losses within an entity may be offset by income or capital gains tax payable at the ownership level.

The value of tax losses depends upon the specific circumstances pertaining to the valuation. For example, tax losses are subject to complex 'continuity of business' and 'continuity of ownership' tax act tests. Where tax losses can be utilised, the value of tax losses will normally be discounted, taking into account the likelihood of utilisation, the time delay to utilise the losses and the degree of uncertainty that exists as to their availability.

Valuing excess imputation franking credits

Where an acquirer is able to increase the amount of franking credits that can be attached to dividends paid, the acquirer may be prepared to pay a consideration for those excess imputation credits. The value of the franking credits will be dependent upon the ability of the acquirer to utilise the excess franking credits and the time frame over which the excess franking credits may be used.

The value of 'normal' levels of franking credits is implicit in the share price and thus the PER, so should not be double counted. However, regulators of infrastructure assets take a different view to commercial operators and value 'normal' franking credits separately.

Special issues

When valuing a business (either equity or total capital), premiums or discounts may attach to voting rights, the ability to control the company and the degree of marketability of the entity or security being valued. All other things being equal, a parcel of shares in an unlisted company will be less (generally much less) valuable than in a listed company due to the higher risks associated with having less liquidity and marketability and, hence, being more difficult and taking more time to sell.

Special circumstances which require consideration include:

- shares of the same class paid up to varying amounts;
- funding of additional capital requirements;
- arrears of dividend payment on preferred shares;
- sales of equity interests near dividend distribution dates; and
- classes of shares with differing or variable rights.

In the case of unlisted shares, empirical evidence, both in Australia and overseas, indicates that a discount of 25% to 35% is appropriate when comparing the value of an unlisted company to that of a listed company. In addition, a further discount for minority interests applies. Where there are other restrictions, such as non-dividend-paying shares or restrictions on voting rights, further discounts apply.

Synergy

Consideration needs to be given to whether there are any material synergy benefits for acquirers. Synergy benefits may be generated from streamlining of administrative and marketing functions, economies of scale through increased buying power, cross-selling revenue enhancement opportunities, increased market visibility and brand recognition from increased market share and so forth. Potential synergy benefits may be general (i.e. available to many potential acquirers) or specific to one buyer.

Investors will not pay full value for synergy benefits due to the risk in achieving the synergies, the risk of dis-synergies and the natural commercial desire to retain at least some of the benefits generated as compensation for having made the acquisition and taken the risks.

In the case of unique synergy benefits, rational acquirers should not have to pay a significant premium for them.

Rules of thumb and their accuracy

Particularly in smaller businesses, some industry participants use rules of thumb (ROT) to assess value. Whilst these ROT are interesting, they are often either out of date and/or materially misleading indicators of value and/or rely on the bigger fool theory (that is, it does not matter if you pay too much for a business if you can sell it to a subsequent bigger fool who will also overpay).

ROT should be treated with extreme caution and should not be relied on as a stand-alone method of valuation.

Rorting the ROT

Generally, being revenue based, most ROT are simple to calculate. They are also susceptible to being rorted.

For example, if the relevant ROT is (say) turnover based, less scrupulous vendors will maximise turnover even if this means selling at a small loss so as to maximise the ROT value.

Replication cost comparison

Knowledgeable WBNAB and WBNAS are naturally cautious about how much goodwill value should be paid. Indeed, goodwill is often cynically called 'blue sky money', the value of which can rapidly disappear if things do not go well.

There is a natural limit on the amount a rational purchaser will pay for goodwill. At the very small end of the market, a purchaser may be prepared to pay no more than replication cost plus (say) the equivalent of one year's profits as goodwill. The basic logic being that the purchaser is prepared to lose (say) a year's profit but mistakenly expects to be able to recover most of the value paid for tangible assets. For much bigger businesses, the goodwill value may be very high.

The value of goodwill should always be checked for reasonableness.

Investment alternatives for small business owners

It is important in all business and equity valuations that proprietors are paid, or an allowance is made for, market salaries. Due regard should also be had to investment alternatives available to small business owners. For example, the return available from a leveraged investment in a residential property may offer a better return, with a lot less risk and a lot less effort, than an investment in what, by comparison, is an overpriced small business.

Barriers to entry

As a general rule, the higher the barriers to entry for new competitors, the more likely it is that the business or entity will be more valuable (and vice versa). Such barriers may be licence barriers (e.g. abalone licences or taxi licences (pre-UBER)), first mover advantage barriers (e.g. telephony and microwave towers), technical, technological and so forth.

Common errors

The following are some examples of common areas in which errors of judgement are easily made when performing business valuations:

- too much emphasis on the past performance of a company when performing DCF or earnings-based valuations. The value of a company is dependent on its future performance. While recent historical performance may provide an indication of the future operations of the company, the valuer must consider the possibility that the future will be different from the past;
- frequently, insufficient consideration is given to what drives PER multiples for listed companies. A proxy company's multiples may be affected by company-specific factors not applicable to the company being valued, such as gearing levels, management issues, market share, growth prospects and a host of other factors. Analysis of the 'comparable' companies, therefore, is important in determining the appropriate multiple for the business being valued. This same challenge occurs when estimating a required rate of return with CAPM, in that betas may be affected by many of the same company-specific factors which need to be considered prior to using a proxy company's beta in a DCF valuation;
- business valuation methodologies require a degree of judgement. As a result, valuation conclusions or opinions will often be stated as a range, rather than as a point estimate. The range of values should represent the range of uncertainties and the sensitivity of the valuation to changes in key value drivers. When required, a point estimate may be derived, but should take into consideration the position of the business being valued within the range of sensitivities, as well as a quantitative and qualitative comparison of relative strengths and weaknesses to any proxy companies or other industry comparatives used in the valuation process. Too often, valuations either 'average' the range of values without justification or a single point estimate fails to consider the sensitivities of the value to key value drivers; and
- where a bidder is offering shares as consideration in a takeover offer, frequently valuers accept the listed price/stated value of the shares being offered as the value of those shares without further investigation or consideration. The same principles of valuation applied to the valuation of the target shares should also be applied in assessing the value of the shares being offered as consideration, to ascertain that the market value reflects all relevant information about the shares and has not been affected by unusual speculative forecasts or other factors.

Excessive reliance on a single valuation approach, or 'backing into' a corroborating value using alternative methods, rather than performing independent analysis using a variety of methods can often lead to inaccurate results. It is important to consider other relevant methodologies and attempt to reconcile differences, rather than to pre-select a single approach. Exclusion of approaches should be explained, so that subsequent users of the valuation will understand the reasoning behind the exclusion of certain approaches. Likewise, all critical assumptions should be documented so that the recipient of a valuation can understand any material uncertainties attaching to certain key inputs to the valuation.

Summary

Business valuations are a specialised, technical and potentially litigious area of valuation practice with the valuation maxim that 'all value is the present value of future cash flows' being prescient.

Whilst other methods of valuation are widely used, these are surrogates for the DCF method of valuation with the underlying technical basis of a properly conducted business or equity valuation having interesting implications for commercial property valuers.

This is hardly surprising as the source of investment capital for commercial property, equity and businesses is generally the same. To such investors, property is just another investment class. Hence such investors find it difficult to understand why a commercial property valuation should not be based on the same basic principles as other business valuations.

This chapter comprehensively addresses the four principal methods of business valuation, drawing parallels with the property valuation process particularly thorough the inputs to the respective methods. Applicability of different methods to different types of businesses is considered together with a range of significant valuation issues and common errors arising in business valuation.

In the first section of the second part of the book, valuation practice for residential, office, retail, industrial and rural property was considered. In this second section of the second part of this book, valuation practice for specialist property sectors is considered comprising leisure property, retirement property and plant and equipment with business and intangible asset valuation considered in this chapter.

The third and final section of the second part addresses valuation practice for specific purposes, including rental, financial reporting, secured lending, insurance and statutory valuation purposes.

References

Lonergan W 2003, *The Valuation of Businesses, Shares and Other Equity*, 4th ed, Allen & Unwin, Sydney.

Biography

Wayne Lonergan is a director of Lonergan Edwards & Associates Limited. His qualifications include Dr Sc Ec, BEc, FAPI, SF Fin, FAICD, AIAMA, Adjunct Professor, Sydney University.

While based on a previous edition, this chapter has been extensively revised and rewritten to reflect current valuation principles and practice.

Wayne is a highly experienced and widely recognised practising valuation expert. He has published over 110 articles on valuation and related accounting topics and 3 valuation texts.

Section Three
Valuation practice for specific purposes

16 Valuation for rental purposes

Greg Preston

Acknowledgement

This chapter draws heavily on chapter 15 in *Valuation Principles and Practice* (2007) (Second Edition, Australian Property Institute, Deakin) which is duly acknowledged here rather than individually referenced through this chapter and to which readers are referred for a deeper consideration.

Introduction

With the first part of this book addressing the principles of valuation, the second part addresses the practice of valuation being grouped into three sections comprising conventional property sectors, specialist property sectors and specific purposes. Conventional property sectors include residential, office, retail, industrial and rural property valuation practice. Specialist property sectors include retirement, leisure, plant and equipment and business and intangible asset valuation practice. Specific purposes include valuation practice for rental, financial reporting, secured lending, insurance and statutory valuation purposes.

This third section of the second part of this book addresses specific purpose valuation practice with this chapter considering rental valuation purposes while financial reporting valuation purposes, secured lending valuation purposes, insurance valuation purposes and statutory valuation purposes are considered in the following chapters.

This chapter addresses the concept of rent, the IVSC definition of market rent together with alternative terminology, demised premises and outgoings, key issues for consideration including make good, lease incentives and restrictive user together with retail lease legislation, rent review and rental determination.

Background

Both property as an investment and property for occupation are often dependent on the assessment of rental.

From the lessor's perspective, rental valuations underpin performance and capital valuations of real estate investment properties and from the lessee's perspective, rental valuations assist in understanding the total occupancy cost of premises required for the lessee's business.

The need for assessment of market rental arises in numerous circumstances, including:

- to assist either a lessor or lessee negotiate the terms and conditions of a new lease;
- to assess the rental under an existing lease for a mid-term certain market review;
- to assess the market rental under an existing lease at the exercise of options included in the initial lease; and/or
- in undertaking capital valuations of single or multi-tenant investment properties to assess the likelihood of rental reversions relative to passing rentals.

The process of assessing market rental for valuation, submission and determination purposes may be more formalised when the requirement for the market rental valuation is included in an existing lease, such as mid-term or option rental review assessment, as the lease itself will typically define:

- the date of the market rental assessment;
- directions to valuers acting for the parties and or a determining valuer (what is to be taken into account and what is to be ignored);
- the required qualifications of the valuer;
- whether or not the valuers acting for a party and/or a determining valuer are acting as experts or arbitrators;
- time of the essence provisions; and
- the process for assessment in the event of any disputed rental including appointment of a determining valuer or umpire.

Market rent

It is important to note at the outset that whilst market rent is defined in valuation standards, lease rent can be and often is somewhat different, specifically because of the directions to the determining valuer requiring them to take into account or not take into account certain specific matters.

In Australia, the International Valuation Standards Council (IVSC) Valuation Standards January 2020 Edition has been adopted by both the Australian Property Institute (API) and the Royal Institution of Chartered Surveyors (RICS).

The IVSC define market rent as:

> Market Rent is the estimated amount for which an interest in real property should be leased on the valuation date between a willing lessor and a willing lessee on appropriate lease terms in an arm's length transaction, after proper marketing and where the parties each acted knowledgeably, prudently and without compulsion.

The conceptual framework for market rental is the same as that for market value (capital value), which is defined by IVSC as:

> The IVSC definition of **'market value'** is applied in accordance with the following conceptual framework:
>
> (a) *'The estimated amount'* refers to a price expressed in terms of money payable for the asset in an arm's length market transaction. Market value is the most probable price reasonably obtainable in the market on the valuation date in keeping with the market value definition. It is the best price reasonably obtainable by the seller and the most advantageous price reasonably obtainable by the buyer. This estimate specifically excludes an estimated price inflated or deflated by special terms or circumstances such as atypical financing, sale and leaseback arrangement, special considerations or concessions granted by anyone associated with the sale, or any element of special value available only to a specific owner or purchaser.
>
> (b) *'An asset or Liability should exchange'* refers to the fact that the value of an asset or liability is an estimated amount rather than a predetermined amount or actual sale price. It is the price in a transaction that meets all the elements of the market value definition at the valuation date;
>
> (c) *'On the valuation date'* requires that the value is time-specific as of a given date. Because markets and market conditions may change, the estimated value may be incorrect or inappropriate at another time. The valuation amount will reflect the market state and circumstances as at the valuation date, not those at any other date.
>
> (d) *'Between a willing buyer'* refers to one who is motivated, but not compelled to buy. This buyer is neither over eager nor determined to buy at any price. This buyer is also one who purchases in accordance with the realities of the current market and with current market expectations, rather than in relation to an imaginary or hypothetical market that cannot be demonstrated or anticipated to exist. The assumed buyer would not pay a higher price than the market requires. The present owner is included among those who constitute 'the market';
>
> (e) *'And a willing seller'* is neither an over eager nor a forced seller prepared to sell at any price, nor one prepared to hold out for a price not considered reasonable in the current market. The willing seller is motivated to sell the asset at market terms for the best price attainable in the open market after proper marketing, whatever that price may be. The factual circumstances of the actual owner are not a part of this consideration because the willing seller is a hypothetical owner;
>
> (f) *'In an arm's length transaction'* is one between parties who do not have a particular or special relationship, e.g. parent and subsidiary companies or landlord and tenant, that may make the price level uncharacteristic of the market or inflated. The market value transaction is presumed to be between unrelated parties, each acting independently;
>
> (g) *'After proper marketing'* means that the asset has been exposed to the market in the most appropriate manner to effect its disposal at the best price reasonably obtainable in accordance with the market value definition. The method of sale is deemed to be that most appropriate to obtain the best price in the market to which the seller has access. The length of exposure time is not a fixed period but

will vary according to the type of asset and market conditions. The only criterion is that there must have been sufficient time to allow the asset to be brought to the attention of an adequate number of market participants. The exposure period occurs prior to the valuation date;

(h) **'Where the parties had each acted knowledgeably, prudently'** presumes that both the willing buyer and the willing seller are reasonably informed about the nature and characteristics of the asset, its actual and potential uses and the state of the market as of the valuation date. Each is further presumed to use that knowledge prudently to seek the price that is most favourable for their respective positions in the transaction. Prudence is assessed by referring to the state of the market at the valuation date, not with benefit of hindsight at some later date. For example, it is not necessarily imprudent for a seller to sell assets in a market with falling prices at a price that is lower than previous market levels. In such cases, as is true for other exchanges in markets with changing prices, the prudent buyer or seller will act in accordance with the best market information available at the time;

(i) **'And without compulsion'** establishes that each party is motivated to undertake the transaction, but neither is forced or unduly coerced to complete it.

While the IVSC defines the conceptual framework for assessing market rent generally, lease rents often require careful consideration of how markets function and operate relating to matters such as:

- lessee incentives (face and effective rentals);
- whether or not the whole lease term or the remaining term only is to be considered;
- outgoings recoveries (net leases, semi-gross leases, gross leases and hybrid outgoings recoveries);
- discounts for bulk for multiple floor lettings;
- space to be considered as if vacant generally;
- space to be considered as if vacant and available for fit out;
- what market rental evidence can be considered or is to be excluded;
- whether the mid-term or option review is to be considered differently when compared to the lease commencement rent and any incentives applying to it from an incentive viewpoint;
- inclusion or alternatively exclusion of rent review evidence within the building as market evidence;
- where a multi-floor office letting is to be assumed to be single floors only;
- whether caps and or collars apply to rent reviews and/or outgoings recoveries; and
- whether ratchet clauses apply.

The above list is not conclusive but serves to reinforce why a lease needs to be carefully reviewed when undertaking market rental assessments in the context of the market for the specific asset class.

Undertaking rental valuations for market review purposes fundamentally requires the careful consideration of the general terms and conditions of any lease and in particular the directions to a determining valuer setting out matters to be considered or 'taken into account' and those which are not to be considered or 'not taken into account'.

The lease document represents the culmination of negotiations between the lessor and the lessee at the time of commercial agreement, reflecting the position of the parties and the market prevailing at the time.

Despite attempts by the IVSC, API and RICS to promote the use of standard lease definitions, such as market rent, leases often get drafted by lawyers/solicitors with different and/or alternative naming conventions for market rental and definitions for what attempts to be tantamount to the IVSC definition of market rent.

Some leases may use alternative naming conventions for market rent and go a step further to define the rent for the lease purpose. The lease terms and conditions and the mechanisms contained therein can have a profound impact on the rentals and therefore capital value of a real estate investment, either positively or negatively.

Valuers should always ensure the lease is a complete representation of the document executed between the parties including all variations. Ultimately, if a formal market rental assessment is required under a lease, the valuer should only rely on a signed, stamped and registered (in States which register leases on title) copy of the lease.

Another important matter for consideration in assessing market rent is whether the actual lease document is silent on how to deal with issues which regularly form part of the negotiated rentals and leases in the marketplace. An example is whether a lease requires a face rent or an effective rent assessment in circumstances where the lease is silent or has no directives as to face rent or effective rent.

There are many interpretative decisions or established Court precedents dealing with the interpretation of leases and assessment of market rent where leases are silent on certain matters or, in the alternative, are ambiguous in their descriptions of those matters.

In addition to reviewing lease documentation, it is important to note that lessee incentives in the form of fit out allowances, rental abatements and rent-free periods are often documented in separate deeds to the lease itself. To understand the initial lease rental, it is imperative that the valuer obtain and review any side deeds (such as incentive deeds or fit out deeds containing incentives) to the lease which may not be registrable in certain jurisdictions.

Variations on market rent

Lease agreements over time have adopted a wide range of terms to describe that rental payable under the lease at rent review or lease option, with some leases defining the term used while others do not. If undefined in the lease, Court precedent may assist in interpreting the meaning of the phrase used in the lease document.

Examples of the terms used to describe that rental payable under the lease at rent review or lease renewal include, but are not limited to:

- market rental value;
- open market rental value;
- current rent;
- current rental value;
- annual rent;
- fair market rent;
- fair rent;
- reasonable rent; and
- yearly rent.

The Courts have considered various alternative terms used in leases as, in many cases, very large sums of money are dependent on the interpretation of the terms used. For example, is reasonable rent that rent which is reasonable to the lessor or to the lessee?

Reasonable rental was considered in *Ponsford v. HMS Aerosols* [1979] AC 63 where a rent review clause requiring the rent to be assessed on review to 'a reasonable rent for the demised premises' was held to require a review of the rent based on market value without reference to the particular parties or how the premises were built and paid for.

Fundamental issues for consideration

For valuers undertaking rental valuations, particularly for mid-term and lease option rental reviews under an existing lease, it is important to first check the status of the lease.

Obviously, a lease which is signed by both parties, stamped and registered on title (based on the requirements of the State jurisdiction) is a lease that can be relied on for rental valuation purposes.

Once the lease is available, the next important matter to be considered when acting for a party or as a determining valuer under a lease is whether any time of the essence clauses apply to the provision of the valuation or determination.

It is then necessary to check the fundamentals of the tenancy documented in the lease including:

- the description of demised premises;
- the lettable area of the demised premises based on the lease definition of lettable area, be it the Property Council of Australia (PCA) or International Property Measurement Standard (IPMS) and whether a lettable area survey is available;
- the name of the lessor;
- the name of the lessee;
- the commencement date of the lease;
- the term of the lease;
- the expiry date of the lease;
- any lease options;
- the basis of rental reviews (e.g. ratcheted or un-ratcheted market, CPI, fixed percentage, caps and collars);
- the frequency of rent reviews (e.g. annually on a fixed basis and to market on expiry or at exercise of option);
- is the market rent review a face or effective rent review;
- whether ratchet provisions or cap and collars on rent reviews apply;
- the basis of outgoings recoveries (e.g. net, semi-gross, gross or hybrid);
- concerning outgoings recoveries, if a semi-gross lease, whether the base year for the outgoings recoveries is brought forward at any time during the lease term certain and particularly on the exercise of option;
- whether any caps or collars apply to outgoings;
- the lease commencement rental;
- the rent commencement date (if different to the lease commencement date);
- the passing rental prior to the market rent review;
- the basis upon which the passing rental has been escalated since commencement and whether or not there has been a mark-to-market review during the lease term certain or prior to the current review;

- whether or not the lessee is obligated to make good the premises upon lease expiry;
- the market rental provisions of the lease noting that some leases may have market rent review provisions for mid-term reviews and different market rent review provisions for option lease rental establishment within the original lease;
- the process and timing (including whether time is of the essence) for the notification by one or both of the parties of the review, reply dispute notices, process and appointment of determining valuer, delivery of submissions to the determining valuer on behalf of the parties, handing down of a determining valuer's decision etc; and
- the directions to the valuers acting for the parties and/or a determining or umpire valuer.

Demised premises

The demised premises in any lease are usually defined by whether they are the whole or part of the title to the land. For leases of part of a building, they are normally defined by the suite and floor or level number in the case of offices, the shop number in the case of retail tenancies or the unit number in the case of multi-tenant industrial premises.

It is commonplace in real estate investment management to obtain lettable area surveys of the demised premises based on the current PCA Method of Measurement for different types of real estate. Generally speaking, the PCA Method of Measurement adopts the defined Net Lettable Area (NLA) for commercial office accommodation, Gross Lettable Area (GLA) for industrial accommodation and Gross Lettable Area Retail (GLAR) for retail accommodation.

Most lease documents refer to the appropriate PCA lettable area definition for two principal reasons. One is to establish the lettable area of the tenancy. The other is to establish the relativity of the lettable area of the tenancy to the total building lettable area for the distribution of outgoings to the tenancies based on area which may vary from time to time in some leases, particularly in office buildings. The total lettable area of an office building can vary when floors are converted from whole floor lettings to multi-tenant lettings on a floor and vice versa because the creation or removal of common areas varies the total lettable area of the building. Most modern leases make provision for this change from time to time.

Outgoings (statutory outgoings and operating expenditure)

To properly consider the market rent of any tenancy, either for the purposes of a mid-term review, option renewal or a new lease, it is important to understand the basis of outgoings recovery from lessees.

Firstly, it is necessary to understand the basis of outgoings recovery for an existing lessee/lease. Secondly, it is necessary to understand the basis of recovery for comparison to letting transactions if they are to be applied in the assessment of market rent.

In considering outgoings, it should, at the outset, be remembered that the comparison in the assessment of market rent should always be the total occupancy cost to the lessee. Adjustments can then be made either to comparable transactions or the subject property to relate the market analysis to the subject lease or tenancy.

Outgoings are best defined by referring to the PCA recommended Chart of Accounts for property management. This Chart of Accounts includes the following items for Statutory Outgoings and Operating Expenditure.

Statutory Outgoings typically include:

- council or municipal rates;
- water and sewerage rates; and
- land tax.

Operating Expenditure typically includes:

- electricity;
- fire protection;
- gas and oil;
- lifts and escalators;
- pest control;
- repairs and maintenance;
- building intelligence systems;
- energy management systems;
- security;
- insurances;
- energy costs;
- management and administration;
- landscaping; and
- sundry.

The basis of outgoings recoveries from lessees can vary and typically fall into the following four categories:

- net outgoings recoveries (total recovery);
- semi-gross outgoings recoveries (increases over a base year – partial recovery);
- gross or true gross (no recovery); and
- a hybrid of any one of the above.

Typically, a net lease is one where the lessee pays a percentage of the total outgoings based on the percentage represented by its lettable area relative to the aggregate lettable area of the building. Obviously, if it is a single lessee building the lessee would pay 100% of the outgoings.

A semi-gross (increases over a base year) lease is one where a lessee pays a gross rent in year one of the lease and then pays a percentage (represented by its area over the total lettable area) of increases in outgoings over a base date. For semi-gross leases, is important to establish whether the base year is brought forward at any time during the lease term certain. In some leases with mid-term market reviews, the base year is brought forward to the lease year prior to the market review date.

A gross or true gross lease does not provide for recoveries of outgoings from lessees. In other words, the lessee pays a rental which is inclusive of the net amount of rent plus outgoings. Ostensibly, but for in the case of retail or for other costs such as marketing and promotion or in office accommodation for afterhours air-conditioning use, this represents the total occupancy cost to the lessee.

To consider a hybrid outgoings recovery lease, those characteristics considered for a net lease, semi-gross lease or a gross or true gross lease would normally apply. In addition to defining the type of outgoings recovery, leases typically include a list of outgoings items (statutory outgoings and operating expenditure) such as that set out above for the PCA Chart of Accounts. Hybrid lease recoveries occur when not all items of outgoings are recoverable. For example, a lease may be a net lease where only statutory outgoings are recoverable, or in the alternative, property management may not be recoverable for example.

Typically, net leases apply in industrial accommodation and some office accommodation although office accommodation can also be let on a semi-gross basis. Retail shops and shopping centres are often leased on a gross or true gross basis because of lessor obligations regarding disclosure statements to be provided to lessees under State-based retail leases legislation.

Hybrid lease recoveries can also be brought about by either caps or caps and collars on recoveries of certain items of outgoings, for example property management in industrial accommodation.

It is important to analyse rental evidence on a common basis to permit comparison of like with like, with gross occupancy cost often used to accommodate all relevant variables between properties. Gross total occupancy cost is defined as the total cost of occupying premises by a lessee, for example, rental obligations plus outgoings commitments under the lease relating to the building, such as air-conditioning, lift, insurance and so forth. It would not include the specific costs of the business such as light, telephone and so forth. While the collation of rental evidence can be time-consuming and challenging, it forms the fundamental basis for rental valuations.

Other issues for consideration

In addition to the fundamental issues for consideration, which are common to most leases, there may also be other issues requiring consideration in rental valuation.

Make good obligations

The obligation to make good the demised premises at the expiry of the lease imposes a burden on the lessee that would be reflected in the rent that the lessee is prepared to pay. Conversely, if the lessee does not have an obligation to make good, a higher rental may be applicable.

Accordingly, depending on the make good obligations in the lease of the demised premises and in the leases used for comparable evidence, some adjustment may be required to ensure consistency.

Lease incentives

The provision of incentives to lease property has become an accepted feature of the Australian property market. It may be common for a lessee to agree to pay a 'face rent', being the rental recorded on the lease document, but then to accept an incentive to enter into the lease which results in the effective cost of the lease to the lessee ('effective rent') being lower.

While governed by the exact wording of the lease document, notions of market rent at rent review are now generally considered to mean 'effective rent' (*Colonial Mutual Life v. HW Tasal Services Pty Ltd*, Supreme Court of Queensland, 6 June 1992, unreported; *Australian & Overseas Telecommunications Corporation Ltd v. Colonial Mutual Life Assurance Society Limited* [1992] V ConvR 54–450), being the rental rate after allowance for incentives.

Accordingly, in the analysis of comparable rental evidence, it will be necessary to quantify the incentive provided (fit out, rent-free period, rent abatement, etc.) and apply an appropriate time value of money adjustment if necessary.

GST

While most modern leases will expressly address GST, those leases which commenced before the introduction of GST in A New Tax System (Goods and Services Tax) Act 1999 should be carefully considered in the context of the transitional provisions, both when forming the subject property lease or leases for comparable rental evidence purposes.

Lessee's improvements

The relationship between lessee's improvements and rental payable under the lease requires careful consideration and close reading of the lease document. Similarly, the distinction between lessee's fixtures and fittings, lessee improvements and improvements provided as part of an incentive package also requires careful attention in determining whether they should each be included or excluded in the rental valuation.

Purpose built premises

The assessment of rental for premises either built to the express design and requirements of a lessee or in a location required by a lessee (which may not otherwise be a location typical for such development) requires very close attention to the exact wording in the rent review clause.

While the rent review clause may link to the cost of development of the property, if the rent review clause links to a notion of market rent this may be challenging to implement. Comparable evidence may be very limited for buildings of an unusual specification or for buildings in an unusual location, such that there may be a very limited market from which to draw market evidence.

Restrictive use clauses

Limitations on the permitted use under the lease should be considered in the totality of the lease and its limitations on the rights to assign. *Plinth Property Investments Limited v. Mott Moy and Anderson* (1977) 38P and CR361 discussed this issue. The rent was affirmed by the Court of Appeal and by an arbitrator, who reduced it by 30% to consider a covenant that the premises could not be used other than for offices in connection with the lessee's business of consulting engineers.

This needs to be balanced against the review provisions where reference may be made to market rent and rental based on vacant possession and open market. Such terminology may override the user provisions.

Breach of lease covenant

Generally, it is assumed that all lease covenants are complied with by both parties for the purposes of rental valuation. A distinction should be made between a remediable breach of covenant under the lease and an issue that is not a breach of covenant but a building design or property management issue.

For example, a common complaint from lessees is that the air-conditioning within the demised premises is not functioning correctly. If the responsibility for the air-conditioning is a lessor requirement, generally the lease would provide for such a matter to be addressed. It would be unfair to penalise the lessor by way of a rental reduction reflecting this issue if, in fact, the problems with the air-conditioning system were remedied immediately.

This problem should be contrasted with demised premises where the air-conditioning is totally inadequate and not able to cope satisfactorily within the accepted standards currently prevailing. Where it is obvious that the physical features of the building such as this are inadequate, this would be a factor that should be reflected in a rental review.

Rent review term and unexpired term

While many modern leases in Australia will have a regular rent review pattern of every three years or every five years, some older leases may have rent review cycles of every 7, 10, 15 or 25 years. Accordingly, the valuer seeking to undertake a rental valuation for a lease with a 15-year rent review cycle but with evidence only from leases with 5-year rent review cycles will need to make adjustment for the differing rent review terms.

Concerning the term of the lease to be assumed at rent review, the issue may arise whether this is to be the term of the whole lease or the term of the unexpired portion of the lease. Essentially, the argument relates to the position to be taken at rent review – does the valuer assume that, at a rent review, the term of the lease is the initial commencing term or does the valuer assume the remaining term certain of the lease at the time of rent review, that is, in a ten-year lease at year five rent review, do you assume a ten-year lease or do you assume a five-year term certain remaining? While practising valuers have differing opinions on which approach should apply and the exact wording of leases may vary significantly, *Burns Philp Hardware v. Howard Chia* (1987) VIII NSW LR 642 indicates an inclination by the Courts to assume the unexpired term.

Retail leases legislation

Most States and Territories now have some form of retail leases legislation that impacts upon rental valuations for those premises defined as 'retail' within the legislation. It is essential, therefore, that the valuer fully understand the legislation and its application before undertaking such a retail rental valuation.

Rental determinations

A lease with a market rental based rent review may include provisions for the determination of that rent at review, should the parties be unable to agree, by an independent party. The lease will generally provide for the framework of the rental determination, including:

- appointment of a party to undertake the determination, which is usually a valuer appointed by the President for the time being of RICS, API, Law Society or similar body or as agreed between the parties;
- to act as either an expert or as an arbitrator, with appointment as an expert more common; and
- a timeframe within which the determination is to be undertaken and concluded.

When appointed to undertake a rental determination, the independent valuer should:

- request and collate all relevant documents from the parties, including the lease and relevant agreements, floorplans, outgoings information and so forth;
- scrutinise the lease and all relevant documents to fully understand exactly what is to be determined and any conditions attaching thereto;
- consider submissions from valuers representing the lessor and lessee detailing each party's case and evidence relied upon;
- consider response submissions from each valuer, if submissions are exchanged for consideration by the other party's valuer;
- inspect the subject property; and
- issue a rental determination which may be non-speaking (comprising only the rental determined) or speaking (including rationale).

Summary

This chapter addresses valuation for rental purposes which is a fundamental issue for both investment property and occupied property. While the IVSC definition of market rent provides a helpful conceptual basis and a terminology common in many modern leases, other leases exist that require the valuer to quantify fair rent, reasonable rent and so forth at review. This challenge is compounded in the event that other lease terms such as make good and restrictive user require expression in the assessment of rent together with other issues such as incentives and GST, as considered in this chapter.

The first section of the second part of this book addressed valuation practice for conventional property sectors comprising the residential, office, retail, industrial and rural property sectors and the second section of the second part addressed valuation practice for specialist property sectors comprising retirement, leisure, plant and equipment and business and intangible asset valuation.

This third and final section of the second part addresses valuation for specific purposes, with this chapter addressing rental valuation purposes and the following chapters addressing financial reporting, secured lending, insurance and statutory valuation purposes.

Biography

Greg Preston is a founding Director of Preston Rowe Paterson and has extensive experience in real estate valuation, advisory, asset management, acquisitions, disposal and leasing, covering all facets of real estate and infrastructure. He has been involved in numerous major investment property transactions and has advised on a number of significant developments in the Sydney CBD.

Greg acts for major REITS, corporations, trusts, funds, government, banks, superannuation funds, private investors and developers in relation to commercial, retail, industrial, residential, hotel and leisure property. He has also acted for clients in relation to major infrastructure asset classes including airports, shipping ports and other infrastructure projects.

Greg, who has a Bachelor's degree in commerce and Master's degree in applied finance, is a Life Fellow of the Australian Property Institute (API) and Fellow of the Royal Institution of Chartered Surveyors (RICS). He recently won the API Colonel Alfred Clifford Catt Award for services to the property profession. Greg sits on the Executive of the Property Funds Association of Australia and is also a graduate member of the Australian Institute of Company Directors.

17 Valuation for financial reporting purposes

Richard Stewart

Introduction

With the first part of this book addressing the principles of valuation, the second part addresses the practice of valuation being grouped into three sections comprising conventional property sectors, specialist property sectors and specific purposes. Conventional property sectors include residential, office, retail, industrial and rural property valuation practice. Specialist property sectors include retirement, leisure, plant and equipment and business and intangible asset valuation practice. Specific purposes include valuation practice for rental, financial reporting, secured lending, insurance and statutory valuation purposes.

This third section of the second part of this book addresses specific purpose valuation practice with rental valuation purposes considered in the previous chapter, financial reporting valuation purposes considered in this chapter and secured lending valuation purposes, insurance valuation purposes and statutory valuation purposes considered in the following chapters.

In this chapter, key accounting standards are itemised and considered in the context of relevant valuation standards, with a detailed consideration of working with auditors which also serves as a helpful and comprehensive check list of matters for attention when undertaking valuations for financial reporting purposes.

Background

Financial reporting is one of the most frequent contexts where professional valuers will be appointed. Major valuation issues are central to the reported results and financial position of most organisations.

Valuations for financial reporting cover many diverse asset and liability types. This chapter gives a short summary of the key valuation issues and requirements that arise.

Valuers engaging in financial reporting work need to be familiar with the specific Australian Accounting Standard under which they are engaged and the general requirements of the key Accounting Standards that set the rules of the game for financial reporting valuations. This chapter explains the key standards and their requirements, with a focus on Australian accounting requirements (and touches on the US and public sector requirements) and the interaction with valuation standards.

The purpose, basis of value, disclosures, assumptions and review processes for financial reporting can markedly differ from valuations prepared in other contexts, like those valuations for capital raisings, advisory, security or insurance purposes. This chapter outlines the key differences that valuers need to be aware of.

DOI: 10.1201/9781003049555-17

Because of the centrality of valuation outcomes to financial reports and the concerns raised around values in financial statements in the run up to and aftermath of the GFC, valuations prepared for this purpose are subject to far more risk and scrutiny than ever before.

A critical part of this scrutiny is the relationship with the audit firm of the client. This has implications for valuers in terms of relationship, process, risk, documentation, disclosure and importantly costs. This chapter explains this relationship and how to manage it.

Valuation is pervasive in financial reporting

Financial reporting has evolved from its origin in using the historic cost approach to the measurement of assets to a framework where many assets and liabilities are recorded at Fair Value.

This change, which evolved over many years, is not without controversy. Some laid the blame of the Global Financial Crisis (GFC) at the feet of Fair Value Accounting, either because of the way in which asset values collapsed after the crisis or because of revaluations of assets before it. Still others say that to use historic cost ignored reality. (For a balanced and reasonable exposition of both sides of the argument, see Posen, 2009.) Either way, nobody disputes that valuation now plays a major role in outcomes in financial reports all around the world.

Many valuers who focus on one asset class will often be familiar with just a small part of the way that valuation impacts these financial reports. To provide an idea of how widespread valuation issues are in determining accounting outcomes, Table 17.1 identifies those Australian Accounting Standards where valuation is a central concern.

The standards listed in Table 17.1 are just those for companies and private sector organisations but they cover many different assets. Generally, fair value is used in these standards to establish initial transaction values and then restate them annually.

The public sector also has its own standards, similar to the above, called IPSAS. These follow a similar pattern in relation to valuation issues as the above standards. The most relevant of these for valuers is IPSAS 17, *Property Plant and Equipment*. This is quite similar to AASB117, with some specific differences in relation to heritage and infrastructure assets. (For more detail, see CPA, 2013.)

Valuers may also be instructed by clients who provide their financial reports under US (known as Statements of Financial Accounting Standards or SFAS) or International Accounting Standards (IAS), which have very similar requirements to Australian Standards (the differences in requirements relate mainly to intangible asset valuation, see Mard et al. 2007). As most valuers in Australia will be instructed to prepare reports under Australian Standards and as the practical differences in most cases between IAS, SFAS and AASB are limited, for the sake of brevity, the differences are not elaborated upon herein.

For valuers preparing valuations for financial reporting, it is essential that they aware of under which standard their report will be used. Valuers should download and read a copy of the relevant standard to understand exactly the requirements, particularly concerning disclosure. However, if there is any difficulty in interpreting the standard, the valuer should seek to be instructed as to the valuation questions that they are answering rather than being drawn in to attempting to provide accounting advice.

Table 17.1 Australian Accounting Standards and valuation issues

AASB No.	Title	Key valuation issue
2	Share-based Payments	Securities issued as consideration for service to be fair valued (para 10, specially defined in Appendix B)
3	Business Combinations	All assets and liabilities to be fair valued and separately allocated as part of Purchase Price allocation on a business combination (para 18)
5	Non-current Assets Held for Sale and Discontinued Operations	Assets held for sale to be held at lower of carrying amount or fair value less costs to sell (para 15)
9	Financial Instruments	Financial instruments to be carried at fair value (para 5.2.1)
16	Leases (supersedes AASB 117 for periods on or after 1/1/2019)	Rights of use and leases can be fair valued at the present value of lease payments (para 26)
116	Property, Plant and Equipment	Assets can be revalued at fair value (para 31) and applies AASB 136 (para 63)
136	Impairment of Assets	Assets may be impaired ie written down if higher of fair value less costs to sell (para 25) and value-in-use (para 30) is less than carrying amount
138	Intangible Assets	Can revalue intangible assets at fair value, if an active market exists (para 75)
140	Investment Property	Investment property must be carried at fair value (para 33)
141	Agriculture	Biological assets (para 12, e.g. an orchard) and Agricultural produce (para 13, e.g. a crop) must be valued at fair value
1051	Land Under Roads	May elect to value land under roads at fair value (para 13)
1056	Superannuation Entities	Assets held by (and liabilities of) superannuation funds must be held at fair value (para 13)

Source: Author

In most cases, Australian Accounting Standards refer to the basis of value described as fair value. So frequently is this term used, that a specific standard was developed in order to clarify the accounting requirements of Fair Value Measurement – AASB 13.

AASB 13 Fair Value Measurement

In the 2013 edition of IVS, fair value was defined as the 'price between identified knowledgeable and willing parties … that reflects their respective interests'. Unfortunately, this is not what fair value is from the perspective of Australian (and US, and IAS) Accounting Standards.

However, all valuation practitioners would be aware of the plethora of valuation bases that exist like fair value, fair market value, market value, investment value, etc. Because of the legal origin of many of these terms, they often differ by jurisdiction. The accounting regulators, like the IVSC, wanted a version that was consistent across the board, so this led to the birth of AASB 13 – Fair Value Measurement.

This Standard defines fair value, setting out in a single Standard a framework for measuring it and requires disclosures about fair value measurements (para 5).

This Standard applies when most other standards use the term fair value except AASB 2 Share-based Payments, AASB 117 Leases and, inter alia, value-in-use in AASB 136 Impairment of Assets (discussed below).

Importantly, AASB13 defines Fair Value as:

> the price that would be received to sell an asset or paid to transfer a liability in an orderly transaction between market participants at the measurement date (para 9)

So, effectively, AASB13 defines the basis of value to be used. It does go further in terms of describing what should be taken into account, including:

- characteristics – like condition and location of the asset and restrictions, if any, on the sale or use of the asset;
- assumptions – those that market participants would use when pricing the asset or liability, assuming that market participants act in their economic best interest;
- purchase or sale price – the exit price under current market conditions ie sale price, regardless of whether that price is directly observable or estimated using another valuation technique;
- market for the asset – principal (or most advantageous) market;
- use of the asset – highest and best use;
- techniques – shall use valuation techniques consistent with..[market, cost or income] … approaches to measure fair value; and
- inputs – shall maximise the use of relevant observable inputs and minimise the use of unobservable inputs.

AASB 13 categorises inputs on a scale of 1 to 3 as follows:

- Level 1 inputs – Level 1 inputs are quoted prices (unadjusted) in active markets for identical assets or liabilities that the entity can access at the measurement date (para 76). Valuers will seldom be engaged if the entity has access to these inputs for the asset in question;
- Level 2 inputs – Level 2 inputs are inputs other than quoted prices included within Level 1 that are observable for the asset or liability, either directly or indirectly (para 81). Examples includes comparable prices or market yields; and
- Level 3 inputs – Level 3 inputs are unobservable in a market. Examples might include future income forecasts or cost analyses.

As might be obvious, valuers will typically work on engagements where they are using a mix of Level 2 and 3 inputs.

In terms of disclosure, the entity needs to disclose the technique used, the type of inputs used and where recurring valuations are used with Level 3 inputs, how much changes in those valuations have affected profit.

Value-in-use

As noted in the foregoing section, Fair Value is used in most Australian Accounting Standards, often in conjunction with an estimate of costs to sell the asset. The largest exclusion from this general trend is the option to use a different basis of value for the purposes of assessing impairments, if it is higher than Fair Value. This alternative basis of value is described as Value-in-Use.

Valuation for financial reporting purposes

For not-for-profits, there is the possibility of using depreciated replacement cost as a mechanism to estimate Value-in-Use. This option is available where the benefits of holding the asset are not dependent on cash inflows and, if deprived of the asset, the entity owning the asset would seek to replace the benefits it brings.

Whether or not this option is available is not a question for the valuer as it is an accounting question, so the valuer should seek to be instructed that an estimate of depreciated replacement cost is required. The standard also defines depreciated replacement cost as replacement cost less depreciation assessed on the pattern of use of these non-cash benefits over the life of the asset.

For most circumstances, however, Value-in-Use is a specialised interpretation of a type of income approach to valuation, a little akin to the investment basis of valuation cited in the IVS.

According to AASB 138, the relevant accounting standard, the value-in-use income approach should reflect the following:

- an estimate of the net future cash flows the current owner (not the market) expects to derive from the asset or its disposal;
- the risk of those future cash flows;
- the time value of money and the price the market would charge for bearing the risk inherent in the future cash flows (essentially the discount rate); and
- other factors, such as illiquidity, that the market would reflect in pricing the owner's estimate of future cash flows.

AASB 138 goes further in prescribing detailed requirements concerning how the owner's expectations about cash flows should be developed, including that they should be:

- based on reasonable and supportable assumptions that represent management's best estimate of the range of economic conditions that will exist over the remaining useful life of the asset. Greater weight shall be given to external evidence that supports these judgements;
- based on the most recent financial budgets/forecasts approved by management, but excluding the cash flow impact of future restructurings or from improving or enhancing the asset's performance;
- based on these budgets/forecasts which shall cover a maximum period of five years, unless a longer period can be justified; and
- extrapolated from the most recent budgets using a steady or declining growth rate for subsequent years, unless an increasing rate can be justified. This growth rate shall not exceed the long-term average growth rate for the products, industries, or country or countries in which the owner operates or for the market in which the asset is used, unless a higher rate can be justified.

Essentially, Value-in-Use is a management valuation, with certain specified limitations imposed by AASB138. Accordingly, valuers should consider whether:

- they are in a position to prepare a valuation report described as an estimate of Value-in-Use, when they are not management; and
- if they do prepare a report that estimates Value-in-Use, it might better be described as a limited scope valuation, or a valuation calculation (as defined in APES225 – Valuation Services).

The financial reporting valuation difference

As may already be apparent, financial reporting valuations differ markedly from those for other purposes. Clearly, the objective is to support a financial reporting outcome, rather than anything else, but there are some other notable differences:

- standards are law: for most valuations, basis of value, approaches, methods and disclosure are a matter of professional practice. For financial reporting, the standards bind clients with legal force (Australian Accounting Standards are mandatory by law) which effectively binds the valuer regardless of their professional background;
- valuation standards and guidance are secondary, but important: IVS and APES valuation standards (and guidance) exist (with the API Valuation Standards Committee having developed guidance on Financial Reporting Valuations for Property, Plant and Equipment) and the standards should be followed if members of professional bodies are bound to do so. Because of the legal force of the Accounting Standards, where there is a conflict the Accounting Standard prevails. However, for matters where there is no conflict, even if a valuer is not bound to do so, it would be considered good practice to adopt the standards;
- valuation basis and other valuation issues prescribed: in most valuation engagements, the valuation basis, method, approaches, disclosures and so forth are defined by valuation standards, but the valuer and their client are free to agree which are to be used in the particular assignment. For financial reporting, the action of AASB13 means that this is not the case; and
- subject to independent real time review by auditors: in most cases, valuer's work is not subject to real time review by a third-party. Because of the assurance role played by auditors, the valuer's work will be subject to more scrutiny than in most applications. This will be explored further in the following section.

Working with auditors

As noted in the preceding section, one of the key differences between financial reporting and other valuation purposes is the involvement of another party in reviewing your work – the auditor of your client. This involvement can have a major impact on the scope, timeframes, project planning and disclosures of this type of valuation compared to any other.

To understand the role and impact that an auditor can have on your work, it is important to understand the way in which valuations for financial reporting interact with the entire financial reporting process.

In short, the process is as follows:

- the client decides that they need to obtain an external valuation to support the estimate of Fair Value in their financial report. Once appointed, the valuer has the status for audit purposes of a 'management's expert'. Management reviews and accepts the valuation as appropriate to use for their financial report;
- the auditor reviews the work of the 'management's expert' and determines whether it provides sufficient evidence to conclude regarding the Fair Value of the item valued; and
- the auditor uses this as a part of informing their view of the financial report as a whole.

Valuation for financial reporting purposes 217

There is authoritative guidance (GN005 – Using the work of management's expert) about how the auditors are likely to approach the review of your work. The discussion below describes the key aspects of that guidance.

It is important to note that the auditor retains sole responsibility for the audit opinion expressed and that responsibility is not reduced by the auditor's use of the work of a management's expert.

Based on this guidance, there are three key aspects that the auditor has to be satisfied with in relation to your valuation report:

- your competence, capability and objectivity in preparing the report;
- how you went about the work; and
- does your work contain appropriate evidence for them to conclude that the item valued in your report is appropriately carried by the client at Fair Value?

How auditors assess your competence, capability and objectivity

Auditors will use their professional judgement in assessing these factors, but key considerations are:

Capability and competence:

- do you possess appropriate education and credentials?
- are you a member of a professional body that subjects you to testing, review, continuous education, valuation standards and codes of professional practice? and
- does your organisation possess appropriate quality control procedures and other practice that connote professional quality?

Objectivity:

- are you employed by or substantially economically dependent on the commissioning client?
- are there any ethical, professional or legal requirements governing your work that promote objective and impartial advice?
- is your work subject to a contingency fee? and
- is your work commissioned by the board as opposed to management?

The auditor's conclusions on these questions will dictate whether they will ultimately accept your work, whether in their opinion another expert is required as well as you and also the amount of audit work required in relation to both understanding and evaluating your work.

What is important for the auditor to understand about your work

The auditor will seek to understand:

- the terms of your engagement, including whether the scope of your valuation is consistent with the asset recorded in the client's financial statements;
- the nature, timing and extent of work performed;
- the form of any report to be provided by that expert;
- the expert's field of expertise or the auditor's firm's previous experience with you;

- how risky your conclusions are given the economic and competitive conditions impacting the entity and its operating results;
- whether there is evidence of undue management pressure on you to reach certain conclusions;
- what level of management review your report has been subject to; and
- whether you have been authorised to discuss your findings and report with them or provide your working papers (this is not normally required).

How the auditor will evaluate your work

Generally, auditors will think about:

- how relevant and reasonable are your conclusions, assumptions, source data and methods;
- how complete and accurate is your source data;
- how consistent are your conclusions, assumptions, source data and methods compared to other audit evidence; generally this other evidence will include databases of other valuations performed for similar businesses in your client's industry; and
- whether or not your work has been included correctly in the Financial Report.

Factors the auditor may consider in relation to your report are as follows:

- are the facts and assumptions in your report consistent with the auditor's understanding of the client and its environment?
- is your report clearly expressed, including reference to the objectives agreed with management, the scope of the work performed and standards applied?
- is the report consistent with the results of other audit procedures?
- are your conclusions cross-checked against one or more other methodologies?
- is the report conducted at an appropriate period/point in time for the relevant use?
- what reservations, limitations or restrictions on use does your report contain and whether this causes issue for the auditor's purposes?
- is the report based on appropriate consideration of issues identified by the valuer?

In relation to the data, assumptions, models and methods within your report, the auditor may consider the following:

- Whether these are generally accepted in the practice of valuation?
- Whether you have justified your choice of valuation methodology?
- Whether you have been consistent with the requirements of the applicable financial reporting framework?
- How much uncertainty is there in relation to key assumptions and what stress testing have you undertaken?
- How robust is your valuation model (i.e. does it add up)?

Using their professional judgement, the auditor (either within the audit team or using valuation experts from the audit firm) may conduct a number of procedures in relation to your report, including:

- asking you questions;
- comparing drafts of your report to the finished product and making enquiries of any significant changes;
- checking how accurate your previous reports have been relative to subsequent transactions in the relevant assets;
- examining the change in your valuation from previous valuations of the same asset;
- accompanying you on-site visits or observing your other procedures;
- verifying a selection of your source data or assumptions back to reputable sources;
- re-performing certain analyses and conducting sensitivity analysis on your key inputs; and
- discussion of your report with management and board of your client.

The auditor's conclusions

If all goes well, the auditor will accept your work. If not, the following could happen:

- you have to re-perform or significantly alter your report to address the deficiencies identified;
- another expert may be appointed;
- the auditor may perform more shadow calculations to become comfortable with your conclusions; or
- the auditor may alter their opinion on the financial statements.

None of these outcomes are positive experiences. Accordingly, it is best to get ahead of this and actively manage this part of your engagement.

Managing the audit relationship around valuation

There are several things you can do to make the process and outcomes smoother for you and your clients in dealing with your auditors. Some of the questions that can be asked at each stage of the valuation are set out below:

Engagement:

- does your engagement refer to the use of your report and does it imply or express consent for use of your valuation in the financial statements?
- does your engagement letter refer to your responsibilities versus those of the auditor and the legal status of your relationship with them?
- do you have clarity on how the client would like you to engage (if at all) with the auditors during the valuation and financial reporting/audit process? and
- have you clearly articulated the basis of value, the type of valuation report you will issue, the standards you will comply with and your likely procedures?

Planning:

- have you scheduled and costed liaison points with the auditors? and
- have you designed your valuation process cognisant of the likely audit review that will be undertaken on your report?

Conducting the field work:

- what are the opportunities to involve the auditors during the valuation process (e.g. site visits) to expedite their conclusions?

Reporting:

- have you included your qualifications, professional memberships, experience and other credentials in your report?
- have you indicated the standing of your professional accreditation with references to the likely concerns of the auditor?
- have you conveyed the extent of quality control procedures you undertake in the report?
- have you clearly articulated the Accounting Standards under which you are reporting, and how you have complied with (usually) AASB13?
- how have you indicated whether you have complied with valuation standards (where they do not conflict with the AASB) and professional standards (for example the IVS or APES 225)?
- how have you demonstrated your independence and objectivity in your report?
- how have you justified your choice of approach and methodology?
- have you provided sufficient detail in your report to allow re-performance (or at least recalculation) of your valuation by the auditor?
- have you included sufficient evidence regarding the assumptions in your report?
- have you provided the source of your data, such that it is easy for the auditor to verify back to the data?
- have you performed cross checking and other reasonableness analysis in the report?
- how have you documented client review procedures in your report? and
- how have you justified any material changes in drafts of your report?

Considering these factors as you undertake the valuation assignment will make your audit process experience much smoother and headache free.

Conclusions

Twelve Australian Accounting Standards contain significant requirements for valuations. These 12 include requirements for the estimation of value for assets and liabilities including financial instruments, businesses, intangible assets, contingent liabilities, provisions and property, plant and equipment.

Typically, valuations are used either to establish the initial value of assets, revalue them annually or to assess the initial value for impairment. These estimates are fundamental to the assessment of both financial performance and position of most, if not all, Australian organisations. These valuations are particularly sensitive, not merely because of their impact but also because of the criticisms of fair value accounting during the GFC.

The general principles for Australian accounting purposes are set out in AASB 13 Fair Value Measurement. This standard sets out the predominant basis of value, Fair Value, and key assumptions about how the valuation might be assessed including the highest and best use, predominant market and the exit price assumption. It also describes the type of evidence that is preferred and how results should be disclosed to users of the Financial Reports. It is most important that valuers read and understand the requirements of this standard and the particular Australian Accounting Standard that they are being instructed under.

In addition, valuers may be instructed to perform an analysis of value-in-use under AASB 138 *Impairment of Assets*. It is important to distinguish value-in-use estimation from a typical valuation basis in terms of the use of management assumptions and exclusion of certain attributes that may be customarily used for other bases of value. If an entity is a not for profit or government entity, the valuer may be instructed to perform a depreciated replacement cost valuation of property, plant and equipment in certain circumstances, which may not be equivalent to estimating market value using a depreciated replacement cost methodology.

Valuers should understand if the client is operating under different jurisdictional requirements for financial reporting. The most common example in this country will be use in US GAAP or IPSAS based financial reports which operate under similar but not identical standards. In these cases, the valuer will need to prepare their valuation not in accordance with Australian Standards but with those of the relevant jurisdiction.

Valuers are also expected by their clients and their auditors to comply with relevant valuation standards but, where there is a conflict, the Australian Accounting Standards will be expected to prevail.

Financial reporting valuations differ from other valuations in context, purpose, basis of value, standards that apply, procedures, documentation and the level of third-party scrutiny that may be applied. Valuers need to understand these differences in considering engagement acceptance, contracting with their clients, planning and costing their work and drafting their deliverables.

Auditors are a major stakeholder in financial reporting valuations. Whilst the valuer is not responsible for the auditor's conclusions, by understanding the nature of audit review they can do many things to ease engagement, reduce costs of liaison and make their valuations more robust upon audit review.

Summary

This chapter comprehensively addresses the inextricable link between financial reporting valuations and the interaction between accounting standards and valuation standards, requiring the valuer to have a detailed knowledge of the operation of each and their interplay. Subject to a high level of scrutiny by boards, investors, auditors and analysts, valuations for financial reporting purposes are a key element in the transparency of Australia's financial reporting system.

The first section of the second part of this book addressed valuation practice for conventional property sectors comprising the residential, office, retail, industrial and rural property sectors and the second section of the second part addressed valuation practice for specialist property sectors comprising retirement, leisure, plant and equipment and business and intangible asset valuation.

This third and final section of the second part addresses valuation practice for specific purposes, with the previous chapter addressing rental valuation purposes, this chapter addressing financial reporting valuation purposes and the following chapters addressing secured lending, insurance and statutory valuation purposes.

References

Accounting Professional and Ethical Standards Board [APESB] 2012, *APES Valuation Services*, Melbourne, www.apesb.org.au (accessed 1 November 2016).

Accounting Professional and Ethical Standards Board [APESB] 2013, *APES GN20 Scope and Extent of Work for Valuation Services*, Melbourne, www.apesb.org.au (accessed 1 November 2016).

Accounting Professional and Ethical Standards Board [APESB] 2016, *APES GN21 Valuation Services for Financial Reporting*, Melbourne, www.apesb.org.au (accessed 1 November 2016).

Auditing and Assurance Standards Board [AUASB] 2015, *GS005 Using the Work of a Management's Expert*, Canberra, www.aasb.gov.au (accessed 3 November 2016).

Australian Accounting Standards Board [AASB] 2016, *AASB 2 Share-based Payment*, Canberra, www.aasb.gov.au (accessed 1 November 2016).

Australian Accounting Standards Board [AASB] 2016, *AASB 3 Business Combinations*, Canberra, www.aasb.gov.au (accessed 1 November 2016).

Australian Accounting Standards Board [AASB] 2016, *AASB 5 Non-current Assets Held for Sale and Discontinued Operations*, Canberra, www.aasb.gov.au (accessed 1 November 2016).

Australian Accounting Standards Board [AASB] 2016, *AASB 9 Financial Instruments*, Canberra, www.aasb.gov.au (accessed 1 November 2016).

Australian Accounting Standards Board [AASB] 2016, *AASB 13 Fair Value Measurement*, Canberra, www.aasb.gov.au (accessed 1 November 2016).

Australian Accounting Standards Board [AASB] 2016, *AASB 16 Leases*, Canberra, www.aasb.gov.au (accessed 1 November 2016).

Australian Accounting Standards Board [AASB] 2016, *AASB 116 Property Plant and Equipment*, Canberra, www.aasb.gov.au (accessed 1 November 2016).

Australian Accounting Standards Board [AASB] 2016, *AASB 136 Impairment of Assets*, Canberra, www.aasb.gov.au (accessed 1 November 2016).

Australian Accounting Standards Board [AASB] 2016, *AASB 138 Intangible Assets*, Canberra, www.aasb.gov.au (accessed 1 November 2016).

Australian Accounting Standards Board [AASB] 2016, *AASB 140 Investment Property*, Canberra, www.aasb.gov.au (accessed 1 November 2016).

Australian Accounting Standards Board [AASB] 2016, *AASB 141 Agriculture*, Canberra, www.aasb.gov.au (accessed 1 November 2016).

Australian Accounting Standards Board [AASB] 2016, *AASB 1051 Land under Roads*, Canberra, www.aasb.gov.au (accessed 1 November 2016).

Australian Accounting Standards Board [AASB] 2016, *AASB 1056 Superannuation Entities*, Canberra, www.aasb.gov.au (accessed 1 November 2016).

Australian Accounting Standards Board [AASB] 2016, *AASB 1056 Superannuation Entities*, Canberra, www.aasb.gov.au (accessed 1 November 2016).

CPA Australia, 2013, *Valuation and Depreciation: A Guide for the Not-for-Profit and Public Sector under Accrual Based Accounting Standards*, Melbourne, viewed 1 November 2016, <http://www.cpaaustralia.com.au>

International Public Sector Accounting Standards Board (IPSASB), *IPSAS 17 Property Plant and Equipment*, New York, www.iasplus.com/en/standards/ipsas (accessed 3 November 2016).

International Valuation Standards Council, 2013, *International Valuation Standards 2013: Framework and Requirements*, London, www.ivsc.org (accessed 1 November 2016).
Mard, MJ, Hitchner, JR and Hyden SD, 2007, *Valuation for Financial Reporting: Fair Value Measurements and Reporting, Intangible Assets, Goodwill, and Impairment*, Wiley, Hoboken.
Posen, RC, 2009, 'Is it fair to blame fair value accounting for the financial crisis?', *Harvard Business Review*, https://hbr.org/2009/11/is-it-fair-to-blame-fair-value-accounting-for-the-financial-crisis (accessed 1 November 2016).

Biography

Richard Stewart OAM is a Corporate Value Advisory Partner based in PwC's Sydney office. He has more than 30 years' experience in providing advice to national and international clients. Richard was awarded an Order of Australia Medal in January 2015 for services to social welfare organisations and the accounting profession and authored the books, *Strategic Value: Value Analysis as a Business Weapon*, published in 2012 and *Hitting Pay Dirt: Doing Mining Deals*, published in 2017.

Richard specialises in providing value advice for disputes, financial reporting, taxation, transaction pricing and other commercial purposes. He has provided independent experts reports, fairness opinions, purchase price allocations, property, plant and equipment valuations, impairment reviews, financial reporting valuations and value improvement advice across a wide variety of industries. His experience also crosses national boundaries including Australasia, Europe and the USA.

Richard's expertise in valuation has been externally recognised through his appointment as an Adjunct Professor in Business Valuation at the University of Technology, Sydney. He is also a board member (and Chair of the Audit and Finance Committee) of St Vincent De Paul Society NSW, serves on the Business Valuation Board of the International Valuation Standards Council, previously sat on the Standards Committee of the API and was a previous Chair of both the NSW Council and Business Valuation Specialisation of the ICAA (now Chartered Accountants Australia and New Zealand).

18 Valuation for secured lending purposes

Ross Turner

Introduction

With the first part of this book addressing the principles of valuation, the second part addresses the practice of valuation, being grouped into three sections comprising conventional property sectors, specialist property sectors and specific purposes. Conventional property sectors include residential, office, retail, industrial and rural property valuation practice. Specialist property sectors include retirement, leisure, plant and equipment and business and intangible asset valuation practice. Specific purposes include valuation practice for rental, financial reporting, secured lending, insurance and statutory valuation purposes.

This third section of the second part of this book addresses specific purpose valuation practice with rental valuation purposes and financial reporting valuation purposes considered in previous chapters, secured lending valuation purposes considered in this chapter and insurance valuation purposes and statutory valuation purposes considered in the following chapters.

In this chapter, valuation practice for secured lending purposes is considered with particular regard to the International Valuation Standards references to scope and reporting structure, together with issues associated with investment, owner-occupied and development property for secured lending purposes.

What risks do lenders take and how does secured lending offset this?

Lenders are in the business of selling money, ultimately at a higher margin than they can buy through either customer deposits or wholesale markets. When looking at the risks taken by banks and other financial institutions in the process of making a profit on their core business (i.e. the lending of money), the key risk taken by lenders is known as credit risk.

Credit risk is the risk of default on a debt that may arise from a borrower failing to make required payments (Basel Committee, 2000). In the first resort, the risk is that of the lender and includes lost principal and interest, disruption to cash flows and increased collection costs.

As with all businesses, lenders take steps to mitigate key risks in their profit generation process. The concept of secured lending is when a lender uses an asset as collateral to provide 'security' against the loan to mitigate against credit risk.

Collateral is something pledged as security for repayment of a loan, to be forfeited in the event of a default. Apart from cash, real property is widely used as collateral to secure against a loan facility. Security is usually taken in either the form of a mortgage or a general security agreement under the Personal Property Securities Register (formally known as a fixed or floating charge).

The inclusion of collateral secured against a loan provides the lender with a mitigant to its credit risk exposure. In the event of a potential default where the lender is seeking to call in its loan to be repaid, if collateral is secured against the loan the lender can sell the asset in order to be repaid.

A valuation for secured lending is an important decision-making document for a lender to understand the type of collateral being provided for security. When a lender requests a property valuation for secured lending, they are ultimately seeking to understand if the asset, should it be used as collateral for security, would repay the loan and any outstanding interest and expenses should an event of default occur.

As the purpose for a valuation for secured lending allows the lender to understand the collateral position to mitigate credit risk, there are often variances in instructions to valuers to ensure the valuation report clearly describes the type of collateral security (in this case a property) being considered for the loan facility. This will assist with the lenders internal decisions on how much debt can be extended in a secured facility based on the type and quality of the collateral provided.

Though replaced by IVS (2019), considering IVS (2017) informs an understanding of valuation for secured lending purposes. Under IVS (2017), IVS 101 provides guidance on the required scope for a valuation with IVS 103 focusing on reporting requirements and IVS 310 providing more clarity on the scope, structure and additional reporting necessary for secured lending. IVS 310 also touches on the importance of foreseeability for a lender over the loan facility period, as well as providing a broad discussion of how different property types are viewed for collateral purposes and what steps the valuer can take to assist the lender with their credit decisioning process when assessing the suitability of the collateral offered.

Scope and reporting structure

IVS 101 and IVS 310 in IVS (2017) identify nine key issues for consideration.

Conflict of interest

Concerning conflict of interest, IVS 101 paragraph 2 (a) notes:

> The scope of work shall additionally include a disclosure of any material involvement that the valuer has with either the property to be valued, the borrower or a prospective borrower. The materiality of existing or past involvement is a matter of professional judgement for the valuer but the principal criteria is whether the involvement would be likely to give rise to doubt in the mind of a reasonable person as to the ability of the valuer to provide an impartial valuation if it were discovered after the valuation had been carried out.

An example of this is if the valuer provided advice to the vendor for the sale of the property and was now being requested to value for the purchaser. This would represent a conflict of interest and would need to be disclosed to the lender. In most cases, the valuation for the purchaser would have to be declined.

Property identification

To comply with the requirement to identify the assets to be valued in IVS 101 para 2(d), the real property interest to be used as the collateral for securing the loans or other financing arrangements shall be clearly identified, together with the party in whom the interest is currently vested.

Assets being valued must be clearly identified as they are then linked to a lenders security schedule for the facility being offered for collateral management purposes. It often occurs that lenders or intermediaries managing the valuation process will request even the smallest of changes if property identification is incorrect, due to the important nature of this issue.

Title search – define the interest

The lender will normally require the valuer to search and comment on the title and clarify the interest of the property being valued (e.g. a freehold or fee simple interest). Application Guidance for IVS 310 (IVS, 2017) states that where detailed information on title has not been provided or is unavailable, the assumptions that have been made concerning the real property interest should be clearly stated. It is also good practice to recommend that these matters be verified before any loan is finalised.

The interest being valued forms a basis for the financier's decision-making process in assessing reliance on the collateral (together with the party in whom the interest is currently vested).

When determining the strength of the collateral being provided for security, lenders may potentially consider a freehold interest to provide a strong collateral security position, whereas a leasehold interest (depending on the lease term remaining) could be regarded as either suitable or unsuitable collateral for security. Financiers may also adopt a different lending margin or loan to value ratio (LVR) depending on the interest being valued to allow for a change in risk position.

As well as the property interest, adverse notations on title also need to be discussed in a valuation report as they may impact on the property's suitability as collateral security. Examples of notations on title potentially impacting security include:

- a noted lease on title that, due to its term, may delay and defer the development potential of the property;
- a notation on title that part of the asset is subject to a future resumption for road widening;
- an easement on title restricting utility or future development potential; or
- the building is subject to conditions of a building management statement requiring the sharing of common property which may reduce the overall utility, marketability and value of the property.

It is important for the valuer to comment on notations and to assess, in their opinion, whether they would potentially impact on the marketability or value of the asset in the current or foreseeable future.

Valuation date

The lender would normally require that the date of valuation is current when they receive a report. The issue of currency relates primarily in Australia to clauses in valuations required by professional indemnity insurance providers, which require a 90-day reliance period within their reports.

While providing a 'current' valuation is not normally an issue for simpler properties, for more complex assets where there can be a substantial lead time for the valuer to receive information, the valuation may be approaching three months old when it reaches the credit approvers desk.

To offset this, the lender may place a requirement in the valuers scope, as well as the loan facility agreement, that the report must be received with two months of currency (i.e. approximately a month from the valuation date) so that the lender can rely and use the valuation as a key tool in its credit approval process.

Identification of client, basis of value and purpose

When instructed to undertake a valuation for secured lending, IVS 101 (2e) states the basis of the valuation will be market value.

Guidance Note G4 in IVS 310 (IVS, 2017) expands on the valuation approach for secured lending, noting that if a property is so specialised that either a market approach or income approach is not suitable (due to the lack of evidence), it would be unlikely that the property would be suitable security.

The purpose of the valuation in an instruction letter for secured lending will usually be for (first) mortgage security purposes and the lender would also require that the lender be noted in the report for reliance purposes.

It is important for the valuer to specifically address who can rely on the report and for what use for the following reasons:

- so the report is not relied upon out of the context for which it was intended;
- so the report not be extended to lenders that the valuer does not wish to extend to; or
- so the report is covered under the conditions of their professional indemnity insurance agreement.

Assumptions

A situation may arise where both the lender and client may have different requests to include in the scope of a valuation required for mortgage lending purposes.

However, both the lender or the client (if they are instructing the valuer directly) may ask that the valuer allow for specific assumptions to be included in the valuation report. Examples of such requests could include:

- market value assumption given a specific marketing and sales period;
- alternate use assumption where there is no clear market for the existing use;
- assumption that a draft lease, agreement for lease or heads of agreement has been executed;
- assumption that renovation, rectification or development works have been completed; or
- that the site is assumed to be clear of contamination.

These requested assumptions may not be consistent with the definition and intent of market value. When forming an opinion of the security value of the collateral, client requested assumptions may not be suitable to the lender. Assumptions that are inconsistent with the intent of market value are called special assumptions.

IVS 101 para 2(i) states that any special assumptions that are considered necessary shall be included in the scope of work. When reporting special assumptions for secured lending purposes, IVS 310 (IVS, 2017) highlights that, where the market value is provided subject to a special assumption, the report should include:

- an explanation of the special assumption;
- a comment on any material difference between market value and the market value subject to the special assumption; and
- a comment that such value may not be realisable at a future date unless the factual position is as described in the special assumption.

Foreseeability

The concept of foreseeability is widely discussed within the IVS guidance framework and is an important aspect of the lender's decision-making process when deciding if an asset is suitable collateral to provide security for a loan facility.

IVS 310 (IVS, 2017) provides guidance on the point of foreseeability indicating 'the valuation report shall also include comment on factors that are relevant to a lenders assessment of the performance of security over the life of the proposed loan'. Examples of these factors include:

- current activity and trends in the relevant market;
- historic, current and anticipated future demand for the type of property and location;
- any potential and likely demand for alternative uses that exist or can be anticipated at the valuation date; and
- the impact of any events foreseeable at the valuation date on the probable future value of the security during the loan period. An example would be a lessee exercising an option to renew or surrender a lease.

Foreseeability is very important from a lenders perspective as it provides the lender with guidance on not only the sustainability of value but also income, sustained demand for the asset class, the ability for environmental risks to be controlled and the existence of potential alternate uses. The suitability of the asset for collateral is as important to the lender at the time of valuation as it is at the time the loan facility is required to be repaid in the future.

With the term of a commercial loan facility typically being one to five years, foreseeability is an important part of the process of deciding if the proposed collateral will be suitable security over the loan's life cycle.

The concept of foreseeability is once again raised in IVS 310 Application Guidance G7 (IVS, 2017), which states that:

> consideration should be given to the expected demand for and marketability of the property over the life of the loan and appropriate advice on current market conditions provided in the report. This advice should not involve predicting future events or values but should reflect current market expectations of the future

performance of the investment based on current trends. However, if such information suggests a significant risk to future rent payments, the impact of this risk on the valuation should be considered and commented upon in the report.

Some examples of how a valuer could provide feedback and foreseeability to the lender concerning potential future performance of an asset include:

- the building is fully leased to a single lessee, however the lessee has vacated the building or it is known in the marketplace that the lessee is looking to relocate;
- the asset reports high levels of occupancy due to a number of accommodation contracts; however, there is no sign of guests at the property, which may warrant further enquiries;
- a new shopping centre is under development in the same catchment as the subject property being valued, with the new centre potentially impacting the trade of the property being valued;
- a commercial strata unit is leased to a lessee for five years on a gross rental below market parameters; conversations with the building manager reveal major works in the next 12 months to the common area lifts and façade of the building will increase outgoings by 20%, potentially reducing the net return from the strata investment; or
- the property is located in an area subject to a draft planning proposal that potentially improves the development potential of the property.

Comments from the valuer to note and identify potential future risks to the security allow the financier an opportunity to structure the transaction in a manner that allows for these risks, to potentially reduce their exposure to the asset or to decide to monitor the asset more frequently.

Guidance Note G8 of IVS 310 (IVS, 2017) indicates

> it is normally outside the scope of the valuation assignment to advise on the ability of a lessee to meet future rent payments and other lease obligations beyond reflecting the information available on the lessee that is in the public domain and available to all market participants.

Whilst taking the above Guidance Note on board, the valuer may be aware of information surrounding the broader market that could impact on the valuation of the property asset not confined to that lease information provided.

In either case, reporting non-reasonable foreseeability within the valuation report provides the financier with the ability to control and mitigate potential foreseeable events that may impact the income, marketability and value of the proposed collateral.

Incentives

Guidance Note G3 in IVS 310 (IVS, 2017) states that 'it is not uncommon for a seller of property, especially a property developer or trader, to offer incentives to buyers'. This is also commonly the case with new lease agreements.

Incentives may be in many forms including rent abatement, fit out contributions for new lease agreements and rental income guarantees and stamp duty contributions for buyers.

When valuing an asset for lending security, the basis of value is market value. As confirmed in IVS Guidance Note 3, '*market value* ignores any price inflated by special considerations or concessions'.

Where incentives are offered as an inducement to a sale, IVS 310 indicates that it is appropriate to comment on the effect that any incentives being offered have on the actual selling prices achieved as the incentives may not be available to the lender in the event that it had to rely on the security. With regard to leasing incentives, any outstanding value should be deducted for mortgage security purposes.

Contract of sale

Where an asset is under contract it is a requirement for the valuer to comment on the contract of sale and also understand the positioning of any under bidders and the conditions of any other known offers. IVS 310 (IVS, 2017) states that enquiries should be made to establish the sale price and the result of those enquiries referred to in the report. Where there is a difference between a recent or pending transaction price and the valuation, the report shall comment on the reasons for this difference.

Property types

It has been established that valuations for secured lending help determine the suitability of collateral as security for a loan facility. This will assist with the lender's internal decisions on how much debt can be extended in a secured facility based on the type and quality of the collateral provided.

A lender's opinion on the quality of collateral provided depends heavily on the property type and interest valued. IVS 310 (IVS, 2017) provides guidance on specific requirements based on the type of property/interest being valued. The guideline states that it is important that the valuation of the relevant interest addresses these requirements in order to properly provide the lender with adequate information on the suitability of the property as security and to help the lender identify any risk factors associated with the property over the duration of the loan.

Investment property

Guidance Note G6 and G9 of IVS 310 (IVS, 2017) consider investment property for secured lending.

When a financier is looking at the suitability of an investment property asset for proposed collateral, the reporting of an investment asset's income, the term certain of that income and the quality of the lessees providing that income are all important components in deciding the suitability of the collateral. Whilst the Guidance Notes are not intended to provide full guidance on how to prepare a valuation of investment property, key items that a lender would be looking to identify when assessing the suitability of the collateral for security purposes would be:

- quality of the lessee profile – are any lessees from industry sectors that are undergoing uncertain economic conditions that may potentially cause uncertainty of future income?
- length of term certain of lease or weighted average lease expiry profile (WALE) and the identification of any potential threats or potential uplift to the expiry profile;

- identification of which lessees passing rentals are below market rentals, with reversionary calculations and commentary on when they will revert to market rents; and
- identification of profit rental for over-market rentals and commentary on whether the potential wasting nature of this value component is material in the context of the overall value of the asset.

Guidance Note G9 from IVS 310 goes on to further state:

> if the income from a property is critically dependent on a lessee or lessees from a single sector or industry or some other factor which could cause future income instability, the impact should be considered in the valuation process. In certain cases, an assessment of the value of the property based on an alternative use, assuming vacant possession, may be appropriate.

When looking at investment valuations forming part of a portfolio, it is notable in Australia and New Zealand that such investment properties are normally requested to be valued on an individual basis with no regard to any premium paid for a portfolio for collateral purposes.

This is supported by Guidance Note 6 from IVS 310 which states that:

> Investment property is usually valued for lending purposes on an asset-by-asset basis, although some lenders may lend against the value of a defined portfolio. In such instances, the distinction needs to be made between the value of the individual investment property, assuming it is sold individually, and its value as part of the portfolio.

Owner-occupied property

The intent of IVS 310 (IVS, 2017) is that owner-occupied property should be valued on a vacant possession basis and that the buyer or lender calling on its collateral would be entitled to full legal control and possession. A key point for valuers in this area is to have regard to leases between related parties of the owner of the property and, if these are identified, they are required to be outlined in the report and disregarded with the property to be valued on a vacant possession basis.

Development property

The approach to the valuation of a development property for secured lending will depend on the amount of certainty surrounding a development concept as the quality of collateral varies greatly given the position of the property in the development life cycle. Whilst not an all-inclusive list, the following points represent a basic development life cycle. It is considered that a lender would take a different view as to the quality of the collateral at each stage of the cycle:

- no approvals; however, zoning or planning information indicates highest and best use for development;
- development approval or planning consent (providing certainty of a specific development concept);

- appointment of builder/contractor, verification of costs by a quantity surveyor, achieved pre-sales, building/construction approval;
- practical completion of construction, building occupancy certificate received, pre-sales settlement process, balance completed unit stock remains (if not fully pre – sold).

Guidance Note G14 of IVS 310 (IVS, 2017) indicates that:

> *properties held for development or sites intended for development of buildings are valued taking into account existing and potential development entitlements and permissions. Any assumptions as to zoning issues and other material factors need to be reasonable and reflect those that would be made by market participants.*

Based on the above basic life cycle of a development, it may be contended that the highest level of assumptions and the highest risk to collateral would be at the first stage of the development, with assumptions and risk to collateral decreasing as the life cycle progresses.

The point where a development sits in the development life cycle influences the type of valuation approach to be used as at the date of valuation. Guidance Note 15 provides requirements for consideration:

- estimating the development period from the date of valuation, and the need to reflect any intended phasing of the development project;
- determining the effect of additional development requirements on costs and revenues, using present value discounting where appropriate;
- identifying anticipated market trends over the period of the development;
- identifying the risks associated with the development;
- considering the impact of any special relationships between the parties involved in the development.

Where a completed development will consist of multiple individual units, Guidance Note 16 requires the valuation method adopted to reflect the anticipated timing of both the completion of the construction of each unit and a realistic estimate of the rate at which individual sales will take place.

If a development has been completed but is not proposed to sell down stock individually, such that there is balance stock, a lender may take a different position on collateral and may instruct an 'In Line Assessment'.

Guidance Note 16 (IVS, 2017) confirms that:

> when reporting, a clear distinction should be made between the value of the completed development to a single buyer who would assume the cost and risk of onward sales of the individual units in return for a profit margin, and the sum of the individual anticipated prices for each individual unit.

Wasting assets

Guidance Note 18 (IVS, 2017) provides commentary in relation to wasting assets. A good example of a wasting asset is a caravan park subject to a non-renewable leasehold interest with a short term remaining.

The Guidance Note states that:

> the estimated life and the rate of value erosion over that life should be identified and clearly stated in the report.

In the absence of directly comparable market evidence, a comparable capitalisation rate could be achieved through a dual rate calculation to reconcile a capitalisation rate from other market evidence or, if an investment or going concern asset, calculating the present value of the income/net profits from the remaining term of the lease at an applicable discount rate to reflect the risk.

Summary

This chapter addressed valuation practice for secured lending purposes with particular regard to the International Valuation Standards references to scope and reporting structure, together with issues associated with investment, owner-occupied and development property for secured lending purposes.

Given the role of the property valued as collateral for lending, the importance of identifying the property and defining the interest held are emphasised, together with the valuation date and any assumptions or special assumptions that may have been made. Further, the challenging issue of foreseeability is addressed in the context of the life of the loan for which the subject property is collateral.

The first section of the second part of this book addressed valuation practice for conventional property sectors comprising the residential, office, retail, industrial and rural property sectors and the second section of the second part addressed valuation practice for specialist property sectors comprising retirement, leisure, plant and equipment and business and intangible asset valuation.

This third and final section of the second part addresses valuation for specific purposes, with the previous chapters addressing rental valuation purposes and financial reporting valuation purposes, this chapter addressing secured lending valuation purposes and the following chapters addressing insurance and statutory valuation purposes.

References

International Valuation Standards Council 2017, *International Valuation Standards*, International Valuation Standards Council, London.
International Valuation Standards Council 2019, *International Valuation Standards*, International Valuation Standards Council, London.
Basel Committee on Banking Supervision 2000, *Principles for the Management of Credit Risk – Final Document*, Basel Committee on Banking Supervision, Basel.

Biography

Ross Turner is the National Director, Commercial, Agribusiness and Advisory at Opteon, being a property valuer and consultant with over 18 years' experience across regional and metropolitan markets in Australia and New Zealand.

Ross has held previous roles in property risk oversight and review at Commonwealth Bank of Australia in its institutional bank, along with other valuation roles at Savills and Herron Todd White. He holds a Bachelor of Business Management (Real Estate and Development) from the University of Queensland and is an Associate of the Australian Property Institute as a Certified Practising Valuer.

His areas of expertise include commercial office and childcare valuations (both individually and on a national portfolio basis), property risk review advice and research and advisory for national markets outside of those traditionally covered by PCA Research.

Ross believes in the importance of training future valuers in the most current, effective and accurate methods of property valuation to give them a solid foundation in an ever-evolving industry.

19 Valuation for insurance purposes

Cameron Dunsford, Mark Klenke and Ashley Grant

Introduction

With the first part of this book addressing the principles of valuation, the second part addresses the practice of valuation being grouped into three sections comprising conventional property sectors, specialist property sectors and specific purposes. Conventional property sectors include residential, office, retail, industrial and rural property valuation practice. Specialist property sectors include retirement, leisure, plant and equipment and business and intangible asset valuation practice. Specific purposes include valuation practice for rental, financial reporting, secured lending, insurance and statutory valuation purposes.

This third section of the second part of this book addresses specific purpose valuation practice with rental valuation purposes, financial reporting valuation purposes and secured lending valuation purposes considered in previous chapters, insurance valuation purposes considered in this chapter and statutory valuation purposes considered in the following, final chapter.

In this chapter, valuation practice for insurance purposes is considered with particular regard to the central concepts of reinstatement value and Indemnity Value, focusing the valuer's attention on the important differences from the concept of market value on various bases.

ANZVTIP4 – *Valuations for insurance purposes*

The Australia and New Zealand Valuation Technical Information Paper 4 (ANZVTIP 4), *Valuations for Insurance Purposes*, provides:

> Reinstatement Cost
>
> Where property is lost or destroyed, in the case of a building, the rebuilding thereof, or in the case of property other than a building, the replacement thereof by similar property in either case in a condition equal to, but not better or more extensive than its condition when new.

However, as insurance policies require declarations on other likely costs incurred following an insured loss, valuations should also give consideration of assessment and allowances for the following:

- demolition and removal of debris costs;
- all building services and foundations;
- any Extra Cost of Reinstatement;

DOI: 10.1201/9781003049555-19

- compliance with Australian and local building codes;
- compliance with relevant authorities;
- cost escalations during the policy period;
- cost escalations during planning, approval and rebuilding lead times; and
- heritage implications (where applicable).

This chapter addresses the issues raised by the above definition of Reinstatement Cost.

Reinstatement value

In general, Reinstatement Value of physical assets is an assessment of value used in determining the Total Declared Value under an insurance policy.

Whilst at times interchangeable, Reinstatement Value and Declared Value can differ with the latter including values for items such as Loss of Rent, Business Interruption (Loss of Profit) including increased cost of operation, Stock and Work in Progress.

Application to plant, machinery and equipment

Reinstatement Value of plant, machinery and equipment is generally assessed using either an individual asset summation (bottom-up approach) or an overall cost of capacity (top-down approach).

Individual asset summation (bottom-up approach)

The bottom-up approach aims to create a profile of the totally installed cost of the assets whether as stand-alone, process area or functional units from an individual asset perspective. That is, to build up a total installed cost of the site assets.

This method involves the following steps.

Prepare detailed major asset listing

A detailed listing of assets is established through site inspections, review of relevant documentation such as process flow diagrams (PFD's), fixed asset registers, engineering equipment listings, specification sheets and interviews with site personnel.

Obtain details of 'ex-works' costs of major assets

The manufacturers and suppliers of the assets are contacted to establish 'ex-works' costs of the major assets. Both firm and budget quotations are typically obtained.

Determine appropriate multiples and total installed cost

This method requires taking the sum of the ex-works cost of the assets and multiplying them by an industry standard multiple/factor to determine a total installed cost of the assets, inclusive of its associated services and minor assets. The multiple/factor considers:

- associated minor assets;
- design costs;
- freight and transport costs;

Valuation for insurance purposes 237

- erection costs;
- installation and commissioning costs;
- instrumentation and electrical costs;
- civil works costs; and
- piping and services costs.

Further engineering costs and contingencies

Cost overruns in relation to budgeted or estimated costs arise on construction contracts because of many factors such as bad weather, unexpected material cost increases and the inevitable inability to forecast future events with complete accuracy. Allowances for contingency costs are made to account for those unforeseen costs which may be incurred in addition to the budgeted or estimated reinstatement cost of an asset.

The following are not included in the multiple/factor and are added as a percentage to ascertain the overall reinstatement cost:

- engineering, procurement and construction management costs;
- owner's costs; and
- contingencies.

When determining the reinstatement costs of individual assets, the 'expected capacity in use' of the existing assets must be considered. 'Expected capacity in use' is the required level of service potential or output consistent with the site's current configuration and the objective of minimising the whole of life cost of assets under 'total asset management' concepts and business planning horizons.

Overall cost of capacity (top-down approach)

This approach seeks to establish an estimate for the total overall group of assets making up each location based on comparisons.

The most reliable means of determining an estimate of reinstatement, for a top-down approach, is from either factoring known costs of recently built similar projects or from establishing capacity-based rates of each functional unit and applying these to the subject current configuration and asset base.

From the analysis of available data and in consultation with appropriate construction firms, a reinstatement cost can be established, after suitable adjustments are made for site specific factors such as the slope of the land, location and overall capacity.

Application to buildings and site improvements

Reinstatement value of buildings and site improvements is typically assessed using a limited quantity surveying approach.

This approach involves the individual calculation of building quantities for the major components of an asset, such as basement/underground areas, car parking, warehousing, office areas and so forth. A suitable determined construction cost rate can then be applied to the individual areas.

Caution must be taken to ensure that the determined rates include not only the shell but also all services such as air-conditioning, sprinklers, ventilation and lighting together with goods and passenger lifts, if appropriate. The valuer should ensure that all special features are listed and measured separately and included in the overall reinstatement calculation.

This approach considers the following:

- modern equivalent construction methods where appropriate;
- quantities of materials used in the building;
- architects, engineering and survey fees, including a contingency allowance; and
- Extra Cost of Reinstatement to comply with current building and fire regulations.

Extra Cost of Reinstatement

The extra cost of reinstatement clause was added to insurance policies to cover for any statutory authorities' requirements, following a loss, to bring not only the damaged portion but also any undamaged portion up to current standards. Extra cost of reinstatement is sub-limited within an ISR insurance policy and is not subject to the co-insurance clause. However, it is important when undertaking an insurance valuation that an assessment for these costs be made so that the adequacy of the existing sub-limit amount can be made.

Important factors to consider when assessing the extra cost of reinstatement include any Federal, State or local government regulations that control construction and development, the most significant being the National Construction Code/Building Code of Australia which is typically enacted in each State and Territory by a Building Act and associated regulations.

This Code provides the minimum requirements for safety and health, amenity and accessibility and sustainability in design, construction, performance and liveability of new buildings and new work in existing buildings in Australia. It categorises buildings and structures into different classes and sub-classes (Class 1 to 10), with the regulations controlling the construction of buildings then based on this classification – it is, therefore, important to correctly classify the building being valued and to understand the minimum requirements for that class of building. Should the property being valued not meet these minimum requirements, then the valuer will need to make an assessment as to the cost of bringing the building up to the required standards as part of the hypothetical rebuild.

Examples of some of these requirements could include the cost of a lift to provide access for mobility impaired people, the provision of fire sprinklers or the provision of additional sanitary facilities within a building. The assessment of these additional costs is required on an elemental cost basis.

The Code also enforces Australian Standard 3959 *Construction of Buildings in Bushfire-Prone Areas*, which specifies minimum construction requirements for certain buildings that are constructed within declared bushfire-prone areas. The cost of complying with this Standard will depend on the individual Bushfire Attack Level (BAL) for the property. Any valuer making an extra cost of reinstatement assessment will need to first know if the property is located within a bushfire-prone area, next know the BAL rating for the site and finally be aware of the relevant construction requirements and associated costs for that BAL level.

Finally, a valuer needs to be aware of the requirements for development enforced by local governments through their planning/development regulations. Such plans may stipulate boundary setbacks, building heights and size as well as parking requirements and these may have changed since the existing improvements were constructed. Should the existing improvements to a property not comply with these requirements, a valuer will either need to assess the likely cost associated with making the improvements comply or, alternatively, where applicable, the fees payable to the council for non-compliance with these requirements.

Removal of debris

An Industrial Special Risk insurance policy may include a removal of debris sub-limit cover for the:

> removal, storage and/or disposal of debris or the demolition, dismantling, shoring up, propping, underpinning or other temporary repairs consequent upon damage to the property.

In assessing the likely costs incurred in removal of debris from a site following a loss, five main factors need to be assessed, namely:

- size of the asset;
- type of construction;
- location;
- nature of occupancy; and
- presence of contaminants.

The size of the asset is the starting point for any removal of debris assessment, with smaller buildings generally costing less to demolish and remove than larger buildings. The size of the building will not only establish the length of time it will take to demolish the structure but also the volume of material that will need to be removed and disposed of. Although a smaller structure will cost less to demolish than a larger structure, it is important to remember that a scale of economy does exist so that, when measured against the square metre size of the building, the demolition cost of a small building will likely cost more per square metre than for a larger building.

The type of building construction to be demolished and disposed of also impacts on the cost of demolition and removal, as this affects the time taken and the volume of material that can be recycled and removed for disposal. Factors to be considered when looking at the type of construction include:

- number of levels, both above and below ground;
- type of building, for example factory/warehouse as compared to an office building; and
- materials used in the construction, for example the steel in a shed may be able to be sold as scrap so offsetting the cost of demolition.

All other things being equal, a multi-level building will cost more to demolish and remove than a single level building, a factory will cost less per square metre of building area to demolish than an office and a steel shed would cost less than a brick structure.

The location of the asset also impacts on the cost of removal of debris. Factors to be considered in this regard include:

- country v metropolitan location – country locations may have lower dumpage charges than metropolitan areas for the material to be disposed of; however, travel costs for appropriately qualified contractors to undertake the work may negate this saving; and
- location of the asset on the site – is the building or asset set back or built on the site boundaries? This will impact on the ease of access that demolition contractors have as well as the requirement for other costs, such as shoring up adjacent buildings or the need for traffic management plans.

The nature of the occupancy of the building can also impact on the removal of debris cost for a site. Environmental Protection Authorities across Australia often insist on very stringent procedures to remove and dispose of debris from certain occupiers such as paint or chemical manufacturers. In some cases, the compliance with these requirements, which are designed to minimise the impact of potential contaminants to the site, can cost more than the actual construction cost of the improvements themselves.

The final factor to be considered when assessing a removal of debris cost for a site is the presence of contaminants, especially asbestos. This material was not officially banned in Australia until 31 December 2003 and so any asset constructed prior to this date could contain asbestos. In undertaking an insurance assessment for a building constructed prior to this date, the valuer should ask for a copy of the site's hazardous materials register which will highlight where, how much and what type of material is present on the site. If more than 10 sqm of non-friable asbestos material is present on a site, then this must be removed by an appropriately qualified and licensed contractor. The cost to safely remove and dispose of asbestos material is significant and can be up to four times the cost of an equivalent site without asbestos.

Limit of Liability

In an Industrial Special Risk insurance policy, the total liability of an insurer is capped to the stated Limit of Liability within the policy. This amount therefore needs to reflect the worst-case situation loss for a site and so needs to be the sum of the Reinstatement Value of the assets, any Extra Costs of Reinstatement, the removal of debris costs associated with the site as well as incorporating any anticipated cost increases between policy start date and the final date that the asset is replaced.

In establishing the anticipated cost increases between the policy start date and the final date that the asset is replaced, three time periods should be considered, namely:

- the period covered by the policy – this is usually one year;
- the anticipated time taken following a loss to clear the site and gain all necessary approvals to begin rebuilding on the site; and
- the anticipated time it would then take to rebuild the assets.

The assessed allowance for any cost increases over these time periods will be impacted by not only the extent that prices are anticipated to increase over the period but also by the total length of time it would take to achieve the replacement of the asset.

In determining the extent of anticipated price increases over the three time periods stated above, the valuer will need to form an opinion, based on appropriate research, on factors including the future level of construction activity, supply and demand impacts and potential exchange rate movements (which would impact any imported assets). Based on these and any other relevant factors, the valuer will typically establish an anticipated annual percentage cost increase (compounded) over the forecast period.

In establishing the likely time it would take to clear the site, gain all necessary approvals to allow a rebuild of the assets as well as the time to rebuild the assets, the valuer would need to not only take account of the type/nature of the assets in question but also any constraints on the site such as:

- heritage listings of assets – these can significantly extend anticipated time periods;
- is it a complying land use within the local planning controls? – if not, this can also extend approval times; and
- prevailing construction conditions – if construction pipelines are full, then rebuilding times may be longer.

Based on the relevant site specific and general market factors, anticipated planning approval and rebuild times need to be established. For some assets, the Limit of Liability will represent an estimated value of the asset several years in advance.

Once these time periods are established, then the Limit of Liability for the site can be calculated using the following formulae:

$$DV = RV + ECR + RD$$

Where:
DV = Declared Value
RV = Reinstatement Value
ECR = Extra Cost of Reinstatement
RD = Removal of Debris

therefore:

$$LL = (DV \times (1+PYI)) \times (PP \times (1+PPI)) \times (RP \times PPF \times (1+RBI))$$

where:
LL = Limit of Liability
PYI = Policy Year Inflation Rate
PP = Policy Period (expressed as years)
PPI = Policy Period Inflation Rate (expressed as an annual percentage)
RP = Rebuilding Period (expressed as years)
PPF = Progress Payment Factor (factor to allow for progress payment factors during construction)
RBI = Rebuilding Period Inflation Rate (expressed as an annual percentage)

Indemnity Value

Indemnity Value may be defined as:

> The cost necessary to replace, repair and or rebuild the asset insured to a condition and extent substantially equal to but not better or more extensive than its condition and extent at the time that the damage occurred, taking into consideration the age, condition and remaining useful life of the asset.

In plain-speak, this is the value of an asset at the time of the loss. Payment of the Indemnity Value is designed to put you in the same financial position that you were in immediately before the loss occurred. Indemnity Value must, therefore, take into account deprecation.

Because Indemnity Value must recognise deprecation, the determinants of Indemnity Value include those associated with both the Cost and Market Approaches.

The phrase Indemnity Value is often open to interpretation, as exemplified by the following actual policy wording excerpts:

Example 1

Basis of Loss Settlement

... Provided that if the Insured elects to claim the indemnity value of any physically lost, destroyed or damaged property, the Insurers will pay to the Insured the indemnity value of such property at the time of the happening of the loss, destruction or damage or at their option reinstate, replace or repair such property or any part thereof. In any event the Insurers will pay any costs incurred by the Insured in accordance with the provisions of the Extra Cost of Reinstatement Memorandum.

For the purpose of this Memorandum, the term 'indemnity value' shall mean:

a   the cost necessary to replace, repair or rebuild the Property Insured to a condition substantially the same as but not better or more extensive than its condition at the time of the happening of the loss, destruction or damage taking into consideration the age, condition and remaining useful life of such property;

or, where such property is not to be replaced, repaired or rebuilt:

b   the value of the Property Insured to the Insured at the time of the happening of the loss, destruction or damage; taking into consideration the location, market value (if any), age, condition and remaining useful life of such property having regard to the nature of the property and the purpose(s) for which it is owned, maintained or used by the Insured.

Example 2

4. Basis of Settlement for the purpose of this Clause 4:
   4.2 Indemnity Value is:
   4.2.1 where the Damage to any Property Insured can be repaired, the cost necessarily incurred to restore the property to a condition substantially the same as but not better or more extensive than its condition at the time that the Damage occurred taking into consideration age, condition and remaining useful life,

including the cost of dismantling and re-erection incurred for the purpose of effecting the repairs. Deductions will not be made for depreciation in respect of parts replaced, but the salvage value of such parts shall be taken into account;

4.2.2 where the property is totally destroyed, lost or stolen, abandoned or cannot be satisfactorily repaired at a cost not exceeding the Market Value immediately before the Damage, the Market Value of the item at the time of the Damage. If due to the nature of the property, it is not possible to readily ascertain a Market Value, the Basis of Settlement shall be the replacement cost of the damaged property less due allowance for depreciation taking into consideration age, condition and remaining useful life.

Market Value is the estimated amount for which the Property Insured should exchange immediately before the Damage, between a willing buyer and a willing seller in an arms-length transaction, after proper marketing, wherein the parties had each acted knowledgably, prudently and without compulsion

Example 3

Construction Risks – Material Damage Project Insurance Policy
Indemnity Value means:

i where the Damage to property can be repaired, the Insurers will pay the cost necessarily incurred to restore the property to its former state of serviceability, plus the cost of dismantling and re-erection incurred for the purpose of effecting the repairs. Deductions will not be made for depreciation in respect of parts replaced, but the salvage value of such parts shall be taken into account;

ii where the Insured Property is totally destroyed, lost or stolen, abandoned or cannot be satisfactorily repaired at a cost not exceeding the market value immediately before the Damage, the Insurers will pay the market value of the item at the time of the Event. If due to the nature of the Insured property, it is not possible to readily ascertain a market value, the basis of settlement shall be the replacement cost of the damaged property less due allowance for depreciation taking into consideration the anticipated useful life of the property and the nature of its usage;

iii if the Insured Property is reasonably abandoned because the cost of recovery would exceed the amount payable under this Policy in respect of such property, it shall be deemed to be a constructive total loss and settlement shall be made in accordance with clause i.

The concept of Indemnity Value and the determinants of it require differing treatment for buildings and for plant, machinery and equipment (P&M).

In the case of the Indemnity Value of buildings, valuers need to consider depreciation based at the very least on the current age and condition of the asset, or in other words a Depreciated Replacement Cost (DRC) approach.

In the case of the Indemnity Value of P&M, if there is no market evidence either on an in-situ or and ex-situ basis for an asset, valuers also need to consider depreciation based at the very least on the current age and condition of the asset.

If adopted, a DRC approach must seek to measure the economic benefits remaining in the asset.

Examples of P&M assets where an Indemnity Value assessment might normally be based upon a DRC approach include:

- integrated process lines;
- energy assets (although some assets such as gas turbines and transformers are readily traded);
- oil and gas assets;
- transmission lines;
- water and sewerage assets;
- mining process assets;
- infrastructure; and
- large quantities of identical items (such as computers and office furniture, where it would not be reasonable to expect to see such quantities in the used market).

If, however, there is a secondary market for the P&M asset, Indemnity Value must reflect that market.

Examples of P&M assets where an Indemnity Value assessment might normally be based upon market evidence include:

- stand-alone manufacturing assets (e.g. toolmaking, woodworking, plastics, food) – such an assessment would require allowances for installation where applicable;
- earthmoving plant;
- trucks and trailers; and
- agricultural machinery.

Summary – Indemnity Value approaches and determinants

Category	Cost Approach	Determinants of Indemnity Value – Cost Approach	Market Approach	Determinants of Indemnity Value – Market Approach
Building	Yes	Replacement and Reinstatement Value Age (either since new or perhaps since major refurbishment) Depreciation Type (straight-line, diminishing value etc.) Condition (Valuers may need to deviate from an age-based calculation if the asset's condition does not mirror such a curve) Salvage Value (the value of any scrap or salvageable items) Remaining Useful Life (this is typically limited by physical life) Remediation Cost at end of life (Valuers should consider whether such costs should be recognised in an Indemnity Value calculation)	n/a	

Valuation for insurance purposes 245

Category	Cost Approach	Determinants of Indemnity Value – Cost Approach	Market Approach	Determinants of Indemnity Value – Market Approach
P&M	Yes	Replacement and Reinstatement Value	Yes	Market Transactions (auction, wholesale, retail)
		Age (either since new or perhaps since major refurbishment)		Cost of transport, installation, commissioning (these costs may exceed the Market Value of the asset itself and are critical to any measure of Indemnity Value)
		Condition (Valuers may need to deviate from an age-based calculation if the asset's condition does not mirror such a curve)		Location (proximity to or remoteness from active markets must be considered and adjusted for if applicable)
		Depreciation Type (straight-line, diminishing value, units of production method, etc.)		Condition (adjustments may be necessary if sales data relates to differing condition assets)
		Salvage Value (any DRC calculation should only apply to the depreciable component with residual or salvage value excluded then added back)		Technological obsolescence (is an equivalent asset traded in the used market or only newer ones)
		Remaining Useful Life (this may be limited by physical life, technical life or economic life, or even by planned re-use of the land. Note, valuers should seek clarification from insurance valuation clients' brokers in respect of depreciation factors applicable to Indemnity Value on plant under the Policy)		Capacity (adjustments may be necessary if sales data relates to differing capacity assets)
		Cost of Transport, Installation, Commissioning (these should be considered within the Replacement and Reinstatement Value assessment)		
		Remediation Cost at end of life (Valuers should consider whether such costs should be recognised in an Indemnity Value calculation)		

(Continued)

Category	Cost Approach	Determinants of Indemnity Value – Cost Approach	Market Approach	Determinants of Indemnity Value – Market Approach
		Physical, Functional & Economic Obsolescence (the depreciation calculation should consider all forms of obsolescence. Note, valuers should seek clarification from insurance valuation clients' brokers in respect of depreciation factors applicable to Indemnity Value on plant under the Policy) Overcapacity or Overengineering (an Optimised Depreciated Replacement Cost may be used in such cases so as not to overstate Indemnity Value)		

Current trends in Indemnity Value

Among the tragic stories arising from the Christchurch earthquake, some interesting developments in the way insurance policies are interpreted are emerging. Recent cases are considering what the term 'Indemnity Value' means (in relation to buildings at least). Many insurance companies, when calculating the indemnity figure they are required to make, will simply ask a valuer to provide a market value estimate. Unfortunately, most valuers are used to providing market value estimates for sale and purchase purposes and some will calculate the market value based on the land and buildings less the land value. This is not the correct basis for calculating Indemnity Value for an insurance policy.

This has been widely accepted by the Courts in New Zealand and Australia. In the United States, the Courts are used to calculating Indemnity Values based on what is called the 'broad evidence rule'. This is where the Indemnity Value (or 'actual cash value' as it is called in the United States) is based upon a consideration by the Court of many factors including the cost of replacement of the building less depreciation, the age of the property, the economic value of the property, the income derived from the property, the profit likely to accrue on the property and any other evidence which may possibly throw light on the actual value of the building at the time of the loss.

Summary

In this chapter, valuation practice for insurance purposes is considered with particular regard to the central concepts of reinstatement value and Indemnity Value, focusing on the valuer's attention on the important differences from the concept of market value on various bases.

The application of valuation approaches not only to buildings but also to plant and machinery in a wide range of industry contexts, from museums to chemical plants, highlights the inherent complexity of valuation for insurance purposes. Further, the added costs of installation, additional engineering, removal of debris and so forth extend conventional valuation considerations through an understanding of the operational considerations of the specific industry.

Valuation for insurance purposes 247

The first section of the second part of this book addressed valuation practice for conventional property sectors comprising the residential, office, retail, industrial and rural property sectors and the second section of the second part addressed valuation practice for specialist property sectors comprising retirement, leisure, plant and equipment and business and intangible asset valuation.

This third and final section of the second part addresses property valuation for specific purposes, with the previous chapters addressing rental valuation purposes, financial reporting valuation purposes and secured lending valuation purposes, this chapter addressing insurance valuation purposes and the following, final chapter addressing statutory valuation purposes.

References

Australian Property Institute and Property Institute of New Zealand, *Technical Information Paper TIP4 – Valuations for Insurance Purposes*, https://propertyinstitute.nz/Attachment?Action=Download&Attachment_id=2093 (accessed 7 August 2020).

Fire and Emergency New Zealand Fire, Circular 1998/2 (revised February 2012 and July 2017) *Fire Service Act 1975 – section 48 Guidance note – 'Indemnity value, valuations and declarations'*, https://fireandemergency.nz/assets/Documents/About-FENZ/Levy-and-payment-forms/Indemnity-value-valuations-and-declarations-guidance-note.pdf (accessed 7 August 2020).

Hooker, A 2013, https://www.interest.co.nz/personal-finance/63081/andrew-hooker-reveals-what-courts-have-ruled-how-indemnity-and-replacements (accessed 7 August 2020).

One Underwriting Pty Ltd, Industrial Special Risks Policy Wording October 2015, https://oneunderwriting.com.au/OneUnderwriting/media/Products/Hospitality%20and%20Leisure/Policy/leisure-ISR-policy-wording.pdf (accessed 7 August 2020).

Self Insurance Corporation of NSW (icare), *Construction Risks – Material Damage Project Insurance Policy*, https://www.rms.nsw.gov.au/business-industry/partners-suppliers/documents/specifications/pai-primary-cw.pdf (accessed 7 August 2020).

Walters Kluwer CCH Pinpoint, *McCONNELL DOWELL MIDDLE EAST LLC v ROYAL & SUN ALLIANCE INSURANCE PLC [2008] VSC 501, Supreme Court of Victoria*, 25 November 2008, https://cchpinpoint.wolterskluwer.com.au/ (accessed 7 August 2020).

Biographies

Cameron Dunsford is a Managing Principal with Aon Valuation Services – Aon Global Risk Consulting (Australia), having received his degree in Business at the University of Technology Sydney. In a career spanning 28 years, Cameron is an expert in plant and machinery valuation.

Cameron has extensive experience in valuations in industries as diverse as power generation, transport, engineering, mining and quarrying, concrete batching, hotels, earthmoving, petroleum, hospitality, woodworking, office fit-outs, information technology, cars and boats, materials handling, logging and sawmills, communications and medical. While these are his specialist areas, Cameron has undertaken significant work in a wide range of areas related to non-real property assets and has completed valuations encompassing up to 300 sites and $28b in asset value.

Cameron has completed major valuations of plant in a wide range of industries including Hanson, Boral & Rinker's combined 9,000 strong mobile plant fleet,

150 quarries and 600 concrete batching plants, the Sydney Ferries fleet, 5,000 public and private buses, 50 thermal, hydroelectric and wind-turbine power stations, Vodafone's Australian Mobile Phone Network, Shell's Australian Distributor Network, Star Track Express' 2,200 strong fleet, 5-star hotels, museum collections, hundreds of sawmilling and logging entities and Councils.

Mark Klenke is a Managing Principal with Aon Valuation Services – Aon Global Risk Consulting (Australia), having begun his valuation career in 1992. He is both a Licensed and Certified Practising Valuer, being one of only a handful who are Associate members of both the Australian Property Institute's Land and Buildings as well as the Plant and Machinery valuation streams.

Mark has extensive experience across a broad range of industry sectors including investment funds, commercial property and infrastructure, agribusiness, educational institutions, healthcare, oil, gas, power, mining and cultural and heritage assets.

Through this experience and further educational studies, he has become an expert in valuation methodologies including those for market, financial reporting, taxation, statutory and insurance purposes and the project management of large assignments.

He has an intimate knowledge of insurance valuations (both pre and post loss) and understands the intricacies of policy wordings and the impact these can have on establishing correct sums insured.

Ashley Grant is a Director with Aon Valuation Services – Aon Global Risk Consulting (Australia), having begun his valuation career in 1994. He is a widely experienced valuer and his work covers the full range of machinery, plant and equipment valuations, with a special understanding of the resources and heavy industry fields. Ashley is also a leading expert in educational institutions, health and aged care facilities, energy and mining.

He has expertise across the public and private sectors in market, replacement, indemnity and auction values for financial reporting, insurance purposes and asset disposal, as well as asset register audit and reconciliation.

Ashley has particular expertise in the valuation of refinery and petro-chemical assets for insurance purposes on an optimised basis and the relationship to policy wording and response, having undertaken valuation assignments throughout the Middle East, Asia Pacific and the Americas.

20 Valuation for statutory purposes

David Parker

Acknowledgement

This chapter draws heavily on:

Parker, D 2015, 'The 2012 metamorphosis of the common law of compulsory acquisition valuation in Australia', *Common Law World Review*, vol. 44, no 3, pp. 175–191;

Parker, D 2016, *International Valuation Standards: A Guide to the Valuation of Real Property Assets*, Wiley-Blackwell, Chichester; and

Parker, D 2018, 'Compulsory Acquisition Compensation Issues in Australia', in *Routledge Handbook of Contemporary Issues in Expropriation*, Plimmer, F and McCluskey, (eds), Routledge, Abingdon,

which are duly acknowledged here rather than individually referenced through the chapter and to which readers are referred for a deeper consideration.

Introduction

With the first part of this book addressing the principles of valuation, the second part addresses the practice of valuation being grouped into three sections comprising conventional property sectors, specialist property sectors and specific purposes. Conventional property sectors include residential, office, retail, industrial and rural property valuation practice. Specialist property sectors include retirement, leisure, plant and equipment and business and intangible asset valuation practice. Specific purposes include valuation practice for rental, financial reporting, secured lending, insurance and statutory valuation purposes.

This third section of the second part of this book addresses specific purpose valuation practice with rental valuation purposes, financial reporting valuation purposes, secured lending and insurance valuation purposes considered in previous chapters and statutory valuation purposes considered in this final chapter.

In this chapter, the Australian approach to valuation practice for statutory purposes is considered in the context of valuation for rating and taxing and valuation for compulsory acquisition which will be considered, sequentially, below.

As the name would suggest, statutory valuations draw their basis and legitimacy from the application of an underlying statute. Accordingly, a key difference between valuations for statutory purposes and valuations for other purposes is that the former may be subject to objection, appeal and decision by an independent Court whereas the latter may not.

DOI: 10.1201/9781003049555-20

250 David Parker

Valuations for rating and taxing

Given the very significant variations in bases of value for the purposes of land-based taxation between the various Australian States and Territories, it is proposed to first generally summarise the various approaches adopted across Australia and then consider New South Wales (NSW) in more detail as a case study prior to considering future trends in rating and taxation.

State and Territory variations

As land-based taxation is a State or Territory power, the basis of valuation upon which to levy land-based taxes varies for each State and Territory as summarised in Table 20.1 (Hutley, Chapter 4, this volume).

Further variations also arise between the various States and Territories, including:

- the ACT using site value to determine the uplift in value based on differing highest and best uses before-and-after a lease variation, with most land in the ACT being leasehold title rather than freehold title;
- Queensland, NSW and Western Australia adopting mass valuation methodologies, whereas other States and Territories do not; and
- frequency of valuation differing significantly between the respective States and Territories.

Case study: New South Wales

The Valuation of Land Act 1916 governs the valuation of land for rating and land tax purposes in New South Wales. The valuation of land is undertaken annually on 1 July by the Valuer General who is an independent statutory officer with land valuations provided to local government bodies who then levy rates based thereon and State Government who then levy land tax based thereon.

The valuation of land is based on its unimproved value which is defined in s6A(1) as:

> The land value of land is the capital sum which the fee-simple of the land might be expected to realise if offered for sale on such reasonable terms and conditions as a bona-fide seller would require, assuming that the improvements, if any, thereon or appertaining thereto, other than land improvements, and made or acquired by the owner or the owner's predecessor in title had not been made.

Table 20.1 Methodologies for land taxes and council rates

	NSW	VIC	QLD	WA	SA	TAS	NT	ACT
Land Tax	LV	SV	UV	UV	SV	LV	Not levied	UV
Council Rates	LV	SV, NAV, CIV	UV	Rural: UV Non-rural: GRV	LV, CV, AV	LV, CV, AAV	UCV, AV, ICV	UV

Notes: AV = Annual value, AAV = Assessed Annual Value, LV = Land Value, CV = Capital value, CIV = Capital Improved Value, GRV = Gross Rental Value, NAV = Net Annual Value, SV = Site Value, UCV = Unimproved Capital Value, UV = Unimproved Value, ICV = Improved Capital Value.

Source: Henry, K et al. (2009).

with s6A(2) notionally permitting the assumed continuation of existing use or a higher and better use for the purposes of valuation.

New South Wales adopts a mass valuation approach to the assessment of land value through the use of outsourced contract valuers (Part 1A), subject to quality assurance by the Valuer General.

The Valuation of Land Act 1916 makes provision for special circumstances including protected archaeological and wildlife areas (s14D), community schemes (s14E), mines and minerals (s14F), heritage properties (s14G), improvements to the land (s14L-s14N), subdivision (Div 4) and mixed development (Div 5).

The Valuer General is required to issue a notice of valuation to landholders (s29) who may object to the valuation on the grounds specified in s34 within 60 days of service of notice with the Valuer General having discretion to accept late lodgement. The land valuation is then reviewed by a valuer different from and not subordinate to the original valuer and the Valuer General may allow or disallow the objection (s35B) through the issue of a notice of determination (s35C).

A landholder may then appeal the Valuer General's determination of objection to the Land and Environment Court (s37) within 60 days of the issue of the determination (s38) (or later at the Court's discretion). The appeal may be heard by a Judge and/or Commissioner of the Land and Environment Court who may uphold or dismiss the appeal, make a decision in place of the decision to which the appeal relates or remit the matter back to the Valuer General for determination in accordance with the Court's finding or decision (s40).

Current trends in rating and taxation

Levying tax based on land is undertaken in a wide variety of forms around the world and around Australia, each of which is subject to criticism by local taxpayers but often protected by other forms being no better. Following the UK Government's introduction of poll tax to replace rates in the early 1990s, riots and public disorder ensued leading to its abolition and providing a salutary example to other governments of the risk of amending land-based tax systems.

While, for example, the NSW system of rates and land tax based on unimproved value is a relic of a different century when land regularly transacted for the purposes of building thereon (rather than the current situation where existing completed buildings and land transact together), the community is familiar with the basis and while it may not consider it optimal, preferable alternatives are elusive.

The benefits of land-based taxation include that it spreads the tax base widely, taxpayers are easily identifiable through land ownership records and the link to current values allows the tax base to move in line with the property market. Conversely, stamp duty, being a duty payable on the transaction of a property, is often contended to distort the operation of the property market and disadvantage certain parts of the community. Accordingly, phasing out stamp duty and replacing it by a land-based tax has considerable appeal and has been adopted in the Australian Capital Territory, with a proposal opened for public consultation in late 2020 in NSW to introduce a choice between stamp duty or a land-based tax.

Valuations for compulsory acquisition

Given the variations in approach to compulsory acquisition by the Commonwealth and the various Australian States and Territories, it is proposed to first generally summarise the statutory power for each jurisdiction and then consider NSW in more detail as a case study.

Commonwealth, State and Territory variations

While both the Commonwealth and each of the States and Territories have their own statutory framework, there is considerable conceptual commonality though with some small differences in detail.

The principal Commonwealth, State and Territory statutes for compulsory acquisition and compensation include:

Commonwealth and ACT	Lands Acquisition Act 1989
New South Wales	Land Acquisition (Just Terms Compensation) Act 1991
Victoria	Land Acquisition and Compensation Act 1986
Queensland	Acquisition of Land Act 1967
South Australia	Land Acquisition Act 1969
Western Australia	Land Administration Act 1997
Tasmania	Land Acquisition Act 1993
Northern Territory	Lands Acquisition Act 2016

In this chapter, the NSW Land Acquisition (Just Terms Compensation) Act 1991 (NSW Act) will be used for the purposes of illustration of the concepts and principles of compulsory acquisition and compensation.

Case study: New South Wales

Upon the publication of a notice of compulsory acquisition as required under the respective statutes, all specified interests of specified persons in the land are thereupon vested in the acquiring authority (Hemmings, 1997).

The effect of the compulsory acquisition is to convert an interest in land to a claim for compensation, assessable in accordance with the statute as at the date of acquisition. (Hemmings, 1997). Effectively, therefore, the land owner cannot hold up the project for which the land is acquired as the concept of acquisition is severed from the concept of compensation.

Compensation for compulsory acquisition is not a right vested by the common law, but is solely a matter of statutory entitlement in Australia and its assessment is limited by that legislation. All acquisition legislation seeks to provide the dispossessed owner with the full money equivalent of the property acquired by compulsion (Hemmings, 1997).

The current statutory framework is premised on compensation, having regard to all relevant matters permissible under the legislation, being an amount that will justly compensate (Hemmings, 1997). Section 54(1) of the NSW Act specifies:

54 Entitlement to just compensation

1 The amount of compensation to which a person is entitled under this Part is such amount as, having regard to all relevant matters under this Part, will justly compensate the person for the acquisition of the land.

The principle that, in the assessment of compensation, doubt should be resolved in a more liberal estimate in favour of the dispossessed has been established for 80 years (*Commission of Succession Duties (SA) v Executor Trustee Agency Co of SA Ltd* (1942) 74 CLR 358 at 374).

The respective compulsory acquisition and compensation statutes follow the principle established in *Pointe Gourde Quarrying Transport Co v Sub-Intendent of Crown Lands (Trinidad)* 1947 AL 568 that the purpose for which the land is being compulsorily acquired is disregarded in the assessment of compensation.

Such a public purpose disregard is specified in s56(1)(a) and (b) of the NSW Act:

56 Market value

1   In this Act: 'market value' of land at any time means the amount that would have been paid for the land if it had been sold at that time by a willing but not anxious seller to a willing but not anxious buyer, disregarding (for the purpose of determining the amount that would have been paid):

   a   any increase or decrease in the value of the land caused by the carrying out of, or the proposal to carry out, the public purpose for which the land was acquired, and
   b   any increase in the value of the land caused by the carrying out by the authority of the State, before the land is acquired, of improvements for the public purpose for which the land is to be acquired,

Generally, in a before-and-after valuation approach to the assessment of compensation, regard may not be had to the public purpose in the before scenario but regard may be had to the public purpose in the after scenario (Hemmings, 1997).

Heads of compensation

By way of indicative example, the NSW Act specifies the following alternative heads of compensation which are generally mirrored in the other relevant statutes:

55 Relevant matters to be considered in determining amount of compensation

In determining the amount of compensation to which a person is entitled, regard must be had to the following matters only (as assessed in accordance with this Division):

a   the market value of the land on the date of its acquisition,
b   any special value of the land to the person on the date of its acquisition,
c   any loss attributable to severance,
d   any loss attributable to disturbance,
e   the disadvantage resulting from relocation,
f   any increase or decrease in the value of any other land of the person at the date of acquisition which adjoins or is severed from the acquired land by reason of the carrying out of, or the proposal to carry out, the public purpose for which the land was acquired.

The alternative heads of compensation may be considered as follows.

Market value

By way of indicative example, the NSW Act specifies the payment of market value for the interest in land acquired, on a prescribed basis and definition, with consequential adjustment to any compensation for disturbance:

56 Market value

1. In this Act: 'market value' of land at any time means the amount that would have been paid for the land if it had been sold at that time by a willing but not anxious seller to a willing but not anxious buyer, disregarding (for the purpose of determining the amount that would have been paid):

   a any increase or decrease in the value of the land caused by the carrying out of, or the proposal to carry out, the public purpose for which the land was acquired, and

   b any increase in the value of the land caused by the carrying out by the authority of the State, before the land is acquired, of improvements for the public purpose for which the land is to be acquired, and

   c any increase in the value of the land caused by its use in a manner or for a purpose contrary to law.

2. When assessing the market value of land for the purpose of paying compensation to a number of former owners of the land, the sum of the market values of each interest in the land must not (except with the approval of the Minister responsible for the authority of the State) exceed the market value of the land at the date of acquisition.

3. If:

   a the land is used for a particular purpose and there is no general market for land used for that purpose, and

   b the owner genuinely proposes to continue after the acquisition to use other land for that purpose,

   the market value of the land is taken, for the purpose of paying compensation, to be the reasonable cost to the owner of equivalent reinstatement in some other location. That cost is to be reduced by any costs for which compensation is payable for loss attributable to disturbance and by any likely improvement in the owner's financial position because of the relocation.

As the definition of market value is central to compulsory purchase compensation, it will be considered further below. However, fundamental to the definition is the assumption that a sale will occur with the existence of a buyer at a fair price (Hemmings, 1997), as stated in *Minister of Public Instruction v Turner* 1955 20 LGR (NSW) 85 at 91:

> a voluntary bargain between a vendor and a purchaser each willing to trade but neither of whom was so anxious to do so that he would overlook ordinary business considerations.

Also fundamental to the definition is the assumption that the value of the land is that of its highest and best use or 'most advantageous purpose' (*Minister of State for*

Home Affairs v Rostron 1914 18 CLR 634), the property being valued at the relevant date in its existing condition with all its 'potentialities' (*Yates Property Corporation Pty Ltd (in liq) v Darling Harbour Authority* (1991) 24 NSWLR 156 at 175–176). While not specified, the International Valuation Standards elements of physically possible, legally permissible and financially feasible may be considered likely to be applicable, with such use being probable and not merely speculative. This has been of particular significance in recent NSW rail compulsory acquisition cases where rural land, which would ultimately, at some undefined point in the future, become residential development land, was acquired at various stages of that journey. In *Chircop v Transport for NSW* [2014] NSWLEC 63, it was held that such land must be 'ripe' (para 10) for such potential higher and better use in order for that to be compensable, with 'ripe' in this case being likely to occur within 15–18 months of the acquisition.

Special value

By way of indicative example, the NSW Act specifies the payment of special value, significantly in addition to market value, where there is financial value for an advantage incidental to the person's use of the land:

> **57 Special value**
>
> In this Act:
>
> **'special value'** of land means the financial value of any advantage, in addition to market value, to the person entitled to compensation which is incidental to the person's use of the land.

In Peter Croke Holdings Pty Ltd v Roads and Traffic Authority of NSW (1998) 101 LGERA 30 at 38, Bignold J said:

> Special value is an element of the concept of 'value to the owner', and is the additional sum above market value which the owner would have given for the land sooner than fail to obtain it at the time of the hypothetical sale.

The benchmark example for special value in NSW is generally considered to be the decision by Callinan J in *Boland v Yates Property Corporation Pty Limited [1999] HCA 64; 74 ALJR 209; 167 ALR 575* where His Honour cited the example of a blacksmith's shop adjacent to a racetrack:

> 292 The special value of land is its value to the owner over and above its market value. It arises in circumstances in which there is a conjunction of some special factor relating to the land and a capacity on the part of the owner exclusively or perhaps almost exclusively to exploit it. None of the examples given by the Full Federal Court are true examples of special value. There will in practice be few cases in which a property does have a special value for a particular owner. Obviously neither sentiment nor a long attachment to it will suffice. The special quality must be a quality that has an economic significance to the owner. A possible case would be one in which, for example, a blacksmith operates a forge in the vicinity of a racetrack on land zoned for residential purposes as a protected non-conforming use, the right to which might be lost on a transfer of ownership

or an interruption of the protected use. Such a property will have a special value for its blacksmith owner, and perhaps another blacksmith who might be able to comply with the relevant requirements to enable him to continue the use but to no one else.

While this fulfils the tests of incidental to the use of land and an advantage of financial value, the example is rare and unusual, consistent with the concept of such value being special. Essentially, special value is a notion of worth or value to the owner, rather than a notion of value between a hypothetical vendor and purchaser, which may ground payment of compensation greater than that payable for market value provided the statutory tests can be met especially that the property is put to some use for which it is specially well suited.

As the Courts have extensively explored and clarified the concept of market value, it may be anticipated that future applicants may be keen to explore the potential for claims under special value.

Severance

By way of indicative example, the NSW Act specifies payment for the reduction in market value of land retained by the landholder as a result of the acquired land being severed:

55 Relevant matters to be considered in determining amount of compensation

In determining the amount of compensation to which a person is entitled, regard must be had to the following matters only (as assessed in accordance with this Division):

(f) any increase or decrease in the value of any other land of the person at the date of acquisition which adjoins or is severed from the acquired land by reason of the carrying out of, or the proposal to carry out, the public purpose for which the land was acquired.

58 Loss attributable to severance

In this Act:

'loss attributable to severance' of land means the amount of any reduction in the market value of any other land of the person entitled to compensation which is caused by that other land being severed from other land of that person.

The assessment of compensation is usually based on a before-and-after method, whereby the value in the before acquisition scenario is assessed and the value in the after acquisition scenario is assessed and the difference determined. Such difference may be negative, resulting in compensation being payable, or positive resulting in a windfall gain or betterment which is deducted from compensation paid for severance or disturbance (*G&R Wills & Co Limited v Adelaide City Corporation* 1962 HCA 61; *Moloney v Roads and Maritime Services (No 2)* [2017] NSWLEC 68). (Hemmings, 1997)

Related to severance, where compensation may be payable for the effect on the retained land of being severed from the parent parcel, is the notion of injurious affection where compensation may be payable for the effect on the retained land of the public purpose. Similarly, the assessment of compensation is usually based on

Valuation for statutory purposes

a before-and-after method, whereby the value in the before acquisition scenario is assessed (disregarding the public purpose) and the value in the after acquisition scenario (having regard to the public purpose) is assessed and the difference determined. Such difference may be negative, resulting in compensation being payable such as arising from the development of a sewage plant (Hemmings, 1997).

Disturbance

By way of indicative example, the NSW Act specifies payment for nominated forms of disturbance:

59 Loss attributable to disturbance

1. In this Act: 'loss attributable to disturbance' of land means any of the following:
   a. legal costs reasonably incurred by the persons entitled to compensation in connection with the compulsory acquisition of the land,
   b. valuation fees of a qualified valuer reasonably incurred by those persons in connection with the compulsory acquisition of the land (but not fees calculated by reference to the value, as assessed by the valuer, of the land),
   c. financial costs reasonably incurred in connection with the relocation of those persons (including legal costs but not including stamp duty or mortgage costs),
   d. stamp duty costs reasonably incurred (or that might reasonably be incurred) by those persons in connection with the purchase of land for relocation (but not exceeding the amount that would be incurred for the purchase of land of equivalent value to the land compulsorily acquired),
   e. financial costs reasonably incurred (or that might reasonably be incurred) by those persons in connection with the discharge of a mortgage and the execution of a new mortgage resulting from the relocation (but not exceeding the amount that would be incurred if the new mortgage secured the repayment of the balance owing in respect of the discharged mortgage),
   f. any other financial costs reasonably incurred (or that might reasonably be incurred), relating to the actual use of the land, as a direct and natural consequence of the acquisition.

Each of the heads of disturbance has been subject to extensive litigation with myopic focus on the exact wording of the NSW Act. For example, legal fees and valuation fees generally need a clear connection with the compulsory acquisition itself rather than fees attributable to advice on related issues or issues arising. Relocation costs and stamp duty costs need to be reasonably incurred with case specific debate about whether losses are costs.

As may be anticipated, s59(1)(f) is generally the most contentious, being that subsection within which a wide range of costs (or losses) could potentially be claimed. Despite the NSW Act clearly requiring a series of hurdles to be overcome for a successful claim for compensation, including that such costs to be financial, reasonably incurred, relating to the actual use and arising as a direct and natural consequence, the creativity of claims under s59(1)(f) has increased since the common law around compensation for market value became more settled.

As Hemmings (1997) notes, disturbance is an element of personal loss not related to the market value of the land. Disturbance may include costs incurred in the purchasing of comparable property, bridging finance, increased rents, increased building costs, removal expenses, diminution in the value of fixtures, loss of goodwill, loss of profit reinstatement, repairs and alterations to buildings and repairs to fences.

Solatium – disadvantage resulting from relocation

By way of indicative example, the NSW Act specifies the payment of solatium where the acquisition concerns the principal place of residence:

60 Disadvantage resulting from relocation

1. In this Act: 'disadvantage resulting from relocation' means non-financial disadvantage resulting from the necessity of the person entitled to compensation to relocate the person's principal place of residence as a result of the acquisition.
2. The maximum amount of compensation in respect of the disadvantage resulting from relocation is $75,000. Schedule 1A provides for the amendment of this section to enable the maximum amount of compensation to be increased by regulation and for the automatic indexation of the maximum amount in line with inflation.
3. In assessing the amount of compensation in respect of the disadvantage resulting from relocation, all relevant circumstances are to be taken into account, including:
    a the interest in the land of the person entitled to compensation, and
    b the length of time the person has resided on the land (and in particular whether the person is residing on the land temporarily or indefinitely), and
    c the inconvenience likely to be suffered by the person because of his or her removal from the land, and
    d the period after the acquisition of the land during which the person has been (or will be) allowed to remain in possession of the land.
4. Compensation is payable in respect of the disadvantage resulting from relocation if the whole of the land is acquired or if any part of the land on which the residence is situated is acquired.
5. Only one payment of compensation in respect of the disadvantage resulting from relocation is payable for land in separate occupation.
6. However, if more than one family resides on the same land, a separate payment may be made in respect of each family if:
    a the family resides in a separate dwelling-house, or
    b the Minister responsible for the authority of the State approves of the payment.
7. If separate payments of compensation are made, the maximum amount under subsection (2) applies to each payment, and not to the total payments.

It is interesting that, in principle, the NSW Act recognises that dispossession from the family home is a separate head of compensation, presumably reflecting the connection between the dispossessed, their family home, its memories and significance to the family unit. This may be contrasted to the dispossession of indigenous Australians where their land may be acquired but where, unless there is a family home upon the land, such aspects of spiritual connection are not specified as a separate head of compensation.

Current trends in statutory valuation methodology

For over a century, the approach to the valuation of land for compulsory acquisition matters in Australia has been overshadowed by the High Court decision in *Spencer v Commonwealth* (1907) 5 CLR 418 (*Spencer*). The decision in *Spencer* not only explicitly determined the basis of market value but also implicitly determined the comparable sales method of valuation to be the preferred method for application in compulsory acquisition matters.

Despite the widespread acceptance of the hypothetical development method, the capitalisation method and the discounted cash flow method of valuation by the valuation profession and the property industry for decades, the Courts find enormous difficulty adopting such methods if there is even the remotest possibility that the comparable sales method of valuation could be applied.

The spectre of Spencer

The basis of market value, for the purposes of compulsory acquisition matters in Australia, was determined by the High Court decision in *Spencer* being, essentially, similar to the definition of the International Valuation Standards Council:

> **Market value** is the estimated amount for which an asset or liability should exchange on the valuation date between a willing buyer and a willing seller in an arm's length transaction, after proper marketing and where the parties had each acted knowledgably, prudently and without compulsion. (IVSC, 2019)

While *Spencer* has assumed almost mythical status in Australian litigation and case law, for the purposes of valuation for statutory purposes, the definition should be seen through a 1907 lens and recognised as constrained by its context and circumstances:

- it concerns a block of vacant, undeveloped land rather than a high-rise building in the CBD or other form of property;
- it occurred at a time when the currency of conversation in the community was the frequent sale of blocks of land providing extensive comparable evidence, not of land upon which income producing structures were built and acquired for investment purposes which may sell infrequently;
- it occurred at a time when the hypothetical parties were private individuals in a local market, not international multi-billion dollar investors acting in a global market;
- it requires conversance, perfect acquaintance with the subject property and cognisance of circumstances affecting the value of a vacant block of land, not a comprehensive knowledge or some concept of market efficiency.

Accordingly, while very useful as a statement of principle, it is often challenging to apply to modern investment property where the vendors, purchasers, marketing process, role of information in price formation and so forth differ radically from that for a vacant block of undeveloped suburban land.

Valuation methodology within the statutory framework

The decision in *Spencer* not only explicitly determined the basis of market value but also implicitly determined the comparable sales method of valuation to be the preferred method for application in compulsory acquisition matters. Despite the unsuitability of the comparable sales method of valuation for certain properties, the Courts have been reluctant to embrace hypothetical development or income methods, including discounted cash flow, except as a last resort.

Though Wells J stated a general principle of willingness to consider alternative methods:

> ... I am not disposed to reject any method of valuation adopted by either valuer on the ground that it is not worth considering; it seems to be that if Spencer's case is to keep its practical worth in this jurisdiction, this court should be slow to reject any method that, in expert hands, is capable of yielding a result within bounds that are not unreasonable. The limitations of every method must, of course, always be kept clearly in mind. (Bronzel v State Planning Authority (1979) 44 LGRA 34v at 38)

while Hemmings (1997) observes:

> Valuation based upon proper analysis of comparable sales must always be preferred to any hypothetical or capitalisation approach. (p. 439)

Comparable sales method of valuation

Hemmings (1997) describes the comparable sales method of valuation as follows:

> Value may be best ascertained by inference from the price at which 'comparable' land has been sold in the market. Whilst no sales of identical land are likely to be available the test is prices obtained in arms' length recent sales on usual terms of land 'capable of being compared' with the subject land. An expert is entitled to apply adjustments to take account of differences, unusual or unique features and special potentialities of the acquired land. (p. 439)

While the comparable sales approach may appear straight forward, the Courts have attached a range of conditions to its application:

- concerning offers, while not evidence of a concluded sale, may be taken into account as evidence of a market and some evidence of value, being at least evidence of the interest of the owner in selling and others in negotiating the sale of the land (Hemmings, 1997);
- concerning subsequent events, while not impacting value at the date of acquisition, may be admissible if confirming a foresight (Housing Commission of NSW v Falconer 1981 1 NSW LR 547);

Valuation for statutory purposes 261

- concerning sales to the acquiring authority, whilst not impermissible as evidence should be treated with considerable caution (Hemmings, 1997);
- concerning the process of adjustment of comparable sales:
  - a preference for as few adjustments as possible in a consistent manner (*Holcim (Australia) Pty Ltd v Valuer General* [2009] NSWLEC 225 at 31);
  - caution where large explicit and/or implicit adjustments are required with particular caution required for large implicit adjustments (*Graham Trilby v Valuer General* [2008] NSWLEC 217 at 36);
  - a preference for separately itemised and reasoned explicit adjustments to an implicit process comprising a single adjustment (*Tomago Aluminium Company Pty Ltd v Valuer General* [2010] NSWLEC 4 at 45);
  - a preference for a transparent process of explicit adjustment leading to an explicable assessment of value rather than an opaque process of implicit adjustment leading to an assertion of value (*Jessica Investments Pty Ltd v Valuer General* [2008] NSWLEC 1375 at 6);
  - a preference for an adjustment process that works forwards from the comparable sales to derive an opinion of value, rather than working backwards to justify an opinion of value previously formed (*Graham Trilby v Valuer General* [2008] NSWLEC 217 at 35); and
  - an acknowledgement that insufficient transparency in the adjustment process risks rejection of the valuation evidence (*Tomago Aluminium Company Pty Ltd v Valuer General* [2010] NSWLEC 4 at 45). (Parker 2015)

While such an extensive range of conditions might be expected to bring transparency to the application of the comparable sales valuation process, the continued simple unsupported assertion of value by expert witnesses led to a series of decisions in the NSW Land and Environment Court commonly identifying four steps to be explicitly undertaken in the comparable sales valuation process, summarised in *Adams v Valuer General* [2014] NSWLEC1005:

1 accumulation – the accumulation step seeks to identify and establish a pool of relevant comparable sales from which information may be deduced concerning the value of the subject property (at 32);
2 analysis – the analysis step provides a common basis of measurement by seeking to convert all potentially comparable sales to a common basis of expression such as a unitary rate (rate per square metre, rate per hectare, etc.) improved or unimproved (through allowance for the absence or existence of improvements, etc.) (at 38);
3 adjustment – the adjustment step acknowledges the fact that no two properties are ever identical and seeks to convert those analysed potentially comparable sales to a hypothetical expression of value as a unitary rate in the context of the subject property through the reflection of differences (such as size, location, use, date, etc.) between the respective potentially comparable sales and the subject property (at 40); and
4 application – the application step seeks to determine the value of the subject property through a consideration of the relevance (such as being limited, indirect or direct) of the unitary rate derived from those adjusted comparable sales relative to the subject (at 56).

Capitalisation of income method of valuation

The capitalisation of income method was accepted by Mitchell J for the valuation of income producing land and property:

> [I]t was necessary to fix the net rental value of the premises on the basis of a rack-rent, taking from that rack-rent proper deductions to arrive at a net annual value to the owner, and then to choose a rate of capitalisation. (*Hill v Commissioner of Highways* (1966) 13 LGRA 369 at 375)

Hypothetical development method of valuation

Being dependent on the assessment of numerous interactive variables, the hypothetical development method of valuation is relatively controversial, being described by Sugarman J as the derivation of land value through the assumption that a party:

> ... erects a hypothetical building upon the subject land, capitalises the anticipated net return therefrom, and subtracts the estimated building cost from the capitalisation, the balance being treated as the value of the site. (*AG Robertson Ltd v Valuer General* (1952) 18 LGR (NSW) 261 at 262)

with a preference, where possible, for valuation by comparable sales:

> It has been said that because many estimates and assumptions must be made the hypothetical development method ought not be used where some use can be made of a comparable sale. (*Gwynvill Properties Pty Ltd v Commissioner for Main Roads* (1983) 50 LGRA 322 at 326)

and:

> ... the residual approach involves a higher risk of reaching unrealistic results than the direct comparison approach. (*Graham Trilby Pty Limited v Valuer General* [2008] NSWLEC 217 at 32)

but may be considered in 'the absence of directly comparable sales' (*Graham Trilby Pty Limited v Valuer General* [2009] NSWLEC 1087 at 41) or the very limited availability of relevant comparable sales evidence (*Gwynvill Properties Pty Ltd v Commissioner for Main Roads* (1983) 50 LGRA 322). (Parker 2015)

Discounted cash flow method of valuation

While discounted cash flow may be used as an income method of valuation or as a dynamic hypothetical development method of valuation and despite its global use in property valuation, the Courts are disinclined to accept it if any other alternative may be available.

The source of such disinclination may be found in a common misunderstanding of the findings in *Albany v Commonwealth* 1976 60 LGRA 287 where Jacobs J considered and rejected the use of discounted cash flow in the valuation of urban and residential development land. However, His Honour clearly stated:

> However, I would not consider it safe to adopt the indicated figure as a correct valuation of the lands, because I am not satisfied of the suitability in this case of a method of valuation based on discounted cash flow.

such that discounted cash flow methods were not rejected in principle but only '*in this case*'. The decision, however, constrained the acceptability of discounted cash flow methods of valuation by the Courts for the next four decades.

In more recent years, discounted cash flow has become more common and has been accepted as a method of valuation of land and business, including by Talbot J in *Collex Pty Ltd v Roads and Traffic Authority of New South Wales* [2006] NSWLEC 579, His Honour commenting at para 82:

> 82 Although Courts have clearly experienced difficulty from time to time in accepting the DCF method due to the unreliability of the assumptions made for the purpose of the analysis, it is nonetheless a method which can be accepted where the special facts and circumstances pertaining to the subject land make it appropriate to do so.

This was supported by Pain J in *Allandale Blue Metal Pty Ltd v Roads and Maritime Services (No 6)* [2015] NSWLEC 18, a case concerning the valuation of a quarry, where Her Honour commented at para 304:

> 304 The Court accepts that the DCF method can be usefully applied to value the resource in the land in the before and after scenarios.

Accordingly, while the principal of acceptability of the discounted cash flow method of valuation appears settled, the comparable sales method of valuation remains the Court's preferred approach.

The impact of COVID-19 on statutory valuation

Significant reliance is placed on the availability of comparable sales to undertake statutory valuation in Australian States and Territories. Currently, Australia is emerging from the COVID-19 pandemic which has significantly impacted property markets across the country since March 2020, with a resultant downturn in the level of transactions.

This was of particular significance in NSW where the Valuer General was required to undertake a valuation at 1 July 2020 (being mid-pandemic) and had no statutory power not to undertake a valuation. Accordingly, the Valuer General undertook a major investigation into the NSW property market during COVID-19 to determine if there were enough transactions with which to undertake a valuation and, if not, how the valuation may be conducted (Valuer General, 2020).

The Valuer General found that, while the level of residential transactions in the period March–May 2020 was 37% below the same period in the previous year, there was still a sufficiently large volume of transactions upon which to base the 2020 valuation for residential property.

Concerning non-residential property, the Valuer General found that, while the level of non-residential transactions in the period March–May 2020 was 41% below the same period in the previous year, the absolute volume of sales had fallen to such a low number that there may be an insufficient volume of transactions upon which to base the 2020 valuation for non-residential property. Following an extensive interview-based research project with major property owners and industry representative groups, the Valuer General found that the impact of COVID-19 varied by non-residential sub-sector, with major short-term revenue impact on hotels and serviced apartments, lesser impact on retail and office property and effectively no impact on industrial and rural property.

For those sub-sectors where there were no or very few sales and following extensive hypothetical development valuation modelling, the Valuer General proposed a series of percentage deductions to the 2019 land values to apply to specific non-residential sub-sectors for the purposes of the 2020 valuation if:

- there were no comparable sales upon which to rely;
- there was no higher and better use for the property;
- there were no other changes relevant to the valuation; and
- the valuation is consistent with the Valuation of Land Act 1916.

The report was circulated among the contributors, made available on the Valuer General website and covered by NSW media channels, receiving wide stakeholder and community support. While the Valuer General has outlined a clear approach to addressing valuation in a market with limited transactions and received support for the approach, this will only be tested through the level of objections received following the issue of land value notices in early 2021 and any appeals that may then flow to the Land and Environment Court where not only the Valuer General's approach but also the hypothetical development method of valuation will be under review.

Trends in dispute resolution

Within the principal Australian jurisdictions, alternative dispute resolution has become a popular approach to the just, quick and cheap disposal of land valuation and compulsory acquisition proceedings, avoiding the need for a full Court hearing.

Alternative dispute resolution is particularly useful where the landowner or the dispossessed is self-represented or of limited funds, where there is ambiguity or misunderstanding between the parties concerning facts, opinions, calculations or reliance on certain comparable sales or where the difference in dispute is disproportionate to the cost of litigation.

Conversely, alternative dispute resolution may not be useful where there is a genuine difference between the parties concerning the interpretation of a point of law or where the parties have fundamentally different approaches to the matter, necessitating resolution by a full Court hearing.

The most common approaches adopted to alternative dispute resolution for statutory valuation purposes in Australia include neutral evaluation, mediation and conciliation.

Neutral evaluation

Neutral evaluation is a process of evaluation of a dispute in which an impartial evaluator seeks to identify and reduce the issues of fact and law in dispute. The evaluator's role includes assessing the relative strengths and weaknesses of each party's case and offering an opinion as to the likely outcome of the proceedings, including any likely findings or the award of damages (LEC Annual Review 2019).

Mediation

Mediation is a process in which the parties to a dispute, with the assistance of an impartial mediator, identify the disputed issues, develop options, consider alternatives and endeavour to reach an agreement. The mediator has no advisory or determinative role in regard to the content of the dispute or the outcome of its resolution, but may advise on or determine the process of mediation whereby resolution is attempted (LEC Annual Review 2019).

By way of example, the NSW Land & Environment Court may refer matters to mediation at the request of the parties or of its own volition, with Table 20.2 showing the number of matters referred to mediation over the last five years in Class 3, being the rating valuation and compulsory acquisition class, with the numbers being relatively low because of the ready availability and use of conciliation by the Court (LEC Annual Review 2019).

Conciliation

Conciliation is a process in which the parties to a dispute, with the assistance of an impartial conciliator, identify the issues in dispute, develop options, consider alternatives and endeavour to reach agreement. The conciliator may have an advisory role on the content of the dispute or the outcome of its resolution, but not a determinative role. The conciliator may advise on or determine the process of conciliation whereby resolution is attempted and may make suggestions for terms of settlement, give expert advice on likely settlement terms and may actively encourage the parties to reach agreement (LEC Annual Review 2019).

By way of example, the NSW Land & Environment Court may refer a compulsory acquisition matter to conciliation under s34 of the NSW Act, to be conducted by a Commissioner with valuation expertise, prior to going to hearing. The parties have a duty to participate in the conciliation conference in good faith (s34(1A)). If the parties are able to reach agreement following conciliation, being a decision that the Court could have made in the proper exercise of its functions, then the Commissioner may record the decision as a decision of the Court and dispose of the proceedings

Table 20.2 Matters referred to mediation 2015–2019 in Class 3

	2015	2016	2017	2018	2019
Total referred	2	5	1	4	4
Number finalised Pre-hearing	1	5	1	2	4
% Finalised pre-hearing	50%	100%	100%	50%	100%

Source: LEC Annual Review 2019.

Table 20.3 Matters referred to conciliation 2015–2019 in all classes

	2015	2016	2017	2018	2019
S34 Conferences	1,500	2,035	1,534	1,465	962

Source: LEC Annual Review 2019.

(s34(3), s34(8)). If the parties are unable to reach agreement, the Commissioner terminates the conciliation conference (s34(4)) and may only adjudicate a later hearing with the agreement of the parties (s34(13)) (LEC Annual Review 2019).

Table 20.3 shows the number of matters referred to conciliation over the last five years in all classes, including but not limited to rating valuation and compulsory acquisition matters, with the total number of matters being relatively high reflecting the popularity of this form of alternative dispute resolution. (LEC Annual Review 2019)

Summary

In this chapter, valuation practice for statutory purposes is considered in the context of valuation for rating and taxing and valuation for compulsory acquisition, focusing the valuer's attention on the fundamental interaction between governing statute, binding Court precedent and valuation practice. With a case study of practice for each in NSW, current trends in rating, taxation and compulsory acquisition valuation are explored and the potential impact of COVID-19 considered.

While the governing statute may differ for each of rating, taxation and compulsory acquisition in each of the States and Territories around Australia, there is significant commonality in concepts and principles, particularly around the understanding of market value. While statutory valuation is evolving over time through the interaction of valuation practice and Court decisions, the pace of evolution is much slower than in the valuation profession generally. For example, while discounted cash flow has been accepted by the valuation profession and their clients as a form of valuation since the early 1990s, it has still to gain favour with the Courts in some States and Territories for statutory valuation purposes.

The first section of the second part of this book addressed valuation practice for conventional property sectors comprising the residential, office, retail, industrial and rural property sectors and the second section of the second part addressed valuation practice for specialist property sectors comprising retirement, leisure, plant and equipment and business and intangible asset valuation.

This third and final section of the second part addresses valuation for specific purposes, with the previous chapters addressing rental valuation purposes, financial reporting valuation purposes, secured lending valuation purposes and insurance valuation purposes. This final chapter addressing valuations for statutory purposes concludes the second part and so concludes this book.

References

Hemmings, N 1997, *Compensation in Valuation Principles and Practice*, 1st ed, Australian Institute of Valuers and Land Economists, Deakin.

Henry, K et al. 2009, *Australia's Future Tax System*, Report to the Treasurer, Part Two Detailed Analysis, Commonwealth Government, December 2009.

International Valuation Standards Council 2019, *International Valuation Standards*, International Valuation Standards Council, London.
Land & Environment Court 2019, *Land & Environment Court of NSW Annual Review 2016*, State of NSW, Sydney.
Parker, D 2015, 'The 2012 metamorphosis of the common law of compulsory acquisition valuation in Australia', *Common Law World Review*, vol. 44, no. 3, pp. 175–191.
Parker, D 2016, *International Valuation Standards: A Guide to the Valuation of Real Property Assets*, Wiley-Blackwell, Chichester.
Parker, D 2018, 'Compulsory Acquisition Compensation Issues in Australia', in *Routledge Handbook of Contemporary Issues in Expropriation*, Plimmer, F and McCluskey, W (eds), Routledge, Abingdon.
Valuer General 2020, *Review of the Impact of COVID-19 on the NSW Property Market*, Valuer General NSW, Sydney.

Biography

David Parker is an internationally recognised property industry expert focusing on compulsory acquisition, valuation standards and REITs, being a director and adviser to property investment groups including real estate investment trusts, unlisted funds and private property businesses (www.davidparker.com.au).

Dr Parker is currently a Visiting Professor at the Henley Business School, University of Reading and a Visiting Fellow at the University of Ulster, having been the inaugural Professor of Property at the University of South Australia, an Acting Valuation Commissioner of the Land and Environment Court of New South Wales and a Sessional Member of the South Australian Civil and Administrative Tribunal adjudicating compulsory acquisition compensation and rating disputes.

Author of the authoritative *Routledge REITs Research Handbook*, *International Valuation Standards: A Guide to the Valuation of Real Property Assets* and *Global Real Estate Investment Trusts: People, Process and Management*, David Parker may be contacted at davidparker@davidparker.com.au

Index

Aboriginal and Torres Strait Islander people 46–7. *see also* indigenous peoples
absentee owners 42
absolute common property 5
absolute private property 4–5, 7–8
accounting approaches 160–1
accumulation step 71, 261
acquisition, concept of 252
Activity Based Working (ABW) 106
Adams v Valuer General 71
adjustment processes 15–7, *16*, 22–5, 59, 261
adjustment step 71, 261
after-tax cash flow and profits 53, 183, 187, 188
Aged Care Act 1997 152
Aged Care Assessment Team (ACAT) 153
Aged Care Funding Instrument (ACFI) 152–3
aged care valuation 158. *see also* retirement and aged care property valuation
agglomeration 36
agriculture. *see* rural property valuation
American Society of Appraisers 175
analysis step 71, 261
Anglo-Australian (Western) culture 3–12
anthropology 4–8, *6*, 8
anticipation of benefits 70
apartment living and investment 86, 89
application step 71, 261
appraisal-based indices and de-smoothing 58–9
Aquinas, Thomas 8
Aristotle 5
asset-based methods of valuation 183, 185–6, 190–1
asset betas, vs. equity betas 62
asset class specialisation 129
asset pricing, the Security Market Line (SML) and beta (β) 60–2, 61
atomistic theory 8
auditors 216–20
Australia and New Zealand Valuation Technical Information Paper 4 (ANZVTIP 4) 235–6

Australia CBD office market performance *57*, 57–8, **58**
Australian Accounting Standards (AAS) 172–5, 211–3, **213**; AASB 138 Impairment of Assets 221; legal force of 216; requirements for valuations 220–1
Australian Bureau of Statistics (ABS) 113
Australian Capital Territory 251
Australian Heritage Council 45
Australian Property Institute (API) 199
Australian REIT (A-REIT) sector 61, 62, *62*
Australian Stock Exchange (ASX) data 61–2, *62*, 184
average daily rate (ADR) 160

Ball, M 16, *16*
before-and-after method 256–7
behavioural economics 92
beta (β) 60–2, *62*
Bethell, Tom 5, 6
Bianchi, RJ 61
Big Bang 8
Bohr, Niels 96
bond yields 19
breach of contract 208
broad evidence rule (United States) 246
Bruhl, M 67
buffer strip 37
builders 30, 33
building codes 44, 84, 236
Burns Philp Hardware v. Howard Chia 208
Bushfire Attack Level (BAL) 238
business and intangible asset valuation 182–96; asset-based business 185; asset-based valuations 190–1; barriers to entry 195; business valuation methodologies 184; capitalisation of future maintainable dividends (FMD) 184, 191; capitalisation of future maintainable profits (FMP) 184, 188–90; common errors 195–6; determinants of value 184; diversified groups, valuing 192; excess imputation franking credits, valuing 193; income

tax losses, valuing 192; intangible assets 192; investment alternatives for small business owners 194; other significant valuation issues 192–5; property valuation and corporate finance 182–3; public documents, methodologies for 186; range of values vs. point estimate 195; rules of thumb (ROT) and their accuracy 194; selecting appropriate methodology 185; service industry 185; special issues 193; start-up businesses 185; synergy 193–4; underperforming business 185

Capital Asset Pricing Model (CAPM) 50–3, **51**, *52*, 60–1, 187, 195
capital availability 18–9, 23–4
capital expenditure ('capex') 96, 119, 122
capital gains tax (CGT) 40, 41; deferred management fee (DMF) 147, 148, 152
capitalisation of future maintainable dividends (FMD) 184, 191
capitalisation of future maintainable profits (FMP) 184, 188–90; determination of the capitalisation rate 189–90; limitations of 190; normalising income levels 184, 188–9
capitalisation of income approach 70, 99–101; and industrial property valuation 129–30, 132; and retail property valuation 116–7
capitalisation rate xv, 53, 63; and industrial property valuation 128; and investment market 16–20; and office property valuation 96, 98, 99–101; in perpetuity 13, 99, 100, 101, 116, 130, 131; traditional property valuation approaches reconsidered 63; of vacant assets 130–1, *132*; weighted average cost of capital (WACC) 18, 52–3, 187
capitalism, defences of 4–5
capital markets xv, 18, 63, 182; overview 49–50, *50*
capital stack 50, *50*
capital values 16, 19, 23, 25, 49, 92, 98–9, 102, 104, 106, 108, 127–8, 131, 200, 202
Caring for Older Australians 153
cash-flow valuation 17, 20, 22–3, 53, 185
cash-generating unit 174–5
CBRE Research 125
Central Business Districts (CBDs) 57, *57*, 94; and industrial property 126; and office property 105, 106, 110; Sydney 108
central place theory 20
check approach 130, 131
Christchurch earthquake 246
Christianity 8, 9, 13
cities 20–1, 24, *24*, 129; capital 125–6; town planning 84. *see also* urban development and planning

city centres 20, 21, 24, 110–1
climate change 44–5
collateral 224–5, 228
commerce 6
commercial property market: development market 15, *16*, 17; investment market 15, *16*, 16–7; occupier 15, 16, *16*; quadrant model of *16*, 16–7, 20. *see also* economic principles
commercial value 3–4, 10
Commissioner of the Land and Environment Court 251
common property 5, 226
communal spaces 89, 164
communistic socialism 4
comparable sales: and business and intangible asset valuation 189–90, 195; and industrial property valuation 128–31; and plant and equipment valuation 175–6; and retail property valuation 118; and retirement property valuation 151; and rural property valuation 135; and secured lending purposes 233; and statutory valuation 259–64
compensation: before-and-after method 256–7; categories 10; concept of 252; heads of compensation 10, 253–5; injurious affection 10, 256; severance 10, 253, 256–7; solatium 11, 258–9
compulsory acquisition 249, 251–66; Commonwealth, State and Territory variations 252; entitlement to just compensation 252–3; heads of compensation 10, 253–4; and market value 253–6; New South Wales case study 252–9; special value 255. *see also* statutory valuation
conciliation 265, **266**
conditional private property 5
Construction of Buildings in Bushfire-Prone Areas (Australian Standard 3959) 238
Consumer Price Index (CPI) 114
contamination 45, 84–5; and removal of debris 240; and rural property 137–8, 151
'continuity of business' 193
'continuity of ownership' 193
conventional property sectors xv, 81. *see also* industrial property valuation; office property valuation; residential property valuation; rural property valuation
Cook, James 7
corporate finance 17, 182–6; basic approaches from perspective of 183–6; and property valuation 182–3
cosmology 8
cost xv, 68–9
cost approach to valuation 69–70, 98, 104, 175, 176–9, 242

Index 269

court cases: statutory valuation 254–6, 259–60
COVID-19 pandemic xvi, 61, 66; effect on industrial sector 125, 126; effect on residential property valuation 86, 88, 89; and leisure property valuation 168; and office property valuation 106; and statutory valuation 263–4, 266
credit risk 224–5
Crown Land 135
culture and belief xiv, 3, 5–7, *6*
current use/existing use 73, 85
customary property rights 3, 7, 9–10
cyclone adaptation strategies 45

Daily Accommodation Payments (DAP) 153–4
Dawson, Christopher 5
DCF method of valuation. *see* discounted cash flow (DCF) method of valuation
debt, cost of 50–2, **51**, *52*
decentralisation 47
default, order of claims 50, *50*
deferred management fee (DMF) 147, 148, 152
demised premises 203, 204
democracy 6
density 21, 86, 105, 120, 152
Department of Health 153
departure 93
depreciated replacement cost (DRC) approach 174, 176–7, 215, 221, 243, 246
Depreciated Replacement Cost (DRC) approach 243–4
depreciation 17, 19, 101, 176–9
deregulation 25
designated use 36
de-smoothing 58–9, *59*
DeSoto, Hernando 5, 6
development: economics of commercial property *23*, 23–4; on-site and off-site 34–5
development control/development assessment 33–4
development market 15, *16*, 17
development property 231–2
DiPasquale, D 16, *16*, 17
direct comparison 130–1, 132, 135
discount department stores (DDS) 110
discounted cash flow (DCF) method of valuation 70; and business and intangible asset valuation 183, 184, 185, 186–8; contraindications for 130; and industrial property valuation 128, 129; inputs 186–7; and office property valuation 96, 99, 101–3; and retail property valuation 117–21; and retirement property valuation 149, 151–2; and statutory valuation 262–3; terminal value 187–8

discount rate xv, 12, 17; and business and intangible assets valuation 187; and industrial property valuation 128; and office property valuation 96, 102, 103; traditional property valuation approaches reconsidered 63
dispute resolution, current trends in 259–64
disturbance, loss attributable to 253, 257–8
diversified group, valuing 192
dividends 19, 186–8, 191–3; future maintainable dividends (FMD) 184, 191
Drew, ME 61
dual theory of property 5
due diligence, occupier 104–5

earnings before interest, taxation and depreciation allowances (EBITDA) 150, 155, 161, 183, 188
e-commerce sector 125
economic principles xiv, 15–27; adjustment processes 15–7, 22–5; commercial property development *23*, 23–4; economics, valuation and the market 15–7; occupational demand and rent 20–3, *22*; and property market processes xiv, 15, 25–6; rational investment decisions xiv, 15, 20, 25–6; rational valuation process 15. *see also* commercial property market
effective rent 201, 202, 203, 206–7
Efficient Frontier 56, *57*
English economic history 5
Enlightenment thought 4
entrepreneurs 30, 33–4, 37
environmental considerations 30, 44–5, 84–5, 105
Environmental Protection Authorities 240
equations: appraisal-based indices and de-smoothing 58, *59*; asset pricing and the A-REIT sector 62; Beta (β) and the Equity Risk Premium (ERP) 60, 61; capitalisation rate 19; limit of liability 240; portfolio risk-return trade-off 55; Security Market Line (SML) 60, 61; weighted average cost of capital (WACC) 18, 52–3
equilibrium 15–7, 23; price equilibrium 70
equitable value 71, 72, 73, 76
equity, cost of 50–2, *52*
Equity Risk Premium (ERP) 60–1
excess imputation franking credits, valuing 193
exclusivity 114–5
externalities 34–8
extreme weather events 44–5, 85, 134

fair value 36, 69, 93, 172–4, 212–7; AASB 13 Fair Value Measurement **213**, 213–6, 220–1
Fair Value Measurement 172, 213–4, 221
family home, dispossession from 258–9

family loyalties 8
Federal Court of Australia 47
feudal system 5, 8
Fiji leasehold system 10
finance: deregulation 25; sources and uses of 50, *50*
finance principles xiv, 49–64; appraisal-based indices and de-smoothing 58–9; A-REIT sector 61, 62, *62*; asset pricing, the Security Market Line (SML) and beta (β) 60–2, 61; Capital Asset Pricing Model (CAPM) 50–3, **51**, *52*, 60–1, 187, 195; capital stack 50, *50*; Efficient Frontier 56, *57*; leverage 18, 25, **51**, 51–3, *52*; portfolio risk-return trade-off 54–7, 55–7; 'property is different' considerations 63; real estate capital market overview 49–50, *50*; risk, return and modern portfolio theory (MPT) 54–9, *55–9*; weighted average cost of capital (WACC) 18, 52–3, 187
financial determinants of value 85–7
financial reporting purposes valuation xvi, 93, 172–9, 211–23; and auditors 216–20; background 211–2; difference from other types of valuation 216; 'managements expert' 216–7; pervasiveness of valuation in reporting 212–3; value-in-use 214–5
financiers 30, 32, 33
First Home Buyers (FHBS) 42
flipping 36
forced sale 73
forecasting 20, 22–3, 64; and business and intangible asset valuation 187–9, 195; and financial reporting purposes valuation 214–5; and insurance purposes valuation 237, 241; and leisure property valuation 163, 167–8; office property market 95–7, 102; and retail property valuation 117–20
foreign investment 46
Foreign Investment Review Board (FIRB) 46
foreseeability 228–9
foundations to property rights 5–10, *6*
Freidman, Milton 4–5, 13
future, visualised xiv, 28, 32, 38. *see also* forecasting
future maintainable dividends (FMD) 184, 191

Galbraith, John Kenneth 96
garden buffer strip 37
gearing 40–1, 51
genesis theory *6*, 7–8, 13
geocoding 82–3
George III 7
Gilbertson, B 66
Global Financial Crisis of 2007–2008 19, 22, 24, 61, 66, 125–6, 212
globalisation 65–6, 75, 124

going concern: and business and intangible asset valuation 182–3, 185, 187, 190, 191; and plant and equipment valuation 173, 175; and retirement property valuation 147, 151, 153–5; and secured lending purposes 233
Goods and Services Tax (GST) 54, 118, 150, 207, 209
goodwill 74, 75, 117, 183, 185, 192, 194
government xv, 5–6, *6*; as lessee 12, 33; third-party regulation 29. *see also* policy principles; statutory valuation
government bonds 19, 62
Greek philosophy 5, 13
Gross Current Replacement Cost (GCRC) 176–7, 180
Gross Lettable Area (GLA) 127, 129–31, 204
Gross Lettable Area Retail (GLAR) 110, 204
Gross Operating Profit (GOP) 161

heads of compensation 10, 253–5
Hemmings, N 258, 260–1
heritage and conservation 45, 241
heritage floor space (HFS) offset 45
High Court of Australia: Mabo decision *6*, 10, 46; *Spencer v Commonwealth* xii, xiv, 3, 76, 259–60
highest and best use principles 20, 36, 38; and financial reporting valuation 214, 221; and industrial property 126; and office property valuation 92, 100, 102; plant and equipment assets 173; and residential property valuation 82, 88; and secured lending purposes valuation 231; and statutory purposes valuation 250, 254–5
Hobbes, Thomas 8
Home Care Packages 153
hotel 85, 160, 161, 162, 164, 166, 167. *see also* leisure property valuation
housing, social 47
human behavior 4–8, *6*, 92, 95
Hume, David 4
hypothetical development method 259, 262, 264

improvements analysis 83–4
income approach to valuation 70, 98, 99–103, 108; capitalisation of income approach 99–101, 116–7, 129–30, 132t; and plant and equipment valuation 179
income tax losses, valuing 192
indemnity value xvi, 235, 241–6, **244–6**
Independent Expert Reports (IERs) 183, 186
indigenous concepts xiv, 3; connectedness 7–8; customary property rights 3; genesis theory *6*, 7–8, 13; leasehold tenure 10; spiritual beliefs linked to property rights 5
indigenous peoples: dispossession of 259; native title 46–7

individualism 4, 8
industrial property valuation (I&L property) 124–32; application 127–8; background 124–6; building 127; definitions 124; determinants of value 126–8; direct comparison 130–1, 132; Gross Lettable Area (GLA) 127, 129–31; location 126–7; methodology for larger investment property 130; methodology for smaller vacant possession property 130–1; pricing 125–6; prime property 126; transportation 126–7; valuation methodology 128–32; valuation process 128
Industrial Special Risk insurance policy 239
infrastructure policy 43, 47–8
injurious affection 10, 256
instruction 81–2, 128
insurance valuation xvi, 180, 235–48; ANZVTIP4 235–6; buildings and site improvements 237–8; extra cost of reinstatement 238–9; indemnity value 235, 241–6, **244–6**; individual asset summation (bottom-up approach) 236; Industrial Special Risk insurance policy 239; limit of liability 240–1; overall cost of capacity (top-down approach) 236; plant, machinery and equipment 236–7; reinstatement cost 235–6; reinstatement value 236–8; removal of debris 239–40
intangible assets 75, 192. see also business and intangible asset valuation
intercultural land use 10–1
Internal Rate of Return (IRR) 17, 97, 102, 103, 118, 167
International Accounting Standards (IAS) 65, 75, 212
International Accounting Standards Board (IASB) 93
international financial centres 20–1
International Financial Reporting Standards 2013 (IFRS) 65, 69, 74, 172, 190
International Property Measurement Standard (IPMS) 203
International Valuation Standards (IVS) xv, 12, 65–6, 75–6, 213; Asset Standards 66, 67–8, 76; and compulsory acquisition 255; General Standards 66, 67, 76; IVS (2017) 225; and leisure property valuation 172–3, 175; and office property valuation 98, 108; and rental properties 199–200; scope and reporting structure xvi; and secured lending valuation 224, 233; and *Spencer* 259; structure of 66–8
International Valuation Standards: A Guide to the Valuation of Real Property Assets (Parker) 65
Internet 65–6

intuition 87–8, 96
investment grade real estate 19, 94, 97, 130
investment market xvi, 15, *16*, 16–7, 38; rents, prices, and required return 17–20
investment property 74–5, 230–1
investment value, risks to 121
investment value/worth 41, 69, 71–3, 93, 109, 121
IPSAS (International Public Sector Accounting Standards) 212, 221
IRR (Internal Rate of Return) 17, 97, 102, 103, 118, 167
Islam 8, 13
iTaukei Land Trust Board (Fiji) 10

Jackson's Airport, Port Moresby 12
Jewish religion 8

Kennedy, Anthony 8
key value drivers 195; in office property valuation 91–2, 95, 96–7, 99, 102–3

Land and Environment Court 77, 251, 261, 264, 265
landholders 30
land tax 40, 42
land use zoning 35–7
land values 21
leasehold tenure 11–2
leases: agreement terms 97; agreement trends 107; appropriate lease terms 71; breach of lease covenant 208; government as lessee 33; gross or true gross lease 205–6; and I&L property 126; incentives 206; leisure property 162; lessee's improvements 207; mid-term or option rental review assessment 199, 204; net lease 201, 205–6; relationship 10; residential 85; special conditions 114–5; Wik people's leasehold 11–2. see also rental valuation
legal determinants of value 84–5
legal principles xiv, 3–14
leisure property valuation 159–69; capital expenditure 164; disruptive technologies 165–6; ensuring operational efficiency 165; forecasting 163, 167; historical trends 163, 167; investment market and purchasers 166–7; management structures 161–2; operators 166; supply and demand issues 162–3; trends in operations and developments 164–6; types 159–60; understanding the financials 160–1; valuation 167–8
leverage 18, 25, **51**, 51–3, *52*, 188, 194
Leviticus 8
licensed securities advisers 186
Lim, Hilary 9

Lintner, J 60
liquidation based valuation 190
liquidation value 65, 71, 73, 76
Living Longer Living Better Reforms (2012) 153
Lizieri, Colin 16, *16*
loan security and disposal 180
loan to value ratio (LVR) 226
local bubble 89
local taxation 40, 43
location 126–7
location analysis 82–3
London, City of *24*, 24–5

Mabo, Eddie 7, 10
Mabo decision 6, 10, 46
major lessees 121
make good obligations 206
'managements expert' 216–7
managers 29–30, 161–2
manufacturing sector 124
marginal cost of debt 18
marginal tax rate 18, 41, 53
market approach to valuation 70–1, 98–9, 175–6, 242
market failure 29
market rent 85, 93, 96, 199–202; defined 71, 93, 199; variations on 202–3
market rent review 85, 114, 203–4, 207
market research/analysis report 112–3
market return 59, 60, 187
market trends, residential property valuation 88–9
market value xii, xv, xvi, 10, 69, 71; and compulsory acquisition 253–6; defined 93, 173–4, 199–201, 254, 259–60; and lending security 230; of office property 91–3; of residential property 82
Markowitz, HM 56, 60
Marks, Howard 95
materialism 4
material values 4
mature demographic locations 121
mediation 265, **265**
Melbourne 126–8
metaphysics 4, 5, *6*
Miller, Merton (MM) 51
MM theorem 51–3, *52*
Modigliani, Franco 51
monetary terms, used to express ownership 11
money 4; time value of 102
moral systems 6–7
mortgage 51, 84, 147, 154, 225, 227, 257
Murray Islands 7, 10

National Construction Code/Building Code of Australia 238

National Trust of Australia 45
National Water Initiative (NWI) 44
Native Title Act 1993 47
natural property rights 7, 11
negative externalities 34–8
negative gearing tax concessions 40–1
neo-liberalism 29
Net Current Replacement Cost (NCRC) 177
Net Lettable Area (NLA) 204
Net Present Value (NPV) 101–3, 174
Net Realisable Value 175
net tangible assets 190, 191
New South Wales: Land and Environment Court 77, 251, 261, 264, 265; statutory valuation considerations 250–9
New South Wales Land Acquisition (Just Terms Compensation) Act 1991 252–9
Nobel Memorial prize in Economic Sciences 92
Novak, Michael 5

Oaktree Capital 95
obsolescence 17, 49, 96, 101, 104, 178–9, *246*
office property valuation 91–108; adjusting for capital expenditure 101; allowances and adjustments 101; analysis and application 91–2; background 91–2; capitalisation of income approach 99–101; cost approach 98, 104; demand for office space 20–1; and discount rate 96, 102; future trends in occupier use 105–7; highest and best use principles 92, 100, 102; and income approach 98, 99–103, 108; interpreting market 95–6; key value drivers 91–2, 95, 96–7, 99, 102–3; and market approach 98–9; market participant behaviours 92, 95; market structure 94–5; matters relevant to purchasers 97; and Net Present Value (NPV) 101–3; occupier due diligence 104–5; occupier needs 104–7; reversionary values in leases 101–2; sub-markets 94–5; Time Value of Money (TVM) 102, 103; value drivers 95–7; vendor and purchaser decision-making 92; weighted average lease expiry profile (WALE) 101, 230
online retail sales 125
Operating Expenditure 205
Optimised Depreciated Replacement Cost (ODRC) 176, 191
orderly realisation of assets 190
outgoings 86, 96, 130, 204–6
outgoings expenditure 116
owner-occupied property 231
owner's corporation minutes 86
ownership xiv; absentee owners 42; conflated with use 3; and customary property rights 10; freehold 11; of industrial property 125;

investment alternatives for small business owners 194; as 'last metaphysical right' 4; by maker 7, 11; monetary terms used to express 11

PCA Method of Measurement 204
peppercorn rents 12, 85
personal interest 11–2
Personal Property Securities Register 225
personnel costs 160
physical determinants of value 82–4
planning controls 25, 241
planning permit 34–6
planning principles xiv, 28–39; planning process 31–5; processes of urban development 29–30; urban development, urban planning and land 28
plant and equipment valuation 170–81; bases of value 172–5; depreciated replacement cost (DRC) approach 176–7; depreciation 178–9; effective lives or useful lives 178; and materiality 171–2; Product Specific Items 178; purpose and scope of 170–1; residual values 178; Special Purpose Machinery 177–8; valuations for financial reporting purposes 172–9; valuations for other purposes 179–80
Plato 5
Plinth Property Investments Limited v. Mott Moy and Anderson 207
pluralism, politics of 8
policy principles xiv, 40–8; compulsory acquisition 45–6; environment and climate change 44–5; foreign investment 46; heritage and conservation 45; infrastructure 43, 47–8; native title 46–7; social housing 47; taxation 40–3, 47–8; utilities 43–4; water access 44
Ponsford v. HMS Aerosols 203
portfolio diversification 54
portfolio risk-return trade-off 54–7, 55–7
positive externalities 34–6
Possession Island 7
Powerhouse Museum (Sydney) 45
practice of valuation xv–xvi, 3. *see also* valuation principles; *specific practices of valuation*
present value 70, 92, 99, 155; and business and intangible asset valuation 183–4, 187, 196; and cultural beliefs 11, 12; and economics 18; Net Present Value (NPV) 101–3, 174; and secured lending purposes 232–3
price xiv, xv, 68
price equilibrium 70
producers 29, 30
Productivity Commission 153
professional agents 30, 33

property: absolute common 5; absolute private 4–5, 7–8; as 'bundle of rights' 3; common 5, 226; conditional private 5; defences of private 4–5; dual theory of 5; English private 5; as term 11
Property Council of Australia (PCA) 203, 204
property interests 3–4, 11, 74–6, 226
property markets xvi; economic principles and processes in xiv, 15–6, 25–6
PropertyPro valuations 84
property rights 192; customary 3–13; foundations to 5–10; held by supernatural forces 7; and intercultural land use 10–1; natural 7, 11; real 3–5
property yield. *see* capitalisation rate
Proudhon, Pierre-Joseph 4
proxy companies 195
public documents 186
public interest 29
public sector 49, 211, 212
pubs 161

Quan, D 58
Queensland 7; Wik people 11–2
Quigley, J 58

rate of return: Internal (IRR) 17, 97, 102, 103, 118, 167; required 17, 100, 103, 191, 195; target 17–9
rational investment decisions xiv, 15, 20, 25–6
rational self-interest 8–9
Reagan Administration (USA) 29
real estate 76; cycles 23–5; defined 74; investment grade 19, 94, 97, 130. *see also specific types of real estate*
real property 76; defined 74
redevelopment 17, 19, 21, 47, 113, 120, 140, 151
redlining 32–3
Reeve, Andrew 3, 10
Refundable Accommodation Deposits (RAD) 153–4
regulation: land use zoning 35–7; and risk 54; of site development 37–8; and urban planning 33–4
regulatory pricing 180
reinstatement cost 235–6, 235–7
reinstatement value 236–8
relocation 253, 254, 258–9
rent: effective 201, 202, 203, 206–7; face rent 96, 202, 206; freehold interest 11. *see also* commercial property market; market rent
rent, concept of xvi, 10
rental growth 19–24, *22*; and key value drivers 96; long-run and short-run 18–21, *22*, 25; and office property valuation 96, 100–1; and retail property valuation 118, 126
rental structures (gross versus net rents) 96

rental valuation xvi, 11, 17; background 198–9; breach of lease covenant 208; demised premises 203, 204; fundamental issues for consideration 203–4; lease incentives 206; lease rent 99, 199, 201, 202, 204; lessee's improvements 207; market rent 199–202; market rent, variations on 202–3; market rent review 85, 114, 203–4, 207; other issues for consideration 206–8; outgoings 204–6; purpose built premises 207; rental determinations 208–9; rent review term and unexpired term 208; restrictive use clauses 207; retail leases legislation 208. *see also* leases
rental villages 146, 147, 150, 152
replacement cost 70, 192; depreciated replacement cost (DRC) approach 174, 176–7, 215, 221, 243, 246; Gross Current Replacement Cost (GCRC) 176–7, 180; Net Current Replacement Cost (NCRC) 177; Optimised Depreciated Replacement Cost (ODRC) 176, 191
replication cost comparison 194
Report on Foreign Investment in Residential Real Estate (2014) 46
required rate of return 17, 100, 103, 191, 195
residential aged care (RAC) 150, 152–7
residential property valuation 81–90; balancing data with intuition 87–8; competing uses 86–7; and COVID-19 pandemic 86, 88, 89; current use 85; environmental considerations 84–5; financial determinants of value 85–7; highest and best use principles 82, 88; instruction 81–2; legal determinants of value 84–5; market trends 88–9; outgoings 86; physical determinants of value 82–4; and town planning 84
resort 163, 166. *see also* leisure property valuation
restrictive use clauses 207
retail property valuation 109–23; capital expenditure ('capex') 119, 122; car parking 122; discounted cash flow (DCF) method 117–21; income and outgoings 115–6; inspection 112; issues and pitfalls in 122; owner supplied information 114–5; platform 111–2, *112*; redemption or terminal yield 119–20; rental income growth expectation 118–9; risks to investment value 121; shopping centre classifications 109, 110–1; tenancy mix 121; trade area analysis 112–3; vacancy risk 120–1; valuation methods 116–21. *see also* shopping centres
retirement and aged care property valuation 146–58; and consultancy companies 157; deferred management fee (DMF) 147, 148, 152; housing 146–52; independent living apartments (ILA) 147; independent living units (ILU) 147; interests valued 153–4; main types of properties and interests valued 146–7; major issues 150–1, 155; manufactured home estates (MHE) 146–7; preliminary information required 149, 154–5; purpose of valuation 147–50, 154; rental villages 147–52; residential aged care (RAC) 150, 152–7; retirement villages 147; serviced apartments (SA) 147; uncommercial arrangements 154; valuation methods 151–2, 155–7
returns to investment 40, 54–5, *55*, 167, 177; Beta (β) and Equity Risk Premium (ERP) 60–1; Internal Rate of Return (IRR) 17, 97, 102, 103, 118, 167
revaluation model 172, 212
reversionary values 17, 96, 101–2, 199, 231
RevPAR (revenue per available room) 160
RICS Valuation – Global Standards 2017 93, 98
risk xv, 49; Australia CBD office market performance example *57*, 57–8, **58**; diversifiable and non-diversifiable 54; Efficient Frontier 56, *57*; to investment value 121; portfolio risk-return trade-off 54–7, 55–7; trade area 121; vacancy risk 120–1
risk, return and modern portfolio theory (MPT) 54–9, *55*–9
risk-free asset 56, 60
risk-free rate 18–9, 62, 96, 100, 126, 187
risk premium 18–9; Equity Risk Premium (ERP) 60–1
Rogers, Thorold 5
rorting 194
Royal Australian Air force runway 12
Royal Institution of Chartered Surveyors (RICS) 199
rules of thumb (ROT) and their accuracy 194
rural property valuation 133–44; basic sales information 136; ex-buildings level of value 138, 142; feedlots 140–1; of grazing and cropping country 137–9; of irrigation land 139; issues influencing 134–5; management practices 134; and not-for-profit (NFP) organisations 147, 148, 150, 155; orchards and vineyards 141–2; piggeries 140; poultry enterprises 141; sales analysis 136–7; of specialised rural properties 140–3; structure of market 133–4; timber land 142–3; valuation approaches 135–7

Salvage Value 175
Schumacher, Ernst 4
Scrap Value 175

secured lending purposes valuation xvi, 224–34; assumptions 227–8; collateral 224–5, 228; contract of sale 230; foreseeability 228–9; identification of client, basis of value and purpose 227; incentives 229–30; property identification 226; property types 230–3; risks taken by lenders 224–5; scope and reporting structure 225–30; title search 226; valuation date 226–7
Security Market Line (SML) 60–2
self-interest 29–30, 34–8; and externalities 34–5; rational 8–9
self-managed superannuation funds (SMSFs) 41, 97
seniority 50
separation/dispersion 36–7
servicers 30
setback strips 37–8
severance 10, 253, 256–7
Sharpe, WF 60
Shopping Centre Council of Australia 110
shopping centres: city centres 110; classifications 110–1; defined 109; major regional centres 110–1, 113; neighbourhood centres 111, 117; subregional centres 111; super regional centres 110. *see also* retail property valuation
site development, regulation of 37–8
slums, bank role in creation of 32–3
Small, William 5
small area plan *31*, 32
Smith, Adam 4, 8, 13
social evolution 4
solatium 11, 258–9
space adjustment *16*, 17, 21
spatial analysis 83
spatial modelling 83
specialist property valuation xv. *see also* business and intangible asset valuation; leisure property valuation; office property valuation; plant and equipment valuation; retirement and aged care property valuation
special value 69, 72, 73, 173, 200, 253, 255–6
specific purpose property valuation xvi. *see also* financial reporting purposes valuation; insurance valuation; secured lending purposes valuation; statutory valuation
Spencer, Herbert 4
Spencer v Commonwealth xii, xiv, 3, 76, 259–60
stakeholders 32, 38; managers 29–30; producers 30; self-interest 29–30, 34–8; users 29
stamp duty 40, 42, 47, 118, 179, 181, 229, 251, 257
standard deviation (SD) 54–5, *55*, 57, *57*
State Heritage Authority 45
Statements of Financial Accounting Standards (SFAS) 212

Statutory Outgoings 205
statutory plan 28, 33–4
statutory valuation xvi; for compulsory acquisition 249, 251–9; court decisions 254–6, 259–60; and COVID-19 pandemic 263–4, 266; discounted cash flow (DCF) method 262–3; dispute resolution, trends in 264–6, **265**, **266**; hypothetical development method of valuation 262; methodology, current trends in 259–64; methodology within the statutory framework 260–3; for rating and taxing 249, 250–1; relocation, disadvantage resulting from 253, 254, 258–9; severance 10, 253, 256–7; solatium 11, 258–9; special value 253, 255–6; and *Spencer* 259–60; state and territory variations 250; subject to objection, appeal and decision 249. *see also* compulsory acquisition
strata titles 42, 147, 149, 229
strata units 42
strategic plan 28, *31*, 32
subjective values 4
sub-markets 19, 94–5, 131, 264
substitution 69–70
suburban setting 89, 126
Suncorp Insurance 45
superannuation investments 40, **213**; self-managed superannuation funds (SMSFs) 41, 97
supply and demand xiv, 15–6, *16*; demand and current use 85; demand and leisure properties 163, *164*; economics of occupational demand and rent 20–3, *22*; and I&L property 125–6; and leisure property valuation 162–3; and residential valuation 86–7
surrogates 183
survival of the fittest 8
synergistic value 71, 72, 73, 76, 193–4
system assets 171

takeover offers 195
tangible assets 171
target rate of return 17–9
taxation 40–3, 47–8; and foreign investment 46; Goods and Services Tax (GST) 54, 118, 150, 207, 209; negative gearing tax concessions 40–1; plant and equipment 179; poll tax 251; stamp duty 40, 42, 47, 118, 179, 181, 229, 251, 257; valuing income tax losses 192. *see also* statutory valuation
technology developments 20, 21, 65–6; digital integration in the workplace 107; and leisure properties 165–6; and residential property valuation 81–3, 89
terminal value 187–8

terminal yield 97, 117, 119–20
terra nullius 7, 46
Thaler, Richard 92
Thatcher Government (UK) 29
time xv, 49
Time Value of Money (TVM) 102, 103, 190, 207, 215
title 6; Certificate of Title 83, 128; searches 84, 226; strata 42, 147, 149, 229
Total Declared Value 236
town planning 84
trade area analysis 112–3, 121
trade related property 75
Traditional Owner Settlement Act 2010 (Victoria) 47
transportation 126–7

UK Government' 251
Ultimo Power Station building 45
Uniform System of Accounts 160
United States: indemnity value calculation 246
The (un)Predictable Equity Risk Premium (Bianchi, Drew and Walks) 61
urban development and planning: construction and investment in implementation 32–3; externalities 34–8; implementation of vision/plan 32; initiating private and public development projects 33; negotiation 34; plan implementation by regulation of land use 35–7; plan implementation by regulation of site development 37–8; planners 28–30; planning approval subject to conformity with planning regulations 33–4; processes of 29–30; process from vision to reality *31*, 31–5; rationale for planning regulation 34–5; time perspective 31; websites 32. *see also* cities
Urbis Pty Ltd. 113, *113*
use, rights to 10
users 29
use value 11–3
US Supreme Court 8
utilitarianism 8–9
utilities 43–4

vacancy 22–3, 150; and industrial property valuation 126, 128, 131, **132**; and office property valuation 96, 116, 120–2; persistent 121; rate 22–3; risk 120–1
vacant possession property 130–1
Valuation of Land Act 1916 250–1
valuation principles xiv, xiv–xv, 3, 65–77; and basis of valuation 69, 93, 213; cost approach 69–70, 98, 104; five bases of xv, 65, 67–8, 71–3, 76; five premises of xv, 65, 67, 73–5, 76; income approach 70, 98, 99–103, 108; and international hierarchy 66; market approach 70–1, 98–9; structure of IVS 66–8; three key concepts xv, 65, 68, 76; three principal approaches xv, 65, 69–73, 76, 98–104. *see also* economic principles; finance principles; legal principles; policy principles; practice of valuation
Valuation Technical and Performance Standards (VPS 4) 93, 94, 98
value xv; actual (nominated) 72; adding of 33, 35–7; and cost approach 69; financial determinants of 85–7; and IVS's 69; legal determinants of 84–5; physical determinants of 82–4; postulated (hypothetical) 71–3; reversionary values 17, 96, 101–2, 199, 231; special 69, 72, 73, 173, 200, 253, 255–6; synergistic 71, 72, 73, 76; use value 11–3; vs. valuation 93. *see also* capital values; indemnity value; investment value/worth; market value; reinstatement value; special value
Valuer General 71, 250, 263–4
Victorian Department of Justice and Regulation 46
visualised future xiv, 28, 32, 38
volatility 52; in demand 24; and portfolio risk-return trade-off 54–6, *55*; stock market 19

WACC (weighted average cost of capital) 18, 52–3, 187
Walk, AN 61
wasting assets 232–3
water access and supply 44; and rural property valuation 134, 135, 136, 139
Water Licences 134
Weaver, Richard 4
weighted average cost of capital (WACC) 18, 52–3, 187
weighted average lease expiry profile (WALE) 101, 230
Western concepts xiv, 3–12; exclusive rights, preoccupation with 10; nineteenth century challenges to 4
Wheaton, W 16, *16*, 17
Wik people 11–2
willing but not anxious buyer (WBNAB) 183
workplace and accommodation models 106–7
Workplace-as-a-Service (WaaS) model 107
worth. *see* investment value/worth

yields, bond 19

Zimmerman, Carle 5, 6
zoning 35–7

Printed in the United States
by Baker & Taylor Publisher Services